BASIC COMMUNITIES

BASIC COMMUNITIES
Towards an Alternative Society

DAVID CLARK

LONDON

SPCK

1977

To my parents

First published 1977
SPCK
Holy Trinity Church
Marylebone Road
London NW1 4DU

Printed in Great Britain by
The Camelot Press Ltd, Southampton

ISBN 0 281 03568 7 cased
ISBN 0 281 02965 2 paper

CONTENTS

Preface   vii

Acknowledgements   ix

1   New Perspectives on Community   1

2   Intentional Communities   21

3   Spirituality   58

4   Environmental and Economic Aspects of Community   91

5   Communities of Learning   125

6   Caring Communities   167

7   Neighbourhoods and Networks   216

8   Yes   265

Notes   284

Annotated List of Basic Communities   303

PREFACE

The opening cartoon in *The Gospel According to Peanuts* shows Charlie Brown pursuing first a preoccupied Patty, then Snoopy, and finally Violet, insistently crying out, 'Believe in me!' He ends up sitting gloomily on the path, resigned to the harsh reality that nobody has even noticed let alone been prepared to believe in him.

In Church and society today there are many like Charlie Brown. Some simply crave undeserved attention. But there are others and this book is about them, who, as Christians but above all as human beings, are convinced that we are failing dismally to make our world and our life within it what they might be. These people have turned their backs on fame and fortune in order to build dreams into realities. They have deliberately set out on a very difficult journey with a destination which is unclear. All they take with them is 'the courage to be'. They do not ask for a great deal except, like Charlie Brown, to be believed in, not so much for what they are doing as for what they are: people attempting to be true to themselves and the humanity within them and their fellows.

Few in Church or society pay much heed; we are busy about our own business. We pass by like Patty, Snoopy, and Violet if not on the other side then very much preoccupied with the world as we see it. So this book is written to draw attention to those, so easily ignored, who are risking a great deal not just on their own behalf but for us all. It is meant as a small gesture of acknowledgement of their vision, courage, and determination.

I have not been uncritical. But in what I have written I hope I have never given the impression of devaluing the people themselves engaged in the exploring of alternatives. Mine has been the armchair; theirs has been the pioneering.

My purpose has been to show that someone believes wholeheartedly in those seeking to create new models of a Church and a society wherein old ones have lost credibility. They may not easily succeed in establishing what they strive after, but they are vigorously alive and filled with a hopeful enthusiasm and an optimism of grace which many of us gave up long ago.

My thanks are due in particular to the many groups and individuals who have allowed me to visit them, share their hospitality, and draw on their hard-earned experience; to those who have freely written articles or sent in news for the magazine about basic communities which I edit and which has drawn me into this important field; and to those who have read chapters of this book and so helpfully commented on them. In the last category I am especially grateful to Stephen Burnett, John Gamlin, Mark Gibbs, Alan Harrison, Jan Hendy, Peter Hocken, David Jenkins, Bill Kyle, John Nicholson, Emmanuel Sullivan, Ian Williams, and Virginia Withey. It goes without saying that the final responsibility for what appears is mine. To Sue, my wife, who has lived with me through a book which became a journey in its own right, I owe more than to anyone.

January 1977   DAVID CLARK

ACKNOWLEDGEMENTS

Thanks are due to the following for permission to quote from copyright sources:

L'Arche: *Letters from L'Arche*, no. 7, Summer 1974.

The Association for Promoting Retreats: *The Vision*, July 1975 and January 1976.

Association of Interchurch Families: *Two-Church Families*.

The British Council of Churches: *Jesus Bubble or Jesus Revolution?* by G. Corry.

Jonathan Cape Ltd and Harper & Row, Inc.: *I'm OK – You're OK* by Thomas A. Harris.

Centrepoint: Centrepoint Annual Report 1974.

Christian Journals Ltd: *Corrymeela – The Search for Peace* by A. McCreary, copyright © Christian Journals Ltd 1975. Reprinted by permission also of Hawthorn Books, Inc. All rights reserved; *A Para-Church in Sheffield*, from *Alternative Church* by J. J. Vincent.

Judy Coleman: Extracts from personal correspondence with the author.

The Editor of *Community*: Extracts from *Community* 1971–6.

The Provost and Council of Coventry Cathedral: *A Common Discipline* by Coventry Cathedral Staff.

Crusade: Crusade, May 1974.

The Cyrenians Ltd: *Cyrenian Principles* by C. Blackwell.

Darton, Longman & Todd Ltd and Abbey Press: *Yes to God* by A. Ecclestone.

Donegal Democrat Ltd: 'Glencolumbkille Report' by J. McDyer, in the *Donegal Democrat*.

The Dove Centre: *Dove One*, 1973.

Faber & Faber Ltd: *The Fat of the Land* by John Seymour.

The Findhorn Foundation (University of Light): Extracts from the Findhorn *Open Letter* and leaflets.

The Grail (England): *A Society of Lay People*.

George Ineson: *Suggestions for an 'Ashram' at Taena* by G. Ineson.

Institute of Christian Studies: Prospectus of the Institute of Christian Studies 1975–6.

Katimavik: *Katimavik* magazine, 1975.

Jean Lanier: *Gestalt Paraphrases* by Jean Lanier.

Laurieston Hall: Articles by Jen Lewis and Gill Harper in *Country Women*, no. 4.

ACKNOWLEDGEMENTS

Lindley Lodge: Article by John Moore in a Lindley Lodge leaflet.

The London Ecumenical Centre: *London Ecumenical Centre* (leaflet).

Maharishi International College: *What is Transcendental Meditation?*

The Methodist Church Home Mission Division: *Team Ministry*, Methodist Home Mission Occasional Paper No. 19.

John Murray (Publishers) Ltd, BBC Publications, and Harper & Row, Inc.: *Civilisation* by Kenneth Clark.

New Covenant, PO Box 102, Ann Arbor, Michigan 48107: 'Steps to Authentic Community' by Jean Vanier, in *New Covenant*, November 1974.

John Nicholson: 'Belief Today' from a talk given at the Evangelische Akademie Arnoldshain, Whitsun 1975.

ONE for Christian Renewal: *Lively Worship*.

The Pilgrims of St Francis: 1976 leaflet.

Post Green Community and the Communities of Celebration (UK): *Towards Renewal*, nos. 1, 4, and 6.

Justyn H. Rees: Extracts from personal correspondence with the author.

Routledge & Kegan Paul Ltd: *Communes in Britain* by A. Rigby, and *The New Liberty* by R. Dahrendorf.

Sheed & Ward Ltd: *Community Journey* by G. Ineson.

C. Percy Smith: *Letters from Pilsdon* by Percy Smith.

Times Newspapers Ltd: 'Consultants Put a Professional Polish on Charities' by J. Miller-Bakewell, in *The Times*, 10 November 1975.

Undercurrents Ltd: 'How the Land Turned Sour' by D. Elliot in *Undercurrents*, no. 11, May/June 1975.

Wildwood House Ltd: *Alternative Scotland*, edited by B. Wright and C. Worsley.

The William Temple Foundation: The William Temple Foundation Bulletin 2, April 1976.

MacGibbon & Kee Ltd and Granada Publishing Ltd: 'Yes' from *Complete Poems* by E. E. Cummings.

SCM Press: *What is Man?* by David Jenkins, *St Julian's* by M. Potts, and *Enough is Enough* by John V. Taylor (US rights by Augsburg Publishing House).

Thanks are also due to the following for the use of copyright material from their publications:

Alternatives Foundation: *Communes in Europe* by R. Fairfield.

BIT Better: 'Self-Sufficient Rural Commune – Special Offer' by G. Crowther in BIT Better, 1975.

Joy Press: *Elements of Encounter* by W. C. Schutz.

1

NEW PERSPECTIVES ON COMMUNITY

Community of place and of interest

It is not many years ago that Britain was a nation of neighbourhoods. Shortly after 1945 a spate of community studies appeared documenting the still rich social life of the Gosforths and the Glynceiriogs, the Barton Hills, and the Bethnal Greens. Despite the industrial and technological revolutions, despite two world wars, people still remained sufficiently rooted to build their community on the basis of place: where they were born and bred, wherein they were married and reared their families. In Robert Merton's words, they were 'locals',[1] literally parochial in orientation and style of life. Though this was true of many sectors of society, it was never more so than of the Church, which saw the neighbourhood as its sphere of operations *par excellence*. In terms of manpower and finance, in terms of worship and ministry, it was the parish or its nonconformist equivalent which was the focus of activity and resources.

Yet signs of fundamental changes in the organization and style of social and ecclesiastical life were already apparent, and their more obvious appearance over the past decade or two a consequence of their increasing impact rather than a new phenomenon. These changes were given impetus by numerous factors but a key feature was 'mobility': never in the history of man has the world become so mobile than over the recent past. Three aspects of mobility are distinguishable. The first is the increase of spatial mobility, where people have actually moved their place of residence. One example which comes easily to mind is that of a fellow college lecturer of mine, born in Derby and with a Spanish wife, who in the last ten years has moved his home eight times. The second increase in mobility is social where, through greater educational opportunity, the slow but sure breakdown of inherited privilege, and not least the coming of the affluent society, people have moved more freely up and down the social scale. Thirdly, there has been the intensification of cognitive mobility where, notably through the mass media, people are now exposed to and often assimilate experiences, ideas, and values which come at them from well beyond their immediate environment. Be it war or peace, sport or fashion, cornflakes or Coca Cola, the world is now everyone's parish.

I make no attempt at this point to evaluate the changes wrought by this rapid increase in all forms of mobility. I simply wish to draw attention to the fact that 'the times they are a' changing' and, as far as one can see, there is no going back. We are a people on the move, though as yet few have asked where to. In Robert Merton's terms we are fast changing from 'locals' to 'cosmopolitans',[2] a people with an 'ecumenical' orientation which affects Church[3] and society alike. This is a statement neither of hope nor of regret; it is, sociologically speaking, one of fact. Of course there is much evidence of cultural lag, indeed stubborn cultural resistance, to the mind-blowing upheavals which have hit especially hard those born at the beginning of this century. There remain 'uprooted locals' and 'nostalgic cosmopolitans', some of them in evidence in the ventures in community-making described later in this book. But the message to our generation is that we cannot hope, Canute-like, to turn back the tide; we must learn to sail with it.

The coming of the cosmopolitan society has played havoc with our understanding of community. It was relatively straightforward to use the word when life was lived out within a self-contained and definable area, but mobility has put an end to all that. We are done with being able to take community as synonymous with this or that neighbourhood, as did so many immediate post-war studies. Since then, sociologists have been struggling to redefine a concept which stubbornly refuses to lie down,[4] so far not very successfully but increasingly coming to realize that community of place has now been joined, though not yet superseded, by community of interest.

This shift of orientation has extremely important implications for the organization of Church and society. The claims of the parish and neighbourhood on the loyalties of men and women have been challenged by the emergence of a whole host of interest groups lying beyond the local. In school and work, in leisure and sometimes in worship, there have arisen organizations and associations, formal and informal, which now command an allegiance and enthusiasm which the neighbourhood cannot hope to match. Meanwhile certain institutions, in particular the Church, struggle on in the naive belief that somehow by their own desperate efforts they can turn the clock back and revive a sense of community based on neighbourhoods which have become increasingly meaningless social units to all but the immobile. To this situation, its possibilities as well as its problems, I return in Chapter 7.

The emergence of communities of interest is of especial relevance to the theme of this book, for it is around interests and issues that people gather with greatest enthusiasm and dedication. Community of place is associated with nurture and the maintenance of tradition; community of interest with action and innovation.

In the past, certain important communities of interest, as in the sphere of industry and commerce, have given rise to the development of new institutional structures, especially of a bureaucratic type. But there are others which have arisen in more recent years, and in which I am especially interested, which neither fit comfortably into the mould of the more traditional kind of institution, nor find themselves at home with great bureaucracies. Their concerns, and more particularly the way in which they operate, do not match the institutional patterns for which our society has currently settled.

These communities of interest find themselves pioneers of an alternative Church and society, not in any grandiose way, but in the sense of pursuing issues and developing a style of life which is set over against much that others, both locals and even cosmopolitans, take to be normative. There has emerged the commune movement trying to discover an alternative to the present shape of family life; those involved in conservation opposed to our squandering of the earth's natural resources; the alternative technology movement seeking to find a means to small-scale, manageable ways of handling the modern discoveries of science; groups concerned with the full participation of workers in industrial management; those disillusioned with the way we educate people and looking for a new relationship between teacher and student; groups attempting to meet far more adequately the needs of the disadvantaged; those challenging the injustices of a world still at the mercy of arrogance, prejudice, and greed. And there are people, too, searching for a fresh and dynamic spirituality which can give meaning and vitality to lifeless forms of public worship and private prayer.

These alternative communities of interest, often linked together in networks across the country, are the subject of this book. Not because they have been established for very long nor because they are very large in number, but because I believe they have a contribution to make to Church and society out of all proportion to their ostensible strength, a contribution I shall examine more closely in succeeding chapters. Alternative communities have arisen before in history, given content and form by the era in which they have emerged. What makes those of our generation particularly important is their extent (for the phenomenon is world-wide), their variety (for they have arisen within every sector of society), the ethos and organization of their group life and their steady growth in number and stability, in spite of the fact that the first flush of enthusiasm which characterized the birth of many in the 1960s and early 1970s has long since faded.

The concept of community

In what has been written so far I have emphasized the shift in communal orientation from place to interest, broadly speaking from the local to the cosmopolitan. There remains the even more basic question as to the nature of 'community' itself. A great deal has been written about this ubiquitous word, but it is useful here to distinguish between what Raymond Plant calls 'community as fact and value'.[5] First, I turn to community as fact, as sociologically definable, even though some would doubt the term ever to be wholly free from value judgements.

The sociological definition of community has run into major difficulties not only because 'fact and value' have been constantly confused, but because the location and pattern of social activity and social relationships have altered so greatly over recent decades. Failing any longer to be able to encompass an adequate definition of community within the boundaries of a given physical area, sociologists have tried to define community as synonymous, on the one hand, with local 'dramatic events'[6] or, on the other, with certain, especially *Gemeinschaft*-type, kinds of structure.[7] None of these approaches really gets to the heart of the matter, for if community is to retain the lively fullness of meaning which most seem to desire, then it must embrace people as whole beings, active and in relationship, and above all, people as feeling beings.

I, therefore, define community as essentially a sentiment which people have about themselves in relation to others and others in relation to themselves; a sentiment expressed in action and behaviour but still basically a feeling. People have many feelings but there are two essentials for the existence of community: a sense of significance and a sense of solidarity.[8] The latter, a sense of solidarity or belonging, is the one which has always loomed large in the literature about community but, taken by itself, it can detract from the importance of the individual and it biases our definition towards only one pattern of communal life. It is, therefore, also crucial to take into full account the individual's sense

4

of significance within the group if an adequate understanding of community is to be gained. Working with these criteria, 'the strength of community within any given group is determined by the degree to which its members experience both a sense of solidarity and a sense of significance within it'.[9]

Two observations need to be made about this approach. The first is that the concepts of significance and solidarity are analytical tools and in reality can never be completely separated. Because man is a social being, some degree of significance will always involve some degree of solidarity, and vice versa. But the need to keep both sentiments in mind is important in order to avoid some of the more value-laden uses of the term 'community' frequently found. For example, community is not a word which can be used to prove that the group has or should have priority over the individual.

The second observation is that such a definition is basically relativistic in that the strength or weakness of community depends on the perception of those involved. If they feel a strong or weak sense of community, in terms of both solidarity and significance, then for them so it is. I see no other way of operationalizing the concept in a way that does justice to the experience of the people concerned. Obviously this leaves us in an amoral position regarding community, for there could be an equally strong sense of significance and solidarity amongst members of the Mafia as amongst members of a religious Order. But though I maintain mine to be a genuinely sociological definition, and one that explodes the myth that community is necessarily 'a good thing', I do not argue that the matter ends there. For in practice the concept of community is used to evaluate as well as describe and it would be naive to turn a blind eye to the former aspect of the term. What is important, however, is an awareness and open recognition of when the discussion moves from community as fact to community as value.

Community and belief

When we move to community as value we step out of the strictly sociological field into the philosophical, the ethical, and, if we so choose, the theological dimensions of experience and thought. We are engaged in giving a meaning to community which is not provable as right or wrong, but which 'rings true' on the one hand and is useful in 'opening doors' to wider horizons on the other. In what follows, I attempt to define the qualitative aspect of community in a way which makes sense

5

to me and which I hope is valuable in the context of the groups and networks examined in succeeding chapters.

Any qualitative definition of community must be founded on what we make of the nature of man. If we wish to ascribe to community a certain quality of persons in relationship, it is utopian or hypocritical to believe that man as an individual has neither the potential nor the power ever to attain this communal state. We are then living in a fantasy world. Alternatively, 'moral man and immoral society'[10] may be an interesting observation from one vantage point, but as an overall assessment of our human situation it is a misleading paradox. For what we affirm about community must square with what we believe about man, and vice versa.

This book is not written by a theologian, though I hope there is plenty of evidence of people 'doing theology' within it. But my stand with regard to the nature of man and thus to community is what I understand to be Christian. It is based on the conviction that

man's nature is fundamentally good (created as good and created to be good), that the central practical key to the human situation is man's responsibility and man's choice, and that, while abuse of this responsibility is the prevailing feature of the human situation as we observe it and experience it, this 'fallen' situation (of *abuse*) does not define or delimit the possibilities of being human.[11]

Such an affirmation springs from and gives rise to, in a mutually inextricable way, certain other basic beliefs which permeate the approach adopted in this book. One such is that 'our Christian convictions and understandings encourage us to be positive, expectant, hopeful, inquiring, energetic, and responsive in our approach to the world and ourselves in it'.[12] From this list I would especially stress the dynamism of hope which is so excitingly characteristic of many ventures described later. It is a feature which is of fundamental importance in our estimation of man in relation to community. It is that which so often brings courage and joy into an otherwise grim world. No wonder that Peter Berger, in describing his five 'signals of transcendence', names three of them as play, humour, and hope.[13]

Such a view of the nature of man is based on 'the optimism of grace',[14] the conviction that any inherent goodness in man and thus within community is a gift of God. This is not to devalue man nor to ignore the skills manifested in his efforts to create community in an imperfect world. It is to affirm that man's struggle is essentially a

6

response to that which is both intrinsically his yet given to him. It is perhaps worthy of note that where this affirmation is denied, man in community seems for ever to be in danger of regression to egocentricity on the one hand, or to immature dependence on some pseudo-religious figure or object on the other.

A final assumption is that God does not stand apart from man. He is 'the end of our exploring'[15] but he is also with us on the journey. As David Jenkins puts it, the universe is 'the experiment of love within which man emerges as a collaborator and migrant on his way to the fulfilment of identity and community within the development and the consummation of that love who is God'.[16] That love has never stood aloof from man; its earthing in the life, death, and resurrection of Jesus Christ being but the supreme example of God's continuous involvement with men seeking to create community in response to that love, or, to put it another way, with those attempting to establish the Kingdom.

Community as a quality of life

From these basic premises about the nature of man and about man in community there follows a great deal which can be said about community as a quality of life. I return here to my earlier (sociological) definition of community as related to a sense of significance and solidarity experienced by participants in this or that group. We must now add a universally qualitative dimension, related to the beliefs and values just outlined, to the concepts of significance and solidarity.

Significance and the personal

In our age, when man can be destroyed in his millions by gas chamber or atomic bomb, when starvation still marches rampant across two-thirds of the globe, and when the explosion of the world's population reaches unimaginable proportions, it seems a sick joke to describe the individual as 'a unique expression of the universe, incomparable, irreplaceable, and of infinite significance'.[17] But this view of the worth of the individual the Christian affirms, even against a vast amount of evidence seemingly to the contrary. By so doing he employs the concept of significance in its deepest sense. Man is not man in general but man in particular, and as such he is both unique and priceless.

But man is more than an individual, even a unique one. He is a person. As Alan Ecclestone points out, we have so forgotten or escaped from the rich meaning of the word 'personal' that 'personalities are outstanding individuals, to get personal is to invade the privacy of the individual, and to receive personal attention is to be singled out for special treatment'.[18] He suggests that we need a new word,

> a word that allows for the uniqueness known to the consciousness within us, which permits growth and change to take place without loss of identity, which can if need be contemplate rebirth and resurrection, which relates us in intimate fashion to others, and which distinguishes between the reality and the falsehood which attend upon our behaviour in the world.[19]

Without such a new term currently available, I take the word 'personal' to describe that which lies at the very heart of individuality and the individual's sense of significance.

To speak of the personal is not to speak of a passive state of affairs. It is an active process of self-affirmation or, in Tillich's phrase, it is 'the courage to be as oneself'.[20] To the extent that we deny or seek to escape our uniqueness, so we also destroy ourselves as persons. Without the courage of self-affirmation and self-realization, our sense of significance will remain enslaved to external conditioning and tied to those impersonal status symbols we covet in a materialistic society.

The search for significance of a personal and fully human kind is today characterized by the quest for integrity and wholeness. It has emerged over against 'perhaps what Western man would himself like to be – a person in total control of himself, analysed to the ultimate depths of his own unconscious, understood and explained to the last atom of his brain, and to this extent completely mechanized', as Alan Watts cynically puts it.[21] The search for personal wholeness is constantly in evidence in the ventures I describe later, but can best be summed up in the quest to affirm the self as fully as possible in the realms of body, mind, and spirit. It may be no surprise that in the groups and networks I deal with, self-affirmation through body and spirit appears to loom larger than through mind. Not that the last is by any manner of means neglected, most people engaging in this movement being extremely articulate. But puritan principles and technological 'objectivity' have for so long denied free expression to the feeling aspects of the personal, especially through the sensual and the spiritual dimensions of experience, that it is no wonder there is now an explosive impulse to redress the balance.

There are two related areas in which the search for personal integrity through feelings has developed with especial power. The first is the desire of men and women for a new relationship with the natural world. As Alan Watts points out,[22] Christianity itself has here been as much a culprit as the other philosophies of Western society. Through an increasing exposure to Eastern religions we are beginning to realize how man has split himself off from nature; has stood apart in clinical isolation, and left himself with only half a world to experience and enjoy. In Chapter 4 I give some examples of the way people are attempting to rediscover their oneness with creation and are seeking to move more in harmony with the rhythms and moods of nature.

The other prominent area of feeling is that associated with the sexual, in its fullest and richest sense. Alan Watts believes that this aspect of the personal is intimately bound up with man's response to the natural world and is coming to the fore in reaction to a religion which has long divided off 'Mother Nature' from a male God.[23] There seems to be evidence that as man feels himself once again to be authentically one with nature, so there comes a sensual and a sexual awakening; likewise, as man is sexually awakened in the fullest, and not commercially trivialized sense, so he finds a new meaning in the beauty and joy of creation, often expressed through art, music, literature, and, of course, worship.

There are other realms too through which this rediscovery of the personal and of a deeper sense of significance is occurring. One, again closely linked to the feeling aspect of experience, is the new urge people have to use their skills in a host of creative activities. There is an eagerness to use natural talents to paint, weave, dye, mould, carve, sculpture, and practise a whole range of crafts.

Another avenue into the personal is different in kind for it concerns time rather than space. It is a new realization of the importance of spontaneity. Our society, not least in its religious behaviour, has for many years championed the cause of strict self-control: yet total self-control means total paralysis.[24] Our error is not in regarding a degree of control as necessary, but in venerating it to the exclusion of that relaxed movement typical of the genuine pianist or dancer and to the detriment of that flexibility of response which is open to the unpredictable experiences of the 'here and now'. If the Spirit really 'blows where it wills' and we 'do not know whence it comes or whither it goes',[25] then it is no wonder that our stereotyped patterns of behaviour allow little opportunity for new experiences to break in upon our pre-packaged way of life, or enable us to 'lift up our hearts' in the exhilaration of an awareness of eternity in the present moment. Maybe the children bouncing all afternoon with total abandon on inflatables, at a gathering of members of communities by the side of Loch Ness, can teach us as much about life and living as a hundred threadbare liturgies.

Solidarity and the interpersonal

Just as the deepest sense of significance comes through the strongest affirmation of the personal, in its wholeness, so the deepest sense of solidarity comes through the strongest affirmation of the interpersonal, in its comprehensiveness. Man not only needs to value himself and to be valued, he needs to belong. And to belong, he needs to encounter others in a way that builds bonds of friendship and affection without destroying identity.

One of the reasons we settle for such a mediocre degree of solidarity within our relationships today is that we have lost the art and appreciation of meeting with people at all but the most superficial level. We do not encounter one another as persons but as those acting out stylized roles, each of which reveals only a fragment of what we really are. The rich potentiality of the I-Thou relationship expounded by Martin Buber[26] has been reduced to an I-It contact wherein the other is seen as little more than an automaton serving our transitory requirements. Harvey Cox suggests that there may be a still personal mid-way encounter which he designates as an I-You relationship,[27] but the fact remains that without the ability to establish adequate I-Thou bonds we remain impoverished people.

An appreciation of the strength of solidarity possible within human groupings can come from a depth of encounter experienced over a long period. But solidarity at its best is extensive and, in qualitative terms, its potential also lies in openness to and co-operation with individuals and groups beyond the chosen core. It is here that deep interpersonal relationships can as easily come to serve the cause of sectarianism as ecumenism, for the introverted group fanatically guards its own sense of solidarity and, in the name of everything from creed to country, damns all those beyond. To be a genuinely open group, to overcome the barriers of class, race, and religion, is a wearing and humbling task made the more difficult by the deep anxiety of losing a corporate identity. But the quality of interpersonal experience I am arguing for here only comes from taking risks; resisting the current flight into massive privatization and claiming the rewards of a solidarity which can encompass the rich plurality of a culturally diverse world. Just as significance is enhanced by a deeper appreciation of the wholeness of man, so solidarity is enriched by a deeper appreciation of the wholeness of mankind.

To enter into this intensive *and* extensive experience of belonging demands what Tillich calls 'the courage to be as a part',[28] one of the hallmarks of which is active participation in the affairs of men. Openness can sometimes mean little more than a benign paternalism; it is the enthusiastic welcome at the door and the vigorous involvement in the world that raises community from a mundane to a dynamic concept. Ralph Dahrendorf is quite right when he states that 'citizenship . . . is not merely about where people stand, but about what they do. It is about participation.'[29] One of the outstanding features of the groups mentioned in subsequent chapters is that they are not just 'standing' but 'doing'.

The quality of interpersonal relationships which makes possible this intensive yet outward-looking sense of solidarity has numerous other features, all interrelated, only a few of the more important of which I can mention here. The I-Thou aspect is characterized by acceptance, an acceptance of others as of as much intrinsic value as oneself. For me this accepting attitude springs from the points made earlier with regard to community and belief, undergirded by our sharing of a common humanity with all men. The situation has been usefully described in Transactional Analysis as the 'I'm OK – You're OK' position, and Thomas Harris writes thus about the approach of the 'Adult' to the interpersonal dimension:

> I am a person. You are a person. Without you I am not a person, for only through you is language made possible and only through language is thought made possible, and only through thought is humanness made possible. You have made me important. Therefore, I am important and you are important. If I devalue you, I devalue myself. This is the rationale of the position I'M OK – YOU'RE OK.[30]

One reference group for this stance is that of 'the early Christians (who) met to talk about an exciting encounter, about having met a man, named Jesus, who walked with them, who laughed with them, who cried with them, and whose openness and compassion for people was a central historical example of I'M OK – YOU'RE OK'.[31] If the Eucharist means anything at all, it is this sense of solidarity through acceptance which is at its very heart.

The qualitative dimension of the interpersonal is also declared through intimacy and love, terms which I use here in the way in which

Transactional Analysis defines them. Eric Berne, the founder of Transactional Analysis, describes intimacy as a candid, childlike (not childish) relationship, a direct and spontaneous response to what a person sees and hears and above all feels, without mutual exploitation. It is 'the delight of opening the gates without fear'.[32]

> Love is Child-to-Child: an even more primitive Child than the intimate one, for the Child of intimacy sees things as they are, in all their pristine beauty, while the Child of love adds something to that and gilds the lily with a luminous halo invisible to everyone but the lover.[33]

Both relationships have a dynamic sexual content, and it is this amongst other things that makes them hard to handle in a society with norms which so powerfully repress genuine sexuality and reinforce jealousy and guilt. Because of this, we are as yet only on the very edge of appreciating how the power of a more open experience of intimacy and love, including its sexual aspect, can enrich solidarity in both an intensive and extensive way, though a number of those involved in the ventures described later have at least set out on this journey.

The more extensive qualitative aspects of the interpersonal include such things as sharing: property, possessions, money, food, and clothing. Many of the groups I am concerned with have stepped aside from a materialistic possessiveness in a striking manner. They have come to share willingly not only amongst their own circle but with the visitor and the outsider too. Caring is also a feature of the outward-looking aspect of solidarity at its best: caring for the sick, the bereaved, the mentally handicapped, the drug-taker, and the homeless, amongst others. And, on a broader canvas, the quest for social justice related to such issues as poverty, racial prejudice, and persecution, is a further feature of those networks striving to affirm the widest meaning of human solidarity.

The personal and the interpersonal

Just as man cannot experience a sense of significance without some sense of solidarity, and vice versa, so it is with the qualitative aspects of the personal and the interpersonal. I have distinguished the personal and the interpersonal as different qualitative components within the concept of community because it is necessary to keep both individual and group in mind, but each needs the other to complement and balance it. To lose the personal in the interpersonal is to court submission and immature dependence; to assert the personal at the expense of the interpersonal is to open the way to irresponsibility and fanaticism. History is the narrative of men seeking to hold the delicate balance between 'being as oneself' and 'being as a part'.

There is in practice no blueprint for success in this search for individuality and diversity within unity. There are theoretical and theological models, not least that of the Trinity. But in the end it is particular people in particular groups in particular situations in a particular age to whom we have to look for examples of what can be achieved. The chapters that follow describe a few ventures in the continuing search.

Authority and autonomy

Where people have really seen a new dimension of the personal and the interpersonal, they become dissatisfied with the sense of significance and solidarity they previously took as normative. To challenge norms is uncomfortable and unpopular for we all depend on the controllable and predictable. No wonder then that some turn a blind eye to the revelation of fresh possibilities and others rationalize them away as utopian. But a few, and in most generations only a few, are not deterred and press on often compelled by experiences they cannot deny without, in their view, denying the meaning of existence.

Their first confrontation is with that authority which has legitimized existing norms and life-styles. In previous eras conflict has frequently arisen between groups with similar styles of leadership and control. Whichever party has won, the nature and method of exercising authority has remained essentially the same. History has thus seen one tradition imposed on another, or one hierarchy deposing another.

However, the quality of community now being sought after has so wholeheartedly espoused the features of the personal and interpersonal described above that the type of authority required to facilitate its development is radically different from that which the large majority assume to be normative: the traditional and the bureaucratic styles. It seems that we are facing a fundamental challenge to old authority patterns on a scale that could be unprecedented. We appear to be in the process, a very painful one, of attempting a change of gear or, to alter the metaphor, of trying a quite new tack. It is literally a 'reformation' concerning a new quality of community life and the nature of that authority which sustains it.

One key to this situation is found in the concept of autonomy, or in such words as Bonhoeffer's, 'man come of age'.[34] The basic ingredient of autonomy is man's right, ability, and opportunity to choose for himself. We are currently entering a world in which men and women are being slowly but surely freed from the shackles of poverty, disease, hunger, superstition, and ignorance. The choices that are opening up are still fearfully limited but, as cognitive mobility in particular gathers momentum, the possibility of autonomy becomes a reality for millions so liberated.

Autonomy as a descriptive term is, like community, neutral. People can choose good or choose evil and still be choosing from themselves. Therefore, in my definition I must again acknowledge my own beliefs outlined in relation to community. Based on this understanding of the nature of man, I see autonomy as indicating an essentially altruistic state in which those who choose freely choose to treat others as persons. This kind of 'altruistic autonomy'[35] is the measure of the morally mature man. It is this kind of autonomy that is causing all the trouble, or creating all the hope, for where it is put into practice it removes authority from 'them' or even 'us' and entrusts it to 'me'. To exercise my authority autonomously I must enable others so to exercise theirs.

There are two major consequences. One relates to the individual as individual, for he now takes not only the right to 'do his own thing' (and for some the process has stopped there, ending up in gross selfishness), but accepts full responsibility for his actions. He can no longer, as an autonomous person, blame his failures or project his fears into others, be they parents, the State, or God. But this also means that he has a right and responsibility to test those authorities which make claims upon him and to reject those which would seek to undermine the new experience of the personal and the interpersonal, of the fullness of community, which he has discovered. He has too the right and responsibility to support his fellow men in the same testing-out process. Because Church and society have been quite unaccustomed to this kind of challenge, there will emerge a mixture of apathy, irritation and, at times, severe conflict. What this book is about is the signs of the growth of this confrontation, as yet hardly realized to be such even by those involved in communal experiments: how it will develop and how it will eventually be resolved, we as yet have few clues.

The second consequence of 'man come of age' is the emergence of an understanding of leadership and control which is worlds apart from current norms. The style of leadership essential to this alternative Church and society is far removed from the regulation of behaviour through custom and ritual, or of relationships through rules and regulations. It is the exercise of an authority on behalf of all involved which allows each individual and each group the maximum opportunity to discover for themselves the rich potential of the personal and the depth yet diversity of the interpersonal. This kind of leadership holds the boundaries secure, not to constrain but to protect those involved in such an enterprise from the intrusion of powers which seek to exploit or manipulate and prevent them from realizing their true humanity. It seeks also to hold the boundaries wide so that people can have the maximum 'space' in which to experiment, make mistakes, and learn for themselves. Percy Smith explains what this means for those living at Pilsdon:

> We see our task largely in terms of providing the space people need to grow emotionally and intellectually and spiritually. We all need space in which to learn to give and receive affection, especially if in early life we have put up barriers to defend ourselves from the pain of lovelessness. We need space to dare to think out and question what we believe without fear of ridicule or abuse, if our ideas are unconventional. We need space to work out what it means to be truly human in personal relationships, and to see all the hidden and unsuspected qualities beneath the surface of men's lives. We need space to hear a voice, more elemental than tradition or custom, of the One, who in the quality of His own being, revealed what God is like.[36]

Leadership of this kind is as determined to prevent immature dependence as it is to encourage and support when really necessary. Its most important wider function is that of passing on information and experience and of co-ordinating resources and expertise. It is essentially non-directive, but is in no sense passive or *laissez-faire*. It does not do away with words like 'should' and 'ought', but helps to make them adult words by choice.[37]

The exercise of authority through this style of leadership is foreign to Church and society. It too will be misunderstood and in the end it too will present a radical challenge to current roles, not least of clergy and laity. Some of those ventures described below, though by no means all, for old habits die hard, are here pioneering a new mode of creating community.

Institutions

The personal, the interpersonal, and that authority which legitimizes their expression, have throughout history been combined in different institutional forms according to how each component has been understood. The way in which community has been translated into social action and social structure has thus varied according to the nature and extent of the individual significance and corporate solidarity expected of it. Attempts have been made to chart certain major organizational forms which have emerged and though, in the Weberian sense, these remain 'ideal types', they are useful in providing examples of overall structures through which community can be expressed.

I shall deal more fully with the features of these organizational models in Chapter 7. Here I simply wish to draw attention to them. I have chosen as most pertinent to my discussion those described by Peter Rudge in his book *Ministry and Management*.[38] He speaks of the *traditional* model based on the faithful maintenance of a common heritage; the *charismatic* linked to the pursuit of an overriding intuition; the *classical* model (one which describes the bureaucratic organization) which he talks of as running a machine; and the *human relations* model associated with self-determining small groups and with fellowship. He mentions a fifth model, the *systemic*, but I do not find it very enlightening as it appears to be one which simply draws on the most attractive features of the other four. It is 'ideal' in every sense, but so much so that it is pragmatically of little value, depending on an omnicompetent leader working with groups of fully autonomous people in a perfectly co-ordinated society.

The model which most closely expresses the quality of community life which I have been describing is the human relations one. This is not to say that some of the groups and networks to be discussed will have no strong affinities with the traditional, charismatic, or classical models, nor is it to claim that certain important features of these organizational types are not needed to complement that of the human relations kind. To assume that the latter approach were all-sufficient would simply be falling into the old trap of making the partial absolute. I believe many mentioned in this book are those whom Mannheim has in mind when he states:

> It is not out of weakness that a people of a mature stage in social and historical development submits to the different possibilities of viewing the world, and attempts to find for those a theoretical framework which will comprehend them all. This submission arises rather from the insight that every former intellectual certainly has rested upon

partial points of view made absolute. It is characteristic of the present time that the limits of these partial points of view should have become obvious.[39]

Yet the fact remains that the shape of those alternatives in community-making currently being pioneered have most affinity with the human relations model, and it is to this that critical attention should be directed in assessing the importance of what is taking place.

Both in theory and practice all institutions have limitations. Yet the quest for a greater depth and wholeness, personal and interpersonal, to community must necessarily concern itself with the realities of some form of organization and control. The endeavour is to create structures that provide man with the maximum space to grow to maturity without losing his identity; those institutions with us at present, religious and secular, are increasingly failing to meet that requirement. However, we must remind ourselves that, at the end of the day, no social order can ensure autonomy any more than it can guarantee community. George Ineson of Taena tells us that 'living and working with other people in the context of the community very soon taught me that denial of life takes place within the individual, whatever the form of the society may be'[40] and Rosemary Haughton observes that 'codes and structures can never do more than approximate to the needs of the individual, and we should therefore try to establish them on the basis of "freedom *from*" rather than "freedom *to*" '.[41] We need much better institutions: but only to enable us the more easily to grow out of immature dependence on them. 'Freedom from' is a risky way to live and many refuse or abuse it. But it is an essential requirement if we are to exercise 'the courage to be' and experience the full quality of being human and thus of human community. The premise on which I base what follows, and upon which many of the people described in this book seek to operate, is that 'man is an open question, directed towards a future of love through present possibilities'.[42]

Basic communities

The material presented in subsequent chapters is about those people who in recent years have been engaged in exploring new dimensions of community. They are radicals in the sense of attempting to return to the roots of being human; they are involved in the establishment of what are coming to be known as 'base' or 'basic communities'.

My concern is mainly with people of Christian persuasion, not because I believe they have a monopoly of the truth, nor indeed because they are the only ones working along the lines indicated, but because I am convinced that they have an enormously important contribution to make in this field. In addition they have the advantage of being reasonably identifiable in belief and practice, as well as being engaged in building a new life-style and alternative structures over against a major institution within our society.

My analysis is not theological, though obviously the stance I have already outlined can be theologically developed and criticized. It is from the sociological vantage point that I write: the focus of attention being the development of new patterns of social relationships and how these are enriching our understanding of the nature and expression of community.

I stress that I am not writing about 'Christian communities', even though I may at times stray into using that term to distinguish between certain groups which have an explicitly religious identity and those which refuse to acknowledge any such affiliation. What I am describing is groups in which Christians are seen to be active in working to establish a new dimension to community life. The basis of their involvement of concern to me, and to most of them, is that their Christian faith deepens and enriches their appreciation of what community is all about; not that they are living in community in order to persuade people to become Christians. It is the quality of community that forms the criterion of my assessment, not whether it is specifically labelled as 'Christian'. Because of this I shall mention a number of relevant ventures in community-making in which Christians and non-Christians are working alongside each other, and a few in which no participants have felt it necessary to make any explicit reference to religious belief.

By definition the sort of ventures I am concerned with have an ecumenical basis in intent if sometimes less so in practice. I shall discuss the meaning of the term 'ecumenical' more fully in Chapter 7. Here I use it to indicate those groups moving beyond denominational alignments in their activities and relationships. I shall not, therefore, be dealing with denominational organizations or societies as such, interesting as their activities may be. Most of those involved in the ventures I describe are lay people (in the non-ordained sense), though clergy too are involved and it will be important to note the latter's position and status in the groups under consideration.

The number of groups now engaged in exploring new life-styles and dimensions of community is growing. I have thus limited my field to Britain; to Britain since 1945 and especially since 1960. Other periods of history have seen similar, but I would argue certainly not identical, movements occur and there are groups such as the Bruderhof, and voluntary organizations like the Settlements, which began well before the Second World War, still very much with us. But it is more recent attempts at community-making which are of interest to me here, above all because they are the ones fully involved in that philosophical change of gear and slow social revolution I spoke of earlier.

I have chosen three terms to describe the wide variety of basic communities in existence: intentional community or just community; group; and network. I was reluctant to employ the word 'community' as such to indicate one kind of venture, but common usage made this virtually unavoidable. The intentional community or community as such indicates those people who have not only contracted to share a common interest but also a common way of life which involves living together in one place; they are a residentially corporate unit. (Just occasionally I follow the wider, non-residential use of the word 'community' when organizations have applied it to themselves: as with the Iona Community or the Corrymeela Community.) The word 'group' I henceforth try to reserve for those people gathered round a common concern or cause, who may meet frequently, but who do not live together in one building nor share so fully in a common way of life. Such groups are involved in a wide variety of interests and concerns, as will be seen later. Finally, in Chapter 7, I draw particular attention to the concept of the 'network': a web of communities and/or groups with similar concerns, linked together often over the country as a whole. All these basic communities (residential and non-residential) are attempting to pioneer *new* expressions of community in the sense described in this chapter. The criteria which characterize their efforts are the quality of the personal and the interpersonal dimensions of experience and the nature of authority being exercised to facilitate the attainment of this.

To highlight the importance of community now associated with interest rather than place I have focused attention not on total communities, groups, and networks as such but on various aspects of those concerns which have brought them together: living in a common household, spirituality, conservation and self-sufficiency, arts and crafts, learning, caring for those in need, and working for the establishment of social and political justice, amongst other things. In this way I hope to escape from the often tedious business of describing each basic community in full and necessitating the inclusion of a lot of unimportant detail. The communal quality of their various activities (in relation to authority, the personal and the interpersonal), will be considered under appropriate headings and one venture may thus appear in a number of different chapters. To give some background information, a final annotated list of basic communities will help the reader quickly to identify and locate the ventures mentioned.

2

INTENTIONAL COMMUNITIES

Our basic purpose is to help ourselves and other people towards true growth and freedom. This means living a full Christian life ourselves and as a group; striving to become a working model of what Christian community could be: a community that exists not just for itself but for others. . . . It involves us in the breaking down of barriers between people generally, between clergy and laity, between classes and cultures. And this process includes in its dynamism healing, the building of bridges, and building communion. . . . It calls us to accept our responsibility for the world, for helping to transform it into a world of peace and fellowship; for making Christ present and active wherever we live and work, and in so doing to see the value of all created realities and, supremely, the value of the human person. In a word, it calls us to take our share in extending the work of Christ, in making all things new.[1]

Thus the Grail describes the purpose of its all-women, all-Roman Catholic community. And at the heart lies 'the breaking down of barriers between people', one of the outstanding marks of the thrust towards a more intentional and intense mode of communal living occurring in a thousand and one places today. Whatever is actually being achieved, and this will be the question to the fore in much that follows, there is now in this country, as elsewhere, a vivid awareness of new territories to explore and a deep dissatisfaction with old horizons.

Though this dissatisfaction extends into the field of national and international politics, unfortunately there expressed more often in rhetoric than in action, it is at the level of the primary or face-to-face group that some of the most significant moves in the breaking down of barriers are occurring. For example, the movement of people into basic communities of every size and kind reveals not just the collapse of old social patterns but a search for new ones. There is not just a revolt against old traditions and stereotypes that inhibit or prevent openness and variety in personal relationships but a determination to experiment with new life-styles. There is not simply anger and frustration at the partial recognition and fulfilment that an impersonal, functional society offers but an attempt to give fresh meaning to words like 'integrity', 'wholeness', and 'completeness'.

PARTICIPANTS

Young people

The most obvious group of people seeking to break down personal and social barriers are the young, as true of the Christian scene as anywhere. The large majority of recent ventures in community-building, in the establishment of intentionally designed and residential primary groups, are initiated by or draw very heavily upon those in their twenties or early thirties.

One of the first groups of young Christian people on the scene in the upsurge of community living in this country at the end of the 1960s was the Blackheath Commune in south-east London which began in 1969 and lasted for some three years. It was made up of eight ex-student friends, including one married couple, some of whom had previously had strong links through the Student Christian Movement. About the same time a similar venture called Newhaven began in Edinburgh.

> Like the members of the London commune, the members of the Edinburgh group had come together as students, and since leaving university, whilst living in the commune, they had pursued their post-graduate careers. Thus, one member worked as an architect, another was doing a Ph.D., another was a teacher, another member was a social worker, whilst an American member was studying Divinity at Edinburgh University.[2]

Indeed since this period the SCM, despite its own fluctuating fortunes, has encouraged student residents living in its regional houses, for example in Birmingham and Oxford and at its own headquarters at Wick Court, to move towards a communal life-style. There are at present two Quaker-based groups, one of half a dozen young people in Glasgow and one called Some Friends, with a dozen residents, in Bethnal Green. Birmingham has seen a number of community houses established with young adult Christians as residents. One in Sparkbrook closely linked with the Methodist Church there, for a while housed six members in their early twenties. In 1975 one Christian Fellowship

House accommodated about a dozen people up to the age of thirty, including three children, and Shenley House community a married couple and three single people aged between twenty-five and thirty-one. The Ashram houses in Middlesbrough, Rochdale, Sheffield, and Kennington reveal a similar pattern though none of the residents is married. Also amongst the more youthful endeavours in community-making lie those associated with the so-called Jesus Movement. 'Whether or not there has in fact been any Jesus Movement in this country', as Micheal Jacob questions,[3] both the sixty-strong Jesus Family based in London and the Children of God colonies, in a recent count numbering nine, with some 200 members overall,[4] scattered throughout Britain, are made up mainly of young people in their late teens and early twenties. Of the 300 members of the Jesus Fellowship based on the village of Bugbrooke in Northamptonshire, at least half are under thirty. And so one could go on with a comparable picture also emerging beyond the Christian scene.

The youthful facet of community-making is perhaps best illustrated by a phenomenon strictly speaking outside our terms of reference – that of the Taizé Council of Youth. In August 1974 some 40,000 young people from all over the world (though only about 300 from Britain) assembled at Taizé to proclaim:

> The Risen Christ comes to quicken a festival in the innermost heart of man. He is preparing a springtime of the Church: a Church devoid of means of power, ready to share with all, a place of visible communion for all humanity. He is going to give us enough imagination and courage to open up a path of reconciliation. He is going to prepare us to give our life so that man be no longer victim of man.

Here were pilgrimage, pop festival, and Church all rolled into one; nobody quite sure what it all meant, except an affirmation of life and the sense of sharing the vision, a largely youthful vision.

Such communal self-determination and vitality on this scale amongst young people would not have occurred within or outside the Church fifty years ago. Whatever their theological or political orientation, the proliferation of close-knit groups of the young putting their convictions into practice and making their voices heard is historically a new phenomenon. Though the mode of expression differs widely, there is here a major section of the population and of the Church not telling us to do as they say but to do as they do.

Many youthful attempts at community-building are of short duration

23

and in numerous cases, even where the unit has survived, the turnover in membership is considerable. But once bitten, bitten for a lifetime seems the appropriate comment and already the young communards of the sixties are beginning to move into or plan groups more suited to the rearing of children and to people of early middle age.

Young and old

As yet it is too soon to say whether communities initiated by the young can easily embrace the old, other than where the homeless or the deprived are currently living in houses, such as in the case of the Cyrenians, specifically dedicated to the work of caring. On the other hand, groups set up by (now) older people still attract the young even if to a rather more structured way of life and work. Lee Abbey and Scargill, for example, encompass within their large communities which staff the centres a wide cross-section of ages including many young people; likewise, the Community of Celebration which is well over a hundred strong, having members ranging from 'newly born to seventy-five'[5] and Post Green, with its membership of about sixty, including several families with older children. In fact the only group of young people notably absent from communal ventures so far are those in their mid-teens, being too old to have been brought up communally and as yet too young to be able to opt in for themselves independently of parents. However, it is interesting to find at the long-established farming community of Taena, where young people have been born and bred and have grown up in a rural communal setting, that some were eager to be at least temporarily free from the intensities of such a way of life, believing that they needed to break away from what for them were the norms of the past, communal and religious, in order to discover their own identity in the present.

Men and women, married and single

If the emergence of a multitude of groups of young people doing their own thing is a break with the past, so is the move towards sexually mixed styles of residential life, especially for the more established communities. Two features are of especial interest here. One is the steadily developing conviction that communities of just men or just women are increasingly anachronistic today, even where celibacy is or has been the rule.

24

A notable example of a shift of viewpoint here is the Grail, since the beginning of its work in England in 1932 composed entirely of women, the core (staff) group of some eighteen living at Pinner in Middlesex, all unmarried. At the end of 1974, *In Touch*, the magazine of the Grail, reported that 'in the future there will be a greatly extended community – married members, priests, helpers, single men and women, who through their commitment to the Grail will be supported and strengthened to live joyfully and in their turn to transform the lives of the people they live and work among'.[6] In March 1975 an appeal went out for ' "volunteers", men and women, aged between eighteen and sixty-five, who would commit themselves to from three months to one year's work and community service and to experiencing community living'.[7] Five such volunteers have linked up with the Grail in the first year of the scheme. A small move in some ways but significant enough to make one wonder how soon other originally all-male groups (such as the Roslin Community) or all-female groups (such as St Julian's or the Farncombe Community), not to mention the religious Orders, will also become involved in 'the breaking down of barriers'.

Another interesting feature is that of married couples and single people living together in the same group. In large communities, such as the Community of Celebration, Post Green, or Findhorn, this seems to work well. In smaller groups, like the Blackheath Commune or Birchwood Hall, where the single members are generally in their twenties and form a large majority, problems have arisen as married couples increasingly look for privacy or the company of their own marital 'status' group, especially when children arrive on the scene.

Lay and religious

Another new but significant move is the tentative reaching out of religious Orders to associate more closely in community with lay people, single or married. At Ammerdown House, for example, a warden and his family share with five Roman Catholic Sisters of Zion in staffing the conference centre. There are problems of denominational allegiance, especially regarding the worship, but an attempt is being made to cross the divide on the basis of a genuine equality of status. At Hengrave Hall in Suffolk an even more ambitious step has been taken in trying to run an ecumenical conference centre with a close-knit, lay/religious team. Eight Roman Catholic Sisters of the Assumption, a Catholic Franciscan who acts as chaplain to the community, an unmarried Anglican, and three married couples with nine children are seeking to work together 'to renew the truth in ourselves and in the Church that we are the people of God and the Body of Christ'.[8] The difficulties have been considerable and one or two couples have not felt at home in the community and have left it, but bridges are being slowly built and, historically speaking, an experiment of considerable significance is here under way. I will say more on this matter at the end of Chapter 7.

Ecumenical aspects

Most of the basic communities I am concerned with in this book are chosen because of their commitment to crossing ecclesiastical boundaries. There are four approaches to this commitment in evidence, each with its strengths and weaknesses. Most common are communities where members' denominational loyalty, expected to be treated as sacrosanct, embraces greater unity beginning from there. Hengrave Hall, for example, encompasses practising Roman Catholics, Anglicans, Methodists, and Greek Orthodox members. The Farncombe Community at one stage included Anglicans, a Methodist, and a Catholic. None the less, many communities still retain a mainly denominational flavour with Anglicans or Roman Catholics usually being the dominant group, though with the interesting exception of the two all-Quaker communities already mentioned. Even in charismatically inspired groups such as the Community of Celebration and Post Green, the Established Church's influence looms large and the stray Baptist or Catholic is pointed to with some pride. Thus old denominational loyalties still count for a great deal.

The second approach is found amongst those communities whose members take the opposite view and sit very lightly to denominational allegiance. Here would come some of the more informal communities where worship is often internally designed, as in the Ashram households, or not regarded as a crucial corporate feature at all, as with the Cyrenian houses, the Kingsway Community, or Wick Court.

The third and least common approach to crossing ecclesiastical boundaries is seen in groups which have actually been flexible enough to change their religious allegiance over time. The outstanding example here is Taena, whose fascinating history saw them moving from agnosticism, through a strictly ordered Roman Catholic way of life, into a wider and freer expression of Christian faith and worship.[9]

The fourth approach consists of those groups seeking to embrace not only the Christian faith but all faiths. This can be, as with Findhorn, in the name of a 'new age' religion of a pantheistic kind, or the more syncretistic style of the five or so 'Open Centres' in this country 'not concerned with religious forms, but with the Spirit of Truth contained within these'.[10] These centres lay considerable emphasis on meditation and prayer linked closely to study of the Christian and Sufi mystics.

I make no attempt at this point to judge whether these attempts at crossing the religious divides are adventurous or tenacious enough to breed a new generation of those who, as the Grail puts it, affirm 'supremely the value of the human person'. All that must be said is that those involved are trying in practice at a deep level of personal involvement to reconcile large differences, and at least some appear to be succeeding.

International aspects

Most communities within this country are through and through British. The exceptions to the rule are the one or two groups sponsored by, or especially attractive to, those from the United States. In the former category is the Community of Celebration which has 'about fifty Americans (all from the Church of the Redeemer in Houston, Texas) plus several Canadians and three Swedes'.[11] The Church of the Redeemer in fact initially 'sent' and still gives considerable financial support to this large group. The Jesus Family is also very largely an American import, the English support they have picked up being minimal.

Of groups begun over here yet now heavily North American in membership, Findhorn is the main example, with probably 100 out of the 175 residents in 1975 coming from the States, and relatively few coming from Scotland where the community is based. At the same time many British groups have a very wide cross-section of people dropping in for occasional days or a few weeks especially during the summer 'tourist' season.

Social class

British communities are strongly middle-class in membership and ethos, whatever age-group one is talking about. Most participants have received a good education and come from relatively affluent backgrounds, even if they have deliberately turned their backs on such a style of life. There are, however, two exceptions.

At one end of the social scale a significant number of the wealthy upper class, including the aristocracy, are directly or indirectly involved in promoting ventures in communal living. For example, Post Green is the home of Sir Thomas and Lady Lees, Ammerdown House is situated on Lord Hylton's estate, and Lady Ursula Burton of Dochfour House near Inverness is keenly interested in encouraging young people in their search for new patterns of community life. The Open Centres in particular have a fairly wealthy and sophisticated group behind them.

At the other end of the social scale, Bugbrooke has a large working-class element, amongst whom are young people who have run into personal difficulties of one kind or another. Other communities exist which have been set up to care for those who are disadvantaged or homeless. For example, the Cyrenian houses and Simon communities contain a mix of the destitute and middle-class 'workers', the Pilsdon staff share their lives with many seeking social rehabilitation, the community at Bystock Court provides for mothers in need of care, and the Kingsway Community contains ex-drug takers. More will be said in a later chapter about such communities dedicated to the work of caring. But there are no intentional communities known to me which have been initiated or are run predominantly by those whom one could call working-class (Bugbrooke, for example, possessing some highly educated and very articulate leaders), though some from this social class, notably skilled manual workers, are here and there carrying considerable responsibilities.

The intentional communities of which I am writing have made little contact with the black population of this country. This is not, I believe, because of any latent racial prejudice within the community movement but because as yet the West Indians, Africans, and Asians are too intent on preserving and strengthening their own cultural and religious identity, the 'colony phenomenon', as it has been called, to want to become involved with white ventures in community-making. Until the black or white person can move out of his own racial grouping without fear of ostracism from those he leaves or of suspicion from those he joins, I see the emergence of communities of a racially integrated kind as still a very long way off. Basic communities do not exist apart from society in the human problems they face.

ORGANIZATION, AUTHORITY, AND LEADERSHIP

To opt for a life-style different from the familiar can appear all too attractive. In the first flush of enthusiasm one can feel the freedom of shaking off those ways of operating which seem to have been so constricting and oppressive. But all those moving away from old structures and behaviour are soon faced with the necessity of establishing some pattern of life to replace the old. The results are in fact never a complete break with the past, if only because the possible ways of organizing the life of a group are limited. What emerges from the many ventures in community-making is, therefore, a mixture of old and new with often the old still looming unexpectedly large.

Space

In the first chapter I mentioned the important concept of social 'space' and the opportunity and ability to operate freely and creatively within it. It is only as groups give members ample space to explore different life-styles that new patterns of community living can emerge. Thus it is necessary for groups as such to have room to manœuvre and, as George Ineson of Taena puts it, to 'find ways of ensuring sufficient inner and outer space for each person separately'.[12]

The amount of space available will depend on various factors, not least on the nature of leadership exercised. One major function of leadership is to define and guard the social boundaries of the group; if these are pulled too tight, for example by a host of detailed rules, there is little room for members to experiment or grow beyond a defined point. If the boundaries are left unclear or no one is prepared to take responsibility for protecting them, then confusion and frustration often arise. The space available in which to establish alternative life-styles is also affected by the decision-making process and the ways in which information is communicated; these features will be discussed later.

The rule

One important factor relating to the total organization of any community is the extent and nature of the rule of life it draws up for itself. The 'contract' can vary from very detailed and explicit to vague and ill-defined. The rule has always been a cornerstone of monastic life, and even in recent times Knowles could write:

> A rule, approved by both authority and the experience of good men, is a necessary safeguard, and this rule must be observed, not with antiquarian or pharisaical precision, but with a faithfulness that maintains its character as an instrument of perfection. If the rule is kept faithfully, in the spirit in which it was composed, all will be well; if it is not kept, individuals may fare well, but the security of a firm standard has gone.[13]

Of the communities I am concerned with here only a minority would today place so much emphasis on a rule. There is a marked reticence to lay down rules in any detail and, in some cases, at all. There seems to be a revulsion against this feature of the classical bureaucratic structures and resistance to obeying a seemingly external and impersonal standard.

Those groups most inclined to some form of rule often have associations with the more established religious Orders. The Roslin Community have a strict discipline which reaches into every aspect of their life. Hengrave Hall, with a group of Sisters of the Assumption being members, has produced 'The Rule of Life of the Hengrave Community' containing aims, an 'Instrument of Government', and 'Statutes' relating to common sharing and common worship. Emmanuel Sullivan makes the point that, in their case, the need to begin 'big', with a large centre and its ongoing life to maintain, meant that some rule was essential to hold the community together in its early stages to prevent wasting precious energy over relatively minor matters. In a quite different cultural context the Children of God also follow a highly structured way of life. Kenneth Leech writes that 'property is given up, and a new biblical name taken. Scripture is memorized and chanted, and the discipline in the communes is quite rigid.'[14] Post Green has attempted to put the commitment of certain members 'as if for life' into a comprehensive document relating to many matters of corporate experience.

Some communities, otherwise quite ordered in their life-style, sit much less tightly to a formal rule than might be expected. The Grail members, for example, writing in *In Touch*, state: 'Recently we re-wrote our Way of Life, but we have been careful to say that it is provisional. Its purpose is to reflect as truly as possible what the basis of our society is and how the society sees itself NOW.'[15] The Community of

Celebration, though in many ways a community 'under authority', as will be mentioned later, believes in informality and pragmatism rather than a routine which is set and orderly. As one elder remarked to me, 'You do one thing today for one reason, and another thing tomorrow for the same reason, so why try and regulate life?'

Groups without an explicit or formal rule of life are still able to promote a well-disciplined community. Lee Abbey and Scargill possess little approaching a rule but operate on a basically hierarchical model. At Lee Abbey, community membership in specific terms embraces only corporate worship, private prayer and Bible study, and conscientious work, with a more general agreement 'to accept the discipline of the Community'. Of Scargill Margaret Leach writes:

> Some, perhaps the younger members, feel that the discipline of the common life is severe, others that it is too lax. There is no written 'Rule of life', no commitment to obedience, and anti-authoritarianism is as common here as elsewhere. Individuals are free to work out their own terms of commitment and their own disciplines, and perhaps these are harder standards to maintain for no one else need know when there is failure, at least not, perhaps, for a long time.[16]

Other groups have attempted to draw up a rule but it has remained much more letter than law. The Kingsway Community, for example, in 1972 set out a full 'agreement' relating to such things as the sharing of food, domestic duties, room rules, and so on. But 'with one or two exceptions these were more in the nature of guidelines for action rather than firmly laid-down orders which a person ignored at his peril', writes Andrew Rigby. 'Of course, if such rules were resorted to it would defeat one of the prime objects of the community, to establish an extended family environment.'[17]

Finally, there are those groups, mainly of a small communal kind, which in this respect operate on little more than the bare minimum of structure. Such would be places like the Blackheath Commune and Newhaven, already mentioned. And beyond the specifically religious scene, such groups as the Shrubb Family reported on by Rigby[18] would be typical.

Overall, the situation reveals an increasing reluctance, at times refusal, by groups to be tied down to hard and fast rules, especially where these intrude on the space that might be called personal. There is much more readiness to set out formal guidelines for administrative and financial matters than, for example, worship and prayer. The old belief that some type of monastic order (literally 'order') is essential for the existence of community is fading, despite the existence of those groups mentioned above which still respect that tradition. Whether the pendulum has swung too far in the direction of freedom and informality remains to be seen. I return to the important question of the emergence of possible alternative structures in Chapter 7.

There is much less concern today for building for a long-term future, much less fear of personal encounter and conflict, much more desire for flexibility and fostering of individuality. Members of many communities have considerable scope for personal choice; bringing with it both the excitement and the fear of freedom. The life of people, especially in community, without rules means that the space is there for the using, for good or for ill. But the gradual abandonment of 'the rule' is only one aspect of creating space; another relates to the nature of leadership and decision-making.

Intentional communities as organizational types

The nature of leadership and decision-making within communities is a crucial issue in relation to the existence and use of social space. In this context 'the rule' may seem to be very important, but in the end it reflects rather than creates the nature of authority.

In the previous chapter I mentioned the four organizational models used by Peter Rudge and of value to us in our current analysis: the traditional, the charismatic, the classical (bureaucratic), and the human relations. The models most closely associated with maintaining the *status quo* are the traditional (akin to the locally oriented way of life discussed in the previous chapter) and the classical (with similarities to the cosmopolitan). It is not surprising, therefore, that we find the life of certain religious communities still clearly reflecting these two models.

One striking feature of certain contemporary communities is that they have been initiated or are led by clergy. This feature indicates the still tenacious link between many new ventures in community-making and the institutional Church. Even though a number of such clergy would be regarded as 'way out' by the local church member, the former still retain close contact with one or other aspect of mainstream Christianity. I do not think this is because more radical clergy fear to go out on a limb. It is because they see the need of a prophetic witness to the Church itself and the grave weakness of sectarianism or separatism. At the same time a contact is also maintained through disillusioned laymen seeking them out to help sustain their own faith and to give them inspiration and a sense of hope in the darkness.

At Pilsdon, for example, Canon Percy Smith, who with his wife Gaynor founded the community there in 1958, spoke of his disillusionment with a Church that seemed unable to care for the needy and deprived in a spontaneous way and of how the search for an open caring community had brought them to this venture. Yet it still remains very much a venture 'of faith', with Percy Smith being vicar of the Pilsdon parish church, linked to the house, and with the community living 'a life of simplicity cast within the framework of the ordered worship of the Anglican Liturgy'.[19] And although it was stated in the annual newsletter of December 1968 that 'the steady, rather inflexible discipline of the early years has mercifully given way to a much greater "spaciousness"', the leadership has remained fairly traditional, with Percy Smith the dominant figure. The core community meets only once a month, and many decisions (such as which referrals of those in need are accepted) are still made by Percy Smith alone. When I visited I was intrigued by the way he firmly instructed each person where to sit at mealtimes.

Another group operating along traditional lines is the Farncombe Community, which began in 1964. Here the women look to external 'authorities' as an important source of wisdom.

> The Community as a whole has a Visitor who is invited by the Sisters to serve for five years at a time. He, in consultation with the Sisters, appoints an Advisor and a Chaplain, who should represent the Anglican and Free Church traditions. Spiritual needs and matters of discipline are referred to one or other of these three and at least two of them are required to interview a prospective Sister.[20]

The classical (bureaucratic) model is also in evidence amongst communities, especially in the case of those linked with Roman Catholicism. Although the Grail is seeking a much greater flexibility in relation to its membership and its 'rule', there still remains a detailed administrative structure outlined in *A Society of Lay People*.[21] A president is elected for four years who guides the life of both staff members (fully committed to the community) through a council of four, and of the Companions (committed to outside responsibilities) through a council of three Companions and one staff member. The classical emphasis also comes through in the matter of decision-making, where issues are divided up into 'major matters', 'matters of concern', 'practical matters', and 'domestic matters',[22] each with the appropriate decision-making procedure.

Another community in this mould is Lee Abbey which, though having a fairly simple rule, has a very well-defined organizational structure of a basically hierarchical type. There is a council which represents outside interest in, and support for, Lee Abbey. There is a management committee meeting monthly and consisting of some members of the community who hold positions of particular responsibility and some qualified people from outside. This committee deals with overall finance and the large-scale management of the estate. Thirdly, there is an inner core or 'chapter' of some eight senior members of the community (including the warden, who carries a considerable authority and has always been a priest). This meets weekly and has executive powers concerning the general running of the house and grounds. A 'Point-Four' group (made up of those who have been at Lee Abbey for a year or more) forms the next tier of authority, while there is a general meeting of the whole community one week and of the house (smaller) groups the other.

Several more recent ventures in community reflect the charismatic model, though an interesting feature is how easily charismatic leadership goes traditional. This is the case with the Children of God who, though associated by the media with the Jesus Movement, have in fact become organizationally very traditional in structure. Each group is highly organized and revolves around the leader or 'shepherd' of the colony who reports regularly on the affairs of his community.[23] Every colony appears to be very much controlled by members of the Berg family, in particular 'Moses' (David Berg), who monitor all major decisions from wherever they are located, often from the international headquarters in London. There seems to be no democratic method of making decisions.

The Jesus Fellowship, with its headquarters in Bugbrooke, is another example. It 'took off' in the early 1970s under the powerful charismatic leadership of Noel Stanton, a Baptist minister baptized 'in the Spirit' late in 1968. As it grew to over 300 people, resident in extended households in Bugbrooke and nearby towns, it became (in their own words) 'a theocracy not a democracy'. The community seeks to follow to the letter the organizational structure of the New Testament Church. The thirty-five male elders, senior and junior, under the guiding hand of Noel Stanton, and 'led by direct revelation and prophecy', legislate for the community, though in principle the Assembly (all members) can test the elders' direction. Beneath the elders, in a more administrative role, come the deacons. Thus, in the words of the Fellowship, 'leadership is from the top down'.

The Community of Celebration, with notable charismatic beginnings, owes its origin and growth very much to the leadership of Graham Pulkingham, originally Rector of the Church of the Redeemer in Houston, and now Provost of the Cathedral of the Isles in Cumbrae, Scotland. He is, however, regarded by many of the community with a kind of affectionate veneration which, with the title 'Father', reflects the traditional rather than the charismatic style of leadership. Again more in line with the traditional model, though there are few 'rules', 'all ministrations are subject to the authority of the elders',[24] a small self-perpetuating group whose influence seems to rest on ascribed status. Even the vital decision to split the English Community in 1975 and move half to the Isle of Cumbrae was taken first by the elders and only then opened to the reactions of the members, who incidentally never meet as a body for decision-making purposes.

Post Green has never had a charismatic leader such as Noel Stanton or Graham Pulkingham, but it owes a great deal of its growth to the inspiration of Sir Thomas Lees and his wife, Faith. In a quietly 'charismatic' way, and supported by dedicated friends, they have led and guided the group since its beginnings in 1968. Yet once again the model of decision-making has so far been quite traditional, with a group of seven elders being fully responsible for all major policy matters. In 1975, an interesting development was occurring with the group under some pressure to devolve authority, one critical issue being just how Tom and Faith, whose estate the community lived on in various households, could fulfil their societal role if their personal control, for example over property, were surrendered. By 1976, there was a strong move, obviously personally costly for some, towards the principle of a common purse in *all* households.[25] It should also be mentioned that true to the traditional style, both the Community of Celebration and Post Green have gone a good deal out of their way to obtain the official blessing of the bishop in whose diocese they are situated.

Though the so-called charismatic communities do not allow much space for members to share in leadership or important decision-making, those groups more reflective of the human relations model certainly do. It is of note here how the influence of the clergy declines and that links with the institutional Church are more tenuous. It is also true that most of these communities are relatively small and have not had to face, for example, the problem of welding a large group together, as has Bugbrooke, the Community of Celebration, or Post Green.

One of the communities coming more or less into this category would be the Blackheath Commune, which sought to order its affairs through a weekly meeting of all residents. Members of the Ashram houses likewise retain full control over day-to-day matters which they organize as a group. The Cyrenian houses work very much on human relations principles with workers and other residents shaping their own pattern of life through a regular community meeting. 'At Kingsway the theory was to involve all members in decision-making with the house-meeting as the sovereign body. In fact, and perhaps inevitably, given the size and the nature of the membership, a leading and determining role in decision-making was frequently played by David Horn.'[26] Here attempts to establish participation and sharing founder at times because of the dependence of the group on one central person with charismatic qualities.

Finally under this heading can be mentioned one group which still retains strong links with the institutional Church, the small Community of the Word of God. Alex Beale writes that their commitment to each other is reflected 'in the super-democracy of their authority structure'.

> 'Authority structure' is in fact a misnomer, since important decisions affecting the community are taken 'by the common mind'. No person can be overruled in the case of a disagreement. It is impossible to act on a majority decision, but there must be unanimous consent. . . . The only 'authority figure' is the Servant of the Community, chosen by the community for a period of three years, to be the 'servant of the servants of God', responsible for day-to-day decisions.[27]

Some organizational problems

A problem in the field of community-making is that to get groups launched, often against the normative tide or on a fragile economic base, is so demanding a task that the charismatic personality is almost essential not only in the initial stage but through the formative period also. But charismatic leadership, though hope-inspiring, can all too easily create a dependent membership and the space for the latter to find themselves is very limited. Writing of Bridge, an East End group of young people which as such collapsed within a year, Martyn Elliott states:

One of our hardest problems has been leadership. Whilst we have claimed to share responsibility, David (the local curate), because of his job and previous experience, is an all too ready-made leader and unfortunately much of the inspiration has been left to him. Though people have complained when he has shown authority, we have been reticent to take responsibility ourselves. This reluctance to take responsibility is a common human failing and only now is the community beginning to come to terms with it. Too often for the house the result has been . . . a stagnation of ideas and action, a decrease in commitment, and a movement towards bitchiness and scapegoating.[28]

Often attempts to move away from the initially charismatic to another organizational model end up in the conservative traditional mould, an over-complex classical system, or develop into a human relations situation which has viability only for small informal groups and promises little for genuine continuity. Groups associated with the Jesus Movement seem to be well on the way from charismatic to heavily traditional; the Grail seems at present to be shaping its structure on classical lines; while the Cyrenians still debate vigorously how to prevent their more human relations type of communities from losing coherence and fragmenting. As Chris Blackwell writes: 'People have referred to the "ordered chaos" of Cyrenian houses, but one suspects that sometimes there is more chaos than order.'[29] The offshoot of the Kingsway Community in Cornwall, Keveral Farm, has also encountered similar problems.

Part of the confusion stems of course from the very divergent expectations of members. The initial 'contract', as in the case of the Bridge Community just mentioned, is never clearly worked out; a fact which makes leadership all the more difficult. For the way in which groups are led and make decisions and communicate are not secondary; they fundamentally affect personal growth and interpersonal relationships to which I shall turn in a moment. As Geoffrey Corry writes of the Jesus Movement, participants have found it all too easy 'to confuse the central function of Jesus communes which is therapeutic, meeting immediate emotional and personal needs, with the task of mobilizing the energies of the group for more sustained work outside their commune'.[30]

One final factor which makes an enabling leadership difficult to establish is the extremely high turnover in communes. The core often remains intact – at Pilsdon, Little Gidding, Bystock Court, Taena – but other members often come and go with rapidity. 'Like a transit camp', commented a Dutchman leaving Lee Abbey after an extended stay as part of the team. 'Like Paddington Station', were John Harvey's words in relation to Iona. It is little wonder that an authoritarian leadership, rules and regulations, or no structure at all are easier options than giving ample space for the community to be self-determining and the members mutually enabling.

None the less, there are numerous examples of basic communities, even amongst those already mentioned, which have tackled these problems with perception and energy. One example is St Julian's in Sussex, the original creation of Florence Allshorn, with a membership of some dozen women. A member writes:

> Five hours in the week are set aside for the Community to meet as a group, for study and discussion, fixing of practical matters, thrashing out questions of policy, and talking out problems arising from our life together. This enables us to discover and work towards resolving the underlying causes of conflict and misunderstanding, so often at first unrecognized. Each member has a day a week completely free, as well as part of Sunday, and we have holiday times. . . . As for the future, we have never had blueprints, as our aim is to be sensitive to the moment of time in which we find ourselves.[31]

Furthermore, the nature of the leadership has changed from the somewhat autocratic approach of Florence Allshorn, through a more 'mothering' style, to the co-ordinating and enabling approach of the present time. To this whole matter of leadership, authority, and organization I return more fully in Chapter 7.

THE PERSONAL AND INTERPERSONAL DIMENSIONS

The nuclear family

The structure of a community – its rules, its style of leadership and decision-making – very much determines the social space available for members to realize their potential in all ways. This may be on the 'political' level, relating to the authority extended to and exercised by the group as a whole, as was my particular concern above. But space not only concerns power and control; it also opens up the whole question of what Schutz terms 'affection'.[32] When authority is considered, the issue is one of the degree to which members are dependent on those who emerge as leaders; where affection is concerned, the question is one of the degree of closeness people desire and for which they are prepared. The polarities here are at one extreme those who seek for 'overpersonal' relationships, wanting to be very much a part of the total group, and at the other those who are 'counterpersonal', seeking to belong but only as long as their personal privacy and individual identity are not seriously threatened.[33] In this difficult and delicate area of interpersonal relationships, each group has to discover its own way forward. Indeed, one of the revelations of community living is that there are no 'right' answers – though some groups still behave as if there were. As each person is unique, so is each group of persons.

Husband and wife: father and mother

It is now commonplace to observe that one of the powerful pressures towards communal living is the breakdown of the close-knit, extended family, in part because of what I have described as spatial, social, and cognitive mobility.[34] There has emerged for many young people, single and married, a sense of rootlessness and a loss of identity. At the same time they have been given exciting and frightening opportunities to choose with whom they will relate and explore the nature and depth of affection. And what better place than in an intentional community where both variety and a degree of mutual support are readily available, and where there is an 'attempt to recreate a wider pattern of intimate relationships'.[35]

At present a pendulum swing is occurring between being a part and being oneself, and back again; between engagement, disengagement, and engagement again. In more specific terms the move is out of the isolated nuclear family into a situation of both openness and loneliness, and then in one way or another back towards a new dimension of relating in a communal context. Of course it can then be out of the latter into even more open and more untested situations.

The move out of the restrictive nuclear family takes various forms, some more and some less linked with old patterns. The Children of God, for example, are well known for claiming the total allegiance of their members and a radical break with parents which in the early days at least meant no, or censored, correspondence and no permission to see mothers and fathers alone. Yet at the same time the Children remain very keen advocates of the monogamous style of family relationships, and sex outside marriage is forbidden. In most other communities of a non-sectarian nature there is very little pressure to break links with the parental home and members are free to retain or relinquish these as they wish. In fact most find that the demands of communal living mean a more tenuous contact with their family of origin, which is frequently as they wish it. At Birchwood Hall, one of the founding families attempted to bridge the gap by bringing their in-laws to live with them: the experiment, shortlived, ended in failure.

As the movement is away from parental control towards greater choice, so it is towards a new experience of affection. It is here that we are entering into a dimension of human relationships which has never been faced in the same way, or at least on the same scale, before. George Ineson of Taena calls it moving slowly away from tribal archetypes into the realm of free association. As yet the community movement in this country has journeyed only a small way along this path; we are only just beginning to experience both the spaciousness and the fear of freedom. For the opportunity to choose openly to whom we relate not only reveals more about others but obliges us to take responsibility for ourselves without the assurance or comfort of tribal approval. This leads to much anxiety for, as Cooper writes, 'what we are socially conditioned to need and expect is not love but security'.[36]

One way to deal with the hazards of intimate or loving relationships in a community has been to insist on the segregation of the sexes, which in practice means celibacy. The monastic tradition of course pursued this way but often, as many would now admit, at the expense of genuine community. Monks or nuns could disengage from 'the world' in an individualistic quest for intimacy with Christ yet, though living in communities, be prevented from finding a loving God through relationships with their fellows. The corporate life could literally and deliberately exclude corporateness.

Of the communities I am concerned with here, some of those consisting of women have also approached the matter of affection on a celibate basis, although with a great deal more openness to each other. Margaret Potts, writing of St Julian's, comments:

We . . . count ourselves fortunate in having, among our friends, psychiatric social workers, psychologists, and psycho-therapists who have been able to interpret for us much in our half-conscious emotions and our thinking about people and circumstances that has divided us. We have begun to discover how to discover the origins and meaning of these emotions and attitudes, to face them more really and so to find our misplaced energies realized and re-directed. We have learnt to begin to recognize a false guilt, which comes from the kind of insecurity that is dependent on being approved of, and that cannot accept and acknowledge ourselves as we are.[37]

The members of the Grail state that their commitment to Christ 'asks us to recognize the importance of sexuality in all relationships, learning to release and redirect our power of loving in warm, deep, and trusting friendships'.[38] But as yet, of such groups, only the Grail seems seriously to be questioning the single-sex basis of its community life.

Within mixed groups there is a greater potential for intimacy and love to be expressed across the sexes. Yet this situation poses further questions of how open both married and single should be in their relationships. For the married couple, moving into community can be a traumatic experience. Even in the Community of Celebration, where personal relationships are worked out with biblical injunctions very much in mind and where there is an almost overwhelming emphasis on loving concern, freedom of association can raise large issues.

This community is currently at a very important stage of development, not least in its working through, as a committed Christian fellowship, the function of the nuclear family and its relation to life in community. On the nuclear family itself, Virginia Withey (a mother of four, a social worker, and a member of the Community of Celebration living in Cumbrae), writes:

I consider that the marriages most of us have and the families we establish are of such a nature as to preclude the building of brotherly relationships. Possessive love, exclusiveness, protection of itself in defensive ways, characterize marriage and the nuclear family in our day. If we have in our local churches a New Testament kind of brotherhood, Christians must re-define marriage and the family and find ways to make them usable as building blocks, as the basic units of Christian community. Instead of warning Christians away from experimentation in this direction . . . we have to find ways to redeem the institutions of marriage and the family.[39]

Virginia Withey and her colleagues are fully aware that marriage at its best can be an immensely supportive and rich relationship. Their concern is not to destroy marriage but, as Christians, to tackle those things that dehumanize it, especially for women whose very individuality is so often threatened, in order that it can realize its great possibilities. It is, therefore, remarkable that the Community of Celebration, with its traditional organizational structure, is under attack from some quarters for seeming to place community before family life. In fact it would see both as of equal and complementary value and claim that each needs to nurture the other.

At Post Green, two of the male members of the community established such a strong bond that eventually their wives and children were drawn in and, after much heart-searching, committed themselves to sharing a home together yet still maintaining the monogamous married relationship. They are still in the process of working out in a mature way the implications of this situation. This kind of situation highlights an important aspect of community life. Quite apart from its creative potential for enabling those of homosexual inclination to discover a milieu in which they can relate without shame and without offence, it points to one thing greatly lacking in our aggressively male-dominated society: the need for men to learn the art of nurturing men in their personal needs and interpersonal relationships.

Although many questions are raised in mixed groups it is remarkable how tenacious, despite the strains and stresses, the continuing one man-one woman relationship remains, be this in (unmarried) pair-bonds or within marriage itself. The idea that communities, at least in our society, are places of unusual sexual permissiveness is quite inaccurate; and even in non-religious situations group marriage is non-existent and 'sleeping around' more the exception than the rule. The reason, however, is not the belief that one man was 'meant' for one woman. Most remain agnostic because so far they feel that far too little is known of more open relationships of this kind adopted by many people through choice, although a mature and thoughtful book on this issue, *Open Marriage* by Nena and George O'Neill, has recently been published in this country.[40] It is much more a matter of the norms and sanctions of our society still weighing so heavily against alternative interpersonal patterns of life that jealousy, fear of disapproval, or plain economic insecurity are likely to be highly destructive. All that can be said experimentally is that alternatives have by no means been fully tested and that what little evidence we have of responsible moves in more open relationships are by no means wholly negative.[41] As Jessie Bernard comments, marriage will certainly remain but 'it has many futures. . . .

The reason is not that marriage itself is becoming any worse. It is mainly because it is getting better and because we face "a revolution of rising expectations".[42]

Just because the monogamous marital pattern for life remains strong in mixed groups, the place of the single person in such communities is all the more important. Segregation or celibacy is one way through; but this cannot be a universally applied solution. At Post Green one delicate issue has been the handling of the relationship of a married couple to a single person where the three have for some years worked extremely closely together. As the single person in this situation commented: 'Put three mature Christians together and it is so easy to end up with an immature trio.' Again we are still only on the threshold of exploring the potential relationship of the single person to the married.

The emphasis above on marriage and sexuality is not meant to beg the question as to how closely they are related to intimacy or love. Many celibates would claim that they could experience the latter at great depth without sexual expression; many married people would say they still feel inhibited and constricted within marriage. Indeed it is quite possible for communities of too small or tightly-knit a kind to prevent a new dimension of human relationships emerging, but to that I return later.

Roles

Communities are places wherein the intention is often to explore a new role relationship between man and woman, husband and wife, father and mother. One could point to changes taking place in non-religious communities like Laurieston Hall, with a very strong contingent of members associated with Women's Liberation, or to Birchwood Hall where some of the women resent exclusion from tasks usually undertaken by men, such as building or accountancy. But, despite good intentions, it takes a lot to overcome well-worn ways, and it is easy even, or indeed especially, in communities for women to get the worst of all worlds. Jessie Bernard writes:

> Women have a hard time in communes, as in so many of the male-designed options, fighting the preconceived ideas about sex roles which the young men bring with them. Unless strong regulations are laid down, they are likely to find themselves saddled with the household chores as ruthlessly as in any conventional household.[43]

A similar danger would seem to exist on the more religious scene. Both Percy Smith at Pilsdon and Alastair Jamieson at Bystock Court spoke to me of the heavy burden of responsibility and work which had fallen on their wives over the years.

With regard to leadership in intentional communities of a religious kind, the paternalism associated for so long with the Church and with the male still looms ominously large. Especially in the more traditional kind of communities, men, often clergy, abound as undisputed leaders: at Pilsdon, Lee Abbey, Scargill, Little Gidding, Bugbrooke, the Community of Celebration and the Community of the Word of God. Certain such communities, like Bugbrooke, take it as a matter of biblical principle that authority should be exercised by men only. In 1975 the Community of Celebration possessed only one woman elder out of seven, though Post Green, its sister community, did much better with several prominent lay women. It would seem, therefore, that though some informal role-sharing goes on, any form of role-exchange or reversal which carries with it a genuine shift in the locus of authority between the sexes is still very much the exception.

Children

It has been suggested that communities are an ideal place for the young family and in many cases this has proved to be true.[44] Reliance on the small nuclear family unit for the socialization of children can at times be desperately inadequate. No wonder that some communities, like the Community of Celebration, find a good number of widowed or separated parents in evidence. At Birchwood Hall a divorced mother who had to go into hospital for a considerable time was greatly relieved to find her young child looked after so well; though one resident did comment on the problem of the house becoming a home for unsupported mothers.

The move from being a part of the nuclear family unit, out towards greater individuality and a link with a wider, extended unit, creates both opportunities and difficulties. Emmanuel Sullivan writes:

Children and adolescents find a new dignity and maturity within community. They are primarily accepted as persons in their own right and not simply as an extension of selfhood for their parents. The experience to date is that, far from negating marital and family relationships and values, community provides the best possible situation for their realization.[45]

Yet Reg East of the Barnabas Fellowship comments:

44

For the parents with families there has also been tension between loyalty to the community and the needs of the children. As this has been realized, they have been released from the demands of the community enough to ensure that children receive attention.[46]

Another problem was encountered by a Roman Catholic commune in Islington where the arrival of a family with young children created frustrating limitations on the more noisy aspects of the social life of the young single members. 'It's impossible to have a real party now', commented one of them. 'To begin with', says Peter Langford of Ringsfield Hall, where there were five young children,

> we tried to be too communal, and the children suffered. Now we have a compromise which in our situation combines family and community life in as satisfactory a way as we can manage. Breakfast is always by families and so is tea except at weekends. Lunch is always communal and so is Sunday tea. When we have small groups to stay we usually have Sunday dinner with them, which the children don't like much![47]

One typical problem for parents is that encountered by a mother at Birchwood Hall who just could not bear her children romping away from her into the arms of other residents. The fact that one's children will be very much exposed to values other than parental ones, such as different approaches to discipline and the sort of presents given at birthday times, is a matter of far more than superficial consequence.

With such things worked through, however, children probably benefit as much as anyone from communal living. Mixing with others of different age and sex and linguistic ability seems to produce a more integrated child. And especially if families in the future have to be strictly limited, as John Taylor suggests may well be the case,[48] then this way of life has a great deal to commend it to young families.

Up to now few communities have seen many children grow through them and leave. In the Israel kibbutzim there have been problems of young people who have difficulty in relating to what appears a strange outside world. But so far in Britain this break seems less traumatic with children moving regularly out of the community at eleven for State schooling, sometimes, as with those from Scoraig in Scotland, spending the week many miles away. Young people born and bred within Taena certainly seemed to us to be well equipped for life beyond and indeed had a very balanced view of the strengths and weaknesses of communal living.

Older people

Older people are evident in intentional communities in three kinds of situation. There are those communities, such as the Farncombe Sisters, in which all the members originally recruited were on the elderly side. This can have the result of producing a rather traditional life-style and make recruitment a very difficult matter: though it should be noted that there is a move to gather the (just) retired into a form of communal life which can be a resource to them and enable them to use their still considerable energy and skills for the sake of others.[49] Secondly, there are communities, such as Taena, where the members started as young people and grew old together, though were rejuvenated by the children who appeared on the scene over the years.

In the third place, there are communities, such as Findhorn and the Community of Celebration, which from the outset recruited both young and old. It has been argued that the older people benefit immensely from living in such 'longitudinal' groups and this seems by and large to be true.[50] But one must not overlook the difficulties of adaptation for them, as well as the acceptance of heavy responsibilities by the young. As yet, we have some years to go before we can fully appreciate both the problems and, I believe, the great potential of intentional communities in which the old play a major part.

The extended unit

The nuclear family living in community has to make considerable modifications to its often narrow, stereotyped function in wider society. Its members are faced with a degree of disengagement from a very close-knit group and engagement with a now wider community. The latter I here call 'the extended unit' (Jessie Bernard terms it the 'affinity group'),[51] for it is in some ways a reflection of the old extended family, though with the fundamental difference that members enter by choice, not by birth.

In the extended unit, the basic interpersonal questions of affection are still the same: how deep should relationships go, not just for the few especially close friends but with all members of the wider group? The tension continues between those inclined towards the overpersonal and those of a more counterpersonal disposition, between being a part and being oneself.

Once again each community has to discover its own balance here. The Children of God on entry formally change their Christian names

46

and adopt those of biblical characters. A contrast to the situation at Bystock Court where a woman from Guyana, variously called Blackcurrant, Whitewash, or Snow White, remained very much her smiling self!

As the circle is widened and a resolution of the interpersonal issues sought, there are inevitable conflicts and crises. It is hard learning to be more open and available to others, risking the hurt of greater intimacy and the stresses of the wider sharing of possessions and domestic duties. Those who join communities in an attempt to escape from the world of tension in human relationships invariably get a rude awakening, for what Jean Vanier calls the period of happy 'illusion' soon passes. He writes:

I have watched a number of communities grow and suffer. During the first period of time everybody is happy. Men who have been deeply wounded come from a lonely, unhappy situation and suddenly find people sharing. They think it is great: everybody is a saint and everything is fantastic. The next few months everybody is a devil. During the first months you could accept not having the biggest piece of meat or not looking at the television program you like. But then you discover that they are looking at all the unintelligent programs, and that they never want to watch the ones that you want to look at. Whenever you want to go to the toilet, they are in the bathroom. This is everyday life. They are always eating spaghetti and peanut butter sandwiches. They accentuate religion too much. For a while religion is great, but not when it is every day. That is fanatical. This second stage, the period of deception, is the crucial moment. It is when my desires are such that I want to see my program and I want my spaghetti. So we say, 'Let's humor everybody. We will have two television sets. Those who want channel number one can go here, channel number two can go there. And we will have self-service so that those who want spaghetti can have spaghetti, those who want fish can have fish, those who want something else can have something else. Then everybody is satisfied. But then we are no longer in a community; we are in a hotel. You have to work at community day by day. During the first stage, the stage of excitement, which is an illusion, you see something which you think is fantastic. Then you get into the period of deception. Finally, through commitment, you come to the moment of reality. During the period of illusion and deception, you are outside of the community. When you come to the stage of reality, you are committed.[52]

47

Margaret Potts, writing of St Julian's, has a deeply perceptive chapter on the 'reality' of community living of which Vanier speaks.

> Living in a community like St Julian's has compelled us to see that the life of Christians is not romantic. They are as much a prey to jealousy, resentment, anger and fluctuating emotions, for instance, as are non-Christians, and the refusal to recognize this produces an impression of dishonesty which discredits their faith far more than the faults they try to hide.[53]

She continues:

> Part of our search for reality stems from our growing conviction that, at every level of life from the Cabinet to the kitchen, one of the main needs is for a Christian witness in relationships. Whether on the mission station or in the office, it is the quality of relationships that tells and that makes for creative action. This is no easier to arrive at in a Christian community than in secular employment. In fact I think we can say truly that it is less easy. For we have no escape from each other. We have no ivory tower to which we can retire. There is no knocking off at 5 p.m. All the small irritations, all the clashes of temperament, are with us every day and all day. We have discovered that to 'cry peace, peace, where no peace is', accomplishes nothing and merely leaves us with a sense of frustration.[54]

Margaret Potts goes on to speak of the problems and opportunities of facing honestly the insecurity, the insignificance, and the anger that so often arise. Of the latter she comments:

> Our suppression of anger was more often than not a result of our fear of its destructiveness, a reasonable fear, for anger, especially violent anger, can destroy a relationship. But within our community life there is hope that there may be a strong enough bond of fellowship to contain the destructiveness. So we may come to learn gradually that, in their proper place anger and love may be two sides of the same coin.[55]

Again and again those experienced in living in community stress the importance of staying with relationships, for 'sometimes these situations or others like them, go on for months, sometimes even for years'.[56] George Ineson of Taena speaks about this process as 'holding the circle'. He describes what this means:

(It is) to contain the opposites, to let the opposites meet so that the new can be conceived and the new life cared for and protected within the circle. The opposites are inner and outer, each reflecting the other – aloneness and togetherness, the discipline of a pattern and the openness to let things happen, to bend like grass in the wind, to SEE, the following of my own thread and the involvement of relating to the other. A group can try and hold the circle only by seeing that its work is to accept the opposites and not simplify them out.[57]

'Whatever the difficulties are,' he writes,

a solution will emerge if you can contain the problem and live through it. Once the community divides into two or more separate organisms, the heat escapes and the meal is uncooked – leaving only partial surface solutions instead of a radical transformation. Living in a town or city offers so many possibilities of escape that it is hardly possible to contain a problem in this way except in the limited sphere of the family; this is one reason why so many of us today never pass beyond adolescence, the spirit imprisoned in a surface adaptation to a particular external context.[58]

Sub-units

The finding of the balance between being oneself and being a part is often made difficult by the size of the community. In this case a helpful way forward for some has been the emergence of 'households' which form a kind of small extended unit within the larger one. At the Community of Celebration, when well over a hundred members were residing at Yeldall Manor, the community was divided up into households or sub-communities of fifteen to twenty in each, eating together and having their own lounge.

Many relationship problems are worked out within such groups which are also felt to be important in maintaining a sense of security and continuity for the children. At Post Green the community of some sixty members actually live, eat, and sleep in five widely separate household units on the estate. Even at Birchwood Hall, with only twenty-five members, the feeling that sub-units were necessary to promote identity and intimacy was so strong that distinct groups were set up, living quite separately in many respects and each creating its own life-style. There was the Coach House group, with a lively interest in arts and crafts; the Blue Kitchen group, living relatively individualistically; and the Yellow Kitchen group, with a strong emphasis on a corporate life-style through such things as income sharing and the breaking down of male/female roles. On the other hand, John Gamlin reports that the sixty or so people living communally at the Old Hall, East Bergholt, would look with suspicion on the creation of such distinct sub-groups.

Privacy

This search for the appropriate degree of togetherness and separation is very much linked with the matter of privacy and the associated questions of tidiness and cleanliness. These are in fact major issues, for the problems of sharing social space are very closely bound up with the sharing of physical space. All that can be said is that participants who cannot live with the communal norm compromise or leave and that this norm, by very definition of the technical problems of managing a large group, tends to be towards lack of privacy, disorder, and dirt, at times to the almost total exclusion of the aesthetic.

At the more disorderly end of the scale lie groups like the Shrubb Family, Laurieston Hall (where the windows have not been cleaned in three years, though there are enough of them to give any window-cleaner heart-failure!), and the Kingsway Community at Keveral Farm where on wet days the place is clogged with good heavy mud. At Birchwood Hall it is disorder rather than dirt that meets the eye, with bedrooms containing a vast quantity of bric-à-brac from cast-off guitars to a basket full of young jackdaws. Pilsdon, Bystock Court, and the Roslin Community are spartan rather than disorderly, having more the atmosphere of institutions and lacking some of the warmth often associated with communal chaos. The sheer size of Bystock Court, for example, with its imposing entrance hall and huge empty ballroom gives one an inevitable sense of the impersonal, though there is life and friendship enough in the parts of the building more fully used. Yeldall Manor, until 1976 the home of half the Community of Celebration, was fairly clean and orderly though a very utilitarian building.

At the more aesthetic end are places like the Open Centres, where beauty of *décor* is deliberately cultivated; for example, at the Salisbury Centre in Edinburgh. Likewise at Findhorn, of which one visitor commented: 'Spotlessly clean. Guests are taken care of superbly and graciously. The gardens are a wonder to behold.'

It is thus really a question of paying one's money (much or little) and taking one's choice. Whether the community operates well in any of these diverse conditions depends on the expectations of members and what one is used to. Andrew Rigby was disturbed in the mornings by the noise of the children at Postlip Hall:[59] I was conscious of children crying late at night and in the early hours at Bystock Court. Expectations can of course change: at Birchwood Hall a married couple who had been there four years were leaving in part because the wife could no longer tolerate the muddle. One thing is certain, however; it is impossible for anyone living in community to avoid at some stage having to come to terms with the question of privacy and order. It is a glorious situation to be farming on the shores of Little Loch Broom, with the majesty of the mountains of Wester Ross surrounding one; but in the long dark winters the Forsyth family, with their four children, have for ten years crowded into a tiny croft with hardly room to swing a mouse let alone a cat and, when nature calls, have had to pick their way outside to the dry toilet in the little shed round the corner.

Meals and meetings

The way in which communities meet for decision-making purposes has already been mentioned. But members also meet regularly for other reasons, in particular to reaffirm in one way or another the identity of the group. This is done notably through eating together. Rosemary Haughton writes: 'Food gives life, but it is a shared life, a common life, and the sharing of food has always been seen as an assertion of community.'[60] Little Gidding members write: 'Our commitment to God and to each other is symbolized in our common meals.'[61] All groups share certain meals. In fact, where this occurs infrequently, it is doubtful whether one can talk of a permanent community at all. In 1972 the Kingsway Community, early on in their life in London, stated this in no uncertain terms in their commitment: 'The first principle is that food is common; the main daily meal is the central act of sharing, and to partake is the unfailing requirement made of everyone who would belong to an extended family in the Community.'[62]

At just one or two places where the community is too scattered or too large to make corporate meals possible, other gatherings gain in prominence. At Post Green, members from all the separate houses meet 'for fellowship' every Thursday evening in the main house. The Community of Celebration at Yeldall had a full evening routine with Wednesday night being an open night, Thursday for the weekly Eucharist, Friday children's and youth night, and Saturday for entertainment and fun. The appropriate rhythm of coming together and separating out is a very important one for communities to establish.

Possessions

In balancing the claims of the individual and of the group, one important matter is that of how to handle personal wealth and possessions. It is interesting that whether communities are self-consciously religious or not, the life-style of the first Christian households in the Acts of the Apostles seems to command universal respect.

One or two communities require that incoming members surrender their all to the group, amongst these being the Roslin Community and the Focolarini, both groups vowed to poverty; the Children of God, and Bugbrooke. The last aim to live at half the average cost of living in this country and use what they thus save to further the work of the community. Other groups permit members to retain their capital, which may or may not be invested in the property owned or used by the community, but to pool all other income and receive back some form of allowance, often very meagre. This is the case, for example, at Pilsdon, the Farncombe Community, Hengrave Hall, and Rostrevor. The Grail follows a similar practice.

> As a symbol of sharing and exchange, as a token of the flowing of life from one to another, we share whatever salaries we earn and whatever income we make through the work of our society. We each receive an annual sum for our personal expenses, but we accept the fact that some of us may need more for various reasons such as health or work demands.[63]

It would, however, be naive to assume that the more total the sharing, the further along the road to a mature sense of community members had gone. Some of those in the religious Orders, for example, would admit that total surrender of possessions can all too easily lead to surrender of economic responsibility and that consequently they can be cushioned against 'the changes and chances of this fleeting world'; whilst opportunities that religious men and women, free from family ties, often have to travel light, see the world, and meet a variety of interesting people, could be regarded as amongst the privileges of the more affluent members of society. In many cases it is wrestling with the responsibilities of money that brings the newer communities to look at the heart of their commitment. It is not easy to share all when salaries or wages earned by members vary a great deal.

Yet some sort of economic pooling is one of the outstanding features of most groups which are seeking to discover a new dimension of togetherness. How they handle this can make or mar their life. There is no blueprint and changes can take place over time even within the same group. At Taena it was found that, after some twenty years of sharing, members wanted to regain a greater degree of independence.

Around 1960 the difficulties increased to a crisis point. The community had expanded to 15 adults and 35 children, and found itself unable to live off the farm. There were school expenses to pay and legal problems over land. The fathers felt irritated because the common ownership system meant that if they wished to take the children out for the day they had to hold a meeting to obtain the money. But the problems were not insoluble. 'After many meetings,' said George, 'we felt that to prevent the institution becoming a prison we should return to a new beginning. So we gave up the Constitution, let the families be independent and through financial independence made it easier for members to leave the community. By separating finance in this way our weekly meeting became voluntary.'[64]

Domestic work

Sharing not only extends to possessions but to domestic duties. The pattern is varied, there being groups which fight shy of any but the most rudimentary system of cooking and cleaning and those which lay down hard-and-fast duty rosters. The need remains, however, for all groups to come to terms with establishing some form of division of labour. Lee Abbey divides its large community into work groups operating in the office, kitchen, house, and on the estate. At Pilsdon each person has a specific daily task in the house or on the farm. On the other hand groups like the Shrubb Family, Keveral Farm (the Kingsway Community), and Birchwood Hall tend to cook and clean as the spirit moves them.

There are, naturally, problems. At Lee Abbey, for example, members initially love the lack of really responsible work but after a while can sometimes become bored and listless just because of this. At Hengrave Hall one difficulty which arose concerned the matter of the extent to which families were responsible for domestic chores in the main house and conference centre. At the Alternative Society's Lower Shaw Farm, Dick Kitto spoke of his feeling of being pushed out when others took responsibility for the market garden he would dearly have loved to look after. Keveral Farm residents have been divided over the effort which should go into work in the house and on the farm, and that which should be directed towards producing their very marketable homemade jigsaw puzzles. The Jesus Family has sought to get outside help with its administration, and Post Green is at times caught between the pressures of internal management and its external ministry.

All these problems only highlight that living in community is a testing ground for working out the meaning of intensive togetherness. Because it is so often washing dishes, cleaning rooms, and keeping the place repaired that reveal basic conflicts of personality and behaviour, the remarkable thing is not that some groups fragment but that so many, more or less happily, survive for so long.

Closed or open?

In true monastic spirit, if not style, most communities place the offering of hospitality high on their list of priorities. Those which are also conference centres – such as Lee Abbey and Scargill, the Barnabas Fellowship, Hengrave Hall, and the Grail – go out of their way to ensure that the permanent residential community mixes as freely with guests as possible. Reg East of the Barnabas Fellowship writes: 'We try to take our guests into a "larger family", welding them and the community into one as much as possible.'[65] The Grail members comment that 'as women we can add warmth to our surroundings and we do this by trying to make the place where we live into a real home. To keep house, to cook and clean, to welcome visitors, is in varying degrees the concern of every one of us.'[66] Yet St Julian's, which as a community is itself so perceptive, in this respect seems to keep more apart from guests, the latter at times feeling the members to be somewhat remote. Nor do they accommodate children. There is little doubt, however, that the example of communal living at the heart of such centres communicates to guests as much, if not more, of the expression of the Christian faith than actual conferences. The medium is indeed the message.

Some communities go in for well-regulated hospitality: the Community of Celebration has one member specially responsible for booking in and accommodating visitors, and at Pilsdon their 'guest master, Sidney, a spastic, is a most capable and erudite guide'. The Student Christian Movement's community at Wick Court holds an open evening for local people to drop in on the twenty-fifth of every month. Other groups allow much more of an open door. Laurieston Hall's summer 'alternative university' gives some 2,000 visitors the chance to come and go more or less as they please, provided they accept the fairly primitive accommodation and pay a nominal amount for their stay. The crofting community at Scoraig, though much less accessible, accommodated some seventy visitors in the summer of 1974. Such 'invasions' can have their problems. The Kingsway Community in London nearly foundered when, in the early days, its house was occupied by some fifty people, a situation that eventually led to much firmer controls.

It is important to note here that so many short-term visitors passing through communities magnifies their influence out of all proportion to their size or numbers. The Blackheath Commune found that in the end they had to give their special energies to coping with those dropping in, some in acute need, at the expense of corporately planned community work in the local neighbourhood. The experience of certain of the Ashram houses has been similar. The Roadrunners, when located in Manchester, accepted this position and made the most of it. One member wrote:

> There is a strong atmosphere of acceptance of people for what they are and this shows itself partly in the large variety of visitors we attract at all times of the day. Visitors are always made welcome and are immediately included in the life of the community. It isn't often that we will sit for hours talking to someone in a polite fashion, pretending that we have nothing to do; more often the visitor is encouraged to help prepare a meal, read one of our books or help with the magazine that we run from the house. This makes for a far more relaxed atmosphere and the visitor generally feels accepted and at ease. One marked example of this is perhaps a lonely and rather nervous old man who now feels that he is quite welcome just to call and to sit down and play the piano, so long as this is not causing anyone annoyance, whether the people who originally made contact with him are there or not. We are pleased that he feels this way. However, with many people it is just a case of them feeling that they are part of the community. In the words of one boy who stayed with us for only a short while: 'You always have the feeling that this is an "open" household.'[67]

CONCLUSION

The question of hospitality raises wider issues than just the caring for or entertaining of visitors. It brings to the fore the whole matter of where communities establish their boundaries, draw the line, or 'hold the circle'. Visitors break the circle in one direction for they bring in with them an external view of life and people, challenging even the value of community living itself. But how open the receiving group is to such questioning, explicit or implicit, will depend on their own philosophy. Findhorn, for example, entertains guests well and for a fee shows day callers round, but mainly to impress on them their own role as the 'Centre of Light' for the 'New Age'. On the other hand, for two years now Laurieston Hall has in the summer 'organized' its free-running series of weeks where people wanting to discuss an alternative society can come and share without any inhibitions.

Can and dare communities, however, break the circle in the other direction by at times deliberately moving out of their enclaves to risk direct encounter with the wider world? Some, such as the Community of Celebration, Post Green, and Findhorn, do this by exercising an external ministry which is supposedly their *raison d'être*, though again one wonders whether it is the actual ministry or the quality of the community expressing it which impresses more. Other groups believe that they have no 'call' to do anything but their own thing within their limited circle, and there is much to be said for inconspicuous living. Family communes as ends in themselves form the main theme of the recent thorough investigation of the secular scene by Philip Abrams and Andrew McCullock.[68] Their inquiry led them to conclude that a random scattering of self-contained units is the best description of the modern commune 'movement' in Britain. From the point of view of this book, however, and especially in relation to those communities associated with the Christian outlook, it must be said that unless they can in some way extend their boundaries, initially perhaps in the direction of other communities, and show that they can live as happily with those as unlike as like themselves, then not much of major social significance has occurred.

Such openness to wider contacts and relationships is a matter of great consequence for the relevance of communities to our time. To move from the potential restrictiveness of the nuclear family into the wider circle of a community may be, though by no means certainly, an initial step towards exploring the possibilities of intimacy and love at a time when free association, for good or ill, is fast becoming commonplace. Jessie Bernard has persuasively argued that the looser co-operative household or intentional community, if not the rather intense commune, has a real future.[69] There is an immense fund of vitality, spontaneity, and sheer enjoyment within many such ventures. Despite all difficulties, one feels that people have discovered a new sense of personal worth and a new depth in interpersonal relationships. Yet to stop there can lead to the establishment of narcissistic groups which teach us little. Philip Abrams and Andrew McCulloch at the end of their inquiry into self-contained secular family communes in Britain suggest that the wisest policy is to leave such groups severely alone.[70] But from where we stand, the value of communal living is not whether it provides happy huddles for hairy or holy ones. It is whether it can train people in the art of living and loving which is able to reach beyond the security of even extended units into the vulnerability of a hostile, lonely, and apathetic world and there demonstrate a new and revolutionary dimension of human relationships. In what follows I examine the ways in which some basic communities are seeking to do just that.

3

SPIRITUALITY

Of fundamental importance to the search for a new expression of community by Christians is the quest for a more meaningful and dynamic spirituality. By 'spirituality' here I mean that which gives human beings the power 'to transcend their immediate needs and to find ultimate meaning and sacredness in all their striving'.[1] For the Christian this is consequent upon what the writer to the Ephesians describes as the illumination of the 'inward eyes',[2] a grasping and being grasped, human opening up encountering divine revelation. The nature of this encounter is a mystery; yet it lies at the very heart of the Christian adventure into new dimensions of self-awareness and human relationships. It seems that any major ferment in society, social or political, is sooner or later reflected in its spirituality, be that 'sacred' or 'pseudo-sacred' (as with the black arts), and thus acts as a kind of barometer of the subtle but often basic changes in the cultural climate.

Spiritual illumination cannot remain a solitary affair; its very nature demands that it somehow be communicated and shared. But in this process of communication words alone often fail and distort, confuse and divide, rather than express the heart of the matter. So today there is a proliferation of diverse forms of expression attempting to translate religious experience into a meaningful 'language'. There is a search for new symbols which are relevant to secular man, symbols which can bring personal poise and communal coherence in a world of bewildering pluralism. Such a search is of basic significance, for, as Mary Douglas writes:

> It is an illusion to suppose that there can be organization without symbolic expression. It is the old prophetic dream of instant, unmediated communication. Telepathic understanding is good for brief flashes of insight. But to create an order in which young and old, human and animal, lion and lamb can understand each other direct, is a millennial vision. Those who despise ritual, even at its most magical, are cherishing in the name of reason a very irrational concept of communication.[3]

58

The first flush of experimentation with new forms of spirituality seems to be over, perhaps itself symbolized by the demise in 1974 of the journal *Living Worship*, a periodical which in one form or another for seven years reported on new ventures in worship. Bernard Braley, who edited *Living Worship*, reports in correspondence that amongst other facts its termination was due to a weariness with new ideas seized on just to 'prop up' otherwise declining congregations, and to the frustration of those trying to introduce fresh forms of worship into situations antipathetic to any departure from traditional ways. It was also doubted by some whether liturgical changes of any fundamental or lasting significance were occurring. The views of those who at this stage still remained unsatisfied are reflected by Michael Walsh who in 1973 wrote:

> It is a long time since I have had a satisfactory celebratory experience. I seldom, nowadays, accept an invitation to participate in 'a liturgy' or 'a worship' or 'a eucharist'. Most of them I find characterized by unresolved paradoxes and contradictions – contrived spontaneity, jovial rather than joyful, affirmations of doubting faith, embarrassed fellowship, a nibbled meal, a studied avoidance of the terminus of prayer, and an anti-human shunning of all ritual.[4]

Yet this kind of disillusionment has by no means prevented the search from continuing. It is merely following other channels of expression of greater significance for the present generation. In this situation the community movement has a great deal to contribute. For what is happening within it is not the imposition of 'contrived spontaneity' on unprepared or unwilling participants. It is an attempt to start where people are, with the reality of human relationships, sometimes as discordant as harmonious, and from that base give expression to the divine-human encounter, through a dynamic and relevant spirituality.

THE RULE
(Authority and control)

As described in Chapter 2, conditions of membership and rules of life associated with communities and related groups touch all aspects of organizational living. The core of the rule, however, is usually about worship and prayer.

In general, communities which have an ordered or comprehensive 'contract' for living normally adhere to a similar type of religious discipline. Thus the Roslin Community is through and through monastic in style, from its 'engagement to poverty, celibacy, and obedience',[5] to its regular daily periods for prayer and worship. Likewise the Farncombe Community, which lives an ordered life, has a rule which

> includes four periods of corporate prayer during the day: morning worship, midday intercessions, corporate silence before supper and evening worship after supper. There is a certain amount of flexibility according to what outside commitments a Sister has. Silence is kept after evening prayers until after breakfast the next morning and on Fridays until 3 p.m. There is a service of Holy Communion in the Chapel once a week, which may be celebrated by ministers of different denominations, and a Community retreat once a year.[6]

At Pilsdon, a community with a traditional type of organization, 'there is a regular rhythm to each day: Matins and Holy Communion at 7.30; breakfast at 8; intercessions at 1; lunch at 1.15; tea at 4.30; Evensong at 6.30; supper at 7; and Compline at 9.15. This is the frame into which the work of each day is fitted.'[7]

Of the mainly non-residential groups, the Iona Community has, in true Presbyterian style, always placed considerable emphasis on the discipline full members accept.

Members are committed

> to give at least 1 per cent of their gross income to developing countries and generally account for their use of the rest;
> to give some account of their use of time;
> to pray daily for the community and its wider concerns.[8]

The community prints a prayer manual and a certain number of members are prayed for on each day of the month. A smaller and very different group, the Coventry Cathedral staff, share 'A Common Discipline', outlined under two headings: 'The Spirit of the Discipline' and 'The Practice of the Discipline'. Items from the latter read as follows:

> Of the one hundred and sixty-eight hours in the week, members of the discipline allot a minimum of one-third, that is fifty-six hours, to

work, study, worship, and prayer. Of this not less than five hours in any week shall be allotted to prayer and worship and not less than five hours to study.

Members provide time for sufficient sleep for good health and neither eat nor drink to excess. Unless prevented by illness or other good cause, they abstain from one meal a week and give money thus saved to the poor.

In addition to breakfast together on Monday mornings members meet together four or five times every six months in smaller groups with not more than seven members in each. Each such meal is accompanied by a period of open talk, the whole occasion lasting for not less than two hours.[9]

Such communities and groups as these have a structure which is based on the virtues of conformity. In principle, members look to the rule to give a sense of purpose and solidarity, being prepared to temper their individual wishes to the decisions of the larger group. However, the degree of cohesion achieved is not always as impressive as at first sight might seem to be the case (for example, amongst the staff of Coventry Cathedral).

There is, however, a move to less defined spirituality. Margaret Potts, writing of St Julian's, states that 'membership of the Community involves a vocation to a way of life rather than submission to a clear rule'.[10] Such an approach can in fact be seen operating in even relatively structured groups. Scargill individuals are free to work out the expression of their own personal religious commitment. The Community of Celebration, with a well-regulated mode of living, eschews any set religious rule of life. Other groups have sought to keep their corporate spirituality from crowding the individual by opting for periods of silence which the person concerned can use as he wishes. Terry Drummond discusses 'a non-compulsory spiritual rule' being considered by the Ashram communities in 1974. He writes:

The group felt that the Ashram Community has a need for some kind of rule of life. The problem was to define a rule that could cover those who felt that traditional spirituality had nothing to offer. It was felt that the best area open to us was that of contemplation and meditation where silence is central to all that is done. Someone said, 'Let there be a space in your togetherness.'[11]

The members of the Servants of Christ the King have a practice called

'Waiting on God', when they seek to give individuals as much space as possible to explore their own style of spirituality.

> Briefly this consists of three parts: first a time of silence in which each member in his own way brings before God the company and the subject of concern for the meeting; next what is called a 'controlled discussion' when everyone in turn is given an opportunity of saying whatever he feels called on to say without interruption; and finally a general discussion when an attempt is made to resolve differences revealed in the controlled discussion. The whole process is repeated, if necessary, until a common mind is reached.[12]

In this context it is interesting to note the attempt of a Greenwich house group of many years' standing, called LINK[13] to move towards some form of corporate religious observance. It typifies the difficulty many people have today in submitting to any corporately agreed religious practice. Patricia Worden writes:

> LINK's second critical point in recent years was more basic to the identity of the group and its *raison d'être*. This was precipitated by consideration of a group Eucharist. The question was mooted for some time before the group could bring itself to discuss it fully. What began as a discussion of a form of service rapidly became an exchange of views on such questions as: Are we a Christian group? How Christian are we? If we are Christian, should we celebrate a Communion together? What more would it add to our meeting, as we already 'break bread' together before discussion in an informal meal? Some felt we were simply seekers after truth and that to celebrate a specifically Christian act would exclude all but committed Christians. The conflict of views was evident and it was obvious that feelings were even more divergent than the ideas expressed. In these circumstances a celebration of the Eucharist was clearly impossible.[14]

It is very few groups that have been flexible enough to be able to change from one type of religious life-style to another. One of the few is Taena, the Gloucestershire farming community which moved over a generation from an agnostic, if not atheistic, orientation, through a strong and corporately acknowledged Roman Catholic phase to, most recently, a pluralism of religious observance and belief. But such is the exception which proves the rule.

WORDS

The use of words, spoken or written, to express and shape spirituality is not peculiar to those engaged in developing new communal forms. But the fact that participants are as near as most to founding worship and devotions on the corporate experience of the group adds a dynamic and a freshness to their endeavours which commands attention. Indeed none of the aspects of spirituality dealt with in this chapter is peculiar to communities; inclusion is justified simply because of the importance of what a vital corporate experience produces in the realm of spirituality.

Authority, leadership, and control

There are those groups which still lay great emphasis on the Bible ('the Word of God') as in itself the ultimate criterion by which communal behaviour and relationships are guided and judged. Outstanding here are the Children of God, with a traditional type of organization, who are out-and-out fundamentalist not only in their approach to the Scriptures, but also concerning the writings of their leader, David Berg, otherwise known as 'Moses'. Geoffrey Corry writes:

> While every disciple gets a solid grounding in the Scriptures, both Old Testament and New Testament, the teachings and writings of Moses would seem to receive a more prominent place than those of Scripture. The crucial question – do the Children have to accept David Berg's interpretation of Scripture without question? As no other books are used other than the King James translation and Berg's writings, alternative interpretations of an informed nature seem to be made impossible.[15]

Many groups influenced by the charismatic movement also place great weight on the Scriptures and their pre-eminent value as a spiritual norm. At Bugbrooke, the Community of Celebration, Post Green, and Rostrevor, a centre for Christian renewal in County Down, Northern Ireland, members rarely gather for worship or prayers without Bibles in hand. At each place a daily 'sharing' meeting occurs in small groups, that at Yeldall Manor, once the home of the Community of Celebration, being described as follows:

> Each weekday at 9.00, a resonant bell gathers into four groups the members of the Community of Celebration. Each group is comprised

of 15–20 members, and they have gathered to share the Scriptures. A song or two may be sung, a simple prayer said; then someone reads aloud a Scripture he's prepared, as the others follow in their own Bibles. The one sharing then relates the particular things the Lord has shown him about the passage. These are related to the individual's life: perhaps to his relationship to the Lord, or his relationship to himself or others; perhaps to his past; perhaps to a current situation. After he has finished, another shares, and so on until each has had an opportunity.

Although the burden of content for the sharings stems from each one's personal reading, and thus rests upon the group as a whole, the responsibility for leadership does not. Each group has established leaders, fulfilling a variety of functions: directing the flow of the sharings, calling upon members to share, making additional comments when helpful, drawing out those who are hesitant or uncertain, summarizing the sharings. Leaders may give some or all of these leadership functions to other members of the group: it is the ideal situation for fledgling leaders to test their leadership in a secure situation. The whole leadership role is one of gentle guidance and sensitive listening, providing encouragement and careful nurturing for those who are troubled or unstable. This is vital, for sharing groups provide an important experience of confidence and security for those who are growing in maturity and health.[16]

These groups have an interpersonal function which will be mentioned later. Here I want to emphasize the way the Scriptures are used to uphold the authority of the community. When I attended a sharing session at Yeldall Manor I felt the strong pressure on me not only to produce my Bible as a kind of passport but also to offer very personal thoughts to the group. Done each day, this can become a powerful means of social control. Or, from another point of view, as the community members would probably argue, 'The facts of stable group composition and established leadership heighten tangibly the security that is so necessary for those who are just learning to live honestly and openly.'[17]

The Focolare, a predominantly Roman Catholic lay movement, is organized on more classical lines. It is Bible-centred in its spirituality and explicitly loyal to the Roman Catholic hierarchy. Friends and sympathizers are similarly inclined, being 'all united in living the "Word of Life", which is a complete sentence of the Gospel chosen each month which everyone tries to put into practice'.[18] There are groups, more on the fringe of orthodox Christianity, which dispense with 'the Word' and shift veneration to 'the words' of some specially regarded member. Such was the case at Findhorn where Eileen Caddy, wife of Peter Caddy the leader, under her spiritual pseudonym Elixir, produced from her meditations volumes of 'guidance' for the community. The language is eclectic and often banal:

> Remember there is a silver lining to every cloud, no matter how dark it may appear at the time. Therefore look for the silver lining and never rest content until you have found it.[19]

> You wonder why some days you go around with rose-tinted spectacles on and see everything in its true beauty, while on another day it is as if you have dark spectacles and nothing seems good. Realize that every hour of every day the choice lies in your hands. Your state of mind is what is different, not your surroundings, the beauty is always there.[20]

Such 'guidance' used to be read out each morning in the 'Sanctuary' at Findhorn until in the autumn of 1971 Eileen, either inspired or exhausted, received a final message that it was henceforth up to each member of the community to develop the ability to tune in on their own personal 'guidance'.

In so many of these situations words are used, often unconsciously, in a way which structures experience into predetermined patterns. The same phrases are used over and over again, the same clichés, until their initial meaning and impact are spent. I was struck in one interview with a minister 'baptized in the Spirit' by his constant and monotonous repetition of the words 'love' and 'healing' in an attempt to describe the obviously key experience which had come to his family and his congregation.

The dangers of using a limited vocabulary, yet talking a great deal, are many. It is a classic way of closely monitoring the life of a community: one only belongs if one uses the 'in' words. I myself feel embarrassed in certain communities because they arc, and I am not, inclined to talk constantly about 'the Lord' and His doings. This sets me apart: I am not one of 'them'. Any in authority are quick to spot the stranger within their gates, however courteous they may be. For all their playing down of the importance of speaking in tongues, even the most liberal leaders within the charismatic movement fail to appreciate the power over a community or a congregation given to them by the mere existence of this phenomenon as a token of membership.

The use of 'in' language also prevents clear communication with the world outside. This destroys any hope of a rational understanding or critique of society or of the community itself. The restricted linguistic code pre-sets the way any conversation will go: with the dehumanizing consequence of limiting the possibility of personal (including spiritual) growth and of leaving members at the mercy of those in authority in the community and of their interpretation of reality. It is a guaranteed means of creating a situation of immature dependence.

A variety of reactions to this state of what Josephine Klein has called 'cognitive poverty'[21] has emerged. One such is to allow a great deal more opportunity for silence both 'beyond words' and 'before words',[22] as Alan Ecclestone puts it. Then there are those communities which shun wordy worship altogether: the Blackheath Commune, the Kingsway Community, and those at Wick Court, for example. They claim that 'The Word of Life' is transmitted through the whole host of informal everyday encounters and exchanges. There exist other communities, such as the Open Centres, seeking to employ not only the language of Christianity but of other religions, notably that of the Sufi mystics. The problem here is in the scale of the operation, with a resulting superficiality and the disappearance of the cultural distinctiveness of words in a sea of esoteric verbosity. Finally, there are those who have been involved in constructing their own Christian liturgies and creeds, as temporary not final formulations of where they are at spiritually. John Nicholson of Dartmouth House described to me a gathering he attended where certain of those present were asked to design their own creed and speak about it. His own ran as follows:

> We welcome life
> as a promise and an invitation.
> We affirm that the time of creation
> is always now.

> In struggle and in conflict we shall receive our name
> and trust in the graciousness of a continual journey
> from what we know to what we may become.

> We have heard the voice of our calling
> among those who have no form or beauty to make them desirable:
> We acknowledge that they carry
> the burden of our blindness,
> and that they embody
> the judgement on our community.

We cannot escape
the discerning exercise of our powers,
and neither have we any claim
to dominate the earth:
The mighty will be put down from their seat.

We are glad
that a man called Jesus has focused these things
in his life and in his execution,
and that he has chosen to go away
so that men and women of this generation
may use their freedom to shape the common life of the world
in the spirit of his self-offering.

We hope for justice in the land of the living.
We expect our idols to be broken
before God
who is the stranger at our gate
and who hides his face a while so that we may live.

Day by day we shall sing
the song of the Lord in a strange land
and make our protest:
Long live God – let us prepare the way of the Lord;
and we confidently expect
the almond twig will blossom again
in peace.[23]

Such 'subjectivism' is anathema to those who, with some justification, fear the breakdown of a common faith without a common language of a prescribed kind. But it demonstrates the desire of those linked to basic communities to discover and speak with an authority which is truly theirs.

The personal and the interpersonal

Words not only reflect the locus of authority within the community but the degree to which the personal is stressed. Those groups which react against a rule, against the authority of 'the Word', are reacting against conformism and impersonality. George Ineson of Taena writes:

Language has become sterile and an increasing number of people have lost any direct experience of meaning and the unfolding of life. So there is the need for us to meet across old barriers, to discover new networks, to open to the world of non-ego through meditation, ritual, poetry, music. And this can happen more easily in the context of small groups.[24]

Jim Nagel, for some years leader of the Greenbus camps at Glastonbury, in private conversation made the pertinent comment: 'It is the space between words that counts.' He adds, 'It is not what we say but what we don't say that matters.'[25] The conviction represented here is the self-awareness which is of the essence of true spirituality can only come through what is initially deeply personal; and words often hinder rather than help.

Others, however, believe that there must be a multitude of words to facilitate the discovery and sharing of a deep and personal spirituality. Despite my previous comments about authority, leadership, and control, members of the Community of Celebration and Post Green would still claim that their sharing meetings operate at a richly personal level:

> The sharing may include struggles of faith or unbelief; burdens of concern; or experienced victories or healings, as any of these relate to the experience of the verses shared. . . . Sharings are not meetings for the sake of meetings but have a real purpose. We can no longer sit back and have a cosy time, uninvolved in each other's lives. We have found sharing meetings one of the strongest methods of allowing love to flow freely between us, to heal and strengthen.[26]

It is certainly true that words can encourage self-awareness and sharing for those groups which look to poetic forms of expression in their spirituality. Katimavik – an organization sponsoring gatherings of mainly Roman Catholic lay people for prayer and worship – often print poetry and prose-poetry in their literature. One example of the latter, referring to Katimavik itself, is as follows:

A Katimavik is an awakening
   to the fact that my heart can be touched
     by the Spirit of Jesus.

In an instant
   it appears to me that my heart of stone
     and of sadness
       is changed into a heart of flesh
         sensitive to the Spirit,
           a heart with hope. . . .

And I am not alone.
    At the same time as Jesus shows himself to me
      as someone living
        I discover brothers and sisters
          awakened and hopeful like me. . . .

I belong to the family of Jesus,
    to His mystical body
      where the Holy Spirit dwells. . . .[27]

A penetrating use of words comes from the field of *Gestalt* therapy, the influence of which on the Church I shall be discussing more fully in Chapter 5. Here a very interesting attempt has been made to rewrite some of the major passages of the Scriptures. I quote the paraphrase of the Beatitudes:

Blessed are the day-dreamers, for they shall find their direction.
Blessed are the *aware* aggressors, for they shall save us from destruction.
Blessed are those who can experience disgust, for they shall discover appetite.
Blessed are those who know they hate, for they shall be able to love.
Blessed are those who can endure the impasse, for they shall experience surprise.
Blessed are those who listen, for they shall hear life.
Blessed are those who can keep silent, for they shall spare us their projections.
Blessed are those who are present in their words, for they shall communicate.
Blessed are those who love their neighbours as themselves, not more, not less.[28]

Perhaps the growing attraction of a language that speaks direct to the personal, especially when it can do so within an impersonal society, is as clearly indicated as anywhere, by the large crowd that turned up to hear Michel Quoist read his now famous 'Prayers of Life' during the 1973 festival of worship, 'That's the Spirit'. 'They came by coach from Haslemere. Nuns arrived in inevitable mini-vans. Those without tickets queued. Estimates put the audience in the University Church of Christ the King at 1,300.'[29]

THE EUCHARIST

The Eucharist is a service which, despite all the changes in life-style mentioned in this book, still remains central to the majority of ventures in community-making in which Christians are involved. From the Grail:

> Paramount among celebrations is the Eucharist. Here we show in word and act our loving dependence on God and our interdependence upon each other. Here we express our continuing intention of giving our lives to God and to the world.[30]

And of a very different part of the Christian scene, John Cooke writes: 'The Eucharist, radically interpreted, informally celebrated and politically understood, is a highly significant aspect of the liturgical life of the Underground Church.'[31]

Authority and leadership

For members of basic communities the celebration of the Eucharist has especial importance, for it is here that an attempt is made to found Holy Communion on holy community. Even if there are failures, these only serve to bear out the genuine humanity of the participants, prepared at least to test the purity of worship in the crucible of real human encounter.

One of the main issues within this encounter is that of authority. The large majority of communities accept the discipline of their own denominations regarding the status of the priest or minister in the administration of the Eucharist, usually meaning his exclusive right to preside over the celebration. Roman Catholic groups in particular, such as the Grail, The Focolare, L'Arche, and Katimavik, fully accept the centrality of the Mass and the necessity of having a priest to conduct it. However, amongst members of other denominations, and even amongst some Catholics, there is a move to explore forms of 'communion' where celebration becomes a corporate responsibility. I am here concerned not with the theology of what is happening but with the *de facto* location of authority in the group rather than in a particular individual. In itself this is nothing new; much of the history of the Christian Church is bound up with attempts to resolve this issue. What today is different is the growing strength of the ground swell towards the

70

sharing of authority and leadership and the fact that this is occurring across ecclesiastical boundaries.

Typifying this situation is the revival of interest in the Agape, the common religious meal which was shared in the early Church in close association with the Eucharist. The Rochdale house of the Ashram Community holds a twice-monthly Agape, the meal being linked to discussion and decision-making about the work of the group. In January 1975 the newly founded Hengrave Hall Community expressed their ecumenical concern during the Week of Prayer for Christian Unity through 'the gathering for the Agape in the Long Gallery on the Thursday evening when some 120 Christians prayed and ate together in a festive atmosphere'.[32] In Birmingham a group associated with ONE for Christian Renewal shares in a regular Agape. Jean Wilson writes:

> In our particular group after a period of four years we found that some members perceived what we were doing together in a fully Eucharistic way, whereas others felt that it was an act of sharing not to be found in a local church, yet not fully Eucharistic for them. It is interesting that although the members have these different perceptions yet there is strong evidence of unity, in spite of the fact that it is this difference in perception which divides the denominations. It does seem that the Holy Spirit is at work, leading us forward we know not where.[33]

In all these cases it is for a new expression of the corporate nature of the Body of Christ, not least of the 'priesthood of all believers', that many appear to be searching.

The personal and the interpersonal

The Eucharist is an intensely personal as well as a corporate act of worship. Because of this, few Christian traditions have realized how much the opening up of the Eucharist to sensitive interpersonal communication can enhance the personal. One example will suffice. At a celebration of the 1976 New Year at Dartmouth House, called 'Midwinter Spring', the midnight Eucharist contained a time of confession when the congregation in pairs shared their regrets and their sadnesses, and a period given to the Peace which involved everyone in a free-flowing act of reconciliation which lasted for over half an hour. It was an attempt to enable personal sorrows and joys to be more fully expressed and met through human relationships infused by the spirit of the Sacrament.

The question of the locus of authority in relation to the Eucharist is closely associated with the interpersonal dimension. No basic community can enjoy creative interpersonal relationships within their own ranks or in relation to others, and not least where the Eucharist is concerned, until the authority issue has been resolved to its own satisfaction.

The dilemma for most of the basic communities with which I am concerned is that they are in the double-bind of trying to remain loyal to their own denominations yet dedicated to the cause of Christian unity. In 1975, for example, a large international charismatic conference was held at Westminster Central Hall, London. The major issue of unity across the Protestant-Roman Catholic divide was highlighted in this otherwise extremely ecumenical gathering at the final communion service when Catholics abstained from receiving the elements. Francis MacNutt summed up the sadness and yet the irony of the situation for many present when he said, 'We may not yet be able to share the same Eucharist, but we can wash each other's feet.'[34] Elizabeth Buckley, leader of the mainly Roman Catholic L'Arche Community for the mentally handicapped in Inverness, spoke to me of the pain she felt was focused in the divisions over the Eucharist in such houses just because all could not participate fully; the Sacrament for her in fact becoming the very symbol of human divisiveness.

On the other hand, the Pilgrims of St Francis, the British branch of the international Les Compagnons de St François, a movement started after the First World War by German and French Catholics and dedicated to reconciliation, seem to feel differently. During their summer pilgrimage across the Isle of Mull to Iona in 1975, they lived a simple life en route in the spirit of St Francis, sleeping in parish halls, cooking their own meals, and celebrating the Eucharist together without any questions being seriously asked about denominational allegiance. The question thus remains, on the community scene perhaps more pertinently than anywhere else at present, as to just how long divisive traditional practice can hold back the conviction of many that Christians who share a common purpose intimately associated with their common humanity should willy-nilly join together in every Eucharist.

The sharing of a common humanity is brought to the fore where Christians see the Eucharist as a Sacrament not just for the Church but for the world, where its celebration is an attempt to express not the divisions but the unity of mankind. For example, those students at Imperial College and Queen Elizabeth College in Kensington sharing in the Sacrament 'may celebrate the Eucharist in a simple way in a bar or common room, TV lounge, or on a lab. bench with the group members sitting, squatting, standing round, and passing the bread and wine from hand to hand, speaking aloud the name of the person to whom it is handed'.[35] On Iona the bread left over from the Sunday morning Communion is shared afterwards by the participants with any they do not know and thereby a deeper sense of community is fostered. And reaching towards wider horizons was the final act of the festival 'That's the Spirit', when on Whitsunday morning 1973 the first ever Eucharist in Trafalgar Square, despite 'the splash of the fountains, the roar of buses, the hazards of marauding pigeons', represented a bold attempt to free such celebration from the confines of a remote institution. 'There was plenty of spirit in Trafalgar Square,' commented Peter Hebblethwaite. 'As for the Spirit, we will have to wait for the consequences.'[36]

PRAYER AND MEDITATION

Authority and responsibility

The prayer life of those living in or associated with communities is often shaped by 'rules' of one kind or another, the nature and function of which has already been discussed. Acceptance of a regular commitment to some form of praying, private or public, is another way in which the group seeks to guide and regulate the life-style of members and to ensure commitment to its purposes.

Although the members of the Grail 'see prayer as central to . . . life, as an atmosphere permeating between, around and within every corner of living, as the presence of the Spirit everywhere, in everything at every moment',[37] specific undertakings are expected of members. They write: 'Each day we set aside some time when we devote ourselves with particular attention to the Spirit within us.'[38] Likewise in the Roslin Community private prayer is obligatory whilst, of the wider networks, Iona Community members are expected to 'pray daily for the community and its wider concerns'. Friends and companions associated non-residentially with such communities as those at Farncombe,

Lee Abbey, and Scargill, are also asked to pray privately for the parent group.

Yet fewer and fewer communities still legislate in any detail for the private prayer life of their members. There is increasing flexibility and a wish to enable people to take responsibility for fashioning their own devotional life-style. Thus, though the practice of prayer, and especially corporate worship, is normative in many communities, there is an increasing growth towards a belief that for good or ill the individual should develop his own personal spirituality, albeit in contact with others.

This is one reason put forward for the recent growth in interest in meditation. Though requiring a good deal of personal self-discipline, its popularity at present rests on its lack of an institutional or formalized context, its practice in small groups, and its emphasis on the individual's self-development. The Open Centres, for example, represent a spirituality, embracing meditation, which lays great emphasis on self-awareness and sensitivity and which at the same time is neither narrow nor conformist. Their houses in Edinburgh and Ettrick Bridge, amongst others, are places open to all who are seeking their own spiritual identity away from established systems. Contemplative meditation is also a central feature of the new network of Julian Meetings, informal small groups wherein people gather to discover for themselves the rich spirituality of the Christian and other traditions. Those concerned are neither passive nor escapist in their spirituality but are seeking for themselves a deeper inward centring in order better, and often more critically, to engage in their work in society. For them prayer and meditation form a check on the minute and frenzied time-structuring typical of a complex technological age, a quiet but determined protest against speed and the clock in the name of the slower rhythms of nature. The practice and teaching of meditation is also developing steadily in connection with certain of the religious Orders, for example through the work of Herbert Slade at the Anchorhold, Haywards Heath, but this, though important, is beyond my immediate brief.

Yet meditation itself is no guarantee of personal freedom and greater individuality. It can all to easily be purveyed as a kind of tranquillizer in a conformist and closed environment. Such appears to be the case with organizations like the Maharishi International College (formerly the Spiritual Regeneration Movement of Great Britain) which in its literature has described its programme of transcendental meditation as follows:

Transcendental meditation provides rest which is much deeper even than the rest obtained from sound sleep. In this way, it makes your mind clearer and your thoughts and actions more effective; it gives you a sense of general well-being.[39]

Will transcendental meditation turn me against the pleasures which I now enjoy?

No, you will appreciate them all the more. Transcendental meditation gives you two hundred per cent life – full inner happiness, full outer satisfaction. It can only add to the satisfaction you get out of life.

Do I have to give anything up?

No. Transcendental meditation always *adds* to what you already have. It does not take anything away.[40]

Suspicions are aroused by the increasing 'secularization' of transcendental meditation through a pseudo-professionalism (Kenneth Leech reports on the establishment in Switzerland in the early 1970s of the Maharishi International University and in Britain by 1972 of the existence of 135 teachers);[41] and commercialization (in 1975 Roydon Hall, the 'National Academy' of the Spiritual Regeneration Movement, was charging about £50 for a week's course).

The First Summer Festival of the Age of Enlightenment which I attended in south-east London in June 1976 was a cross between a Moral Rearmament meeting and a Black Country Sunday School anniversary. Among other events, certificates of merit were awarded from the Ministry of Cultural Integrity, Invincibility, and World Harmony honouring 'the individual whose activity strengthens and unifies the community by upholding the integrity of all individual interest', and from the Ministry of Prosperity and Progress honouring 'the most successful member of the business community'. The Transcendental Meditation Movement has now drawn up a 'Constitution of the World Government for the Age of Enlightenment (which) consists of the ideals of the constitutions of all governments; the ideals embodied in the scriptures of all religions; the cultural values and traditions of all societies and the economic, political, and social ideals of all nations'. Think that out! It would be laughable if the movement did not now command the naive allegiance of so many otherwise apparently very intelligent and articulate people.

Even more dangerous in this respect is the Divine Light Mission, famous for its teenage guru Maharaj Ji, which claims 8,000 followers in

Britain. 'There is no creed, no dogma, no moral codes, no set times of meditation but a listening to the sound within.'[42] Salvation is through receiving 'the Knowledge' about one's true self through various techniques of meditation. Although disciples surrender their entire income to the Mission, the latter, until recently when rapid contraction set in, had been supported by the umbrella Divine United Organization with a host of subsidiary companies including Plain Grain food supplies. Divine Travel Service, Tender Loving Care manufacturing cosmetics, and Mother Nature Products marketing textiles.[43] The last two are now structurally independent of the cult. The overall turnover of the Divine Light Mission in Britain was, in 1975, estimated at £500,000.[44]

A different style of 'protest' spirituality, with considerable emphasis on meditation, is found amongst those groups which believe that the world is just over the threshold of the New Age, that of Aquarius, which began in March 1948.[45] A new planetary adjustment is apparently taking place, an occurrence which it is believed happened previously around the birth of Christ when the Age of Pisces began. Groups associated with this belief system are Findhorn, convinced it is pioneering a fresh life-style for the New Age, and the Wrekin Trust, founded by Sir George Trevelyan, which runs a variety of conferences around the country on such themes as 'Birth of a New Age', 'Performing the Pathway of the Stars: An Approach to Astrology', and 'The Ageless Wisdom Re-emerges' – all these held in 1975. Such groups live in the rarefied but complex world of angels and nature spirits and over against our materialistic age which has become 'a real threat to the very existence of the earth of which we are a part'.[46] Yet, however opposed to established institutions and ways of life without, there remains within as great a degree of adherence to the wishes of leaders and to the rules of the group as in any of the more traditional and orthodox Christian communities. Exclusiveness and conformity threaten to be the last if not the first word.

The personal and the interpersonal

As already mentioned, prayer, meditation, and silence are intimately concerned with personal development. A major emphasis in a great deal of spirituality associated with communal living is on the individual's inner life, on what Happold, following its long history in Catholic ascetical theology, calls 'acquired contemplation', where 'the self is content to rest in a new level of vivid awareness, marked by a deep peace and living stillness'.[47] Groups like the Open Centres place this aspect of prayer at the heart of their concern. The Grail members follow a similar path with their 'days of solitude' and occasional weekends exploring 'Ways into Meditation'. The Julian Meetings began in 1973 in an attempt to fill the spiritual vacuum felt to exist within the institutional Church. By the end of 1975 nearly thirty groups existed, each one pursuing its own style of meditation.

The Cambridge group meets in a church, monthly. They start with a short address, followed by thirty minutes' silence. They are ecumenical and have been on pilgrimage to Walsingham. At Exeter meditation is linked with intercession for the sick. A Roman Catholic priest leads the Brixton group and it is unstructured. A sentence, silence, the liturgy, intercession, and occasionally a meal are all used. At Chichester the group meets in the Cathedral near the site of the Shrine of St Richard of Chichester. A sentence from the Bible is chosen and repeated at the start of the meeting, together with an invocatory prayer. It is expounded theologically for ten minutes. Then follows ten minutes' silence, after which the text is expounded devotionally. Then follows ten minutes' silence, after which the text is expounded with volitional requirements in mind. The meeting ends with everyone saying the prayer of St Richard of Chichester. . . . Members of this group are encouraged to use the month's text for daily meditation. . . .[48]

In such situations the individual lay person gains a great sense of significance through developing his own power to pray, his own openness to God in silence, and a wholeness of life summed up in the final words of a prayer used by those associated with Katimavik:

Teach me, Lord, that perfect silence
So that my life may no longer be anything
But a continual 'Yes', full of faith, hope, and love.[49]

Another association whose members set a good deal of store by silence is the Servants of Christ the King. Their 'Waiting on God', including a half-hour period of silence, has for many years been a focal point of group meetings. More recently some confusion has arisen as to the main purpose of the silence; to help decide God's will for a company, to focus thoughts before a 'controlled discussion', or a technique associated with Bible study or group meditation. However, most members still uphold the great value of the silence.

The heightening of personal consciousness usually leads to a deeper sense of the interpersonal, a sense of solidarity with those also participating in prayer and meditation. Such is certainly the experience of the members of the Julian Meetings and the Servants of Christ the King companies. So too with the 'sharing meetings' at the Community of Celebration and Post Green. When staying at the latter I was impressed early one morning at a simple prayer meeting round the breakfast table, not by the intensity and solemnity of the occasion but by the quite spontaneous and unembarrassed laughter which broke out all round at one point; sharing was genuine at many levels of experience.

Where one of the main functions of communities is to staff and run centres providing conferences or retreats, their corporate life of prayer not only enriches the experience of permanent residents but of visitors as well. Reg East of the Barnabas Fellowship writes: 'Prayer is at the centre of our life, and so we have at least one hour a day for community devotions. Before conferences and retreats we increase this whenever possible during the three days preceding, and include fasting.'[50] One consequence is:

> The Holy Spirit has led us into many lovely things. One such is willingness to be told the truth about ourselves. Not only are we learning to receive the truth from each other. Even more important is the self-knowledge which God gives deep in the heart as one waits upon Him. As a result we are learning to accept others for what they are, and conversely to realize that we ourselves are accepted by the others. This requires grace to 'see' others and hence to have sensitiveness towards them and a sympathy for their problems. Perhaps much of this can be summed up as the willingness to give others the freedom to be themselves.[51]

At Burrswood, a 'home of healing' founded by Dorothy Kerin, their special ministry is closely linked to intercessory prayer. 'Not only does the whole community pray, but it is the special work of some; in addition the name of the sick person is put on the altar. Dorothy Kerin regarded prayer as the most powerful ray in the world.'[52]

An experience of the richness of the interpersonal dimension of the spiritual in a situation of temporary community is being fostered through the 'Houses of Prayer Ecumenical' (or HOPE for short). The venture began in 1975 when 'six surprisingly assorted shapes and sizes of people who knew each other virtually only by a few hours' introduction, descended on a little house near Peterborough for an adventure in prayer. Two weeks had been set apart to share deeply in the gift of life in prayer, work, relaxation, and fellowship together in Christ,'[53] writes Helen Allan. She continues:

> Each day a 'President' was chosen from amongst us to integrate and plan the functions of the day. We shared everything equally, including the responsibility of cooking, housework, laundry, etc., so that no one person was burdened unduly. Usually we had a theme which ran through the whole day. . . . The group opted for silence for the greater part of each twenty-four hours, but there was still plenty of time for getting to know each other, for sharing handicrafts or stories, music and laughter, brisk walks or gentle strolls together in the nearby bird sanctuary – in short, time for just being ourselves, and letting others 'be'.[54]

So inspired were the small group by their experience that in 1976 three more HOPES were arranged for others to share a similar time together.

There are a few situations where communities and related groups are deliberately seeking to extend their ministry of prayer beyond their own circle; very difficult because prayer is so often regarded as an in-group activity. The Open Centres, typified by the Salisbury Centre in Edinburgh, throw their doors open to all comers. A leaflet on the Edinburgh Centre ends:

> Come, come whoever you are,
> Wanderer, worshipper, lover of leaving, it doesn't matter.
> Come, ours is not a caravan of despair,
> Come, even if you have broken your vow a thousand times,
> Come, come again, come.[55]

In 1974 the Servants of Christ the King attempted to find a way of adapting the conduct of their company meetings to the presence of non-Christian participants. One suggestion at the annual conference was that the initials SCK should be interpreted in a new way:

SILENCE
1 To fulfil the need for relaxation.
2 To explore deeper relationships.
3 To explore myself.
4 To experiment with different techniques of silence.

COMPASSION

1 To be geared to love the world into loving.
2 To open out and to learn from those of different or no faith.
3 To act.

KNOWLEDGE

To deal with our own ignorance.[56]

The initial, though not the final, response was a vigorous reaction from those who felt very strongly that this would be the end of the Servants of Christ the King as a Christian movement. But 'in the end, the conference unanimously accepted this idea and offered the support of the movement to individuals and companies who felt called, after waiting on God, to reach out in this way'.[57]

The International Ecumenical Fellowship works on a broader canvas still. It began in 1967 with the intention of uniting Christians of many denominations 'in the simplest possible way', believing that the key to this lay 'in the spiritual field, particularly in prayer and worship together under the guidance of the Holy Spirit; that if people pray together they will live in peace'.[58] The Fellowship aims, through a loose network of contacts, especially in Europe, to keep Christians in touch with each other's traditions of worship and spirituality, with especial emphasis on the Eucharist, and to promote international conferences for study, prayer, and fellowship. So far it is these large, lively ecumenical gatherings which have given greatest impetus to the Fellowship.

MUSIC, SONG, AND DANCE

Authority and leadership

If we were always busy making history but never celebrated it, we would be . . . trapped in an unremitting treadmill from which all detachment, joy, and freedom were gone.[59]

Thus writes Harvey Cox. The explosion of spirituality into music, song, and dance has in part been a reaction, in the name of 'joy and freedom', against that 'unremitting treadmill' characterized in our time by two World Wars and an acute economic depression followed by the self-satisfaction of the 'You've never had it so good' generation. It has expressed itself in a wealth of experimentation ranging from multi-media programmes designed to celebrate the opening of Coventry

Cathedral and of the Metropolitan Cathedral of Christ the King, in Liverpool, to the small inner-belt London church struggling to get its Sunday School scholars to perform 'Joseph and His Amazing Technicolor Dreamcoat'. My concern, however, is not so much with music and movement as such but with their expression of and contribution to new styles of life.

Some of the groups at present most deeply involved in this field are those associated with the charismatic movement. One of the main features here has been the move towards a much more corporate form of worship. Choirs, music groups, dance teams, often play a very prominent role and where possible involve the total congregation in singing, clapping, and movement. The Community of Celebration's choir, The Fisherfolk, is now world-famous; Post Green has its own vocal group, The Post Green People; and Findhorn (which possesses certain charismatic features) has produced The New Troubadours. Within some parishes also a similar emphasis is found; as with the charismatically renewed church of St Cuthbert's, York, where a well-trained choir and dance group involve the people as fully as they can in the worship. At Scargill, more in the evangelical than the charismatic tradition, there is great interest in the use of drama and mime in worship.

No one has outstanding talent, but knowing each other and working together to develop an idea into a play, to give a new angle to an over-familiar story, new understanding comes to the players and something fresh gets across to the audience. Improvised drama . . . has advantages for inexperienced players in obviating the learning of words by heart, in needing relatively little rehearsal and in being adaptable to the exact composition of any particular group.[60]

At the Community of Celebration at Yeldall Manor, the Thursday evening worship often contained an extremely lively combination of music, song, and dance. I attended a Eucharist there when the whole company shared fully in a service which contained a moving African dance sequence on the theme of thanksgiving. None the less, though the members of the Community of Celebration report that they never get the feeling of being onlookers in worship, their ministry in this connection inevitably assumes much more the nature of a performance when they travel farther afield.

The Fisherfolk, for example, state explicitly that their intention 'is not to "perform", but to draw others into the spontaneous, peaceful flow of

81

praise and prayer that is characteristic of their Community's worship'.[61] There is, however, little doubt that many are attracted by the choir's professional reputation and remain more an audience than a worshipping congregation. The same can be said of the earlier efforts of the Jesus Family with their 'multi-media production entitled "Lonesome Stone", portraying the story of a bunch of freaks in the San Francisco of 1967, seeking salvation through drugs, astrology, revolution, and gay times'.[62] More recently, evangelicals have taken the same approach with their 'Come Together' and 'If My People'. And all this of course makes no mention of the commercial productions, 'Godspell', 'Jesus Christ Superstar', and 'Joseph and His Amazing Technicolor Dreamcoat'.

This is not to deny the value of worship as a dramatic event during which trained people perform. Like pop festivals, such gatherings can be extremely moving for all involved. But in such situations the congregation as an audience often remains in an observer role very little different from so much of traditional worship. The music group, choir, or dance team supplements or assumes the role hitherto occupied by the priest or minister.

Within basic communities, however, there do remain occasions when through music and movement of various kinds people take the shaping of worship into their own hands. One example of this is the Pilgrims of St Francis whose national and international pilgrimages are occasions for all to share in worship, a spontaneous and ongoing activity throughout. The British Pilgrims have a National Troubadour whose job is to get the group singing and expressing their ideas in mime, dance, and music. 'He is responsible for overseeing the "*veillée*" or camp fire on pilgrimage and for collecting suitable songs for both the *veillées* and for the liturgy.'[63] At the end of the international 1973 pilgrimage, Kathleen Holford recorded that for the final act of worship 'each group had been asked to prepare a part of the Liturgy, so one presented the Gospel in mime, another the Creed in three dance sequences, and yet another the Thanksgiving in the words of a Dutch pop song, *Let the Sunshine In*'.[64]

In a quite different setting Norwyn Denny describes the same concern to give worship back to the people in Notting Hill:

What we *have* learned in Notting Hill is joyful celebration. All is not weakness: God is not without witnesses; there is so much to make you glad within even the sordid areas of life. Sufficient indeed to bring back joy to community life and to facilitate the establishment of a new order of joyous mendicants. The palm processions, the street parties, the wedding feasts, the community organization pageants, the free participation of the congregation, the spontaneity within liturgy, the baptismal jamborees, all show that gladness is as much a preoccupation of Christian community as is human need. Celebration is the note of discovered community that we would want to strike above all others.[65]

The personal and the interpersonal

The shift of leadership in worship from the clergy or trained groups to the people as a whole carries with it the possibility of the latter's deeper personal and interpersonal involvement. At the personal level this is seen in the increased use of all the senses as, for example, in dance. John Cooke writes:

Dance uses both the body to celebrate, and also celebrates the body. It is such an expressive medium, and offers ways of celebrating the human experiences of pathos and joy, life and death, in a way that is spontaneous and yet as is man himself. It is part of the eroticization of liturgy that is turning worship in the direction of spontaneity, touch, dance, emotion, and noise. It is an appropriation of what Sydney Carter meant when he wrote *Lord of the Dance*. Man affirms flesh in the house of God.[66]

At Taena, George Ineson and a small group have been using the Taoist 'dance', Tai Chi Chuan, to enrich self-awareness and self-expression. 'Hands, shoulders, elbows, fists, legs, knees, toes, sides of feet and soles, even eyes are brought into play in a series of specific patterns of movement, called forms.'[67] The 108 forms blend in a fifteen-minute exercise designed to express the harmony of the human organism and increase awareness of the moment. Though often used without any religious associations, to the Taena group it is closely linked with a meditative form of spirituality. During the 'That's the Spirit' festival in London a 'Mass with Dance' was held, the congregation being invited to make simple gestures during the offertory:

Lord, let me see these hands as you see them. When I am angry (clenched fists), bring me peace (hands folded together); when I am sad (head clutched in hands), bring me joy (hands extended upwards); when I am afraid (hands defend the face), make me calm (hands joined in prayer); when I am grasping (gripping gesture), make me generous (open hands). And let me offer these hands to you (offering).[68]

The rediscovery of the whole person in regard to spirituality has greatly influenced the interpersonal dimension too. 'Decentralization' of worship brings the possibility of a new openness between persons; communication becomes more vital and meaningful. Thus the activities of the Pilgrims of St Francis and the Notting Hill team mentioned above greatly enhance solidarity. The freeing of the sense of touch has also brought a new dimension into Christian worship. The exchanging of the Peace, for example, is now not just a handshake but often a full embrace, as during the Eucharist at the gathering of representatives, many of them previously strangers, of some thirty communities in Birmingham in April 1975. As hands and arms are now more freely opened to God, so they are more readily opened to one another.

CHARISMATIC RENEWAL

Authority and organization

The movement of charismatic renewal which began in the United States in the late 1950s and is best known to us there through the Roman Catholic Ann Arbor Community in Michigan and the Episcopal Church of the Redeemer in Houston, Texas, is already well documented and serviced over here through the work of the Fountain Trust and their magazine *Renewal*.[69] Sometimes termed 'neo-Pentecostalism',[70] it remains (unlike the Jesus Movement) ecclesiastically mainstream, and because of that in practice largely works within rather than fundamentally challenges denominational divisions. Thus it currently remains not only acceptable to the various hierarchies but often commands enthusiastic support in high places. A noteworthy example of this was the Congress in Rome in May 1975, attended by nearly 10,000 Catholics 'from Bogota and Birmingham, Belfast and Brussels, Brisbane and Bombay',[71] during which the Pope addressed the crowds, giving the movement his blessing and encouragement, a gesture hailed by a section of the mass media as of epoch-making significance.

None the less, there remains at the heart of the charismatic movement an experimental dynamic (expressed in tongues, prophecy, and healing amongst other things) inherently inimical to institutionalism. It is nurtured by a genuine attempt to be open to the Spirit, and the conviction that those who are cannot be other than one in Christ. The Grail, reflecting this mood, writes:

We know that Christ's work of redemption was done once and for all, yet the Spirit constantly bears it into the unknown future. We want to be caught up in this great dynamic movement which is transforming creation and building the kingdom of God.[72]

This kind of affirmation by Catholics led the editor of *Renewal* in June 1974 to write an outspoken article challenging members of that Church to re-examine some of their basic beliefs, such as the doctrine of papal infallibility and the question of intercommunion, in the light of their charismatic experience.[73] At the same time the so-called 'charismatic divide' was causing friction between many of those within the charismatic movement and evangelicals, especially in the Church of England. Although both charismatics and evangelicals are strong on experience, the former tend to emphasize the visible expression of each member's spiritual gifts for and through the total congregation, the latter to stress the individual's 'rightness' with God as an intensely personal and private affair. At the local level too, the emergence of a charismatic congregation can be somewhat divisive. Its obvious liveliness soon brings both public attention and the movement of certain members out of their own congregations into what seems a very attractive alternative. This does not of course endear those presenting this very different style of congregational life to the upholders of more traditional ways. Despite movement and deeper understanding on all sides since then, problems remain highlighted by the difficulty of expressing a new or renewed spirituality in organizational and especially institutional terms.

That at least some headway is being made is shown in the international and ecumenical charismatic assemblies held in recent years at such places as Guildford, Nottingham, and Westminster. But perhaps even more significant is the emergence of many small groups sometimes meeting in the face of ecclesiastical and even secular opposition. No more impressive example of this is found than in Northern Ireland. At the Christian Renewal Centre at Rostrevor in County Down, I attended a Monday evening prayer meeting where more than fifty people (sometimes as many as a hundred attend), including Roman Catholic Sisters and Presbyterian ministers, were crowded into the front room. One of the latter reported that his congregation would condemn his participation if they knew he was there. A number of people had travelled for several hours from Belfast, risking the hazards of dark roads in a country where cars can be stopped and drivers sometimes shot. In numerous places in Northern Ireland such a witness continues; one tangible if still fragile symbol of hope. Although in September 1975, nearly 4,000 people gathered in Dublin for a massive ecumenical charismatic assembly, the real test of the dynamic of this still loosely knit movement will be whether the many small cells in the North can sufficiently multiply *and* cohere to challenge the inertia and defensiveness of larger institutions.

The personal and the interpersonal

At the level of the personal and the interpersonal, the charismatic movement has brought a new vitality. Martin Marty 'sees the search for the recovery and reformulation of prayer as part of a quest for immediate experience which will take many shapes – demonstrations, games, liturgies, T-groups and sensitivity sessions, drugs, communes, pop festivals'.[74] Many charismatic affirmations of 'immediate experience', in music, song, and dance, and physical self-expression, have been touched on under previous headings (the matter of healing I shall deal with in a later chapter). Here I simply stress the intensity of that experience born of deep personal involvement. Reg East of the Barnabas Fellowship and a young couple I met at Rostrevor felt that their present communities drew them because others they had been associated with, in these cases the evangelically oriented Lee Abbey and Scargill, lacked something of the sense of corporateness and the depth they sought. This depth is not discovered only through fervour. Emmanuel Sullivan argues that it is not noisy enthusiasm but 'the contemplative level which makes the movement in any way effective as a witness to the action of the Holy Spirit and an agent in the renewal of the Church'.[75] Indeed, though the phenomenon of tongues, a form of ecstasy which also brings home the deeply personal nature of charismatic renewal, is usually associated with loud public utterances, Peter Hocken comments in correspondence that certain of its most powerful manifestations are found at the beginning of contemplative prayer.

But loud or quiet, the charismatic movement has gone a good way towards enriching and opening the lives of many, individually and corporately.

CONCLUSION

When we speak of spirituality we are at the heart of man's deepest desires and acutest needs. The religious forms in which he expresses these, though always inadequate, give some indication of his understanding of the nature of authority, his own and others, of the awareness of his selfhood, and of interpersonal relationships. Where spirituality is fashioned by and fashions a community or group which has related closely together over time, then that understanding has at least been proved translatable into viable social terms and is available for others to accept or reject.

Authority and leadership

In the context of worship and spirituality many communities opt for patterns of leadership closely reflecting those of the main denominations, especially in their traditional and classical forms. A traditional rule of life touching worship and prayer amongst other things is firmly adhered to by such groups as the Iona Community, Pilsdon, and the Coventry Cathedral staff. 'The Word' is made a fundamental reference point in many evangelical and charismatic groups. Eucharistic celebration, for example with the Roman Catholic Grail, Focolare, and Katimavik, is usually in full accordance with denominational tradition.

But there are some significant changes taking place. One is the steady loss of interest by many groups in a rule of religious life which sets out in detail corporately binding regulations about devotions and private prayer. This can be seen, on the one hand, as a reaction to regimentation and, on the other, as a move by the laity to assert their own right to fashion their spiritual life-style in accordance with their own experience, personal and communal. Though the clergy still remains very prominent in community worship, there is a move towards a spirituality designed by laymen for laymen, as in the case of the Julian Meetings. The great interest in meditation can be seen in a similar context; a search for a spiritual wholeness and identity over against a Church which so often seems fragmented and impersonal. The renewed interest in the Agape is an expression of a more corporate lay concern and involvement. Yet another is the emergence of choirs, music groups, and dance teams seeking, if not always easily, to make worship an act of full congregational participation.

It would be foolish to deny the importance of all this for the corporate life of the communities and groups involved. A new emphasis in the conduct of worship and the development of spirituality must begin somewhere. But is what is occurring just a passing fashion for the dedicated or privileged few, or does it have more far-reaching implications for and effect on the institutional Church? There is little evidence that theologically more fringe groups, such as the heralds of the new Age of Aquarius, carry much weight here. Of much more consequence is the charismatic movement. This has already demonstrated its readiness not only to meet on a thoroughly ecumenical and international basis but to challenge openly the divisions of the Church. The movement has not yet reached its ultimate testing, however, and one confesses to some doubts as to whether the all-embracing experiential impetus it has given to ecumenical co-operation will not lose ground as doctrinal presuppositions come more to the fore; for example, relating to Christology, sacramental theology, initiation, and ethics. It will be interesting to see whether it then remains tamed by denominational and cultural constraints or can challenge them in an effective and radical manner.

Spirituality almost inevitably remains an in-group experience for Christians even in its most ecumenical form. If its new communal expressions as yet have made little impression on the power structures of the Church, it would be unlikely if society as a whole were greatly changed. Yet there is a steady strengthening of determination to move from a 'soft' to a 'hard' quality of spirituality, to work for that which is responsive to the social and political events of life and does not escape into unearthed ecstasy or disengaged passivity. And there is the significant witness of the charismatic groups in Northern Ireland, who at risk of life and limb are facing not only religious but political hostility. Their courage is considerable; though it remains a sad comment on our time that ecumenicity at the level of worship and prayer only has immediate political impact in a society so religiously hidebound and intransigent as that of Northern Ireland.

The personal and the interpersonal

At the personal and interpersonal levels the great variety of expressions of spirituality has demonstrated a whole new or rediscovered dimension of personal and communal experience. Of course there is the possibility of the artificiality of staged fellowship. Of course all aspects of spirituality, especially the more sensual or sensational, can be escape routes from reality or perhaps worse, safety-valves to prevent pent-up energies from rocking the ecclesiastical or political boat. It could be that ever-recurring assemblies and 'come togethers' simply help siphon off proper dissatisfaction, thereby ensuring the continuing irrelevance of Christian worship and innocuous nature of Christian witness. But where spirituality is built on a continuing community or group of a kind able to face the cost of corporate living and sharing together, then there appears a new and exciting realization of what the individual is as a whole person.

This is discovered and manifest through many and various forms – prayer, meditation and yoga, song, and dance – but in our time the emphasis is dominantly experiential. 'If God returns,' writes Harvey Cox, 'we may have to meet him first in the dance before we can define him in the doctrine.'[76] The individual comes to feel that he has a much greater religious repertoire and is able to relate these to his whole self in a more liberating way than traditional rituals allow. There is released a new *élan*, until recently acutely missing in Christian worship, a sense of festivity and festival which links man dynamically with his religious past and gives him a vision, personal and corporate, of the future. At its zenith, this vision can be a 'peak experience', vital to man, an experience of which I shall say more in the final chapter.

One problem has been a growing dissatisfaction with words as the only means of communication. The search for new forms of spirituality can in one sense, therefore, be seen as the search for new symbols which can focus and facilitate interrelating at a new depth. Old symbols still remain – for example, the cross carried by Arthur Blessitt during his pilgrimage round Britain in 1971; and ephemeral ones appear – from Jesus stickers to Jesus T-shirts. But now others of a more communally significant kind are emerging: the circle for worship and the celebration of the Eucharist, a new openness in the giving and receiving of the Peace, the use of the hands in many ways, dance rituals and so forth, as well as a whole range of things produced by those skilled in arts and crafts. It is a time of indigenous symbols, their influence lying as much in their significance for the community as in their wider associations.

Such expressions of spirituality can easily be abused, as in the growing commercialization of transcendental meditation, or incestuous, the ultimate danger of doing one's own thing. A strongly experiential spirituality always runs the risk of cultural fundamentalism, especially liable, as we have noted, to suffer from the use of a restricted language code. It is just as easy for a community to idolize its own spiritual life-style as it is for the Church to idolize its organizational structures.

Attempts are being made to share the new-found spirituality of which I have written with non-Christians as well as Christians; from the Harvest Festival in a Methodist church, where public houses on a huge map of the area above the Communion table were indicated by mugs of beer,[77] to the 'That's the Spirit' Eucharist in Trafalgar Square. The celebrations organized by the Notting Hill Team Ministry have also reached out to the neighbourhood. But though these and similar endeavours have gone a good way towards humanizing the worship of the church (and this is of vital importance), their significance for the secular city would appear to be extremely limited. As Charles Davis has said, the ghetto or the desert seems at present to be the unenviable choice.

However, there are other activities and symbols not directly associated with spirituality which do command attention. These do speak to the non-Christian more clearly. In subsequent chapters I shall be drawing attention to them even if they demand a style of life which means 'going into the world, mixing with corruption and sin, dirtying oneself with externals, having some truck with the despised forms, instead of worshipping the sacred mysteries of pure content'.[78]

4

ENVIRONMENTAL AND ECONOMIC
ASPECTS OF COMMUNITY

'Avoid the use of disposable diapers. . . . Learn to cook from scratch.
. . . Cut down on shower time. . . . Stop smoking. . . . Use lunch boxes
instead of paper bags. . . .'[1] Just a few exhortations from the fifty-eight
in a leaflet issued by Dartmouth House in 1975 as part of their
environmentalist campaign. The battle is on: against waste and
pollution and for care and conservation. What but a few years ago was
seen as something of the latest bandwagon has now become a matter of
serious and articulate concern.

Three aspects of society's material well-being are particularly
worrying.[2] There is anxiety that the flow of energy and raw materials,
until recently taken for granted, will slowly cease; there is the realization
that industry and its products have within them the power fatally to
upset the delicate balance of the biosphere; and there is the awareness
that our technology as it is, let alone as it might become, could well do
more to destroy than enhance man's welfare. The response to these
concerns has been kaleidoscopic, ranging from the dissemination of
many erudite or hortatory articles and books to a new zeal for self-
sufficiency and the development of an alternative technology. Linked to
this has been the search for a new life-style, personal and communal,
which has placed a major emphasis on simplicity and moderation
especially with regard to consumer patterns, and on working within
the boundaries set by nature rather than wealth.

Within this movement, for it can by now be called that, the Christian
has been prominent. E. F. Schumacher, author of *Small is Beautiful*,[3]
makes no apology for his own Christian stance and the Bishop of
Winchester's *Enough is Enough*[4] has proved a bestseller. Therefore, in
seeking to use as illustrative material for this chapter ventures which are
Christian in ethos or in which Christians are known to be actively
involved, I do not feel I am distorting the overall picture or underrating
the major contribution of the non-Christian in this field. My aim is not

to produce a treatise on conservation programmes or alternative technology; it is to assess how what is happening reflects or affects the nature of power and authority on the one hand, and the personal and interpersonal dimensions of life on the other. As Ralf Dahrendorf comments in his 1974 Reith Lectures: 'After all, survival is not enough, what matters is life worth living.'[5] (One book in particular has proved relevant to my theme: *Alternative Technology and the Politics of Technical Change* by David Dickson,[6] and to this I would draw the reader's especial attention.)

AUTHORITY, POWER, AND WEALTH

The current scene

A key feature of Western society has been the insatiable desire for more and more wealth and, until very recently, a belief that one major step towards this was to ensure an economy expanding as fast as advanced technology would allow. The post-war years in Britain were marked by an energetic desire to construct a new and affluent society with the 'haves', despite the existence of a welfare state and occasional gestures in the direction of the Third World, too busy about their own business really to heed the dire poverty of the 'have-nots' at home and abroad. The mass media became geared to a consumer-oriented situation in which people's 'needs' were fanned if not created by high-pressure advertising to make certain of a secure market for mass-produced goods. 'Built-in obsolescence' furthered the process. John Taylor writes: 'This society of excessive consumption exists within, and indeed thrives upon, a larger society of excessive need.'[7]

In very recent years the presuppositions on which this way of life is based have received some huge jolts. One is the sudden realization of the fantastic explosion of the world's population:

> It took a million years to produce the first billion human beings. It took only a hundred years to produce the second billion, by the 1850s. It took only fifteen years to produce the fourth billion, by 1973. The next forty years will add to the world's population more people than the whole history of mankind has done to date.[8]

Another jolt is the emergence of the stark fact that if we continue to use up non-renewable natural resources in proportion to the estimated rate of increasing industrial output, then these may well be exhausted during the next century. Add to this the escalating threat of world-wide pollution and there is more than room for thought. Dahrendorf puts the position succinctly: 'The survival of mankind is in jeopardy.'[9] None the less, words still loom larger than deeds, warnings than action, and we in Britain continue to live well beyond our means, be that seen in terms of continuing inflation or mortgaging our future against the hoped-for bonanza of North Sea oil.

Of special concern to me in this chapter is that whatever government has been in power, there has been little shift during the avid pursuit of wealth away from a technology that maintains 'authoritarian forms of discipline, hierarchical regimentation, and fragmentation of the labour force'.[10] The factory system with its paternalistic then classical mode of operating, originating in the Industrial Revolution, steadily became the unassailable norm. Thus 'the apparent need for authoritarian discipline and hierarchical organization of the factory required to operate complex production-line equipment, for example, is held to justify the accompanying relationships between management and workers'.[11] Furthermore, despite a long history of bitter conflict, management and unions have in fact come to collude in this situation, as Dahrendorf points out:

> Capital and labour rose together, they rule together today, and they will decline or at least stagnate and lose relevance together too. . . . The reality of the expanding society then is determined by the common interests of those with a stake in expansion, the industrial classes, to defend their position. It is also determined by their methods of contracting agreements, as they have developed especially in the last thirty years, that is, by a mixture of false autonomy and sheer power.[12]

One issue now emerging, to which those concerned with an alternative society are directly or indirectly turning their attention, concerns the nature of informal or formal organizations which might in some way be able to challenge such 'false autonomy and sheer power' in the name of a social system which takes as paramount 'the right and the force of the general public over all sectoral and technocratic claims'.[13]

Concentration of wealth and power, with its resultant social hierarchism, has also manifest itself in the cult and mystique of 'the expert', particularly where this role legitimates the dominance of technical over other expertise. Early on the scene here was the Church itself, which in the Middle Ages not only established a virtual monopoly of scholastic knowledge but also maintained its control over technical skills through the strongly religious basis of craft guild rules and regulations. The rise of the technological expert which eventually destroyed the economic hegemony of the Church, simply led to the creation of a new 'priesthood' which has come to wield immense influence not just in the technological but also in the political arena. Whilst political parties can now manipulate so-called scientific 'facts' to their own ends, the 'layman' is dismissed from any genuine involvement in important decision-making.

A similar situation exists in the world of the mass media. Though Dahrendorf believes that 'concern about liberty is . . . widespread among the representatives of the fourth power in our countries, the press, broadcasting, and television, the so-called media',[14] others remain much less convinced. The inane rattle of television commercials, presenting the consumer, not least the very young, with a pre-packaged and highly influential view of a society whose values are based on material acquisition and physical comfort, is only one issue.

While appearing to democratize society by disseminating information to all, and 'opening up the insides of politics', what we actually see on television is subject to strict, centralized control experienced through imposed norms of acceptable viewing. The important choices – such as *how* news is presented, or *which* experts are invited to discuss important topics – lie outside the control of the viewer.[15]

In talking to well-informed and open-minded Roman Catholics in Northern Ireland, I felt the deep frustration associated with the mass media which, in many subtle ways, constantly distorts the 'facts' which it publicly presents.

The exclusion of 'ordinary' people from what are made out to be society's extremely complex problems, demanding specialist knowledge and skill, tight control of vital information, and the presentation through the mass media of a politically monochromatic world-view, are coming up against an increasingly educated and inquiring generation refusing to have things done for it or to it. As in the past, much of the response to this has so far been containment. On the industrial front it is aided by our inheritance of a division of labour and general fragmentation of production tasks within single firms, and between different firms in the same field. Divide and rule have been the basis of capitalistic control and 'scientism . . . legitimates a process where division of labour, initially emerging as an economic and social necessity, has subsequently become institutionalized in the very design of production technology, while at the same time being fashioned to meet political ends'.[16]

Containment of those articulate enough to question the system has also been achieved by authoritarian forms of discipline with strict control over labour being a major objective. A typical feature of the Industrial Revolution, this situation was created and perpetuated by the demands of competition, as dehumanizing as the machine itself. Even when the organization of the factory became more sophisticated and management techniques were developed, originally by F. W. Taylor, an American, in the 1880s,[17] regimentation of the work force was as important an aim as increased productivity. Technology and social engineering became the means of legitimizing social control. Dickson writes: 'The dominant modes of hierarchical organization and authoritarian control, I maintain, become incorporated in, and hence come to coincide with, the technology that is developed by capitalist societies.'[18]

Dickson also argues forcibly against the myth of the neutrality of technology. Not only is it socially violent, as seen in a hundred and one ways from cutting a new motorway to dropping the atomic bomb, it is politically partisan too. Our technology has been designed to support a society where the profit motive and the market dominate the scene and mean that the welfare of all takes second place to 'producing the goods' and the considerable wealth of the few. As Schumacher states, it becomes increasingly obvious that 'no system or machinery or economic doctrine or theory stands on its own feet: it is invariably built on a metaphysical foundation, that is to say, upon man's basic outlook on life, its meaning and its purpose'.[19] The doctrine of man underlying our technology since the Industrial Revolution has been one which sees him as a means to unlimited economic prosperity and great wealth for a privileged minority rather than as an end in himself. A far cry this from a Christian doctrine of man which, whatever else, sees 'in the individual as an individual a unique expression of the universe, incomparable, irreplaceable, and of infinite significance'.[20]

Alternatives

In response to the current scene a whole host of groups have recently emerged, seeking, often in and through some form of alternative technology (also known as 'soft technology, radical technology, low-impact technology, intermediate technology . . . people's technology, liberatory technology, and so on'),[21] to express and communicate a new style of life which challenges the institutionalization of authority, power, and wealth already described. One such challenge comes from those groups opposed to squandering and polluting the world's natural resources.

Conservation and pollution

Many of those working for alternative life-styles hold the ecological integrity of the environment very dear. This concern stems from deep regard for the natural world and its creatures, an attitude which has much in common with the Franciscan love of nature and a doctrine of Creation which emphasizes man's solidarity with and stewardship of the world rather than, as in certain Judeo-Christian writings, his separation from and mastery over it. It is a powerful emotion which takes many communards out into some of the wildest parts of Britain, like the small crofting community at Scoraig on the north side of Little Loch Broom in Wester Ross. The 'Letter from Pilsdon' in Dorset, in July 1960, reflects this mood:

> Midsummer; a 'flaming June' that has lived up to its name; lunch on the lawn day after day; haymaking with scythes and pitchforks, stripped to the waist; cheesemaking, planting, watering, endless hoeing. And, in contrast, the conflicts and contradictions of human personality. Yet it is all a necessary part of the pattern – the peace of the garden and the beauty of Albertine roses round ancient archways; martins flying in front of the house and swallows nesting in the stables; bees swarming; and a small community of men and women, a microcosm of society, working, praying, groping, stumbling, picking themselves up again.[22]

At times such oneness with nature and the seasons is taken to extremes, as in the pantheism of the Findhorn Community, where the 42-lb cabbage grown on the sand-dunes of Findhorn Bay became an object of veneration rather than a matter of simple horticultural pride, a sign of the presence of Pan and his nature spirits rather than good husbandry and good soil despite the sand. But in its more 'orthodox' form, care for the natural world remains a major concern within many communities in which Christians are involved, from Little Gidding in Huntingdonshire to Lothlorien in Kirkcudbrightshire, from Taena in Gloucestershire to Glencolumbkille in Donegal.

This concern is not a romantic sentiment resulting from great proximity to nature, though feelings are strong, but is something which results in action. This may be farming the land and caring for animals in a way which neither pollutes nor destroys. Tom Forsyth, who with his family has lived at Scoraig for ten years, spoke about his hatred of strontium fall-out, poisonous fertilizers, soil exploitation, lead in man's diet, and battery rearing. Much cultivation carried out by such groups is organic, rejecting artificial fertilizers and treatments, as at Findhorn, Laurieston Hall, and Scoraig itself.

Another form of action is focused in more direct protest. One massive item on the agenda here is the consequence of extracting oil from the North Sea; it is surprising that Christians so far have said little about the social effects of this enterprise. However, the Scottish SCM conference on ecology in 1975 did produce the following declaration:

> It is the opinion of the conference that the oil under the North Sea should not be extracted now, with the minimum of delay, at the maximum rate, with anybody's capital and to anybody's profit, especially not to the profit of the big oil companies. Instead we believe that the oil should be extracted at a modest rate, with national capital even if this means long delays, and only for certain purposes, which implies strict controls over the final use.[23]

A more broadly based organization, Friends of the Earth, which started in the United States in 1969, have been especially active protesters. They state:

> In the UK, we have successfully attacked RTZ's plans to mine in the Snowdonia national park. We have initiated a national debate on the absurdity of over-packaging, and we are urging major manufacturers to reverse their marketing policy on non-returnable bottles. We have helped ban the import into the UK of whale meat and products from other endangered species. We are also increasing pressure on the International Whaling Commission, of which Britain is a member, to institute a ten-year moratorium on the catching of all species of whale.[24]

Friends of the Earth form some 150 local groups in this country, most characterized by a young and enthusiastic membership. They have also produced a number of 'well-researched documents aimed at confronting governmental or industrial decision makers and winning support from the media and the public'.[25] Although Dave Elliott sees the main *raison d'être* of Friends of the Earth as 'saving the planet from eco-catastrophe, as opposed to the more political goals',[26] and feels that some of its campaigns (as with Save-the-Whale) have faded somewhat innocuously away, there is no doubt that the network is doing a great deal to raise the level of ecological consciousness of people working at the grass-roots.

A body with similar concerns, the Conservation Society, states of its aims: 'Our first tasks are to stabilize population and to devise an economy that does not wreck the environment and make our lives not worth living.'[27] This group tends to be more of an educational instrument operating through working parties and disseminating information, and less concerned with active participation and direct action at the local level.

Amongst other objects of attack by conservationists has been motor transport, increasingly cluttering towns and cities, demanding more and more land for motorways and belching out polluting fumes. And to these problems John Taylor adds the one of the car as an infantile status symbol for grown-up children.[28] Perhaps such factors made the Shrubb Family begin getting together horse-drawn vehicles as an alternative to motor-power.[29] However, conservation is sometimes more difficult to practise than to preach. At a large community in Scotland where one was asked to urinate in a bucket in order that the contents could be used as fertilizer, electric lights were left blazing and a good deal of food was seen lying about in the communal kitchen all day, going to waste.

For those who are unable to live out their ecological concerns on a large scale and are not well placed for effective protest, numerous guidelines for aspects of a conservationist way of life have appeared recently. One example of this was the Dean of Bristol's attempt in 1972 to promote a discipline called 'Life Style'. The aim was to provide guidelines 'whereby we may live more simply that others may simply live',[30] and amongst the items of personal commitment were these:

To make our decisions about the level and the character of our consumption of goods and services as responsible citizens of the planet Earth.

In our purchases to resist obsolescence, to scrutinize advertisements and challenge wasteful packaging.

To be generous without ostentation and hospitable without extravagance.[31]

Other groups have followed suit. Dartmouth House, whose conservationist leaflet was mentioned at the outset of this chapter, in 1975 set up an open (and ill-fated: see the next chapter) group called Beginning Now, committed to living out and developing such ideals in practice. The Ashram Community in 1975 gave over a whole edition of *ACT* to discussing and suggesting, through a workbook approach, a simple life-style.[32] George Ineson at Taena writes along similar lines:

> The primary elements of any attempt to change our direction are (1) to use only tools which we can control and not those which control us; (2) to reverse the present addiction to the new as a status symbol — to care for the things we use so that they will last as long as possible and to use as little as we can instead of as much; (3) to be more aware of the results of our actions on other people and on the natural world so that we can reduce the harm we do; (4) to remember and rediscover the creative relationship between man and the work he does on and to the natural world.[33]

There are, however, problems associated with these kind of suggestions about our use of the world's resources. As with 'Life Style', the initial impact of which has rather faded, there is often lacking a core group which can sustain enthusiasm. It is the vitality of the basic community rather than the conservationist guidelines which give continuing impetus to self-discipline. Dartmouth House, the Ashram Community, and Taena have gained here, but even so their ideas for a personal conservationist code are at times so numerous and so all-embracing as to be overwhelming, in the sense that it would take the utmost, indeed almost obsessive, vigilance not to infringe the code regularly, as well as a great deal of time and even expense to be fully loyal to it.

One other difficulty is that few communities (be they specifically dedicated to ecological concerns or not) attempting to live out a simpler life-style, would have been unable to get off the ground at all, and in certain cases survive, without drawing on wealth acquired through working the capitalist system. Centres such as Post Green, Ammerdown, and several groups in the Inverness area, as the monasteries before them, have wealthy and generous patrons. Others, such as the Community of Celebration and more recently Findhorn, are backed by funds from the United States. Numerous communities have members who have been able to make their move on the basis of capital acquired in a world they now wish to question in one way or another. Of the fragmenting secular Commune Movement, Geoff Crowther makes a more generally relevant comment:

> The Commune Movement became a predominantly middle-class oriented body since it was only people from this background who could collect the necessary assets, both in terms of money and education, to be in a position to even consider taking off for the country. In this way they highlighted their privileged position and many 'communes' became glorified weekend cottages. 'Forming a commune' became another form of consumer fetishism.[34]

Crowther does not believe all such ventures worthless, but he does point out the inherent dualism of alternatives which to survive have to draw heavily on the resources of the society criticized. Some communities, such as Findhorn, can even become affluent, and their enterprise border on commercialization, as a result of their popularity and professional publicity. On the other hand a conference of the Network for Alternative Technology and Technology Assessment in 1976 generally accepted that to refuse all State aid or the support of patrons was naive and that the criterion was not the source of funds so much as the extent to which 'the project or campaign helps to shift the balance of power'.[35] None the less, in whatever way set up and backed, no one can ignore the dedication and often considerable personal sacrifice of those determined to build some model of a society which does not exploit, pollute, or look upon the creation of more and more wealth as the God-given right of man.

Small is beautiful

'Small is beautiful' has for many become the rallying cry of the alternative technologists, although the theme itself is much more low-key in Schumacher's book of that title than might be expected.[36] The real issue is not so much that of 'beauty' as the affirmation of the importance of the personalized unit of production, as far as possible self-managed and self-contained, over against the impersonalism and complexity of modern technology and factory life.

One attempt to operate at the 'small is beautiful' level is found in those basic communities devoted to some degree of self-sufficiency. In the 1920s and 1930s, groups with a strong Christian and often pacifist ideology were already exploring such a way of life. One still continuing is the Distributist Community, a group of predominantly Catholic families which settled in Laxton, near Corby, in 1935 and is now corporately farming the land. Of their particular philosophy Harold McCrone writes:

> Distributism proclaims that the happiest condition of a nation is that in which *productive* property is as widely distributed as possible; that every father of a family who has the energy and sense of responsibility necessary should have the opportunity (even if he does not seize it) of being economically independent; that is to say, of being his own boss. Since the nation's sustenance is based on agriculture, then its economic health should be based on a vast network of farm small-holdings, thus leading to a drift away from huge conurbations back to the countryside and the restoration of life in our thousands of beautiful villages which lie beyond the 'commuter belts'. This is not to deny to industrialism its proper function and the preference for it by many men who regard a secure wage as better for themselves than the uncertainties of frugal independence. But in sharp contrast to the shocking centralizations of 'big business', leading as it has done to the emergence of the 'tycoon' and to ever-larger business takeovers of recent years, Distributism asserted that the duty of government is to protect the *small* independent business or factory, and to see that its ramifications are spread widely over the whole of the country instead of concentrated in industrial cities. The conversion of free Englishmen to an industrialized 'proletariat' is a serious curtailment of their innate sense of independence; it may well be that recurrent strikes are basically an instinctive revolt against an unhuman system. Distributism called for the small farm, the small shop, the small factory, the small professional practice; the multiplication of small independences until a sizeable proportion of our countrymen were genuinely, economically *free*.[37]

The modern rural prototype was the Suffolk farm operated by John and Sally Seymour. In 1961 John Seymour wrote:

> Here we all sit, Sally my wife, Jane who is five and a half, Ann who is two and a half, and Kate who is seven (days), a mile from a hard road, with no electricity, no gas, no deliveries of anything at all

excepting coal, provided that we take at least a ton, and mail, and the postwoman gets specially paid for coming here. And we are self-supporting for every kind of food excepting tea, coffee, flour, sugar, and salt. We have no car – we drive about with a pony and cart. If the rest of the world blew itself up tomorrow we could go on living happily here and hardly notice the difference.[38]

Scoraig, the crofting community which in 1974 consisted of some twenty adults and fifteen children is of a similar kind. When I visited it, Tom Forsyth talked with great enthusiasm about his small pine plantation, the fields with a good 'ley' won from the barren hillside, the fruit trees and the beehives, the huge rye stalks and wheat grown as never before in those parts.

Other ventures believe the small unit is ideally suited for promoting communal participation and self-determination, but with a variety of ends in view. The New Villages Association, set up by Lin and Don Warren and, in 1975, having a membership of 200, has as its main aim the establishment of 'land-based villages, where people can live and produce as much as possible of their own food, clothing and other necessities locally, and recycle their wastes'.[39] Each village is planned to consist of between 500 and 1,500 people on as many acres, being largely self-sufficient communities subsisting on organic farming and a small industry or two for trading purposes. Ecology, participatory democracy, and co-ownership are other guiding principles. Despite these laudable aims Geoff Crowther regards the Association as presenting the image 'of an exclusively rural, self-sufficient group whose intention was to cater for the "good life" of its members with little expressed concern for or interaction with other groups and individuals in "straight" society other than some vague statement about "reducing demands on others so as to minimize their exploitation"'.[40] It has as yet no working groups on social or political structures and Crowther believes it to have 'a thinly disguised but very definite paternalistic line and a power élite composed largely of those who dreamt up the idea'.[41] Whether such criticisms are pertinent, only time can tell.

At Bugbrooke in Northamptonshire the Jesus Fellowship owns a fifty-acre farm which, together with the grounds of the large hall, is used to help support the large community living in the village, with a view to its being as self-sufficient as possible. To this end the Fellowship also runs small building and car maintenance enterprises and has two shops in Northampton, one selling jeans and the other wholefoods. Their declared intention is to be a model Christian community in their own right, as little dependent on the outside world as possible.

Bugbrooke would see itself as separatist, never as élitist; but the Children of God are quite definite about the élitist nature of their beautiful world. They too have the vision of a village society:

> Each village will be virtually completely self-controlled and self-sufficient unto itself, like one big happy family or local tribe. . . . (The villagers would) till the surrounding land, grow their own crops, harvest their own food, make what few necessities they need, clothing, housing, implements, tools, etc., right there in their own little villages.[42]

So far so good, but they go on to add:

> God's government is going to be based on the small village plan, each one circular with radial streets like the spokes of a wheel centring at the hub of God's local administration by you and me (that is, the élite members of the Children of God) ruling in love over the villagers of this world. . . . It will take supernatural administrators to run it, the angelic saints we will then be, with superhuman bodies and miraculous powers to use when necessary to enforce God's Will upon any who dare to defy His wise, loving and caring angelic administration.[43]

However, there is in fact evidence that the small can reflect human relations rather than a traditional or sectarian organizational model. The Catholic parish of Glencolumbkille is situated on the south-western tip of Donegal in the Republic of Ireland, 130 square miles in size and having a population of some 1,800 people.[44] Constant emigration over a century reduced the economic viability of the area disastrously. After the Second World War, Father James McDyer was appointed parish priest. Despite some opposition he was gradually able to engage voluntary labour to build a community hall, to get electricity installed, to improve the water supply and to exploit the natural resources of the area, notably farming, fishing, and the tourist industry. Co-operatives were established to promote small industries around vegetable processing, machine knitting, jewellery, and homecrafts, and a folk museum was set up. In all these ventures Father McDyer made every effort to revive the economy on community-development principles which he himself outlines as follows:

1 Widest possible diffusion of the fruits of development within the community. This entails that:
   (a) enterprises be generated and promoted by co-operative means.
   (b) the sources of wealth be owned by the community and be exploited by and for the community to the exclusion of middlemen.
   (c) the exploitation of all local resources be carried out first, in farming, fishing, small industry, homecrafts, and tourism.
2 That vocational education be programmed to serve the needs of and produce skills for local enterprises.
3 That the message be carried throughout the community both extensively and intensively that unless they co-operate to save themselves nobody is going to come in to save them.
4 The local Community Council be endowed with some authority under the law so that all decisions be not made at national or county level.[45]

He is, however, quite open about the difficulties: conservatism, fear, and prejudice led to antagonism or lack of co-operation from many parishioners, so that they 'have really travelled only half the way'. He, himself, remains much more central to the success of the undertaking than he would wish, according to the principles just quoted. His final comment speaks for itself:

> Most of all I have been sustained by my religion. Were I not working for God I could not be bothered working for man. People are very lovable but they are also very irritating and disloyal and ungrateful. God has been called the Man of Sorrows. Ireland could be called the Land of Sorrows. I have striven to give Him a little honour and to Ireland a little joy.[46]

In Northern Ireland in particular, other small-scale self-help and self-determining co-operative ventures, often associated with Catholic initiatives but with their possibilities being increasingly explored by Protestants, have been established. Father Desmond Wilson, very much involved in Ballymurphy Enterprises, Belfast, a co-operative concerned with knitwear, expresses his conviction that such ventures must remain small-scale in order to retain their dynamic. Other similar experiments relate to crystal in Dungannon, farming co-operatives in Swatragh, the Lough Neagh Fisheries, and the Whiterock Industrial Estate in Belfast. Father Wilson states that these ventures have 'proclaimed that the people at large can have a hand in making decisions about what kind of industrial development, what kind of economic theory, what kind of ownership of property they should have'.[47] His deep regret is that the Church has failed to be associated with these principles, not only within its own organization but in its attitude to the whole production process. Instead there has been 'the acceptance by Christians of the principle that growth is of first importance and that profit is the first, perhaps the only, motive for entering business or industry. It is a disastrous surrender to materialistic principles.'[48]

In England, an organization called the Alternative Society has been actively involved in promoting similar projects. Its other activities will be referred to in the appropriate chapters, but in 1975 it set up a Centre for Alternatives in Urban Development at Lower Shaw Farm near Swindon, with the help of funds from the Anglo-German Foundation. The intention is to use the Centre amongst other things for experimentation and training in self-building, energy conservation, and growing food organically.

Through its ubiquitous co-ordinator, Stan Windass, the Alternative Society has also been associated with initial attempts to establish a Community Land Trust. Based on the belief that 'the system of private ownership of land which once led to high productivity and personal independence has become a major source of economic and social inequality',[49] the Trust is meant to hold land for the common good, which may or may not be combined with common ownership. Such land would be held in perpetuity and leased to users with the expectation of preserving or enhancing its long-range resource value. The residents have secure use-rights to the land and are free to control and build their own community through co-operative organizations or individual homesteads. The purpose is to give groups, perhaps such as the New Villages Association, physical and social space to shape their own community and control their own lives.

Nearly all these ventures are either rural in nature or prospect or closely linked to the use of skills and the giving of services rather than to the production of goods. Other attempts have been made to translate the basic principles of small-scale decentralized units, controlled by those concerned with a particular production process or using the services or commodities concerned, into the more fully urban industrial situation. The Co-operative Movement itself is such an example. Although outside the purview of this book, it is perhaps worth noting that its failure to arouse much enthusiasm today, even among those strongly committed to the idea of an alternative society, is twofold. On the one hand, the Movement has never succeeded in establishing a strong producer co-operative side, in part due to the fact that in redistributing a large proportion of profits to shareholders it weakened its ability to develop competitively enough in a capitalist economy. On the other hand, the consumer, as well as the producer, side lost popular appeal as shares were transferred or bequeathed and passed out of the hands of working or otherwise closely associated members. Bureaucratization set in and the image of the faceless corporation and far-away head office appeared.

Another and more immediately relevant example of workers' participation on the production side is the Industrial Common Ownership Movement.[50] The origin of the Movement lies in the establishment in 1951 of the Scott Bader Commonwealth, a Wellingborough firm which produced polyester resins, on what Ernest Bader believed were fully Christian principles: 'a concrete contribution towards a better society in the service of God and our fellow men' and an 'effort to establish the Christian way of life in our business'.[51] The ownership of the firm was transferred to the employees who operated on the basis of certain ground rules. These were: a firm of limited size (in 1975 it was 400 strong), a strict limit on differentials between the highest and lowest paid, security of employment other than for personal misconduct, full accountability of the Board of Directors to the Commonwealth, and the apportionment of half of the profits to outside charitable purposes. Since then and especially after 1970, more companies have moved over to common ownership by one means or another and in September 1975 thirteen firms, with from ten to 400 employees, belonged to the Movement. Most of these companies are run on similar lines to the Scott Bader Commonwealth, limited by guarantee and having no share capital. In 1976, the Industrial Common Ownership Movement, which links these ventures, was hoping to expand into a full-time staff, encouraged by the Government's increasing recognition of the possibilities of common ownership, and in part stimulated by the energetic campaign which backed an Industrial Common Ownership Bill (now become law) introduced by a private member, David Watkins, in March of that year.

Critique

It would be naive to imagine that any of the projects discussed above are *the* key to the future. There are many peculiarities about their situation which prevents easy translation to our economy as we know it at present.

A fundamental difficulty is that of seeking to establish any style of genuinely participatory socialism within or over against an economy which, whether a Conservative or a Labour government be in power, is dominated by the profit motive, the market, and consumerism. Only the benevolent, the wealthy patrons of certain communities, or the philanthropic like Ernest Bader, are prepared to step somewhat out of line. Even here, as Schumacher notes,[52] the backlash is not far off with even Bader's 'quiet revolution' still unacceptable to many (management *and* unions) in industry.

There are many ways in which this unacceptability becomes obvious, not least in the attempt by such enterprises to raise capital, which Father McDyer at Glencolumbkille states as one of his outstanding problems; though Glencolumbkille is fortunate for it does have an abundance of land, a commodity which in England is less available than in nearly any other country in the world. (This fact, incidentally, is probably one of the main reasons for the relatively few intentional communities here, especially in the ecological field, compared, for example, with the United States.)

It is thus easy for cynics, let alone outright antagonists, to employ the adjective 'parasitical' of such ventures. Geoff Crowther writes about the Commune Movement:

> Great lip-service was paid to the concept of self-sufficiency, yet this disguised a strong element of bourgeois escapism. Almost without exception these self-sufficient groups continued to be reliant on piped water, grid electricity, gas, transport and the petrochemical industry, etc., etc., all of which presupposed the continued existence of the things they had wanted to get away from.[53]

There is some truth here and a few groups live in a kind of fantasy world until the need for medical services or schooling becomes acute. The older children from remote Scoraig have to travel sixty miles across Scotland to Dingwall on the east coast where they board for the week while attending school. At Little Gidding, itself a group dedicated to an ecologically acceptable way of life, questions were raised in the 1975 autumn newsletter about the appropriateness of the word 'self-sufficiency' and a suggestion was made that a better and less exclusive, indeed less possessive, phrase would be 'sufficiency through sharing'.

Where alternative ways of operating do emerge within the system, it is often in niches left by mass production which just cannot cater for certain more specialized services and commodities, often of a 'luxury' nature, such as candles, pottery, jewellery, and woodcarving. The Industrial Common Ownership Movement is in reality a drop in the ocean set against the massive national and even more massive multinational companies at present using up the earth's resources on a vast scale.

The projects discussed, simply because they depend on specialized skills, whether in agriculture or in producing resins and plastics, attract workmen who are well trained or highly educated and therefore able to have a go at something new. There is thus an élitist feel to some projects where members, otherwise in a position to be fitted back into the mainstream, can for a while enjoy the privilege of doing their own thing. On the other hand it would be foolish to underestimate the personal and communal dedication, the readiness to endure considerable physical discomfort, and the sheer hard work required to set up these ventures.

Also problematical is the ability of these groups to survive very long on the basis of genuine all-round participation. There seems to be a slow but steady tendency for authoritarianism to set in, which can be fed either by intense identification with an ideal, sometimes of a religious nature, and a determination to see it survive at all costs (as with the Children of God), or for a *laissez-faire* situation to develop as some form of democratic control proves too demanding or too cumbersome (as with the Kingsway Community). The very *raison d'être* of moving apart from the system then disappears and the results may be technologically interesting – organic farming, constructing solar panels, and so on – but socially unremarkable.

These kinds of issue led Ralf Dahrendorf to criticize the 'misplaced romanticism which claims that "small" is not only "beautiful", but also feasible'.[54] But there is another side to the coin: a view which, recognizing the fragile and sometimes exaggerated claims made for some of these experiments, still sees them as important models for what could be if only. . . . For where else can one look other than to delve deep into history or build castles in the air? At least something tangible is happening and is observable. People are now *seen* to exist in our time who do not go along with the norms of consumerism and affluence; there *are* those who challenge the ravaging of the land and seas; people *do* exist who refuse to take as inevitable the organization of work on authoritarian and socially divisive lines; and we *can* observe groups determined to throw off the weight of impersonal bureaucratic structures. Seeds can grow, but no seeds means barren land.

Even where the small and the alternative are regarded as politically ineffective, the importance of these ventures in seeking to give a new dignity to man is recognized. Harry Newton, a founder member of the dominantly Marxist Institute of Workers' Control, writes: 'Socialism based on materialism appears to result in bureaucratic nightmare. Unless the economic and political structures of "Socialism" are imbued with the spirit of the Brotherhood of Man, they are barren and joyless.'[55] He argues that such brotherhood should be very much the Christian's concern, not just to speak of but to live out. Alternative technology and alternative modes of organization in relation to work must in the end mean an alternative form of society. Many Christians, alongside others, in such enterprises as those I have described, have at least made a courageous and determined beginning, in practice not just in theory.

THE PERSONAL

Sensuality

Alternative ways of life concerned with a new orientation of man to the earth and through this to his fellows, deeply influence the individual's awareness of the world in which he has been set. This is especially true of basic communities living in remote or rural surroundings, such as that which from 1969 until 1974 lived on one of the northern islands of Orkney. One of their number writes:

A word on night skies, deserted sandy beaches in moonlight. Northern lights of mingling purples, greens, reds, blues in indescribable patterns with white flashing lights – silent but roaring with their magnificence and aura of universal power. A lapping moonlight bay out of the window from the bed in the roof. Thousands of birds, seals that swam in so close to you as you walked round the beaches or played the trumpet to them. The time the foal was first born, standing in the field on shaky legs a few hours old. The air, the expanse, the vastness of the universe, right there with me in it and it in me. The long, long sunsets in the summer, the red glow that never died in June; just red for a few hours and then the sun was up again. The smell of harvest as I ride on the top of the trailer, bringing it home for the people who sold us our house. The children who were born there and the beautiful view of the islands on the boat-ride to and from the island. All bring on, again indescribable, a surge of joy and love into me and up out of me. Also some of the fear. The being alone and isolated long, long winter evenings (dark at 3.30 p.m., light at half-9 a.m.). The waves 60–100 ft high, with howling winds. Exciting, thrilling, but frightening too. You see how small a human is. Our largeness is created only in our minds.[56]

Through this sort of experience many people are discovering more about themselves. To echo the American therapist, Fritz Perls, they may seem to be losing their minds but they are coming to their senses. Audrey, whom we met near Inverness, walking barefoot through the woods, kicking up the leaves and curling her toes to feel the soil, may seem a trivial example of 'being earthed' again, but to her this was an existence for which it was worth sacrificing a very great deal.

Nor are such people unaware of the criticisms levelled by the city dweller, half in scorn and half in envy. Jen Lewis writes of herself in Laurieston Hall's magazine, *Country Women*:

She read the 'secret life of plants' and began apologizing to the ground-elder for pulling it out of the strawberry patch. She visited the beech tree that leaned over the beck and rested her cheek on its rough bark and said, 'You have been a good friend to me.' She came home and stood looking out at the mountain and the meadow in the soft green dusk and said, 'Yes, this is how it is meant to be. This feels right. Humans are meant to live like this.' And comes away pondering how to justify it, how to continue to choose to live in the country, how to counter the voice that says, 'No time for all this self-indulgent mystical lyricism and talking to plants. The struggle's in the city with the workers, you middle-class escapist.' But she knows that's not right either. . . . There are workers in the country too; on the farms, in the towns and villages. Trying to maintain a local country-women's group is a start. Giving out leaflets and collecting signatures for the abortion campaign in the local village is another.[57]

Animals are bred by many communities such as Taena, Pilsdon, Little Gidding, Keveral Farm, and Ringsfield Hall. Lothlorien, after only a year and without the main accommodation anywhere near completed, already had hens, a pig, two goats, two cows, and two bull calves. Ray Forsyth writes of Scoraig: 'The environment is a natural heaven for young children and no one has to organize play groups for sand and water play! There are animals about all the time; birth, mating, and death are part of everyday life.'[58] Not all the creatures of nature are, however, attractive and at Scoraig a toughness of hide to withstand the swarms of midges in season is a great asset!

Food obviously looms large on the agenda of most communities. Organic farming is common though by no means universal. But everywhere the emphasis is on as wholesome a diet as possible. Supper at Lothlorien when I visited was a choice from home-grown lettuce, beans, peas, carrots, potatoes, homemade cheese, raspberries, unleavened bread, and peanut butter. In *Country Women* Gill Harper passes some comments on her belief that 'macrobiotics isn't just a diet – it's a way of life'.[59] She writes:

> To have respect for food is to have respect for life, for the food that we eat builds our bodies and minds. . . . To eat natural and wholesome food does make sense not only to our own bodies but to our planet. If we overfill our stomachs with rich unnatural foods we become sick and slovenly and if we rob the earth of goodness and replenish it with crap it too will become sick and cease to supply the foods we need for life. . . . There are three premises for eating macrobiotically: Eat first-order foods. . . . Eat whole foods, as these are balanced plants within themselves. . . . Eat local-grown foods in season.[60]

Vegetarianism is also popular on the grounds of health and the needless butchering of other creatures. In fact a survey carried out by the *Communes Journal* revealed that there were as many as '42 per cent with a positive interest in vegetarianism'[61] amongst their sample, only 10 per cent in any way objecting to it. However, the existence of this high proportion of vegetarians can also bring its problems and any group which underestimates the intensity of the potential clash between vegetarians and meat eaters can be in for a rude awakening. Let the saga of Dartmouth House described in the next chapter speak for itself.

That the food issue is not just confined to the countryside can be evidenced by the large number of wholefood centres or co-operatives now springing up throughout Britain. Small-scale they may be, but they provide a real opportunity for the city dweller to share something of his fellow communards' commitment to doing away with artificial aids to growth and with synthetic processing.

A good deal of store is laid by the physical, and often spiritual, value of hard manual work. Especially noteworthy here is the Iona Community; in the reconstruction of the abbey they sought to enter into a common life based on working together, living together, and worshipping together. Extended work camps continued year after year until the main work of rebuilding was over. In it men of all social backgrounds and with a wide variety of skills, or none, shared as an act of self-expression and communal commitment. Iona is but one group which fostered the idea of the work camp to give participants a sense of achievement, to accomplish socially useful work, and above all to express the value of corporate endeavour and sharing, originally during the depression of the 1930s and, on a more ecumenical and international basis, throughout the years of reconstruction after the Second World War. Such camps have been a continuing example of the creation of temporary but meaningful community through the basic medium of physically demanding manual work. Ray Davey of the Corrymeela Community can still write: 'The work camp movement is Corrymeela's golden asset.'[62]

Yet the work camp, like many other more established 'institutions', is having to face the winds of change. In correspondence, Judy Coleman of the British Council of Churches Youth Unit writes:

> Apart from, say, countries like Italy, where there is still manual work to be done which is *needed*, voluntary work's shift into the sphere of community service, of playschemes, care of the old, hospitalized patients, reconciliation projects between factions (as in N. Ireland), has made the remit of voluntary work much less clear, and the aims and potential achievements wide open to debate. In one sense our ranks of volunteers are far wider than they were (in terms of philosophy, creed, and to an *extent*, socio-economic background, not to mention age and occupation). In another sense, the new community-social style camps *preclude*, by dint of their very nature, a certain group of people (often those without higher education, many of whom feel insecure in situations calling for articulate, rational thinking, self-assurance and a facility for social intercourse).

At the same time other issues have arisen: the problem of volunteers engaged in this kind of work having little energy left for community-making with their fellow volunteers; the difficulty of offering anything of real value to local people during a short stay; and the question of whether volunteers should get involved in any form of political engagement.

There are, of course, schemes (such as that sponsored by the Catholic Institute for International Relations) where volunteers work abroad for as long as a year. But though this may alleviate certain of the difficulties mentioned, others then emerge: the increasing reluctance of Third World countries to accept them and their effective resettlement in this country on their return. I include all this simply to emphasize that work camps and volunteer schemes are no longer about enthusiastic young people painting halls or digging holes and creating instantaneous community en route.

Harry Newton, in an article in *Community*, rightly attacks a certain tendency to over-glamourize the manual aspect of work. He sees as one of man's great achievements the discovery of a technology which first liberated him from physical slavery and now, with automation, can free him from slavery to machines. He writes: 'Those who extol the physical, mental, and spiritual virtues of hard manual labour may "tell it to the Marines" but they will get little response from the fishermen, miners, or agricultural labourers.'[63] Yet though there is obvious truth in the charge of false romanticism, it would be quite inaccurate to conclude that members of communities do not realize how arduous manual work can be. Many established groups have worked incredibly hard, with considerable skill and craftsmanship, to build or renovate property and to make land fertile. Lothlorien's letter to would-be visitors runs: 'You will see that if you come here you will be expected to work as we work. Which is pretty hard. We cannot afford to carry passengers and anyone who comes here must understand that work is a prerequisite of life at Lorien. It is our food.' And this is no idle warning when one sees the 30-ft-long logs, weighing several hundredweight, which are being lifted into position by hand in the construction of the huge cabin.

Most communities would not stop even at claiming that they know what hard work is, not to mention the added strain of living as well as working cheek-by-jowl month after month. They would express a conviction, some in more religious language than others, that work has a spiritual dimension especially where it is not primarily related to the making of profit or to mass production. The almost total work/leisure dichotomy of modern society would be strongly opposed and the emphasis placed on the wholeness of man's self-expression – body, mind, and spirit. This is very much the case, for example, at Pilsdon where 'the work itself is very important – farming and gardening, cooking and cleaning, painting and pottery, and keeping in good repair a large manor house and grounds'.[64] Percy Smith continues:

One of the revealing things is the way most people willingly offer to work without being asked. Work here is not directly related to money, and this in itself is significant. We are fed and clothed and live in quite enough comfort, and our work is seen not as something to do to earn this, but as a necessary contribution to make the life of the community possible.[65]

In the 'Letters from Pilsdon' Percy Smith adds: 'We live in our work, and the day's work is punctuated by prayer, which is also our work. We believe that it is as natural for man to say "Lord have mercy" as to say "I am mucking out the cowsheds".'[66] And again: 'We have come to realize also that prayer is not time taken off from work, nor is work an interruption of prayer, but work finds inspiration in prayer and prayer finds expression in work.'[67] Here then the 'sensuality' of manual work combines with the 'sensuality' of prayer to create a new personal and communal integrity.

Spontaneity

Spontaneity has been crushed out of modern life, amongst other things by our new technologies and the need to serve or be served by them. The mechanical clock, which became popular in England sometime towards the middle of the fourteenth century, was a major step in this process, providing the means to order and control physical activity in order to develop the new production technology of the machine.[68] Though discipline through time-structuring had always been an important part of monastic life, and bell-towers not only ensured devotional obedience but brought regularity into the life of the workman, the steady breaking down of time into smaller and smaller units and the attributing of economic value to such, brought an entirely new situation. Advanced technologies have come to demand of time what Wilbert Moore calls precise 'synchronization' and elaborate 'sequences' requiring highly co-ordinated 'activity rates'.[69] And even if modern man can occasionally escape from direct subservience to these, he is still, as when watching television or listening to the radio, bombarded by news of a mass of external events almost immediately they occur anywhere round the globe. 'The diffusing and cushioning effect of time and space are now almost entirely cut out by modern methods of communication.'[70]

No wonder that many searching for an alternative way of life are also seeking alternative technologies and means of livelihood which give greater temporal space. One way of gaining this is an attempt to return to time structured not by machines, or the economic value of the second, but by nature. Ray Forsyth at Scoraig speaks of 'accepting the discipline which livestock imposes',[71] whilst Margaret Potts quotes one member, in the early days working on St Julian's farm, as saying: 'It is a place where people must forget themselves for the sake of what is alive and needs constant and faithful attention. You have to carry a job through whatever the weather is like or whatever you feel like.'[72] Indeed, working with the seasons rather than racing the clock, though even in rural or remote areas now very difficult to avoid, gives a sense of time being one's partner rather than one's master.

Another way to arrive at this point has been for communities to create synchronization, sequence, and a rate of activity suited to their own particular way of life. This can be irregular and very informal as at Keveral Farm or with the Shrubb Family, or much more structured, as at Pilsdon, where one purpose is to give support to disoriented members. 'But this structured life is also within the context of a great deal of space, where people can work at their own speed without the pressures of a conveyor belt or the boss breathing down their neck.'[73] This situation can also bring a much greater degree of availability: people not always hurrying off to complete the next task or fulfil the next engagement. I am constantly surprised, when visiting communities, at how much time members are ready to give to meeting people without neglecting necessary responsibilities.

The important fact is not that any one community's mode of structuring time is 'best', but that in such situations members are in a position to create those temporal rhythms through which they can meet both the demands of corporate living and their own personal needs in a way which gives the maximum opportunity of experiencing the reality and the vitality of the present. As Theodore Roszak says, 'True time . . . is properly the living experience of life itself.'[74]

Creativity

A new fervour for 'the feel of things' and a temporal rhythm determined by nature or communal requirements provides an ideal setting for the releasing of creative skills, especially through a wide variety of crafts. Though in the context of the economic and technological climate of today, communal crafts may by some be equated with Nero fiddling, this is really to beg the question. For in the field of community crafts small *is* beautiful, and entering into the experience of the creation of things of beauty is a personally enriching process.

The craftsman is a person who has a real sense of the material and of its potential, of what is within that brings order out of apparent chaos and beauty out of formlessness. Many basic communities are creating things of intricate design and great beauty, not just to help pay their way but because they believe craftsmanship in itself to be worth while. One outstanding example of this is the Dove Centre near Glastonbury which began operations in 1972 and, despite a recent shift from the communal to the craft aspect, still emphasizes both. The skills include pottery, woodwork, ceramics, glasswork, painting, and printing. In 1973 one of the members wrote:

> We are grateful that we can pursue artistic interests in such a mutually supportive and sustaining community. There is what one might call a 'creative space' wherein one can follow one's artistic aims. Another great advantage is the opportunity for teaching: for stimulating interest in arts and crafts as a service to the local people and their children. Thus the Dove is becoming a small but energetic cultural centre. We think it is possible in such an environment, to develop a healthy and creative life-style — a balance between individualism and brotherhood through service. The community is not philosophically aligned and our colleagues are from diverse backgrounds — yet we have found a refreshing openness at the Dove. The essential source of inspiration and confidence is the artistic integrity of our fellow artists. Albert Schweitzer said that sincerity is the foundation of the spiritual life. In this sense then, the Dove Centre is establishing its own creative spirit.[75]

At Pilsdon delightful pottery, with a warm brown finish, is produced. Taena is mainly a farming community but it also contains those skilled in pottery, silver, and woodwork, such as George Ineson whose meditation hut is filled with carvings of beauty and deep spiritual significance. Keveral Farm is remarkable for its beautifully painted and stained children's jigsaw puzzles which are of such quality that they won a Design Centre award and are ordered by people from all over the world. Here, however, there are problems as the work of keeping up the farm, and at times the lack of interest of community members in making items on what could begin to seem a mass production basis, have caused strong differences of opinion as to how energies should be spent.

But where community members can get down unimpeded to such

crafts, a great deal of personal fulfilment is experienced. At Findhorn the crafts workshops are amongst the most impressive aspect of community life. Paul Hawken writes:

> There is a studio for weaving and macramé, one for graphics, one for pottery, and one for candlemaking. . . . The creative aspect unfolds at Findhorn in a completely natural way with ease and grace. People who had done 'nothing' creative before coming to Findhorn emerge as great dancers, photographers, potters and carpenters.[76]

The aim is to turn out workmanship of the highest possible quality, with no eye to built-in obsolescence; in the case of Findhorn to bear witness to the nature of life in the New Age just dawning. In this instance, not at all a bad advertisement.

At the Salisbury (Open) Centre in Edinburgh the emphasis is rather more therapeutic. They write:

> We feel that the use of crafts, both as a means of therapy and as creative expression can be part of this growth process, in that to make something in tranquillity and awareness can lead to an enhanced sense of personal identity transcending self-centredness, and that in these days of mass production it is vitally important to keep the love of craftsmanship alive. Thus we have facilities for pottery, weaving, and woodcarving and we are open to any developments along these lines.[77]

Though I am here stressing the matter of ₁ new personal awareness through crafts, the interpersonal aspect is implicit in much that has already been described. As at the Dove Centre, all sections of a community can be closely drawn together through crafts. At Birchwood Hall one of the 'family' sub-groups selected itself predominantly on the basis of an interest in arts and crafts. The Findhorn work teams spend time together in prayer and in ensuring a social harmony which it is believed enriches the quality of their work. As David Dickson comments: 'Small-scale craft industries promise a return to a community-based mode of production, in which every man or woman is in direct control of his or her own life, and work becomes reintegrated with all other areas of collective activity and experience.'[78]

THE INTERPERSONAL

The nuclear family

'The thing is that alternatives to the nuclear family are not *just* about personal relationships. They pose a real threat to the social order, and I think a threat to the whole consumer-based thing as well. Our whole society is structured towards the nuclear family.'[79] So comments one man in his thirties in a discussion which was recorded and then written up in *Community* in 1975. 'The whole consumer-based thing' is intrinsic to the type of society to which we belong and the constrictive effect of this state of affairs, legitimated daily by massive and clever commercial advertising, prevents much genuine exploration of alternatives to the small, closed, nuclear family unit. It is through the advertising business in particular that the myth of technological neutrality, referred to earlier, can be seen for what it really is, for we have here invented a technology and a life-style which are mutually dependent. A competitive, consumer-oriented society needs the isolated, gullible nuclear family to which to sell its many luxury goods as well as the more functional products; the nuclear family needs the mass media to inform it what constitutes 'the good life' and constantly to reaffirm that it is (nearly but of course not quite) 'making it' with regard to social norms.

Many basic communities have reacted very strongly against such pressures. Few of them, other than the more 'straight' conference centres, have television sets, and goods are bought predominantly on a functional basis. The search for simplicity of life-style already mentioned; the refusal to go for the line of least resistance in buying processed or pre-packaged foods; the emphasis on 'do-it-yourself' at the most basic level; and above all communal living itself where sharing space, work, and goods is normative: all these constitute a protest against the nuclear family as the major pillar of consumerism.

Our society also imposes a style of life based on the independent and isolated nuclear family unit in other ways. One is the nature of family welfare benefits, though these do not so easily hinder communal living as such. A more limiting factor is housing. This is a complex subject, but the overall situation is still that reported by a Chimera working group in 1971. They state: 'We have found that the difficulty of borrowing money for a group enterprise, even when all members as individuals would have no difficulty in securing mortgages for themselves, has been the greatest barrier.'[80] The housing association arrangement overcomes some difficulties but not in regard to genuinely communal accommodation, the self-contained unit remaining in most cases the *sine qua non* for raising loans. Hostel accommodation, which may seem an attractive alternative, has the built-in problem of being what the Chimera working group term 'latitudinal'[81] in nature; that is, it can only be used for distinct groups such as students, the elderly, the mentally ill and so on, and not in a 'longitudinal' way, that is, embracing all ages as well as mixing the 'disadvantaged' and the 'normal'.

Of course groups do get round these problems in a variety of ways or there would be no communal living to write about. Postlip Hall in Gloucestershire was bought in 1970 by six families who formed a co-ownership housing association.[82] Birchwood Hall was purchased in 1970 by a group which worked out a trust arrangement with loans from members and friends and with the four people who put up most of the money being trustees.

> Shrubb Family live in an old farmhouse with an acre of land. At the start it was owned by one member, who later wanted to leave, so they spent some time working out the best way to transfer it into collective ownership. . . . They eventually set up a company limited by guarantee, with all members of the commune being shareholders, and the owner agreed to give them a private mortgage to be repaid in full by a certain date.[83]

And Laurieston Hall, which in 1972 cost £25,000, is currently owned in the names of the four women who originally purchased it. On a larger scale, the attempt to set up a Community Land Trust, already referred to, is another attempt to give communal living a secure future. But these and many other exceptions only go to prove the rule that to move away from the concept of the self-contained nuclear family unit as the basis of obtaining living accommodation is to meet not only genuine administrative problems but vested interests head-on.

Less obvious yet even more insidious is the way that a competitive society, depending on the market to establish criteria of value and on the legal contract as the basis of trust, can influence the whole concept of what family life is about. As Eric Fromm points out, the ideal marriage can all too easily be portrayed as a romantic paradise (the commercial world thriving on the sale of canned sentimentality) or reflecting exchange on the market, as a contract with each person seeking the best bargain, an exchange of 'personality packages'.[84] 'Fairness' rather than love is the most this kind of agreement can offer. And if the whole force of our economic system against valuing things or people for their intrinsic worth does not prevent a couple from genuinely loving and sharing with each other, it can so easily isolate them from other couples as they struggle to set up and equip *their* house and to establish *their* family life on the basis of a kudos associated with material possessions or social status.

It is against the inherent competitiveness and individualism of our economic system, not least with regard to the nuclear family, that so many communal experiments are a protest. Alienation is not just man being separated from the product of his labour, it is man being separated from open and meaningful relationships with his fellows at work *and* elsewhere. John Taylor writes:

> Inasmuch as the systems often impose the attitudes, we have to defy them also; and this calls for a counter-culture of families and groups that cannot be conned or manipulated because they simply do not accept the accepted values or pursue the ambitions that are expected of them. We must try to live by the divine contrariness of Jesus. We need a rapidly increasing minority that is entirely counter-suggestible, a minority that calls the bluff of the trend-setters, is a dead loss to the advertising agencies and poor material for the careers advisers.[85]

The communal ventures already described are a demonstration of 'counter-suggestibility'. By keeping in touch with an alternative values system, especially with regard to the physical and material aspects of life, they are reaching out to a new dimension of relationships in which significance and belonging are not regulated by extrinsic worth and achieved status.

Symbolic place

One aspect of the emergence of a new sense of corporateness is the rediscovery of the importance of 'symbolic place' in an urban society which goes through constant physical upheaval and reshaping. Symbolic place has been defined as 'any feature of the physical environment which, in the midst of a world of swift changes, gives a "feeling of meaning and permanence"[86] to social existence'.[87]

G. Herbert here quotes the Smithsons:

> Just as our mental processes need fixed points (fixed in the sense of change over a relatively long period) to enable them to classify and

value transient information, and thus remain sane and lucid, so too the city (and one would add, many other places) needs 'fixes' – identifying points with a long cycle of change, by means of which things changing on a shorter cycle can be valued and identified.[88]

Many communities and similar groups have come to be associated with such 'fixes' as a means not only of giving them a tangible point on which spiritually to reflect and around which physically to gather, but as a way of linking them with a common heritage, be that the glory of the natural world or the Church over many centuries past.

Outstanding in this connection is the island of Iona which has given to the community a vitality and tenacity quite impossible to measure. Kenneth Clark sums up the mood of many visitors:

I never come to Iona – and I used to come here almost every year when I was young – without feeling that 'some God is in this place'. It isn't as awe-inspiring as some other holy places – Delphi or Assisi. But Iona gives one more than anywhere else I know a sense of peace and inner freedom. What does it? The light, which floods round on every side? The lie of the land which, coming after the solemn hills of Mull, seems strangely like Greece, like Delos, even? The combination of wine-dark sea, white sand, and pink granite? Or is it the memory of those holy men who for two centuries kept western civilization alive?[89]

The sheer beauty of the island and its setting, the knowledge that man has worshipped there since St Columba first landed in AD 563, the simple yet compelling austerity of the now rebuilt abbey – all these go to make Iona a symbolic place *par excellence*. And symbolic not just for those calling in, but for many when they return to the concrete confines of the city. In 1975 the English Company of the Pilgrims of St Francis came to Iona to visit its historic places and worship in the abbey as the climax of their journeying together. In this and so many ways the island contains within itself the power to call people together and to send them out renewed in a way which, in the last resort, defies analysis.

But not only Iona. Glastonbury too has this kind of appeal for many, by no means all of Christian persuasion. Though, strangely enough, no permanent community has established itself there in recent years, people are drawn to the town and stay for as long as possible in order in some way to share together spiritually. Because of this a camp was run during the summer months, for three years from 1972, called the

Greenbus,[90] giving food and shelter under canvas to young wanderers and offering a 'non-aggressive' Christian presence in the midst of a welter of other beliefs associated with legends surrounding Joseph of Arimathea (and his visit with the youthful Christ to Glastonbury), stories of King Arthur, astrology, and the occult, and more recently with devotees of the New Age of Aquarius. Even Christians there speak of Glastonbury as a cosmic battleground. Be this as it may, a symbolic place of a compelling kind Glastonbury certainly is. This is the case, whether or not one believes the theory of 'ley lines', a term coined by Alfred Watkins in 1921, referring to the network of straight lines on which many prehistoric sites appear to lie and which some think gives a form of spiritual energy to ancient centres of worship, such as Glastonbury.[91]

Other places too are noteworthy for giving 'a feeling of meaning and permanence' to communities associated with them. In Glencolumbkille, Donegal, it is the country, the rolling hills, and the wild sea, which give the spiritual dynamic, as Father McDyer knows well:

> Donegal County presents many faces to the visitor, but here in Glencolumbkille we find the face that is most varied and rugged. Here one can envisage the awesome and majestic turbulence that must have taken place when the world was young. Here the presence of man can never and will never obliterate the footprints of God.[92]

Likewise the beauty of the North Antrim coast stirs the hearts of those working at Corrymeela; and the grandeur of Little Loch Broom and its surrounding mountains, those living at Scoraig.

More historically, Marygate House on Lindisfarne attracts many drawn there by the Celtic heritage of Northumbria and a sense of Holy Island's ministry over the ages. Little Gidding in Huntingdonshire, too, has roots in the past, being known especially for its association with Nicholas Ferrar, once an MP and Deputy Treasurer of the Virginia Company; in 1625, with his large household, he moved from London to a tumbledown manor house there. They lived and worshipped in a small community, serving all who wished to visit them. Nicholas Ferrar's renunciation of wealth and fame was the inspiration of Pilsdon and less directly of other groups; not to mention of one of T. S. Eliot's *Four Quartets*.

Bearing the scars of rather more recent years is Coventry Cathedral which, bombed and gutted during the last war, was rebuilt on an adjacent site as a church filled with the symbols of reconciliation and renewal. It has become a place constantly visited by people of all nations and extends its influence far and wide, especially through its educational activities and its Cross of Nails (the original stands in the old blitzed church) now presented to some fifty places of note working for reconciliation throughout the world. More recently the international Community of the Cross of Nails was established to link these centres in a creative network. Kenyon Wright, heading Coventry's International Development Centre, believes that the cathedral must now seek to symbolize not the work of reconciliation typical of the immediate post-war period but 'the central issue of world development, of the gap of poverty and injustice between nations and within nations'.[93] He is probably right, but one thing troubles me about the cathedral: its growing impersonality. The symbol seems to have lost touch with an identifiable and dynamic lay community at its heart and one feels that its multifarious ministries may be outstripping the only thing that in the end can make any symbol live.

These symbolic places offer to all the basic communites linked with them an extra potential for enriching the interpersonal dimension of their common life. Their associations, natural or historical, give an added impetus to solidarity, fusing the great events of the past and the vision of the future into one. The Church needs such symbols, as George Ineson of Taena puts it, 'because power . . . attaches to places'.[94] But place only identifies community; it cannot in the end create or sustain it. In the last resort community must be its own symbol.

Openness

One test of the quality of life to which basic communities bear witness is not only the strength of their sense of belonging but their ability to be open to others, whilst not losing their own identity and surrendering their distinctive contribution. Within their own ranks many groups are deeply conscious not only of the ravaging of the earth and of pollution but of a world of human despair. Their simplicity of life-style is rarely an end in itself, just for the sake of health or spiritual alertness, but a protest against a society which can gorge itself to death whilst millions have no option but to arrive at the same point by slow starvation. The members of Lothlorien put it this way:

> We hope that our Lothlorien will not only be . . . a place of re-creation, but also that it will become a source of inspiration to others to make similar places. The need is great in our world today,

threatened increasingly by the shadows of economic collapse, of the pursuit of the 'Big', of the loss of spiritual values. . . . Lothlorien is *not* an attempt to escape from the outside world; it is an attempt to find a positive alternative to some aspects of that world – an alternative that will enable us and others to go on living in it.[95]

But one problem of seeking for a more 'natural' existence on a crowded island, of attempting to be self-sufficient, is that it can bring an isolationism and even exclusiveness which prevents any real interaction with, let alone political impact on, mainstream society. Geoff Crowther puts the point, as ever, forcefully:

> If communes and radical communities are not just to be an end in themselves (and therefore provide a cocoon for middle-class escapism) they should have urban as well as rural bases so that there exists the possibility of exchange between the two. This way we would be moving towards doing something positive about over-coming the alienation and pointlessness of modern urban (and rural) living. Such communities could give the industrial worker a chance to get back in touch with the land and therefore his source of food and give the farmer the opportunity of getting in touch with the industrial means of production on which so much of his material needs and security depend – an idea familiar with the Chinese. They would also make a start in eliminating expertism and professionalism, their resultant hierarchies and the discriminative social values attached to different jobs. If alternative organizations do not direct their efforts towards raising the general level of consciousness about what is being done on their behalf and so encourage confrontation with and resistance to the controlling political forces, then the latter will blithely continue along their autodestructive path until it really is too late.[96]

Yet one sympathizes with groups seeking to survive, quite apart from being seed-beds of revolution, in generally unconducive surroundings. The danger of economic collapse, of absorption back into the system, of being overrun if the doors are opened too wide, is immense. If, as seems obvious now, any major changes required to secure wider acceptance of the life-style presented by these groups must in the end be of a political nature, then it is probably much more the responsibility of those who are disenchanted yet still benefiting from the system, than of those exposed to the risks of living more outside it, to bring such changes about.

5

COMMUNITIES OF LEARNING

The theme of this book is an examination of the way in which basic communities deal with the fundamental issues of authority, personal awareness, and interpersonal relations whilst engaged in a number of key communal concerns. Nowhere is this theme more prominent than in relation to communities, centres, and other groups which have a major interest in some form of educational programme or teaching ministry. For in this context, not only are those involved declaring a great deal about their understanding of the nature of authority and interpersonal relations by the way in which they live and the methods they adopt for teaching purposes, but at many points they may be engaged in imparting material directly related to my basic themes. In trying to sort out the great variety of groups involved, there are thus three main variables to be considered: *the nature of the teaching group itself* and *the environment* in which it operates; the educational *methodology* used; and the *content* of the message which is being imparted. In arranging the sections below I have begun with learning based on intentional communities operating in a residential setting, through certain 'midway' groups, to itinerant teams operating anywhere. Within each section I have first dealt with groups communicating a more specifically religious message and gone on to consider those covering a more open curriculum. Where possible I have looked initially at groups using a more cognitive methodology and then taken those with a more fully experiential approach.

It is impossible to be fully consistent here. There are groups with a dominantly religious message who employ a range of experiential methods; Findhorn, for example. There are groups placing great emphasis on examining important secular issues while relying almost entirely on the cognitive dimension of learning; St George's, Windsor, for example. None the less, in this particular chapter, I have felt it better to treat communities and other groups as entities rather than split off those features which do not quite fit the broad criteria of the order in which they are placed. My survey is not exhaustive. I have selected communities and groups typifying the approaches of various similar ventures in existence, discussion of all of which would simply be repetitive.

TEACHING COMMUNITIES

There are a few communities which give pride of place to their teaching ministry, with their life as a community being very much geared to that end. They usually hold very strong religious convictions in common and feel called to 'spread the good news' they have discovered. Most of these groups tend to work within a fairly closed system of thought which stresses the proclamation or teaching of a definitive way of life and a particular set of beliefs, rather than encouraging critical debate or the close examination of life-styles alternative to that offered by the host community.

One group with features of this kind is Post Green, who describe their main function as being 'a teaching community with a concern to see God's people and local churches experiencing renewal through the power of the Holy Spirit'.[1] Their stance is very much Bible-centred, though not fundamentalist, with a charismatic emphasis. Though a good deal of proclamation is undertaken by their music group, The Post Green People, the main thrust of their work is the responsibility of teaching teams of four or five which conduct courses throughout the country. The course itself was originally written by members of Post Green, each completing a separate section, and has steadily been added to or revised, now covering such matters as baptism, gifts of the Spirit, the healing ministry, prayer-group leadership, and counselling. It is meant to be taught, not undertaken by correspondence, and the community insists on either its own team being present or the lead being taken by those who have themselves been present at training gatherings. Through 'second' and 'third generation courses' some thousand people had been reached in this way by the end of 1975, in such places as London, Birmingham, St Albans, and parts of Yorkshire and Norfolk. The course itself is backed up by tutorial seminars and further residential weekends.

Post Green's teaching ministry is thus didactic in emphasis. My own belief is that the material itself would be unexceptional if it were not for the enthusiasm and personal witness of the team conducting the courses. The demonstration of their own communal life together, with the dynamic of their Christian experience, gives the sessions a vitality which would otherwise be sadly missed. In this case, as in others where the impact of the community carries so much weight, the medium is very much the message.

The Community of Celebration, like Post Green in the charismatic tradition, and seeing its ministry predominantly to the Church, also lays great emphasis on proclamation and teaching. It undertakes this in two main ways, a drawing in and a going out. Of the drawing in, Graham Pulkingham writes:

> We conduct a multi-faceted training programme for Church leaders who come to us to gain experience and knowledge about community life. A part of this training programme is our invitation to them to come with their families and live with us for a year or two, becoming a full part of our community life and developing their leadership potential from within an existing, growing community structure.[2]

Of the going out he says: 'We are committed to participating as fully as possible in renewal of the Church by sending teams out into local parishes and congregations, at their invitation, to share with them whatever insights and skills we have in bringing about Church renewal.'[3]

In the latter situation the real impact has been made by The Fisherfolk, who in small teams of extremely talented musicians and singers have rapidly moved from local coffee-bar to international fame. The Fisherfolk plan their programme in consultation with local church leaders and give effect to their message through personal testimony, in music and in drama. They sometimes initiate worship workshops around dance, mime, poetry, and the graphic arts with an emphasis on exploring new forms of liturgical expression. Follow-up teaching materials have been designed. Once again the medium is very much the message and, though The Fisherfolk figure as leaders and 'experts', their spontaneity and creative skills can result in active and enthusiastic participation by local people.

One other community strongly influenced by the charismatic movement, the Barnabas Fellowship, also regards its educational work as important, though it concentrates its energies on running its centre, Whatcombe House, rather than on conducting many external events. In fact Reg East noted early in 1976 that they were more and more in demand for personal counselling and that an increasing flow of people from their neighbouring area were coming for help. The centre programme is charismatic in nature. Reg East writes:

> Helping others to rejoice in the renewing power of the Holy Spirit is carried out mainly by holding conferences and retreats for up to thirty-five people. Many of these are arranged by ourselves, varying in length – weekend, inside of a week or a full week – and the teaching and personal work is mainly the responsibility of the community. Outside speakers are sometimes invited.[4]

He adds: 'Though we never cease to speak of the Baptism in the Holy Spirit, we are more and more teaching consequences. The subjects most in demand at present are: Prayer and the spiritual life; Healing; Counselling; The local church as centre of ministry.'[5] The dynamic of the gatherings comes very much from the example of a praying core community which offers itself wholeheartedly to guests.

Away from the specifically Christian context, but still operating with its own religious world view, is Findhorn in north-east Scotland. In 1973 the community received divine guidance that it should move from seeing itself as a 'City of Light'[6] to becoming a 'University of Light', spreading the good news of the New Age far and wide through touring speakers, tapes, and a wide variety of publications. It also decided to build a £100,000 university hall with an all-purpose auditorium to seat 300, a recording studio, a sophisticated projection room, and a lounge with refreshment bar. In 1976 a large hotel on the outskirts of nearby Forres was purchased and named the Cluny Hill College, to extend the educational work of the university.

The community runs an ongoing programme of courses and experimental workshops on such themes as:

> *Revelation:* an in-depth study of the significance of the Limitless Love and Truth messages contained in the book *Revelation: The Birth of a New Age.*

> *Esoteric studies:* an exploration into the occult laws and principles underlying the constitution of man and the universe.

> *Sex and identity:* an opportunity to discover the meaning of sex and its relationship to one's personal identity.[7]

The Findhorn members, though operating within the context of their own peculiar pantheistic philosophy, are increasingly employing techniques pioneered by the human potential movement, techniques which they see as integrating with and expressing the life of the total enterprise. They write:

> We are dealing with experience and process. Since we conceive education as a dynamic unfoldment of inner potentials, our programmes cannot be rigid nor too formally structured. The University programme is essentially a series of experiences which, when assimilated by the individual, produce growth and expansion of consciousness. It does not seek to 'fill in' but to 'draw out' and help each person find that attunement to his own inner God-source wherein lies the fulfilment of all his needs. . . .
>
> The way in which this training takes place is through the work programme which integrates the spiritual concepts with daily activity, through the college in promoting mental clarity and synthesis, through relationships which help stabilize and strengthen the emotional patterns and through the gathering together of the whole community to affirm our spiritual vision. All these elements make up the matrix of our education and transformation. This is the essence of the University of Light. We are not concerned with education in the academic sense of intellectual studies, though they have their part. We are dealing with a process of unfoldment on an individual, group, and planetary level.[8]

The actual techniques employed include 'body awareness, dance massage, singing, group discovery, drama, astrology, and writing'.[9] These are experientially excellent tools and one only regrets (sometimes fears) that they are being so effectively used by a community based on such an ethereal philosophy.

Another cluster of small communities dedicated to a prominent educational programme is that embracing the Open Centres of one kind or another. Though these centres are in intention dedicated to a free exploration of a panorama of religious beliefs and practices, in fact they are developing a fairly distinct life-style of their own drawn from a mixture of mysticism, meditation, self-healing, the insights of psychoanalysis, and a strongly positive attitude to manual work. For example, at the Salisbury Centre, Edinburgh, the small residential community share in 'groups involving meditation and prayer, painting, encounter, dream analysis, and the study of the works of the Christian and Sufi mystics',[10] whilst at Ettrick Shaws Lodge near Selkirk the core group runs a programme in which 'meditation and manual work, study and discussion (are) carefully balanced, with time for relaxation'.[11] The Lodge community also seek to encourage good relations with the local people and emphasize service to the neighbourhood a great deal, especially over the summer months.

CONFERENCE CENTRES WITH
A RESIDENT COMMUNITY

The emphasis here is on conference centres which are staffed by communities somewhat less concerned than in the previous section with carrying out a teaching ministry linked to their particular beliefs and way of life. Members of these communities often play a prominent role in the educational scene within the centre, but just as frequently they will be helping visiting groups to run their own programmes. Thus the community itself has as much an administrative and servicing function as a directly educational one. Following the arrangement mentioned at the outset of this chapter, I begin with those groups operating within a definitive theological framework and move on to those working with a very open brief.

Established by the Hildenborough Evangelistic Trust is Hildenborough Hall, near Sevenoaks in Kent. It is run by a core community of some fifteen people, others coming in daily to help with the work. Its general director is Justyn Rees, who writes in correspondence:

> Each weekend we run 'Open House' which means anyone can come and stay from Friday night to Sunday afternoon. We average somewhere between 70 and 80 staying each weekend, during which a different theme is tackled arising from the Bible or some practical aspect of Christian living. In addition to the work done actually in the Centre, we also have a musical team which spend week days going round schools in the S.E. of England taking assemblies, R.E. lessons and lunch hour concerts. The aim and objective of the whole place is to share with people the Christian Gospel.

Lee Abbey is a conference and holiday centre of thirty years' standing which has at its heart a fairly fluid community of some seventy people. The latter spend their energies in maintaining the house and estate and catering for the thousands of visitors, their direct contact with guests being mainly of a social and pastoral kind. Only a small core team, including the warden and chaplains, exercise a distinctively educational role. The summer camp is an important gathering, with 150 young people present throughout August, but though intended to enable participants to 'discover the secret of true living and find Jesus Christ as a personal and powerful reality in their lives',[12] it does so through a social as much as a specifically educational programme.

Scargill works along similar lines to Lee Abbey though with more outside groups using the centre. The core team arranges a number of 'Focus' weekends on themes such as evangelism, as well as organizing a series of young people's events. These have been of a fairly traditional kind in terms of educational method, though a growing interest in the contribution of group dynamics is emerging and affecting both the organization of the community itself and the nature of worship. There is also a move to branch out in the 'Focus' gatherings towards wider topics such as changing life-styles and even political theology, an interesting development for a centre which, like Lee Abbey, is still very much evangelical in ethos. It would, however, be foolish to minimize the more personal impact of both the Lee Abbey and the Scargill communities on the many guests each receives annually, in the case of Scargill 'from parishes, to look at the nature and purpose of the Church, particularly in their own situations; clergy; young people; schoolchildren; Borstal boys; members of the medical profession; people in industry; people in education; many for the holiday houseparties; some privately'.[13]

It is appropriate at this point to mention two predominantly Roman Catholic communities with responsibility for centres sponsoring learning programmes: the Grail and Hengrave Hall. The Grail in particular has a long history of involvement in educational work. The members write:

> The energies of our society require the possibility of many kinds of work. Still, it can be summed up by saying that we work to build community and to provide education. By community we mean a network of loving relationships between God and man and between man and man. By education we mean everything we devise, formal or informal, direct or indirect, to help people become whole and free and self-aware. Our involvement is with Christians of diverse traditions, with all those who seek the Truth, and those for whom God is irrelevant.[14]

Of their specific activities they say: 'We do adult and child catechetics, we run experimental courses of various kinds, on prayer, liturgy, communications, and drama; we organize counselling courses for priests and lay people; we work with family groups and young people; we do local parish work.'[15] In addition they have more recently organized weaving and spinning weekends. Many of the community are not directly engaged in the educational work and in this sense their total ministry is much more diverse than that of, say, the members of the Barnabas Fellowship, but leading or sponsoring gatherings of people of all ages to work through the implications of the Christian faith is an overall and major concern. Their published courses for young people's groups are amongst the most imaginative produced in this field to date. The Grail's work with family groups is outstanding and I shall say more about this later in the chapter. The educational ministry of the Grail is mainly confined to Catholics, though the community is in intent committed to an ecumenical approach.

Hengrave Hall which, though it has a strong Catholic representation within its otherwise ecumenical community, is developing an open kind of educational programme ranging from a consultation on Northern Ireland which was held in 1975 to gatherings to explore the nature and relevance of charismatic renewal. In 1976 they arranged more events run by themselves. As yet, however, Hengrave relies a good deal on 'experts' or 'consultants' leading or conducting gatherings via the lecture and has not gone very far towards employing a more fully experiential and group-centred form of learning.

Two notable communities, with only a small number of their members actually acting as resident staff and ensuring the smooth running of their educational programmes, are Iona and Corrymeela. In both cases their conferences are set up to explore major religious, social, and political themes of the day. They encourage dialogue and debate and seek to bring together those of differing viewpoints.

The Iona Community has two main facets to its educational work; that linked to the training of its members and that directed to its summer programme on the island itself. The initial aim of George MacLeod was to offer young ministers the chance of a new and realistic kind of corporate training before they went out to serve the Church in an industrial society, a training closely linked to the rebuilding of the abbey and sharing the hard work and the fellowship involved. But with the completion of the renovation and the entry into the community of more lay members, a new issue has been raised about both the focus and the nature of the training. Ralph Morton poses the as yet unanswered question: 'How is a Church (including the Iona Community) that has in the past wasted its substance on training its clergy, to begin to let the laity educate themselves?'[16]

The summer programme is much more specifically geared to the interests of the layman and is an attempt to mount what Morton terms 'an open experiment in the education of adults'.[17] The weeks are usually led by an invited guest with expertise on some particular topic; in 1975 these covered such subjects as Personal Relationships, Music and Drama, Worship and Liturgy Today, The Current Alcoholism Problem and Northern Ireland. The weeks are intellectually stimulating and challenging but my experience is that the almost invariable method of lecture and discussion frequently fails to tap the potential contribution or meet adequately some of the basic needs of course members. As Ralph Morton says, Iona still seems to be dominated by the desire to instruct, to have a message, to see results, even to serve',[18] whereas the last thing people need today is to be the objects of instruction and service, if this is at all avoidable. Morton believes that the Iona Community should go all out to enable associates and visitors to the island to learn for themselves, to come to their decisions, and to discover how to live with other people. Whatever else this means in practice, it would certainly necessitate the speakers at Iona each summer being much more prepared to engage their course members in active and experiential learning. (In this connection it was good to see that the programme for the summer of 1976 contained at least two weeks — one concerned with music and drama, the other with the practice of prayer — when the emphasis was on participation.) There are, however, exciting possibilities here which are far from fully exploited.

Iona also runs a series of youth camps, in hut accommodation, with a fully experiential programme, which always attract a large number of young people to the island. They have a fairly primitive adventure centre, Camas, on Mull, with accommodation for some twenty young people.

The Corrymeela Community dedicates much of its energy to providing hospitality and healing for those bereaved or deeply distressed by the numbing violence of Northern Ireland, especially in Belfast. But it has also involved itself actively in bringing together at its Ballycastle Centre many people, including politicians, of wide and often aggressively conflicting viewpoints. Alf McCreary writes:

The Corrymeela Encounter projects have embraced a wide range of issues, social, political, cultural and theological. They have included 'The Generation Gap'; 'The Worker and the Church in a Changing Society'; 'Violence'; 'The Church Inside Out'; 'Ireland, a New Start'; 'Schools in Northern Ireland'; 'Police and Community'; 'Mixed Marriage'; 'One-Parent Families'; 'The Use of Television'; 'Ulster Politics and Christian Morality'. . . . Some of the conferences have led to the formation of an organization to continue the discussion begun at Corrymeela. These include the Mixed Marriage Association, the One-Parent Family Association and the Voluntary Housing Association. Again the conferences at Corrymeela are backed up by continuing study groups in Belfast, and once a month a Corrymeela Focus is held in Belfast to enable everyone who has been at Ballycastle to keep in touch.[19]

Young people linked with Corrymeela also gather at the international Christmas Corrymeet and Easter Eastermeet and the Friends of Corrymeela assemble at Ballycastle from time to time. In *Causeway* the following comment on these consultations appeared:

Often we ask ourselves and others ask us what do these conferences achieve? We believe that the openness of the atmosphere in which they are conducted and the breadth and honesty of the contributions have led and can continue to lead to people going out from Corrymeela conferences to act as catalysts in their areas of influence. We feel the need, however, to provide more continuing support training to these catalysts.[20]

Recently the community has made an attempt not only to meet this situation but also to take much more seriously the 'ongoing search for a relevant theology for the layman in the complex world of the seventies'.[21] The need to carry the spirit of the Ballycastle conferences back into the local church and neighbourhood is one of which the community is acutely aware, and ways of doing this are being developed. For example, a new initiative reported in 1976 concerned

the formation of Open House groups. Corrymeela members and Friends and Supporters and others have been asked to use their homes as places where people in the area can meet for discussion about the situation and what can be done. It is hoped that in this way the ideas of reconciliation and community harmony can be talked about and practical steps taken where possible. The big struggle at present is in the world of ideas and if attitudes are to be changed, dialogue must be started at every level of society.[22]

Ammerdown, near Radstock, an attractive conference centre standing on the estates owned by Lord Hylton, is staffed by a Methodist warden and his wife and a small group of Roman Catholic Sisters of Zion. These provide a central administrative team which seeks to maintain a regular form of worship, supplemented by incoming groups, often in a very imaginative manner. The centre is host to many non-religious groups but its openness to exploring the more experiential approach is shown by the warden's active involvement in setting up courses related to such themes as meditation, life-style, and group dynamics. The declared aim of Ammerdown is to give visitors an exciting yet demanding experience of what the warden calls 'temporary community'. One imaginative happening, not yet repeated, was a family week in which the centre and grounds formed an isolated island. The object was for the families to explore it, find their own corporate identity, and devise their own life-style. It was a week of unexpected events and strenuous activity which at times tested visitors and staff to the limits, but one of exciting experimentation and learning.

The Student Christian Movement headquarters at Wick Court has a resident community of some dozen adults and children at its heart, a number of whom are responsible for mounting occasional conferences, from September 1976 housed in the new Tatlow Centre adjoining the main house. These conferences focus especially on themes of radical concern: 'The Theology of Gay Liberation', 'Careers and Alternatives', 'Feminist Theology', and so on. The educational approach is one of an open exchange of views rather than a working through a formally structured programme.

Other centres with a group of a distinctively communal nature at their heart share a ministry directed towards more specific groups. Such is Ringsfield Hall in Suffolk which in 1975 had a core community of five adults and five children. Their late-Victorian house, with fourteen acres of grounds, is used especially by parties of schoolchildren who, with their teachers, design the programme as they wish using the facilities in and around the Hall and the resources of the staff as required. Church groups also come and, as with the schoolchildren, the community's main ministry to these is through personal contact and friendship.

Lindley Lodge, near Nuneaton, serves a different clientele but has a

Christian group at the centre of operations. It was established in 1970 with the following purpose:

> To assist in the development of the approach, attitude and understanding that the young worker has to his employment in particular and to himself and society in general, rather than in the teaching of practical skills or technical knowledge. The course programmes normally include sessions on industrial relations, unions, management, company structures, communications, safety, moral values, the use of money, health and law and order.[23]

The staff, numbering about forty, many of them relatively young, live on the premises as a Christian community and are employed in educational, administrative, and maintenance work. John Moore writes of their endeavours:

> Those of us who work here feel not only that God has called us to this work, giving us a concern for young people's well-being as well as a concern about the industrial structures by which their working lives are governed, but that what we are doing is by its very nature Christian. It would be sufficient to work here with that as a motive without ever having the chance to share verbally our faith in Christ with those who come to stay here, but we have the added incentive of having many such opportunities, all of which arise naturally from ordinary conversation and confidence built up over several days. We all count it a privilege to be involved in this work for God. Results material and spiritual are ultimately in His hands we know, but we do have the satisfaction not only of sowing but of seeing some of the harvest as well.[24]

The centre is governed by an independent council with a strong evangelical leaning and the community's approach is in this general tradition – definite, structured, and with a healthy respect for the *status quo*. Reflecting this ethos, their publicity material contains the following quotation by John Garnett:

> It is now vitally important that all companies, who are concerned to increase their profits and improve their service to industry, should recognize what the key terms are on obtaining employees' commitment. This attitude of commitment can be trained into people, and Lindley Lodge is a very important resource available to industry and commerce.[25]

Despite (or because of?) this accolade, some 150 companies have sent young people to Lindley Lodge since it opened in 1967, and plans to launch a new centre in North Yorkshire are well advanced.

CENTRES WITH A RESIDENT STAFF

In this section I include centres which, though run to further some aspects of education related to the nature of authority, personal development, and interpersonal relations, have a staff rather than a community with a distinctive life-style at their heart. The staff can operate in a variety of capacities from actively educational to purely administrative.

An occasional but interesting series of gatherings are those which for several years now have been sponsored by John Walters of the Argyll Hotel, Iona – only indirectly associated with the conferences organized by the abbey. The gatherings have attracted fairly large attendances from all over the country and have stimulated thinking in an open and informal way on themes such as 'Healing and the Wholeness of Man', 'Self-Sufficiency', and 'The Practice of Meditation within the Christian Faith'.

The Othona Community, a now long-established group, has as one of its main objectives the stimulation of what it terms 'fraternal dialogue'.[26] Each summer at their two centres, Bradwell-on-Sea in Essex and Burton Bradstock in Dorset, invited speakers lead the participants in daily discussion sessions around a wide variety of topics such as 'peace, reconciliation, ecology, cybernetics, prayer, mysticism and activism, violence and aggression, education and Bible study, faith and reason, and the generation gap',[27] although currently the greatest emphasis is given to themes related to Christian spirituality and life-style. The summer gatherings have provided a valuable assembly place for people of all ages and diverse backgrounds, seeking to gain a deeper understanding of community. There is currently a move to re-equip and open the more primitive Bradwell Centre all the year round, under the direction of Colin and Kate Hodgetts, and to develop gatherings there linked to the themes of self-sufficiency and a simple life-style.

Froddle Crook, near Armathwaite in the Lake District, is a small ecumenical centre which was started late in 1974 and is at present staffed by a team of four people. Two of their objects are to achieve 'a balanced religious life which should help to draw people towards unity' and to make the centre 'a rallying ground for reasonable and Christian friendship, for peace and for prayer'.[28] There is a strong emphasis on the development of a relevant spirituality. A third aim is to work for international peace and justice, in particular through 'The One World Movement', a non-party organization working through the United Nations Association; and in other ways for a reformed United Nations with direct elections. The centre also seeks to support such groups as Pax Christi and Amnesty International.

A number of other staffed centres, mainly located in major cities, are seeking to bring theological study at some depth to bear on major issues through a variety of educational methods, not simply, as is the case with the three centres just mentioned, via the traditional lecture or talk and discussion. One such organization is the Institute of Christian Studies which began in the early 1970s 'to provide an *environment of learning* – a place where men and women can be free to share in the adventure of study, prayer, and fellowship'.[29] At the centre of their teaching method are 'core groups'. They write:

These are groups of about a dozen people who stay together over a period of three years so that they can get to know each other well and share their real doubts and fears as well as their faith and hope. The work of the groups is centred in the experience of the students themselves so that at all times questions of truth and meaning and purpose are related to the realities with which we live day by day. . . . The essential feature of the core group is *corporate responsibility*; members of the groups are responsible to each other for their learning. Each group has its leader who can guide students as they turn to grapple with the Bible or with the history of the Church; but the leaders are themselves part of the learning situation, receiving from others as well as sharing their expertise. Much of the time, it is the members of the groups themselves who will share with others their discoveries after periods of research and reading. The Christian mind and imagination are best formed when the Christian vision can be seen to validate and integrate the student's own experience. . . .

The Institute aims not so much to provide an authoritative answer to questions raised by the groups – a static product at the end of the learning situation – but rather to involve students in the process of discovering what it means for them to be Christians.[30]

Beside the core groups the Institute sets up termly seminar classes raising questions about life and the Christian faith through the study of literature, art, history, and psychology. The desire for the students to take their own initiative after a course of studies has led to the mounting of projects of both an academic ('A Theology for Africa') and a practical kind ('Liturgical Dance' and 'Urban Ministry'). On the dance workshop they comment:

> Dance was once *the* religious art. It is ABOUT grace. And, as when David danced in the sanctuary, it is about large praise. It *is* rhythm, the ritual of heart and body. Only a people condemned to live by reason alone could have excluded it so totally from their worship, or trapped it safely into the confines of clerical procession. The Spirit of Life and Truth is caught as it moves. And it is, as St Bernard says, a 'deft' catching. So dance expresses the Spirit of Christ and when the Church catches that fire once more, it will dance. The workshop at the Institute believes this and seeks to discipline itself accordingly. In the past academic year (1974/1975) we have choreographed two liturgical offerings: one for Epiphany and one for Pentecost.[31]

Despite the development of core groups, seminar work, and projects, the tutors generally adopt an individual rather than a team approach. There is also some concern to achieve a wider and more varied clientele for courses.

The Institute furthers its (non-residential) community life through its restaurant and bar. 'Everyone is asked to help with the preparation of meals; and each core group and seminar group undertakes the serving and washing up twice a term.'[32] Describing outside events furthering the same ends, the staff write: 'The Institute's annual pilgrimage . . . takes place over the Spring Bank Holiday at the end of May. In past years we have walked about 50 miles to Canterbury, Salisbury, Norwich, Chichester, and Wells.'[33]

Seeking to relate theology to the life of an urban society in a more radical fashion is the steadily developing Sheffield-based Urban Theology Unit under the forceful directorship of John Vincent. It organizes long-term training courses as well as conferences and consultations of a shorter duration, attracting a multi-denominational and multi-national clientele. The themes for these gatherings seem at times to embrace mind-blowing areas of knowledge and expertise: 'Modern World through Modern Novels', 'The Sociology of Theology', and 'Urban Mission in Global Perspective'. But the dynamic and enthusiasm of the team make up for biting off more than any man could chew, let alone digest. At the same time there are more focused events and an attempt to relate with increasing empathy to the local downtown neighbourhood and congregations undergoing a period of traumatic change. There is concern to get the local laity more involved in the Unit's courses.

Dartmouth House, on the edge of Blackheath, London, was for five years, under its warden John Nicholson and deputy warden Diana Eeles, one of the most imaginative centres operating. It sponsored conferences on themes very pertinent to major issues of today, not least in the realm of Christian alternatives, at the same time keeping an open door for use by many groups within and outside the Church. Over the years, consultations and training events covered such areas as communication and social criticism, community development, personal growth, and interpersonal development. Titles included 'Theology, Therapy, and Social Change', 'Community Newspapers', 'Television and the People', 'Sexuality and Christian Faithfulness', 'Things New and Old' – the last being part of a continuing exploration into the links and tension between the tradition of Christian spirituality and the contemporary search for personal growth and fulfilment.

During 1974, the warden brought together a small group to form the nucleus of a team within the House. They were to be concerned with discovering ways in which a traditional conference centre might become a working model of an institution in transition, making decisions about the use of facilities and resources appropriate to a world facing ecological and economic crisis. The group were able to make their work known by relating it to the publication of Ronald Higgins's article in the *Observer* supplement (23 February 1975) entitled 'The Seventh Enemy'. They found themselves within two months handling a correspondence from over 700 people interested in associating with the House as in some way providing 'a sign of hope' that thinking *and* action for the future might be effectively combined. From the concerns expressed, a programme of weekend workshops for 1975–6, under the heading 'Beginning Now', was devised. At the same time steps were being taken to make use of the House and grounds to illustrate aspects of alternative technology, alternative food-growing, and craft work, all within an urban centre. In addition, a non-meat menu was instituted and great care was put into the designing of meals to focus visitors' attention on the possibility of eating responsibly and convivially in a hungry world by moving away from a protein-wasting meat diet.

The underlying intention of all this was to make the House, with a committed community at its heart, a sign of the message it was seeking to communicate. This move, an adventurous step towards earthing ideas, ran into immediate opposition from the bishop of the diocese to which Dartmouth House belonged. The expressed objection was to the non-meat menu and the detrimental impact this might have on the potential users of Dartmouth House, though fears of even more wide-ranging innovations were obviously very much present, perhaps understandably so as the project was a comprehensive one. The bishop's initiative led to the recognition that all the consultation with the various bodies responsible for the House had not been sufficient to ensure an adequate and secure base from which to translate ideas into practice in areas of controversy. In such a context the 'Beginning Now' project could no longer be true to the spirit of exploration which had inspired its new constituency: this led to its termination and to the dispersal of a disillusioned core group with the loss of their considerable corporate potential.

I have dwelt at some length on the case of Dartmouth House because the conflict illustrates two issues directly related to my theme of authority: the inbuilt resistance to teaching methods which seek in any really telling way to make the medium the message; and the ease with which ecclesiastical power can be exercised to silence expression of and discussion about matters of critical importance to Church and society.

The London (formerly Notting Hill) Ecumenical Centre has been an active catalyst in the Greater London area, seeking to gather residents from all over the metropolis around issues of major religious, social, and political importance.

In the first ten years the Ecumenical Centre devoted much of its energy to making links between members of the various communities in Notting Hill, to help understanding and tolerance in situations of great stress. The Notting Hill Ecumenical Centre in Denbigh Road, W.11, as it then was, dealt with a layman's world and the problems of people at work: tenants and police striving against vandalism on housing estates; those who care for the dying; sixth-formers and pop music; the future of the social services and how people are affected by them after their re-organization; theological students living and working for a month to gain an idea of inner city tensions; the problem of finding new uses for old church buildings.[34]

As mentioned in an earlier chapter, the centre promoted two major gatherings on spirituality in London, during 1973, called 'That's the Spirit' and during 1975 called 'Exploring the Ways of the Spirit', the latter attended by more than 7,000 people. The spirituality theme has increasingly come to the fore and early in 1976 a Worship and Prayer Resource Centre was set up for visitors to see material available in the field of new forms of worship and prayer. Other ventures being currently developed are the creation of a Christian group for Prisoners of Conscience, closely linking with the work of Amnesty International, a course exploring questions arising from the racial problems of a city such as London and a group to consider the changing roles of men and women in society today. The Ecumenical Centre, with Brian Frost as its programme director, remains alive and vigorous in its response to the many facets of a changing, complex environment.

> The Netherbow, named after the site of the old Eastern Gate of the city of Edinburgh on which it stands, is the Arts Centre of the Church of Scotland. It has a 74-seat, fully equipped studio theatre suitable for drama, film, multi-media, recitals, conferences, and worship services. It also has a restaurant which forms a meeting place for local residents, tourists, church people, and artists. There is also a gallery space for the visual arts and a sound recording studio suitable for the production of cassette tapes and programmes for local radio. The function of the Netherbow is threefold – (1) To encourage Christians to express their faith through the arts; (2) To help the Church to come to a better understanding and appreciation of the world of arts; (3) To help the world of the arts realize that the Church is concerned and that the Gospel may have some relevance to contemporary creativity.[35]

The director of the Netherbow, Gordon Strachan, has a strong interest in the charismatic movement and seeks to express the latter's contribution to the Church through his own paintings as well as through the events and exhibitions in the centre. For the Church of Scotland the Netherbow is an interesting break with its traditional image of Calvinistic austerity.

A small group of centres with strong denominational links have put their energies into making contact with members of the professions and leaders in other walks of life such as commerce and industry. St George's House, Windsor, has two declared aims which sum up its ethos:

1. To be a place where people of influence and responsibility in every area of society . . . come together to explore, to develop and to communicate, freely and frankly, their ideas and anxieties. . . .

2. To be a place where clergy of all denominations can come together for short or long courses adapted to the needs of various stages of their career . . . designed to illuminate ministerial responsibility and functions in the context of modern conditions.[36]

The courses are efficiently run and draw on the services of some extremely competent people. In 1976 weekend consultations were arranged for MPs, civil servants, educationalists, scientists and theologians (together), as well as for the clergy. However, for some of those attending the courses, there is unease that an environment representing what one calls 'aggression (the military presence), role and hierarchy',[37] is apparently seen as quite compatible with a modern Christian life-style which the House is there to explore. On the other hand, as the same person writes: 'Who can really resist a drink before the meal, horse-riding prints all round the room, good conversation with the Dean, and attractive foreign girls serving at table!'[38]

Relating its courses very closely to the world of industry, unions, and management, is the Luton Industrial College, the work of which has steadily developed over the past two decades through the unflagging efforts of Bill Gowland, and which is a monument to his dedication to the Church's involvement in this sector of society. The courses, which cover all aspects of industrial life, with especial relevance to younger people, are staffed with true lay involvement by some 150 honorary lecturers and consultants of all denominations. Bill Gowland has always sought to hold the often separated sectors of life together and the college is thus situated at the heart of the city, with a church and community centre adjoining it. The staff exercise a corporate ministry to every part of the complex, as well as seeking to support the work of some 170 Methodist ministers acting as chaplains to industrial concerns throughout the country.

Another centre which for many years has attempted to combine the concerns of Church and society is Scottish Churches House, Dunblane, an ecumenical foundation which more recently has been handicapped by changes of warden. Both Luton and Dunblane adopt a fairly traditional method of educational approach with the emphasis on expert input, cross-questioning, and group discussion.

There remain one or two ventures relating their educational

programmes to urban issues in a more experiential manner and retaining a close link with their surrounding area as a learning resource. One of these is the Urban Ministry Project, founded in 1968 through the efforts of Donald Reeves and Anthony Dyson, and based on Morden, Surrey, though now an integral part of the Oxford Institute for Church and Society. The aim of the Urban Ministry Project is

> to use the tools of extended study and experience to help the participants grapple with the theological and sociological assumptions behind their work, so that, focusing on the issues in their locality, they may (re)gain courage to get to grips with some positive action in relation both to themselves and their local situation.[39]

The eight-month sandwich course has two especially interesting features: 'the plunge' – a forty-eight-hour period spent out and about in London when the student 'looks, listens and absorbs, testing his perception and developing awareness in strange situations and different environments – without a role';[40] and the detailed analysis over an extended period of the student's own local or working situation, an ongoing activity central to the whole project. There is currently an attempt to extend this kind of approach on an interprofessional basis.[41]

Very similar in intent but especially concerned with groups of students from teacher training colleges was the Community Education Centre in south-east London, begun in 1972 under the auspices of the Student Christian Movement. The centre was thoughtfully developed by Bob and Maggi Whyte and had several particularly interesting aspects. One of these was that the resident group spent a good deal of time establishing a co-operative learning community through shared responsibility for their day-to-day living together. The Whytes write:

> The facilitating of inter-action in the group was much helped at the Centre by the fact that the group lived communally and looked after its own domestic needs. We felt from the outset that it was important to combine the physical and mental work – both in order to get away from the usual division of labour where participants on a course exercise their minds but not their hands (and someone else does the chores), and to ensure that groups would make some collective decisions about the day-to-day running of affairs. We felt that the time spent on chores was generally well worthwhile in the opportunities it gave for personal relationships to be built up. This ongoing mixing of members of the group was often reinforced by a

specific session of 'inter-action games', which were relaxing, encouraged active participation in the course activities, and some of which highlighted the tendency for competition between people even when we are working in informal groups.[42]

The aim of discovering more about the urban community and issues raised by it was also met in as participatory a way as possible. A mini-plunge, similar to that organized by the Urban Ministry Project, was available for those ready to take it, and for everyone a good deal of in-depth observation of the local area was required. Visits to agencies were not pre-arranged, in the belief that the students would benefit from talking on their own initiative to a much wider cross-section of local residents than just members of the helping professions. There was also concentration on more specific issues such as housing, employment, social welfare, and so on. The Whytes sum up their approach thus: 'Our experience highlighted the need for the training of people whose work will involve them with the community (such as teachers, clergy, etc.) to be grounded in practice, and not to be simply a theoretical training isolated from everyday experiences.'[43]

The Community Education Centre was sadly forced to close in the summer of 1976, a year after the Whytes moved on, due to financial difficulties and lack of staff with sufficient experience to maintain the venture. I include the account of its work here because it embodied a type of experiential approach which one hopes will not disappear from the training scene with the centre's demise.

Working along the same kind of lines, but with a much broader programme and greater resources, is Coventry Cathedral. Its educational activities cover work with school parties visiting the cathedral, young people, those working in industry, and a wide-ranging international ministry (mentioned in the previous chapter): all these programmes co-ordinated by a Centre of Studies. Its hostel, intended in particular for young people, is John F. Kennedy House, opened with the hope that it would provide the setting for groups to create their own life and ethos and seize the opportunity for a temporary experiment in Christian community.

The lack of explicit rules in the running of the house also allows groups to develop their own rules and way of living within the house. With larger groups from more formal settings such as schools, the authority of the teachers brings to the house many of the assumptions of the school. However, even with large groups there is room for exploring with staff the possibilities open to them to get to know pupils in a different way or to share decision-making with them. Such attempts almost always increase the sense of worth of the group as a whole as well as increasing their motivation to learn in the course. To put it crudely, 'People learn more from the way they are treated than from what they are told.'[44]

So writes Richard Morgan-Jones. He adds that the cathedral courses are rooted in the conviction that

man's identity is intrinsically tied up with the destiny and quality of life in Cities. When people make comments on the City they live in they are also making comments about themselves. 'The City provides good facilities for shopping', 'It's too busy', 'Everyone looks so worried', 'The buildings are so impersonal', 'The pace is exhilarating'. All these comments are not only statements about the City in which people live, but also express people's feelings about their own perspective on life. If you like, the City is an image or symbol around which people express their hopes and fears, their disappointments and frustrations, their loves and hates.[45]

Thus, as was the aim of the Community Education Centre, the courses are intended, perhaps rather more hopefully than in actual practice, to train people really to listen to the views of city dwellers, the better to understand the opportunities and problems of an industrial society. Visits to a wide range of places are organized, drawing on the many contacts of the Coventry Team Ministry. To further press home learning, role-plays and simulation exercises are set up.

A recently established centre is Glencree in County Wicklow. It was opened in 1974 when Shaun Curran, a Jesuit, took up residence. The programme is action-research oriented and has two main aims: to raise public awareness and the deepening of concern with the basic problems at the root of the conflict in Ireland; and to facilitate attitude changes within the communities in conflict. To this end a series of projects are planned, some more particularly educational, some more action-oriented in nature. In 1976 the following were amongst some of the events planned: Peace Education Conference for Teachers, an International Conference, a competition for the best audio-visual production on 'Why there is Sorrow in our Community', and a Youth Leadership Programme.[46] Work on the building continues and the centre enjoys steadily growing support.

Reflecting the close link of the Church in its educational concerns with urban life is the Social Studies Centre of the Methodist East End Mission in Tower Hamlets, London. Staffed by an ordained minister as tutor-warden and a teacher, both full-time, it seeks to provide young people in the last two years at school with an awareness of themselves as young adults and of the potential as well as the problems of the neighbourhood in which many of them will live and work. This aspect of the centre's programmes is termed Phase I and it began in 1966. Its current aims are 'to help youngsters in their last two years at school to understand and participate in their society and environment' and 'to supplement the pastoral work of the schools'.[47] It works at these aims through three types of course: CSE Social Studies, immigrant courses, and remedial courses. In 1969 Phase II of the centre's activities began involving some twenty resident adult students in courses relating to such subjects as religion, family, and community. The students go out to earn a wage in the afternoons and undertake some form of social work linked with the Mission in the evenings. 'Part of the programme is to learn to live in community and to learn about the mission of the Church in an urban area.'[48] Phase III provides opportunities for adult students and professional workers, coming from many parts of the country for short courses, to gain experience of the social work agencies of the Mission and to enter into discussion with the Mission staff on important issues. The centre is not so much pioneering a particularly new educational method of approach as seeking to bring students of all ages into a dynamic contact with personal and social issues under the guidance of a dedicated Christian team.

One final venture which would not wish to have the label 'religious' attached to it, yet owes a great deal to the energy and drive of a Roman Catholic layman, Stan Windass, its co-ordinator, is the Alternative Society. Originally it promoted weekend conferences on a wide variety of alternatives. More recently, as mentioned in the previous chapter, it has been able to establish a centre at Lower Shaw Farm near Swindon where a good deal of emphasis is on developing self-reliance, especially in relation to building skills, the conservation of energy, and growing food organically. None the less, other projects continue, notably in connection with home-based education and alternatives in such fields as health, prison, family life, politics, and communications. Though prominent resource people often attend the weekends, the gatherings are sometimes flexible and informal to the point of being 'happenings' rather than conferences, with learning going on through multiple encounters and conversations rather than within a structured programme.

CATALYTIC GROUPS WITH NO SET MEETING PLACE

There are a number of groups established for the purpose of stimulating learning which have no residential centre or meeting place of their own to which they can invite people. Theirs is a kind of itinerant educational work which aims to inspire people with energy and enthusiasm 'on the spot'.

The Wrekin Trust, founded by Sir George Trevelyan in 1971, describes itself as 'a kind of adult education of the spirit' and is committed to exploring 'the ageless wisdom of the past' in the light of the New Age into which we are apparently entering.[49] Though many of their courses are led by 'expert' speakers, as at Findhorn with which it is closely associated, it is increasingly involved in employing methods and techniques typical of the human potential movement, such as encounter and awareness programmes, with a 'spiritual' end in view, as yet ill-defined in their literature.

A much more mainstream yet catalytic organization, of Roman Catholic origin, is the Movement for a Better World founded by Father Riccardo Lombardi as an instrument of communal reconstruction after the Second World War and now established in over thirty countries. A small full-time group, together with many voluntary helpers, carries on the work of promoting the Movement, the main method being through a so-called 'Basic Retreat' which Jim Sweeney, its director in this country, describes as follows:

> The instrument Father Lombardi formulated for carrying out this work was a special retreat experience. In a break with the tradition in this field he saw the retreat as a shared experience which a community would go through together rather than as individuals. There is an in-built dynamic in the retreat which works through an intense shared experience of reflection, dialogue, and prayer. The community examines the needs of the world today, and in the light of the Scriptural message – proclaiming the power and presence of God in human history – discerns the concrete events and trends which are signs of the ongoing action of the Spirit, and those events and trends

148

which frustrate and hinder this action. This discernment is the basis for a renewed commitment by the community to work in solidarity with others, within and without the Church, towards the ultimate fulfilment of man's destiny. Then follows an exploration of the qualities of life the Christian requires at personal and community levels to live out this commitment. And finally, a series of practical sessions to determine the future action of the community.[50]

The breadth of the Movement's concerns is demonstrated by the international theme for reflection in 1976 which was 'The Present World and the Kingdom of God'; the idea being that each country attempts to make a structural analysis of its own country at the socio-political, socio-economic, and ideological levels and to look at the movements of change that are taking place.[51]

The Movement's ministry is currently confined to the Roman Catholic Church, especially within parishes or through more open retreats held at conference centres (the latter not now very well supported). It would seem to have even more to offer if it could operate in a more genuinely ecumenical way and further develop its insights into the possibilities of reshaping and renewing parish life (of which I say more in Chapter 7).

Another quite different organization playing a catalytic role is the William Temple Foundation. It was launched in 1947 when it first occupied premises at Hawarden and then later at Rugby where it drew people from all walks of life, but especially industry and the professions, on short and long-term courses to work at the relevance of Christian faith to modern society. In 1971 the Foundation sold its Rugby property and there ended one of the most creative attempts to bring together the study of theology, the social sciences, and the affairs of society to have emerged on the English scene this century. It is an extremely sad commentary on the failure of the Church to be able to sustain such a continuing opportunity for study and dialogue that this step was taken. The Foundation established its new headquarters in the Manchester Business School, as 'a College without walls', from where its reduced staff, under the able leadership of David Jenkins, have developed their activities around several major themes, notably 'Social Responsibility in Industry and Business', 'The Health Service, Provision of Health Care and the Community', 'Community Development', and The Disadvantaged and Deprived in Industrial Society'.[52] One of the most significant developments has been the stimulating of so-called 'operative' groups of Christian laymen, deeply involved in these and related fields, gathered in different places up and down the country to share their experience and thinking, and where appropriate to promote action.

Finally, under this head, should be mentioned CORAT, Christian Organizations Research and Advisory Trust, which was established in the late 1960s as a team of management consultants to service mainly charitable institutions and Christian organizations, as for example, the Benedictine Abbey at Stanbrook, the British and Foreign Bible Society, the Young Women's Christian Association, and Christian Action. They also run intensive three-day seminars and larger summer schools for lay and ordained people, especially in relation to management and organizational principles.

The importance of their work lies in seeking to bring the insights of management theory to bear on often outmoded ecclesiastical structures and practices, for example those of certain religious Orders. John Miller-Bakewell writes:

> Religious Orders devoted to a life of prayer . . . have additional problems with no business parallels. Traditionally they have supported themselves through endowments and by selling handicrafts or specialized products, from pottery and liqueurs, to altar wafers and church vestments. With the average age of their members rising, fewer working hands are available, while the costs of essential purchases, such as electricity and food, are rising. So new approaches have to be found. Although automated production and improved marketing are the nearest answers, this is a hard road to choose for an Order which is founded on a belief in the virtues of manual labour and has little idea of product policy or marketing strategy.[53]

CORAT in such cases attempts to suggest new ways of expressing old ideals and as such can bring searching questions to bear on the structure of authority and interpersonal relations. It is, however, facing the cold winds of economic stringency and the hard fact that a Church, which in any case always regarded consultants as a doubtful resource, is even less likely to commission assistance when it is struggling to make ends meet.

THE CELL

A great deal of learning takes place not only through whole communities or groups dedicated full-time to educational work, but within the small cell, committed to explore often at considerable depth the nature of Christian life-styles and their present-day implications. The cell is as old as Christianity itself and has always played a dynamic part in the history of the Church, but it is only relatively recently that its importance has again been seen, though perhaps still not yet fully grasped.

The Catholics have here been way ahead, especially in their emphasis on the importance of the family unit. The Grail, for example, has been especially prominent in this respect. In 1975 they had some 900 family circle groups, with about eight to ten members in each, meetings being held usually once a month in members' homes. Jackie Rolo writes:

> Many hundreds of people, who are not members of the Society, work at building community with us. Family Circles aim to fulfil a need which very many married couples experience – the need to 'talk things out' and to pray together – through such an exchange, in small groups, they find they are more able to pass on their growing understanding of their relationship to each other as Christian husband and wife, their deepening understanding of Scripture, the liturgy, prayer and their role in the Catholic Church and ecumenically. Often this leads to their becoming more active in meeting their own needs and those of their families, the church, and society.[54]

The Grail organizes weekends and weeks for families to meet and there is an annual Family Circles national conference.

The emphasis on the family is also found amongst other Roman Catholic groups. The organization called Catholic People's Weeks specializes in arranging holidays for Catholic families with an often lively theme and speakers, but plenty of time for participants to enjoy themselves. However, outside the Catholic Church the interest in family groupings is strangely absent, though of late attempts have been made by ONE for Christian Renewal to promote a network of such meetings, and there is some evidence that groups are beginning to emerge through other initiatives, as via the programme on the family currently being mounted by the World Council of Churches. Where these groups have developed, the emphasis is experiential with not only a sharing of typical family problems but also a questioning of the present basis and nature of the current form of nuclear family.[55] The only other similar gatherings are workshops, arranged by the Anglican General Synod Board of Education, for married couples. It seems, therefore, that two movements exist: one seeking to deepen and intensify traditional (Catholic) family life; the other attempting to work at the changing nature of the nuclear family and to examine some personally and socially searching questions.

Outside the nuclear family as such a host of small groups have emerged associated with many communities and organizations already mentioned: the Iona Community, the Servants of Christ the King, Focolare, Katimavik and, more recently, the Julian Meetings, to name but a few. Likewise with the Teilhard Centre for the Future of Man which is a somewhat sophisticated association set up as 'an educational project to encourage study of the thoughts of Teilhard de Chardin and to develop it further. Its object is to make people increasingly aware of their responsibility for directing the future.'[56] The centre does this through numerous conferences and consultations, through its magazine *The Teilhard Review*, but in particular by means of its study groups up and down the country. In 1976 there were some forty of these, together with contact persons in places where no group met.

However, in many cases, groups are not linked with any wider organization or network but remain an *ad hoc* expression of local concern. One such group, typical of the attempt to move towards more ecumenical gatherings, is the LINK house group. Patricia Worden reports:

> The LINK group is made up of people living in or near West Greenwich, South East London, who meet monthly on a Sunday evening for an informal supper together and for discussion. Its membership has over the past four years been drawn mainly from the West Greenwich congregations including Methodists, Presbyterians (from the shared Presbyterian/Methodist church there), Anglicans, and Roman Catholics. In this time probably as many as sixty or seventy people have at some time attended the group, average attendance being about fifteen. Local clergy have met frequently with the group but have never dominated its discussions.[57]

The subject matter ranges widely over many aspects of both Christian faith and current affairs.

Its members are middle-class and articulate, fairly radical both theologically and socially, who are mainly committed to the Christian way of life and the unity of Christians. In brief, they tend to have common traits which are not shared with all other members of their separate churches. They obviously feel a deep need for enduring support and the sharing of common concerns which the local Christian congregations are failing to meet at present. LINK's ability to survive (meetings were still being held in 1976) leads one to think that such groups may well be revealing a great deal about the Church as it is and about the shape of the Church in the future.[58]

It might be added at this point that a new wave of house groups has emerged in the past year or two, inspired by the influence of the charismatic movement, which although very much given over to prayer and Bible study also offer members time for the sharing of personal concerns and problems at some depth. For example, it is reported that between 1973 and 1975 the number of charismatic prayer groups in the Birmingham area rose from three to ninety.[59]

Another situation in which the small group once thrived, though of late a decline appears to have set in, is the world of higher education. Noteworthy here is the West London Chaplaincy based on Imperial College and Queen Elizabeth College, Kensington. The small cell has there been used as a kingpin of the meeting of the students seeking to tune in to what Christianity is all about, creating what Anne Hoad, then assistant chaplain, terms 'a network of roots'.[60] She continues:

> The church in the colleges has over the past six years ceased to put its entire weight behind its Sunday worship and found itself branching out into a cellular structure of some forty groups involving about four hundred people during the week. Considerations of work, travel, and study make it impossible to gather the chaplaincy community together at any one time; and so the pattern has diversified and growth has ensued. . . . The development of each group over the year affects the quality of the community's life as a whole. If the individual group fails to meet the needs of its members or fails to resolve the tensions between authority and freedom, the problems of leadership and responsibility, then the group will remain preoccupied with its own internal relations and be unable to cope with its relations to other groups and with the wider tasks related to the whole community. The same applies to the sort of issues raised. If the issues remain sectional in interest then the group is in danger of isolating itself from the wider

153

concerns and as a result it loses its relevance to the surrounding community.... A growing, developing group begins to ask questions about the other groups; begins to work out means of intercommunication and to reflect upon the ways in which learning has been carried out in the group.[61]

The groups themselves create their own pattern of study, prayer, and worship:

Every two weeks the leaders from all the groups meet to discuss and assess and plan. Every term there is a chance for all the groups to meet and worship together, and once a year a Teaching Week when groups combine as small centres to receive a team member and for general meetings. On Sundays there is a Eucharist in an art gallery in the heart of the administrative complex.[62]

I have quoted Anne Hoad at some length because the West London Chaplaincy exemplifies the diversity and yet the vitality of the small group network. As she later points out, it is sometimes difficult to sustain the identity and coherence of the whole body, but, none the less, the cells retain an essential flexibility and liveliness. Furthermore, as with all the small groups mentioned in this section, there is a sense of corporate leadership and richness of interpersonal encounter so often missing in the larger and more impersonal church gatherings. In many of these instances, the lay and ecumenical dimensions, with members thinking, concerned, challenging, calls into question the clergy-centredness and the still narrow denominationalism of many normal church meetings.

THE EXPERIENTIAL GROUP

At times during the previous discussion I have mentioned learning communities and groups which include in their programmes activities of an intensely experiential nature. Most of these activities spring from a major movement, sometimes known as the Human Potential Movement, which began in the United States after the last war and is now slowly but surely gaining ground in this country. This approach to working with groups is closely associated with what has been called 'humanistic psychology' or 'the Third Force' (over against the rival orthodoxies of Freud and behaviourism), and lays great emphasis on personal growth and interpersonal development.

In Britain, however, the prototype T-group, developed by Wilfred Bion[63] and the Tavistock Institute of Human Relations also after the last war, was more concerned with fostering leadership and organizational skills than promoting personal development. The T-group ('T' usually taken to stand for 'training') is a group with no other agenda than to study its own behaviour as it occurs, the 'leader' being there to facilitate learning around this task. The emphasis is on investigating the group process rather than one's own or other people's feelings. A major aim, and especially pertinent to the issues on which I am focusing in this book, is to enable group members to work through problems of authority and interpersonal relations.

'Encounter', on the other hand, is a groupwork skill much more concerned with personal awareness and growth. It emerged in the United States in the 1960s and began to establish itself in this country in the early 1970s. In fact, 'the encounter group became a social oasis where people could drop the façade of competence demanded by a fast-moving, competitive society, and let loose their doubts and fears and disappointments'.[64] William Schutz writes:

> Encounter is a method of human relating based on openness and honesty, self-awareness, self-responsibility, awareness of the body, attention to feelings, and an emphasis on the here-and-now. It usually occurs in a group setting. Encounter is therapy insofar as it focuses on removing blocks to better functioning. Encounter is education and recreation in that it attempts to create conditions leading to the most satisfying use of personal capacities.[65]

Besides Schutz, the other famous name linked with this approach is that of Carl Rogers.[66] Schutz believes the encounter group to have a notable religious pedigree and *raison d'être*. He states:

> One thread running through the history of encounter is clearly religious. The assumption that God is within, or works from within you, that you are a vehicle for expressing God, is a common theme. As I gain experience with encounter, it becomes clearer that the encounter goal of realizing one's potential is virtually identical with the religious goal of finding God within.[67]

The encounter group has drawn on a wide variety of therapeutic and educational techniques which have greatly transformed its nature, at times moving it fully into the world of individual therapy (with the group as the supportive therapist or 'audience') and away from any concern with group processes as such. The main emphasis of these teaching techniques has been to stress the non-verbal aspects of behaviour, with especial attention being given to the expression of the emotions, vocally and physically. Notable here is *Gestalt* therapy, developed by Fritz Perls in the United States during the same period as the T-group, and bio-energetics with its emphasis on the full and free involvement of the body in the therapeutic process. Both *Gestalt* and bio-energetics owe a great deal to the pioneering work of Wilhelm Reich, particularly in the 1930s.

One other recent development, again in the United States and now in Britain, is the emergence of Transactional Analysis originating in the work of Eric Berne in the 1950s[68] and derived from psychoanalysis, thus emphasizing the cognitive dimension of learning. Its great merit is that its (at times deceptive) conceptual simplicity makes it an ideal educational as well as therapeutic tool for those who would baulk at a more sophisticated and long-term analysis.

I have included this very brief description of groupwork approaches because they are dealing not only with the mentally disturbed but with those whom Perls calls 'well enough' or 'better than well enough' people. He writes: 'In this way psychotherapy is taking over the functions of education, but that is because the customary education, in home, school, university, and church is increasingly inept. What we would hope for, of course, is that education would take over the functions of psychotherapy.'[69] The few groups involved in this field with a Christian orientation and described below are in fact seeking to do just that.

Two important questions are often asked. One is whether such intensive group experiences are really necessary. Many therapists and educationalists would wish they were not. But in a society where mobility and impersonality have reduced the chance of close personal contact, facilitating the spontaneous expression of likes and dislikes, to a minimum and in which the virtues of the rational and the objective have become the hallmark of wisdom, many find themselves deprived of the opportunity to relate at depth with any but a tiny handful of people and of the chance thus to 'find themselves'. As Perls puts it: 'Our times are a chronic low-grade emergency.'[70] The encounter, and related, groups are in effect an attempt to offer insights into an unrealized or untapped dimension of personal potential and a means to bring some kind of wholeness (*Gestalt*) in an age when Church and society seem incapable of offering real life to real people. Such groups provide an experience of temporary community which at least brings an appreciation of what is and thus what might be, as indeed did the original Methodist class meetings. That this experience still needs to be given full expression in everyday life is more a challenge to the educators and educated than a fundamental critique of the approach.

The other question raised is that psychological damage is done. As a still relatively new method of group work, little conclusive evidence is yet available, especially as the criteria of 'damage' and any follow-up inquiry over a long period are very hard to obtain. A recent very thorough examination by Cary Cooper of all the investigations which have been undertaken so far gives little help – the most reliable studies varying from a 0·66 per cent to a 7·5 per cent 'casualty rate'. Cooper concludes:

> At the moment, the cries that T-groups and Encounter Groups are psychologically dangerous . . . has not been proved. In fact . . . there is some evidence that indicates that it may be less stressful than university examinations or perceptual isolation experiments, or indeed, that it may enable participants to cope better with sexual and aggressive stimuli and stressful periods in their life.[71]

It seems, therefore, that given experienced trainers, voluntary attendance at groups, and adequate screening of potential members for previous mental disturbance, the dangers of psychological damage being done are probably no greater than in many other educational situations, not least the trauma of sitting examinations.

The organization of Christian orientation most closely associated with the development of the Tavistock (T-group) style of approach to the study of human behaviour is the Grubb Institute. It originated as the Christian Teamwork Trust in 1957 with Bruce Reed as director, a major concern being 'how it could help ordinary men and women with Christian convictions to carry out their daily work to the benefit of man and the glory of God'.[72] Colin Quine writes:

> From 1957 the staff were aware of the need to understand more fully the human behaviour which it was struggling to describe theologically and was one of the pioneers of the group dynamics movement in this country. In 1963 the staff decided to increase their understanding through collaboration with the Centre for Applied Social Research of the Tavistock Institute of Human Relations. By

1966 they felt the need for an educational and research body to further this work in a Christian context. The Trust therefore set up the Christian Teamwork Institute of Education, which drawing on the experience of the previous general consultative service, now focused its study on behaviour in certain key areas of society. As both Christians and non-Christians found the title misleading, it was changed in 1969 to the present title, taking the name of Sir Kenneth Grubb, one of its founders and a former Chairman of the House of Laity of Church Assembly.[73]

The work of the Grubb Institute is central to the theme of this book because of all the communities and groups so far mentioned a key aspect of its educational programme is directly and specifically concerned with enabling its 'conference members to learn about authority and the inter-personal, inter-group and institutional problems involved in exercising it'.[74]

The focus is not to increase the individual's understanding of himself, but to develop understanding of organizational behaviour which members can use in their working situations, whether as a senior manager of an international company, a probation officer, or a clergyman of an inner city church. In this way it is hoped that the insights members gain will lead to organizational changes which may benefit many other people.[75]

From experience of many such courses, the Grubb has developed its own theory about the nature of society and the function of the Church and its clergy. At the heart of its philosophy is the conviction that 'a major condition for a just society is the existence of a dependable religious institution or institutions'.[76] The emphasis on the importance of mature dependence, closely related to Wilfred Bion's 'basic assumption'[77] of the same name, is a constantly recurring theme in the Grubb literature, and the Institute has made a significant contribution to the debate about the role of the Church in this respect. The latter is seen as having the task of managing regression (in a controlled, not escapist, way) to dependence (especially through worship) in such a manner that people can move out with confidence, without the need to hang on to religious labels or activities, to undertake their work in the world.

I have described this thesis here because the Grubb is one of the very few educational groups associated with the Church, even attempting to formulate a frame of reference within which to operate. However, their championing of the importance of 'going to Church'[78] and their powerful stress on the dependency function of that organization and its ministry seems to me to open the way to serious limitations. It is an approach which encourages the separation of a sacred Church, where God is encountered and depended on, from a secular world outside, where he is not. Even if society does *de facto* define the 'primary task' of the local church as offering security and reassurance through the so-called sacred, does that mean, in terms of the Gospel, that this is what it is meant to do? The New Testament would seem to lay on the Church as a task of equal importance bringing hope to birth (Bion's 'pairing' assumption), a role splendidly illustrated in Harvey Cox's book *The Feast of Fools*:

> Christian hope suggests that man is destined for a City. It is not just any city, however. If we take the Gospel images as well as the symbols of the book of Revelation into consideration, it is not only a city where injustice is abolished and there is no more crying. It is a city in which a delightful wedding feast is in progress, where laughter rings out, the dance has just begun, and the best wine is still to be served.[79]

Cox's words remind us that in this world the Church also has the role of combating evil and injustice (Bion's 'fighting' assumption). My conviction is that, at this point in history, it is above all dynamic hope, not dependency, which is significantly missing and that the emergence of the many groups mentioned in these pages is evidence of this deeply felt need. To this theme I return in my final chapter.

On a purely practical level I also doubt the ability of the Church, as it is at present, to monitor regression to dependence in a way which can prevent it from becoming immature dependence. Furthermore, to expect clergy and ministers to play such a monitoring role is virtually impossible, given the present structures of congregational life and pattern of worship. Instead both clergy and laity seem to be able to collude with ease in an immature relationship which denies either group the opportunity to interact freely as human beings and to give adequate expression to their unique talents and skills. Not that the Grubb Institute would wish it this way; but to break centuries of collusion it seems that both clergy and laity should be encouraged far more energetically to take the engendering of joyous hope and the struggle against social evil as crucial functions of the Church. And such fostering of hope and such a fight against evil can never be authentic unless the Christian congregation itself has for a while set dependence aside to explore and experience within its own life that joy and that struggle as many of the communities described in this book are attempting to do. For me the Grubb's emphasis is unfortunately more likely to be a recipe for passivity than to lead to the attainment of maturely dependent congregations.

If the Grubb Institute concentrates its major educational work around the concepts of authority, leadership, and dependence, the training section of the General Synod Board of Education of the Church of England has moved steadily from a somewhat similar concern and approach, employing the 'straight' T-group, towards a much more varied programme of events, with increasing emphasis on personal growth and interpersonal development. Their courses in 1976 included, amongst other events, encounter groups, games and simulations, Transactional Analysis and *Gestalt* workshops. Their core course is in three stages of five days each, it being suggested that the stages are separated by periods of some six months. There is a movement over the three stages from dominantly small group work to intergroup and large group experiences. Their *Gestalt* techniques in particular have a strong orientation towards personal awareness, the emphasis being on rediscovering, owning, and expressing those aspects of personality pushed into the background because of unpleasant happenings in the past, frequently in childhood. Great attention is paid to the 'fit' between verbal statements and body movements, with an attempt to revalue both the sensual and the spontaneous. It is a pity that the Board of Education, however, has so far published very little about its actual philosophy and methodology. A small Methodist group offering sensitivity training also exists, most of its energies being devoted to the post-ordination training of Methodist ministers.

Recently the Student Christian Movement has sought to set up training programmes combining *Gestalt* techniques with the community action approach designed by Saul Alinsky in the United States. The ambitious, probably over-ambitious, aim is to run an on-off six months' course in which the two methods, the one related to personal development and the other to radical political change, are related and where possible integrated. Follow-up work has, however, proved difficult to monitor. Whatever the eventual outcome, this Student Christian Movement course does point to a growing concern to establish training which provides fully experiential as well as cognitive insights into both personal and political issues. Though outside the immediate scope of this book, such is the recent development of the event known as a 'mini-society', where participants live together for a week or more and are required to build their own society from scratch.[80]

CONCLUSION

Those communities and centres described in this chapter are seeking to communicate some aspect of the Gospel which they believe to be of especial importance to Church or society. My concern is whether they are enabling those with whom they come in touch to explore new aspects of authority and leadership, new depths of personal awareness, and new dimensions of interpersonal relationships. It is especially hard to assess communities of learning in this way because message, method, and medium are inextricably bound up and some groups which appear open and outward-looking in their message may be relying on a fairly traditional educational methodology, such as the Iona Community; while those groups alert to the use of experiential educational techniques and aids may employ them within the context of an ethereal if not eccentric philosophy of life, as at Findhorn. Thus no simple continuum can be constructed to facilitate easy comparison and evaluation of such communities and groups.

None the less, the three aspects of the work of these centres mentioned at the outset of the chapter help to sort out the wide variety of approaches. One is a consideration of the *message* such groups seek to impart. For example, is it one which upholds the religious and ecclesiastical *status quo* or, in terms of attitudes to authority and the interpersonal, one which at least questions it? Secondly, and very important, there is the matter of the educational *method* used. For example, to what extent is leadership of or within the course autocratic and to what extent democratic? Thirdly, there is the *learning environment*, especially the style of life manifest by the educators and the influence which this has on message and method.

Message

The content of the message basic communities attempt to get across varies from those accepting present ecclesiastical and secular structures, yet wanting a new quality of life within them, to those challenging fundamental aspects of the life of Church and society. Many issues here concern *authority and leadership.*

Most basic communities in the former category have little in their message seriously suggesting a move from a traditional or classical pattern of authority and leadership. There is the usual message about the equality of members within the Body of Christ, but little attempt overtly to challenge the hierarchical nature of ecclesiastical organizations. From the Community of Celebration to the Grail, from Lee Abbey to Hengrave Hall, this situation seems to be accepted as normative. The only new explorations being made by some of these groups are into the, at times still autocratic, charismatic movement, though it should be noted that Post Green in particular stresses a human relations style of leadership in the running of its courses. On the secular side of things, Lindley Lodge is apparently concerned with teaching young participants commitment and loyalty to superiors, whilst the 'Establishment' image of St George's, Windsor, gives the impression of a 'restorationist' approach to the value and viability of our present institutional structures.

It is only as we move towards groups with a distinctive stance concerning current patterns of the exercise of power or wrestling with problems of the collapse of society, as in Northern Ireland, that the message contains serious questioning of the nature and exercise of authority today, and is prophetic rather than pastoral or social. Dartmouth House ran a weekend on the art of political lobbying, whilst the Alternative Society has gathered interested persons around the issue of alternative politics. Indeed the stance of the Alternative Society calls into question present-day patterns of power and authority across the board of our institutional life. The Froddle Crook Centre at Armathwaite has a strong concern for world justice and interest in prisoners of conscience, whilst much in the courses run by the Sheffield Urban Theology Unit contains a critical approach to the exercise of power in Church and world. In Northern Ireland the Corrymeela Community has been increasingly engaged in attempts to promote a critique of society on which peace and corporate leadership can be based, Glencree more recently following suit south of the Border.

However, it is mainly those associations directly concerned with human relations training wherein the authority issue is put at the heart of the learning experience. Especially important here is the work of the Grubb Institute, committed to enabling course members, Christian and non-Christian, to face searching questions concerning authority and leadership immediately and intensely. Despite its over-emphasis on the Church's dependency function, the Grubb continues to offer the opportunity for participants to gain extremely valuable insights into institutional structures and organization.

Many basic communities, which may make only passing reference to questions of authority, have the matters of *personal growth* and *interpersonal development* well in the forefront of their message. For example, many aspects of the Post Green and Whatcombe House courses explore at depth the nature of Christian commitment and fellowship, as do the gatherings at Lee Abbey and Scargill. Indeed the main contribution of charismatic renewal seems to be within this context rather than in relation to the nature of authority. The Movement for a Better World has as its major aim the re-creation of community as an earthed experience, beginning at the parish level and extending outwards. The Open Centres stress a new dimension of self-awareness, for example in their study of the mystics, and interpersonal openness. The Iona Community, Urban Theology Unit, Scottish Churches House, the Institute of Christian Studies, the London Ecumenical Centre, and the William Temple Foundation, amongst others, maintain a programme in both the religious and secular areas that is fully cosmopolitan and ecumenical. The Urban Ministry Project, the Community Education Centre in Lewisham, and Coventry Cathedral seek to arouse empathy for all kinds and conditions of men in the urban situation by involving students directly in meeting and talking to city dwellers, Coventry basing a great deal of its course on the theme of reconciliation. Again, Corrymeela and Glencree are giving expression to this theme not only in discussion but also in many ways of practical caring.

Method

The method adopted by communities and groups is as important, if not more so, than the message proclaimed. Though obviously the medium need not always demonstrate the message, where the former is a manifest denial of the latter, credibility is called into question. On the other hand, where method can uphold and illustrate message, credibility is greatly enhanced. This is especially important where the issue of *authority and leadership* is concerned.

It is surprising to find how many centres can mount conferences and courses where the virtues of corporate leadership, participation, and mutual responsibility are extolled using an educational approach quite alien to the themes under consideration. The lecture or talk by 'the expert' with questions and some discussion to follow is still very much the norm, in some situations quite appropriate but in others very inadequate or detrimental to learning. The Iona Community perhaps has hitherto disappointed as much as most groups in this respect, simply because its summer courses are based in a place which gives such a wonderful opportunity for corporate involvement, but many other groups also rely over much on this educational style. A way forward is to impart necessary information through a variety of views and experiences within gatherings of a more flexible kind, such as some of those set up during the London Ecumenical Centre's major summer happenings on the theme of spirituality, and the weekends organized by the Alternative Society.

In this context the cell or small group has a very important role to play, not least the kind of network of family groups stimulated by the Grail. We are still only beginning to grasp the great potential of the small, especially the self-programming, groups along the lines of the LINK house group in Greenwich or those meeting under the auspices of the West London Chaplaincy, for promoting not only interest and enthusiasm but learning about the nature of shared leadership. In a more specifically educational setting, the Institute of Christian Studies usefully employs core groups which meet to explore and share material.

A shift from the expert delivering his speech to experiential learning by the individual or the group can be seen in the growing amount of project work undertaken by students. Particularly interesting here is 'the plunge', the Urban Ministry Project and the Community Education Centre offering participants on courses the chance of learning by roughing it in London for a day or two. The Community Education Centre and Coventry Cathedral are especially committed to using the city – home, street, shop, factory – as a workshop, whilst other groups such as the Institute of Christian Studies and the Urban Theology Unit involve students in project work to an important but lesser extent. The educational model of action-reflection-action is here being well developed.

As yet few communities or centres have ventured into the even more open T-group type of learning situation. Though the focus of concern is in this case very much on the exercise of authority within the group, there is also a great deal of attention paid to *interpersonal development*. The Grubb Institute is noteworthy here, group leaders deliberately refusing to take responsibility for the group's learning about itself yet keeping members strictly to the task: the group becoming the message and the medium for those with eyes to see and ears to hear. The General Synod Board of Education courses also seek to integrate medium and message though with generally more support from, and less confrontation by, leaders. The interpersonal development aspect of the group's life is being stimulated by a variety of approaches, especially associated with the human potential movement, some of which are used by groups with a very different philosophy of life, such as Findhorn and the Wrekin Trust, in their educational programmes. In many of the communities and groups mentioned in previous paragraphs, the shift in the exercise of leadership from the autocratic to the corporate style also helps to enhance interpersonal learning and development: for example, when the Community Education Centre and Coventry Cathedral encourage resident groups to fend for themselves and to design their own communal life-style.

Finally, some groups look very much for the *personal growth* of participants through self-discovery and self-awareness methods. Findhorn places great store by this aspect of its work, its techniques ranging from mime to bio-energetics; the Institute of Christian Studies has a dance workshop; the Community Education Centre makes use of interaction games; whilst Coventry Cathedral uses role-play and simulation a good deal. Together with music and drama, employed by Scargill and the Community of Celebration as well as other places, these approaches move the emphasis on to finding the self through a whole range of affective experiences.

The learning environment

The message of these teaching communities and centres as well as their educational method is further enhanced where the learning environment is conducive and supportive. For example, the teaching of some communities about shared *leadership* is assisted by the teaching or facilitating group itself demonstrating this approach, as in the case of the Post Green teams and the Community of Celebration Fisherfolk. On the other hand, the problem facing St George's House, Windsor, not alone here, has already been discussed. It ought also to be mentioned that the rules and regulations which centres draw up, and above all the way these are conveyed to visitors, have a major effect on the message communicated. Some places exercise a protective, and at times patronizing, attitude out of all proportion to the actual needs of the situation. Centres should appreciate the impression that notices on boards and walls can give for good (as at Dartmouth House) or ill. One healthy trend here is that incoming groups are becoming, and being encouraged to become, more self-sufficient and self-directing, in itself a very valuable learning experience, as the mini-society conferences amply demonstrate.

The living example of the group's life-style gives especial weight to what is communicated at the interpersonal level. The community may be engaged directly in the teaching, as at Whatcombe House, or less directly but still influentially, at a social and pastoral level, as at Lee Abbey, Scargill, Hengrave Hall, the Grail, or Ringsfield Hall. The quality of the interpersonal relationships of the host community further enriches message and method where the group is really prepared to open itself up and share its life with visitors.

Other centres witness to their understanding of the interpersonal dimension by the variety of people attracted to their courses. St George's House, Windsor, for example, seems to opt for a fairly sophisticated type of clientele whereas the Urban Theology Unit, Corrymeela, and the Alternative Society witness to their view of ecumenicity by the cosmopolitan nature of participants.

Many communities and centres are working towards a synthesis of message, method and environmental context. Some are further along the road than others; some, such as Dartmouth House, have gone far enough to show that when an attempt is made to translate vision into reality the possible clash with a Church holding very different ideas about the nature of authority and the meaning of community is a hair's-breadth away. But where such synthesis does occur, then educational credibility and the impact of the message are immensely increased. Particularly when groups are seeking to hammer out a new understanding of authority and the interpersonal in a Christian context, it would seem that some such integration is essential. For too long the Church has failed to practise what it preaches; now its right to preach at all is doubted by many. The sooner, therefore, message and method and medium come together in a courageously experiential way, the sooner we shall be at the heart of the true teaching ministry of the Church.

6

CARING COMMUNITIES

There is an impressive number of individuals, groups, communities, and organizations involved today in caring for those in need – physical, mental, and spiritual. My concern in this chapter is primarily with those exercising such a ministry who call themselves Christians, or who work for or with some group which has a Christian ethos, often derived from its being originally founded by Christians or on Christian principles. This implies no discrimination between Christian and 'humanistic' or 'secular' groups in the sincerity of their commitment or the quality of their service; many who would shun the label 'Christian' give of their time, energy, and concern in a way that would shame many of us who claim that title.

Because my interest is generally restricted to Christian involvement in caring, I shall omit, or only touch on a few of, the large number of other groups and organizations working in this field. Furthermore, my discussion relates mainly to communities and groups which have emerged in more recent years; I shall not, for example, deal with the excellent work undertaken by such institutions as the National Children's Home (a Methodist foundation) or similarly long-established charitable organizations, such as the Settlements. It is to what is emerging at this moment in the realm of Christian caring and to the current content of this ministry that I wish to direct attention.

Josephine Klein has usefully distinguished two approaches to their work adopted by the so-called helping professions which are important in the context of this chapter. One she calls 'responding to need',[1] an approach to social and community work which deals with the crises people face and puts the emphasis on immediate action to remedy ills and right wrongs. She believes, however, that this approach by itself is in the long run inadequate unless accompanied or followed up by another which she terms 'working for autonomy'. In the latter case the helper 'is likely to prefer to take steps which will make him redundant, or to take steps which confirm in his clientele the understanding that they can deal with the situation rather than quickly solve the problem on his own'.[2] Klein stresses that a fundamental distinction must be made between the service itself and the way in which it is rendered. It is true that there are many occasions when needs are so acute that all that can be done is to try to avert crises. This is an essential response and in this chapter, especially in the section on the interpersonal dimension of caring, I shall describe people exercising this extremely important ministry. But in these situations the limelight falls mainly, as with the Good Samaritan, on the person or group doing the caring. Therefore, in the first section of the chapter, I want to draw particular attention to the efforts of those seeking to pursue Klein's second approach, fostering the autonomy of those with whom they work, by enabling them to take responsibility for meeting their own needs and solving their own difficulties, and resisting a passive dependence on the paid services of the full-time helping professions.

Encouraging self-help and self-determination is a very hard task, especially when one is dealing with the sick, the handicapped, the insecure, and the ill-treated. However, caring could produce an even greater sense of self-reliance amongst those in need if the attitude of the helpers were more open to change. We are still very much influenced by a style of caring based on the traditional type of organization, which tends to paternalism, or on the classical kind of organization (now typical of a great deal of provision under the Welfare State), which encourages a functional approach related to narrow and fragmented needs rather than to whole people, and which can produce a debilitating impersonalism. To move from these organizational models towards what Rudge[3] calls the human relations type is both risky and personally costly. If the Church really means business, it of all institutions should be reaching out towards a kind of caring which involves all concerned in mutual acceptance and liberates not only the body, but the mind and spirit of man too. However, some people have found their bearings and some people do care for the total man, amongst these a number who call themselves Christians, and to their endeavours I now turn.

THE AUTHORITY ISSUE

If man is going to find himself, which involves caring for himself and others as people of inestimable value, he must be free from the crippling sense of dependency or inadequacy that misfortune or, worse still, injustice, brings. One way this can come about is by the gradual breaking down of the powerlessness that is a consequence of 'being cared for' or 'being done good to'. There is a number of communities and groups which attempt in their approach to caring to do just this, through the one-to-one relationship or through the establishment of self-help groups both at the level of the neighbourhood and well beyond. (It might be mentioned that in a recent working paper the Cyrenians question the use of the very word 'caring' as smacking of paternalism and antithetical to the creation of community.)[4]

The one-to-one relationship

I shall be dealing in the second section of this chapter with those aspects of counselling which enable people to rediscover the wholeness of life and to enrich interpersonal relationship in the fullest sense. Here I want to mention one movement in the counselling world which has considerable implications for the reshaping of the counsellor-client relationship as such; that known as 'co-counselling' or 're-evaluation counselling'. This developed as an effective means of pastoral care in the United States in the late 1950s, particularly through the work of Harvey Jackins who has pioneered the approach and techniques involved.[5] The 1970s have seen the movement steadily growing in Britain.

Re-evaluation counselling is unusual in that it is essentially based on counselling between peers, not between a professional counsellor (carrying achieved or ascribed authority) and a (dependent) client. There are many other features of the movement, but this is the one that presents the real challenge to the idea of pastoral care being given by those with credentials to those without. It is founded on the conviction that the greatest help one human being can give to another is to listen with caring attention and to allow the speaker time to explore and 'discharge' his deepest concerns and feelings. This is done by first one person listening supportively and then the other for periods of up to an hour each way. The mode of operating is based on a contract mutually agreed before the session starts. Sessions are often monthly and sometimes weekly.

These features of re-evaluation counselling have drawn many Christians into close association with the movement. They have found in it a new appreciation of the caring ministry given to the total Christian Church and not just to priests and ministers. They have also discovered in it many things reflecting the search for a new style of

Christian spirituality. Audrey Shilling describes the situation as follows:

> Forms of spirituality which have been evolved at other times have stressed the need of the soul for a guide or spiritual director. In our day people are much less willing to give another person authority over them. They may sense that to do so would in some way be to diminish their own responsibility for themselves. The co-counselling method emphasizes the responsibility of the client for the work which he chooses to do. The peer relationship between client and counsellor encourages each to explore and develop his own inner freedom to the full.[6]

This peer relationship is sustained and nourished within wider re-evaluation counselling communities. These are non-residential associations of people up and down the country who meet regularly to co-counsel each other. Audrey Shilling comments that 'the warmth and openness which is characteristic of co-counselling communities makes them attractive to those who are seeking new life in the Spirit'.[7] Roy Clements goes further and spells out many links, including the communal one, between the theory and practice of re-evaluation counselling and that of 'the contemplative way'.[8] In the United States, though not yet in Britain, 'liberation' workshops have also sought to apply the principles of peer counselling to such groups as those of different ethnic origins, teachers, the handicapped, and the elderly.[9]

A major anachronism within this movement is the dominant part played by its founder, Harvey Jackins, designated 'the international reference person'. In an attempt to exercise quality-control over the rapid growth of co-counselling, all major articles and statements published on the method have first to receive his imprimatur. This has already caused some division on the British scene, and it is difficult to see how an organization committed to an essentially human relations approach can for very long sustain an autocratic form of monitoring.

A peer counselling group of British origin which seeks to apply the method of mutual support to the field of special needs is the Compassionate Friends. Its founder was Simon Stephens, an Anglican priest, who in his chaplaincy work discovered the immense help parents who had lost young children could gain from companionship with others who had suffered a similar bereavement. The movement grew slowly from 1969 onwards and a network of groups came into existence in Britain (some thirty-five by 1976) and abroad. There is a constant endeavour to establish contact with bereaved parents with religious convictions or none, by personal reference or by scanning the columns of the newspapers, though this still small movement can meet only a fraction of the actual need. Much of the work is private and, by means of personal correspondence, of a confidential nature.

The Compassionate Friends aim to work alongside the helping professions, including the clergy. However, the movement arose through a realization that so often it is those who have suffered who are best able to help others experiencing bereavement for the first time. Many professionals proved unprepared or unable to meet such acute personal need with skill or empathy. Any such movement has its dangers, for example that of living too long in the company of those mourning, but it again underlines the great healing potential of counselling which takes place between 'equals'.

Though I have stressed the one-to-one relationship, the groups mentioned also use the self-help group a good deal and to other illustrations of the latter I now turn.

The self-help group

The last few years have seen the emergence of a large number of self-help groups seeking either to right the social wrongs currently inflicted on their members, such as Gingerbread which brings together one-parent families,[10] or to provide alternative ways of structuring society and especially the professions, such as Rank and File (teachers) and the radical social workers' group which produces *Case Con*. Many include no particularly Christian pronouncements within their stated aims but a good number associate with the humanistic aspects of Christian concern and many have Christians working within their organizations.

One such community is Alpha House in Portsmouth, which has Jean Stubbs, a Christian, as house director.[11] The project was born in 1968, as a social rehabilitation community for ex-drug users based on the Phoenix House prototype in New York. Jean Stubbs states:

Alpha House is a drug-free, residential therapeutic community. It is non-permissive and hierarchical. . . . (It) is a replacement family for people who have somehow failed to grow up adequately the first time round. While demanding the type of behaviour and functioning one would expect from friends and colleagues outside, we do not expect this to come without practice. We create a safe environment in which the residents can make mistakes without being rejected. However, unless we set high standards, the residents will never, on their own, strive to achieve them, but will be (apparently) content with the squalor of their previous lives. By demanding the exercise of their potential we show them what they are capable of achieving.[12]

A person's stay of residence begins with a nine-to-fifteen months' very strict Phase I based on getting to know himself through confrontation: 'For ourselves, confrontation of the individual by himself and his peers is the prime instrument in the reconstruction of attitudes. Without this he is condemned to walk in ignorance, not able to understand himself or those with whom he shares his environment.'[13]

Then follows a more liberal Phase II, living in and working out, in preparation for a full return to society. Jean Stubbs adds deliberately:

This is not a Christian community as such and in the early stages people are not allowed to go to church even if they want to. We are teaching them to be self-sufficient and religion can all too often be another prop. In Phase II, when people have more idea of their own needs and how to satisfy them, they can then choose, knowing that the choice is a real one and not just a crutch.[14]

In some respects this approach would seem to be quite contrary to the implications of what I have previously written concerning the difficulty of combining directive leadership with a mature community life. But with Alpha House there is a different situation for it is a community dealing with, at least initially, normatively disoriented young people who need not only a 'jolt' to stab them awake but security, predictability, and incentive to get them socially moving again. As they grow through the phase of a highly structured existence and maximum confrontation, it is hoped that they will begin to take real responsibility for themselves (the self-help aspect of the work) and slowly move towards personal autonomy. Indeed it could be said that in refusing to use religion as a 'prop' at the outset, the House could in the long run produce young people of greater maturity than are found in some churches. Alpha House demonstrates that in speaking of alternatives one must fully appreciate the initial situation of the people with whom one deals, starting where they are and not where one would hope they would be, and sensitive to the moment when external constraints need to give way or make space for self-managed personal development.

Two other basically Christian organizations running a number of community houses are, like Alpha House, attempting to enable residents to move towards a new sense of their own worth and assume responsibility for themselves. They are L'Arche and the Cyrenians. In this section of the chapter I am concerned not so much with their caring ministry as with their *attitude* towards the mentally handicapped, on the one hand, and the homeless on the other.

L'Arche was founded in 1964 when Jean Vanier, a Roman Catholic Canadian lecturer, was visiting France and was deeply moved by the plight of mentally retarded adults imprisoned in institutions. He bought a small house in the village of Trosly-Breuil and L'Arche began. By 1976 there were over thirty L'Arche houses throughout the world: in Britain one in Barfrestone, Kent, one in Inverness, and plans to open one in Lambeth and Liverpool. Elizabeth Buckley, director of the Inverness House, writes:

> L'Arche is a Christian inter-faith community which creates home-life and work situations with mentally handicapped (retarded) adults. That 'with' is an important key word because the handicapped persons who come to the community are as much members of the community as the assistants and young volunteers.[15]

In fact some of those working with L'Arche shy away from using the word 'handicapped' at all, believing that all of us are handicapped in one way or another and that true community can only be built on a sense of the affirmation of the fundamental value and thus the 'equality' of all human beings, whatever their physical or mental state. From the 'Charter of the Communities of L'Arche':[16]

> We believe that each person, whether handicapped or not, has a unique and mysterious value. The handicapped person is a complete human being and as such he has the rights of every man: the right to life, to care, to education, and to work.

> We also believe that a person who has been wounded in his capacity for autonomy and in his mind is capable of great love, which can be called forth by the spirit of God. We believe that God loves him in a special way because of his very weakness.

> Our communities seek to be communities of peace where handicapped people and assistants live, work, and pray together, sharing their sufferings and their joys like brothers. We know that we are all handicapped: for some the handicap is external, for others it is the handicap of selfishness or pride.

Our communities strive to be communities of hope, where handicapped people and assistants seek to progress together both humanly and spiritually. We seek whatever autonomy of life and work is possible for each person, and to respond to God's call for each individual.

Their communities are committed to 'a levelling-off of hierarchy, so simplicity of relationships and spontaneity (can grow)'.[17]

The British houses are meant to offer a family atmosphere and as such they are kept to about a dozen residents. The assistants themselves are constantly looking for ways of validating and receiving validation from the more retarded, linking their efforts closely to their spirituality, for 'the first aim of L'Arche is to create communities inspired by the Beatitudes and the spirit of the Gospel'.[18] 'The roots of L'Arche are deep in the Beatitudes, and Jesus' love for and identification with the marginal and rejected ones of this world. Its foundations are built solidly on the granite of the gospel spirit: brotherhood, justice, truth, liberty, and peace.'[19]

The communities are also inspired by the words of Jean Vanier now becoming widely known through his numerous publications.[20] At Inverness, Elizabeth Buckley spoke to me of the residents' 'fantastic capacity for joy' and their all being involved in 'a way of life much more than an experiment in social care'.

Akin to the work of L'Arche, though founded on a less explicitly Christian philosophy, are the Cyrenian houses for the homeless, themselves similar not only to the Simon communities from which they originally sprang in 1970 but to a number of similar ventures both in Britain (notably the St Mungo Community Trust) and overseas. Currently the Cyrenians have over forty local projects, night shelters, and residential houses which spread nationwide. Chriş Blackwell states that, as far as is humanly possible, the intention is to relate on the level of mutual acceptance with the homeless, 'identification' being seen as too presumptuous a term to employ. This is achieved through helpers and residents fully sharing the life of the house:

Practices embodying this principle include the sharing of meals, sleeping accommodation, and household chores between workers and other residents alike. Workers also accept as pocket money a sum similar to the Supplementary Benefit personal allowance normally received by the other residents. Of course these elements are simply the skeleton on which Worker Participation is based. The real participation is much less easily defined. Its classic expression has been in the phrase 'a community of the caring and cared-for, living and working co-equally'. It requires of the worker that he recognize that men and women rarely become homeless, poor or socially handicapped through their own faults, but, more usually, through some kind of misfortune – of birth, or later life. In a very real way the worker comes to realize that (literally) 'there, but for the grace of God, go I'. The distinction between 'us' and 'them' is not only anti-therapeutic – it is UNTRUE.[21]

This is not to say that the worker surrenders his own identity, skills or role, for this would destroy the means of genuine communication. Nor does it imply that all is sweetly harmonious; a great deal of anger and aggression has to be coped with in dealing with people in acute need. But it does lead to a style of caring which accepts rather than judges, enables rather than imposes, and so makes possible the slow development of individuality.

More recently a 'Cyrenian Rethink' has been going on. Despite original intentions it has been only too easy to slip from 'community' to 'hostel'. New 'Guidelines'[22] are being worked out to clarify roles and responsibilities, to strengthen the community meeting (involving *all* those running the house) and make it a monthly event, and to give greater autonomy to the house meeting for the day-to-day supervision of domestic affairs. None the less, this is still policy; as ever, the practice is very much harder.

One other group discriminated against so often in our society, now seeking to find both legitimate social and spiritual expression for their abilities and concerns, is the homosexual. The fight is against both legal limitations and social prejudice. 'Reach' is an interdenominational group led by an Anglican priest, at present based in Salford.

(They) believe that as homosexual Christians they can be both fully homosexual and fully Christian and wish to offer fellowship and support to those Christians who are at present isolated within their own church because of their homosexual condition; to work within respective churches to develop understanding of the homosexual condition and the general theology of sex; to encourage the Church towards the ending of all forms of discrimination against the homosexual both within the Church and in society at large.[23]

To these ends they have established a number of working parties on relevant topics, held a series of seminars up and down the country, and produced a pamphlet on the Church and the homosexual.

Seeking to give even more explicitly communal expression to the Christian homosexual is the Metropolitan Community Church (MCC) founded in the USA in 1968. They argue that 'the rapid growth of MCCs in the USA, Canada and Britain, resulted from the need to fill the yawning gap created by those churches that neglected their clear pastoral duty to those who are or feel rejected because of their sexual and emotional orientation'.[24]

The MCC, despite a good deal of latent as well as open opposition both within and outside the Church, is now established in its own right in London, Birmingham, and the south-west. One of the MCC's clergy, Jo McVay-Abbott, writes: 'Homosexuals are commonly deeply religious people. It is hardly surprising therefore, that in the face of the traditional churches' defection from their pastoral responsibility to the homosexual, the Spirit of God should move beyond them to create an alternative.'[25]

The Association of Interchurch Families seeks, through self-help groups, to meet the problems created by a divided Church: in this case of those entering into mixed marriages, particularly involving Roman Catholics.

The Association of Interchurch Families was formed in 1968 by a small group of couples who, having faced the various vicissitudes of a mixed marriage, believed that they would have been helped considerably in their troubles if they could have discussed them with other people in a similar position. Further, it was reasoned that in this age lone voices have difficulty in being heard, whereas concerted action can be turned into a 'pressure group', if the cause is just and the arguments intelligently compiled.

The Association has grown considerably since its foundation. Regional areas have been formed, couples meet and discuss specific problems and form resolutions which are passed on to the leaders of all Churches, and in some cases these have been taken up by responsible church bodies. The Association meets each year for a weekend at Spode House, to which are invited clergy representative of all Churches, and from the number of bishops who have now attended, it may be said that the Association has achieved respectability.[26]

Despite such 'respectability', the Association is operating on a basis which challenges the segregation created by a divided Church, most acutely in Northern Ireland. 'It is the belief of members of the Association, held with humility, that they have become "better" people through their knowledge, understanding, and acceptance of the life of another Church.'[27] Their work is thus that of mutual support, reconciliation, and the search for a richer wholeness of being than the institution can as yet see fit to foster.

The neighbourhood

If Christians have refused to accept the imposition of an unwarranted dependency situation, they have also been prominent in trying to rouse the neighbourhood from the apathy and inactivity which are so often the result of bureaucratic control and Welfare State provision. Three examples of movements in which Christian concern has been evident are the 'Good Neighbour' schemes, Community Development, and the recently established Community Health Councils.

The local church is well placed to mobilize pastoral care for those in the neighbourhood who are in personal need. It is, therefore, encouraging to find that it was a group of local churches in the late 1950s which first awoke to the fact that the Social Services were not catering for a great deal of perhaps less dramatic but none the less real hardship suffered by many caught stranded, physically or socially, in an impersonal society. Between 1957 and 1960 Helen Roberts initiated and guided the first scheme to direct local voluntary help towards unmet need, in south Birmingham.[28] The project was very much based on the churches in the area, one specific aim being to discover 'the extent to which churches and other Christian groups can bring an experience of community to the neighbourhoods where they are at work'.[29]

Offers of service were listed and a liaison officer was appointed to take calls for help from social workers or other people likely to unearth unmet need. The officer then ensured that the person in need and the appropriate helper were matched and linked up. Not only were people thus cared for, but a total dependency on professional help was avoided. Furthermore, where churches were ready and able to co-operate across denominational divides, a deeper sense of both neighbourhood and Christian community was fostered.

Problems remained for the scheme: of recruiting reliable helpers, of locating genuine need, and especially of co-ordination. But despite these, the venture proved what could be done and was developed in other areas (notably in south Sheffield where Helen Roberts went to live in 1961) and under a variety of titles, such as the Ashton-under-Lyne Community Care Scheme and the Old Headington (Oxford) Fish Scheme. In 1966 the National Council of Social Service produced a booklet entitled *The Caring Community*,[30] describing such projects, all of which showed local churches playing a prominent role. The more recent trend has been for schemes to go on to a more 'secular' basis, as with 'Care' in Bushey, Hertfordshire, and with the appointment and payment of a full-time liaison officer by the local authority, as in the case of 'The Link' scheme in Bristol. Though there is a danger of voluntary help being institutionalized and losing the element of freely offered service, the potential advantage of really effective co-operation between lay and professional workers intended by such developments must be acknowledged.

A more full-blooded attempt at neighbourhood self-help has been the Community Development movement which, in its modern form, first got under way in the developing countries, especially made known through the writings of T. R. Batten,[31] and, notably in the form of community organization, in the United States, before it 'took off' in Britain in the 1960s. In Britain community development has had a somewhat erratic career, being very much associated with the rise and, some would say, fall of the dozen major five-year projects sponsored by the Home Office from 1969 onwards. Nevertheless, the ideal of the neighbourhood working to ensure that its own social needs are met and for the creation of a meaningful local identity remains, even if the hope of fuller self-determination has received a number of setbacks.

The Church has so far moved into this field with only limited success, in part because of the lack of resources to stretch its social or pastoral ministry any further, but more so because of perplexity or disagreement about the involvement of an organization which lays claim to a Christian style of life and commitment to mission in a mode of neighbourhood activity where any form of open proclamation or proselytizing would negate the object of the exercise. Indeed even between those Christians committed to community development principles there are differences of emphasis, some seeing the local church, with its multifarious activities and organizations, as an identifiable and 'model' community which should work mainly as a partner with other neighbourhood groups in the community

178

development process; others believing that the local church ought to shed its separate meetings and clubs and free church members to be fully involved in community work within a non-religious setting. Tending to the former approach, George Lovell, and Catharine Widdicombe, a member of the Grail, have worked as full-time consultants to a prototype venture called 'Project 70–75' which has been based on the combined efforts of certain churches in one Greater London borough.[32] However, increasing co-operation is taking place between Christians involved in community development, helped by the thinking of a British Council of Churches working group, and by the efforts of the William Temple Foundation to establish an 'operative' consultative group in this field.[33]

A much more recent attempt to involve people in expressing their views about a very important aspect of life was the establishment in 1975 of Community Health Councils. In no way an exclusively Christian concern, this possibility has sparked the imagination of many Christian people interested in the whole concept of community health and the many failures so far to develop it in a really creative way. Their hope is, as Michael Wilson believes, that 'hospital medicine is giving ground to preventive medicine: preventive medicine is giving ground to community development'.[34] Despite the often cumbersome and politically biased method of appointing Community Health Council members, and the current confusion about the Council's role, there is at least some chance that the more thoughtful Christian voice will be heard in relation to a matter which many realize is closely linked to the biblical concept of 'salvation'.

Wider society

The challenge of caring communities and groups to the established order emerges most conspicuously, yet not necessarily always most effectively, at the macrocosmic level where the cry for social justice can be put in a way that commands attention if not remedy. Charles Elliott, in his searching critique of the failure of the Church to right economic injustice and steer clear of heretical structures, writes:

> The last and best hope (of freeing the Church from doing little but legitimize the *status quo*) seems to be the small, often autonomous, cells of Christians struggling to find new life-styles, new relationships with each other, with the environment, and with national and

international society. It is there, if anywhere, that one will see the activity of God and hear the genuinely prophetic voice, as these groups go inward in radical contemplation and outward in radical action.[35]

The final sentence of his book, 'Radical action begins with radical contemplation',[36] is important in that it reflects a growing desire to link politics and prayer much more closely, an attempt seen, for example, in the Jubilee Group, a network of some 150 priests concerned with the renewal of the Catholic movement within the Church of England and in particular of its social tradition. Kenneth Leech, one of the central figures in this movement, describes its members as 'subversive contemplatives' not 'shallow activists'[37] and emphasizes the inspiration they draw from the life and writings of Thomas Merton.

Few intentional Christian communities, however, have proved ready or able to pursue an active political line. The Blackheath Commune was deliberately established, as Christopher Ross reports, to be

a base for political activity which we thought of principally in terms of community struggle, where people would organize themselves to regain control over resources essential to the full development of their lives. This we hoped would lead us into contact with local shop stewards, community workers, anti-radical organizations, and tenants associations.[38]

This goal was never fully realized, as Ross, whilst still a member of the Commune, reveals:

At the outset with the May Days of Paris 1968 still very much alive to us, we expected that issues which affected the local people could swiftly mobilize them while the causes could easily be traced to the basic question of control. We underestimated the diluting effect of doing different jobs. In the early days of the Commune it required all our efforts just to keep up with what each of us was doing during the day, let alone being able to sort out, plan, and implement what we should be doing as a group in the community! The only issue which mobilized us all was the anti-Springboks and Stop-the-Seventy-Tour campaigns. Apart from that our political work has consisted in two or three people becoming involved with a particular local or national concern. These have varied from work with drug addicts, explaining the unjust trade relations between Britain and the Third World, and highlighting business links with apartheid in the area, to opposition to the anti-Trade Union legislation. Despite our aspirations at the start we have been unable to link up the various issues. We have not developed a clear analysis of the priorities and the decisions of boardroom personnel – both council and commercial – and how they determine the quality of life of ordinary people in the area and direct the area's future development or decline. We know now that such a task requires deliberate and painstaking attention and a long-term commitment to the area.[39]

Explicit and sustained political activity usually comes more from a central organizing headquarters often servicing a network of interested groups, rather than from single intentional communities as such. The Student Christian Movement, for example, though currently attempting to establish a residential community in its headquarters at Wick Court and a number of 'sister' houses elsewhere has really given expression to its radical political views through its (now very few) full-time paid staff and the groups and consultations they are able to convene, and especially via its magazine *Movement* which concerns itself with many national and international issues making the political headlines. The latter's coverage and commentary is often thorough and stimulating though the wide variety of topics dealt with (as in the case of *Roadrunner*, a kind of less sophisticated version of *Movement*) presents an often bewildering kaleidoscope of radical concerns meaningful to only the politically *avant-garde* reader.

Christian Action, founded by John Collins immediately after the Second World War, has for three decades sought to rouse Christian awareness in relation to a number of major political and social issues. The movement was very much involved in, though never finally committed to, the Campaign for Nuclear Disarmament, and championing the cause of those victimized under the apartheid policy of South Africa. In recent years, true to its 'situational' approach to social ethics, Christian Action has turned its attention to the cause of the single homeless woman in our big cities and, especially relevant to my concern with groups questioning traditional attitudes and State provision, to the matter of penal reform in close association with the group known as Radical Alternatives to Prison (RAP).[40] The latter is an information and pressure group calling for an end to imprisonment and the establishment of community-based alternatives. Most of the work is carried out by a London nucleus with the support of a few locally based groups, for example in Bristol and Bradford. RAP is a small but vocal group usefully trying to push back the frontiers of prejudice in relation to the 'criminal'.

There are numerous other groups in which Christians are playing a significant role, active in the quest for social justice and challenging political systems which seem to deny the basic rights of man: notably Amnesty International (to be mentioned again later) with Paul Oestreicher, an Anglican priest, as its British chairman and groups, including Christian Concern for Southern Africa and ELTSA (End Loans to South Africa), seeking to stir people to thought and action on the issue of apartheid. To mention these smaller and focused networks of Christian political concern is not of course to ignore the fact that all the major denominations and the British Council of Churches have well-informed departments or committees producing comment and, less often, initiating action on important issues related to national and international justice.

Comment

Just as most of the communities and groups described above are fully engaged in Christian work of caring and reconciliation, so also do many of those with a major concern for encouraging personal development and enriching interpersonal relationships (see below) frequently call in question situations of cramping social dependency and political injustice. But I have here been especially intent on describing groups giving a good deal of time and energy, in thought and practice, to challenging dependency and injustice, because it is only as man is able to find an authority which gives him space to be truly himself, discover his own worth and that of others, and express himself without fear or favour, that autonomy is possible.

These ventures in earthing the Gospel encompass a few examples of this process of questioning, self-discovery, and growth. However small the number or personal the endeavour, as with the Compassionate Friends, men and women are attempting to break with the childish and inhibiting belief that 'they' have all the skills and all the answers. There is here evident, as throughout the community movement, the emergence of a genuinely lay Church which sees the professional – priest, social worker, local government official, politician – as a resource to be called on when necessary rather than as a *deus ex machina* for whose condescending appearance all must wait with awesome expectation and infinite patience.

Even so, the crises of life, personal, social, and international, all too often dominate the scene and mean that 'responding to need' swamps the more delicate and dangerous task of 'working for autonomy'. Indeed, Christians with a cause are by no means innocent of treating people as means to their albeit noble ends, rather than as ends in themselves. Yet with many of the groups I have described, whether in the sphere of peer support, self-help ventures, community development, or the attempt to tackle broader injustices, both the source and the recipient of care and concern have at least some glimpse of the infinite value of the individual, be he addicted to drugs, mentally handicapped, homeless, or persecuted, and his human right to be seen as a responsible being and treated with dignity.

PERSONAL WHOLENESS

Because care and concern are all too easily linked with the ending of crises or the alleviating of distress, ministry in this field can become pervaded by the idea of 'dis-ease' rather than health or wholeness or, in the Jungian sense, individuation. Michael Wilson makes this point clearly and forcefully in his book *Health is for People* where, though refusing to define health and thus 'to kill it',[41] he argues that we must reorientate medical thought and practice from preoccupation with disease to the fulfilment of our being human. This involves setting health in the context of both personal autonomy and interpersonal co-operation. He writes:

Health is the milieu (human and environmental) which enables people individually and socially to grow towards fullness of life.

Community development is nearer to a model of health care because it is concerned not only with the basic necessities of life, but also with the people's struggle to obtain them and enjoy them together.[42]

Though the search for wholeness involves setting disease in this fuller context of health, it also means taking the darker aspects of life, physical, mental, and spiritual, very seriously as integral parts of ourselves and of our living together, and not seeking to escape from them. Monica Furlong, discussing Jung's concept of individuation, argues that it is only as we become fully aware of our 'shadow', with the

183

tension of opposites and the pain which that produces, and live with that awareness, that we can reach wholeness:

> With our reluctance to endure this painful conflict most of us opt out long before this happens. We seek to dodge it by pursuing a perfection which will allow us to deny the parts of our personality which make us uneasy. But individuation is not about perfection, but about wholeness, completeness, and nothing may be left out of this reckoning.[43]

The Christian ministry of caring and concern needs to be far more than a desperate rescue operation. It should be a ministry that sees suffering and pain, however much demanding alleviation, as personally and corporately meaningful and one that works *through* these things towards the hope of personal and social completeness. I look below at one or two ventures in Christian community-making dedicated to these ends and in doing so take three traditional aspects of the substance of man – body, mind, and spirit – as my pegs.

Body

The Church since its inception has been deeply involved in healing the physically sick, whether through the operation of technical medical attention or through religious practice, such as prayer and the laying-on-of-hands. In the early days of the Church the two approaches were casually distinguished, indeed, were closely associated, for example, in the tending of the sick by the religious Orders. But with the rise of medical science as such they began to part company and, as Michael Wilson points out, healing became a specialized function divorced from the mainstream religious beliefs of Church and society. In recent years there have been some attempts to bring medicine and religion a good deal closer again within the context of communities of healing, two notable ventures being Burrswood in Kent and St Christopher's Hospice in Sydenham, London.

Of Burrswood, founded in 1947 by Dorothy Kerin, with the threefold aim, 'to heal the sick, comfort the sorrowing, and bring faith to the faithless',[44] the late Edward Aubert wrote:

> Burrswood can be described as an intensive care unit in which there is a working partnership between religion and medicine. The chaplain and the doctor see all who are admitted to Burrswood; but

these are also seen by the nurses, and by the members of the community who clean their rooms and bring them their food. The nurses and the houseworkers believe whole-heartedly in this partnership between religion and medicine. There is scarcely anyone, however ill, frightened, shy or withdrawn, with whom at least one member of the community does not establish a bridgehead, and it is through this bridgehead that the therapeutic resources of the community reach the patient.[45]

Edward Aubert saw the resources of Burrswood as, first, 'a loving acceptance of each person as they are', second, 'the trained listener', and third, 'the medical and nursing care of a modern and well-equipped home'.[46] He added that 'the fourth of Burrswood's resources is intercessory prayer. Not only does the whole community pray, but it is the special work of some; in addition the name of the sick person is put on the altar.'[47]

Finally, there are the most important of all Burrswood's resources – the spiritual ones, in particular the healing services with the laying-on-of-hands. These are not a substitute for the appropriate medical treatment, though they do sometimes render it unnecessary. They bring the sick person directly to the source of all healing. But this must be done with proper understanding, with a receptive mind and with an attitude of faith.[48]

Burrswood has something like 1,000 patients passing through per year and can now minister to whole families if the need arises. It offers a number of bursaries, but most patients are fee-paying, which unfortunately confines its residential services to a limited clientele. However, during its three healing services weekly in 1975 some 15,000 visitors received the laying-on-of-hands. Consequently its public relations officer, Ralph Stanbury, now sees the key need as the establishment of a network of parish groups, properly led and able to follow up the wider healing ministry of Burrswood and indeed of similar centres.

Another venture of this kind is St Christopher's Hospice.

St Christopher's is a Christian and medical foundation, caring for those in pain and suffering because of advanced cancer or other long-term illness. They are welcomed into a community planned for them where they can stay as long as they are in need. Its aim is to show the love of God for such people in skilled nursing, in using all that modern medicine has to offer to relieve distress and in seeking to understand and share the problems of those involved.[49]

It is an independent enterprise with two hallmarks: its Christian foundation and its caring community. The latter write of themselves: 'We believe that it is essential that these people [patients] should be welcomed into some kind of community that can complement as far as possible their own homes, while giving them the skilled and experienced attention they need.'[50]

In the case of Burrswood and St Christopher's specialist services and a trained staff are required. In other communities and networks where the emphasis is concentrated more on the contribution of worship and prayer to healing, there is greater opportunity for the layman to participate on an equal footing with the specialist. The Guild of Health, for example, since its foundation in 1904, has evolved as a network of some 300 local groups containing a total cross-section of interested people committed to restoring 'the healing ministry of Christ in His Church . . . [which] involves re-establishing a living relationship with God, with the community and within ourselves'.[51]

The ethos of the Guild within the Church's ministry of healing maintains a balance between:

(i) the approach through the sacramental life of the Church;
(ii) the revival of an understanding of the charismatic gifts;
(iii) the practice of counselling through prayer and care.

The Guild's ethos stresses three levels of healing:

(i) The supra-personal (or supernatural) – an open-ended relationship with God in Christ;
(ii) the personal approach – as God works through people either individually or in groups;
(iii) the impersonal level – as God and His people use things as instruments in healing.[52]

Over the years other bodies of a more specifically educational or co-ordinating nature, such as the Churches' Council for Health and Healing (1944) and the Institute of Religion and Medicine (1962) have been set up to encourage co-operation and improve pastoral skills.[53]

A concern for the healing ministry of the Church is incorporated in the life of certain other more focused communities where all members are regarded as playing an integral part. The Community of Celebration say of their ministry:

> There are no 'healing specialists' at Yeldall. Visitors seeking prayer for healing often attend the weekly praise and teaching meeting held in a local church, after which elders and other community members pray with them. The corporate life of the Community itself provides an environment of great healing power.[54]

On Iona each Tuesday evening during the main season, a healing service is held embracing three elements, 'the symbolic spiritual act, the hoped-for psychosomatic effect and the commitment of the worshippers to social action on behalf of those prayed for'.[55] At the appropriate moment during the service those seeking healing kneel in the chancel of the abbey; they are surrounded and hands are laid on them by as many of the congregation as possible, a moving demonstration of the corporate nature of the act. At the Christian Renewal Centre at Rostrevor in County Down, a similar ministry goes on, this time with informal groups laying hands on any who come, especially after the regular Monday evening gathering for praise and prayer. When I was there this took place in a quietly impressive, personal, and caring manner.

As an interesting aside I want here to move away from the matter of illness and healing to mention a kind of caring ministry trying to express itself through the encouragement of outdoor activities for those who are physically fit yet in some way socially disadvantaged. A small group called COPAS (Christian Outdoor Pursuits and Arts Scheme) has over the last three years run summer camps in Derbyshire and Cornwall for such young people, some also emotionally disturbed. These camps are recommended and sponsored by Social Service agencies in London and Birmingham.

The activities of the fellowship seek to stretch the young people

PHYSICALLY
with pursuits of an outdoor, adventurous nature;

MENTALLY
with involvement in the creative arts;

SOCIALLY
to become aware of other people's needs by sharing in a community life;

SPIRITUALLY

by giving thought to the deeper questions which a person's faith asks of life; not by structured activities, but simply by personal encounter with people who are committed to a personal faith in Christ.[56]

COPAS, though as yet in its infancy, seems to be reflective of a new concern to develop body, mind, and spirit as integral parts of a Christian yet non-directive caring ministry.

Mind

A host of counselling groups and centres has sprung up in recent years, committed to setting counselling in the context of caring Christian relationships and the fullness of life this can bring. The approach to therapy draws heavily on theory and practice not associated with specifically Christian beliefs, but the new techniques are increasingly being related to a Christian philosophy of life.

The Richmond Fellowship for Mental Welfare and Rehabilitation is included here, on the one hand, because it was founded in 1959 by Elly Jansen, a Dutch theological student, though she was highly critical of a religion which was 'too concerned with teaching people dogma and too little with teaching people about people';[57] and, on the other, because of its concentration on therapeutic communities, having some two dozen halfway houses specializing in after-care mainly for those who have been in mental institutions. There are houses for adolescents, for students, for ex-alcoholics and ex-drug users, for older people with a history of emotional disturbance, and even places where whole families can be helped to weather a crisis. The houses are staffed by experienced leaders whose aim is to provide a realistic situation in which members can be assisted, and can help one another, to understand themselves more fully and to find satisfaction through building up relationships and learning all over again the social skills and disciplines of work which they have lost, or never known.

The Richmond Fellowship draws on many modern therapeutic techniques, as do other centres more within the mainstream of Christian counselling. Particularly interesting in this connection is the steady development of the use of Transactional Analysis to facilitate counselling and pastoral work within the Church. As mentioned briefly in the previous chapter, Transactional Analysis (TA) originated with the work of Eric Berne and many believe it has considerable relevance to a

Church for so long dominated by the 'critical parent' image of God and thus by the whole issue of guilt. Recently Transactional Analysis has been pertinently applied to many aspects of Church life, but especially the pastoral.[58] For example, the Church of Scotland's Counselling, Development and Training Centre in Edinburgh, through Archie Mills and Jean Grigor, is very much concerned with applying TA to personal and parish life, viewing 'the total local congregation as the agent of pastoral care rather than seeing this function vested in one man, the minister. Thus the local congregation has the potential to become in a real sense at one level a "therapeutic community".'[59]

Two other centres exercising a similar ministry, this time in London, though in the case of the first trying to establish local counselling centres elsewhere in England, are the Westminster Pastoral Foundation (Methodist) under Bill Kyle; and the Dympna Centre (Roman Catholic), with a particular emphasis on religious problems, under Louis Marteau. The former states that the Foundation 'is a living statement by the Church that it is possible to exert a ministry, bringing together men and women in a mutual ministry established on the belief that man has a spiritual nature and is capable of transcendental experience';[60] whilst the latter writes that 'all true counselling should take into account the individual's Higher Values, and thus their religious commitments'.[61]

The Westminster Pastoral Foundation is now well-established and beginning to take initiatives outside London. It began in 1969 when Bill Kyle, a Methodist minister, was given the support of the Methodist Church to establish in the Central Hall at Westminster a broadly based counselling service. The idea was to provide counselling on a multi-disciplined basis, an approach already put into practice by Kyle through a counselling centre in Highgate (established in 1960 and still operating), which had proved to be of considerable help in ministering to the neighbourhood. The present Foundation seeks to blend the insights of religion and psychology and to integrate these insights in a living experience of counselling with individuals, couples, families, and groups.

A training programme runs in conjunction with the counselling service and there is opportunity for both part-time and full-time training through seminars, group and individual therapeutic experience, as well as through counselling under professional supervision. There are now a number of affiliated pastoral counselling centres in various parts of Britain, such as Newcastle and Redditch, and close links are maintained between the Foundation and the Institute of Religion and Health in the United States.

Numerous intentional communities already mentioned in previous chapters also offer personal pastoral support to the emotionally disturbed and insecure, notably Pilsdon, the Kingsway Community, Bystock Court, Alpha House, and L'Arche; as well as the Samaritans discussed more fully later.

Spirit

It is only a conceptual convenience to talk of the spiritual dimension of personal caring and growth under a distinct heading. As Paul Halmos has persuasively argued,[62] it is impossible to say if and how compassion ends and techniques start or the ministry to the body and mind finishes and that to the spirit begins. I include this heading simply to stress that in the attempt to enable others to find wholeness, there is a growing and explicit move towards acknowledging and exploring a spiritual dimension to life.

In the previous chapter I mentioned the increasing use made of *Gestalt* therapy in certain Christian communities and groups. This too is used in counselling, especially group counselling situations, by various organizations. The *Gestalt* view of life and relationships and its link with Christian spirituality is well expressed in Jean Lanier's '*Gestalt* Sermon from a Level Place', from which these few verses are taken:

> You are a new event. If you remain frozen in the past, you will lose your taste for life, and become predictable.
> What bores we can be, when we blame and complain!
> We are all adulterers. We all betray the one true marriage which is between ourselves and Life.
> Use your senses and stay rooted in the present. No man can be anxious while he is tasting an orange.
> The best communication is *yes* or *no*. All the rest is either elaboration or distraction.
> Your good deeds will be punished, if that is what you think you are doing.
> When we can include all that we see in others as parts of ourselves — both what we like and admire, and what we detest and deny — then we shall know something of what it means to be 'whole'.[63]

Likewise there is a growing literature linking re-evaluation counselling with the spiritual dimension of life. Concentrating here more on the element of personal development than, as previously, on the peer counselling aspect, I feel Audrey Shilling is worth quoting at some length. She writes:

As a Christian I find co-counselling to be a method which both supports and extends what I understand as Christian spirituality.... The theoretical basis is also consistent with Christian theology. Re-evaluation counselling assumes that the universe is a life-affirming, coherent, loving place, and that the task of human beings is to discover and realize in themselves the sources of live and creative energy which they are meant to possess. They are to do this, not by any means of escaping from what they are, but by recognizing the immense power of the constraints upon them, and feeling their impact to the full. At the same time the person sustains (and is helped by his counsellor to sustain) the hope that on the other side of the distress, and its accompanying distortions, lies the new person, the self that he is really intended to be.... The really hard work which is necessary if he is to conquer a 'distress pattern' will lead him, if he knows of them, to take comfort in the sorrows of Christ. At other times he will feel at one with the risen Christ in the new sense of joy and freedom. Repentance, trust, hope, and setting of the will towards the love of God, all these elements in traditional spirituality are given new and active expression where the method of co-counselling is practised by a Christian. He will be doing it alongside and with the help of others who are working for their growth without seeking in God the source of the love they seek, but he will find that his vision of the Kingdom is not so far removed from their aspirations towards a world which is based on the power of love.

The Christian may also find that as a result of his co-counselling experience his whole prayer becomes enriched. He will learn to come before God with a freshly discovered contact with the reality of his own feelings, which brings a new awareness to this as to all his activities....

The considerable popularity of the Growth Movement is an indication that many people who are serious in their desire for personal change no longer expect to find in the churches a spirituality which will enable them to achieve this. Co-counselling offers to those who can use it a radical spirituality which is consistent with Christian teaching, and also a means of communicating to others the values which the Christian learns, supremely, from Christ.[64]

The spiritual dimension of re-evaluation counselling is very much reflected in another growing counselling and therapeutic organization, the Clinical Theology Association. This was founded by Frank Lake, who served as a medical missionary in India and a medical superintendent of the teaching hospital at Vellore, and who on coming to England worked in the Health Service as a psychiatrist. His experience led him to the conviction that the clergy ought to be given access to psychiatric insights to help them both pastorally and personally. The interdisciplinary seminars which Frank Lake began in 1958 met with a welcoming response from clergy, and in many parts of the country groups came into being. The Clinical Theology Association itself was established in 1962 as an outcome of this early work. Its training methods have altered considerably in the past few years, now emphasizing experiential and growth aspects of learning and minimizing the didactic approach formerly used. For example, in 1976, groups were run on such themes as 'Personal Growth in the Small Group', 'Marriage Growth Group', 'Spiritual Direction: Catholic, Evangelical, Charismatic', and 'Body and Soul: Application of Bioenergetics and *Gestalt*'.[65]

The experience and expertise of its staff is now considerable and many thousands of people have so far attended its courses. Its work is based on a Christian theology initially embodied in the writings of Frank Lake,[66] but more recently an increasingly open-ended approach to its Christian thinking has been emerging. For example, in 1975, a note on a 'Christian Awareness Workshop' ran as follows:

> With the help of Christian forms of contemplative awareness and prayer drawn from the Eastern Orthodox as well as the Catholic tradition, together with suitable forms developed by other religious traditions, the group will begin to approach and explore the incommunicable experience which is the Vision of God.[67]

Comment

The importance of the communities and groups mentioned in this section of this chapter lies not only in their response to the particular crises people face, but in setting human problems in the context of health and wholeness as potential learning experiences. Though for convenience I have placed them under the three headings of body, mind, and spirit, one significant feature of nearly every group is that, in spite of special emphases, it is man as a totality they deal with. In no case is the Christian basis of their work pursued in a closed or sectarian way: there is a growing awareness of theoretical and therapeutic contributions of a non-religious kind and of the necessity of keeping counselling and group sessions open to those of any or no religious persuasion.

Yet one warning must be included: that, despite the recent appearance of the Association for Pastoral Care and Counselling as something of a co-ordinating body, the proliferation of too many groups in this field can lead to overlapping interests and waste of scarce resources. A divisive new professionalism, sometimes pseudo-professionalism, can take the place of a divisive old denominationalism, and an element of competition can creep in as each organization attempts to attract clients, extend its sphere of influence, and pursue its own 'line'. In fact, so little has been the readiness to co-operate between certain counselling groups and so little the effectiveness of bodies such as the Churches' Council for Health and Healing, that 'physician heal thyself' would not be a totally inappropriate comment. This situation is even more unfortunate when the Church already pays insufficient attention to such groups and rates their claims on institutional support so low. It seems that sooner rather than later a much more serious attempt to pool expertise and ideas and to rationalize resources must be made if the credibility of the Christian contribution in this field is to be sustained.

THE INTERPERSONAL DIMENSION

Having emphasized the need to see beyond immediate crises and preoccupation with disease to the necessity of facilitating individual autonomy as well as personal and social health and wholeness, I want to state emphatically that I fully recognize the alleviation of suffering and the ending of injustice in themselves as essential and continuing hallmarks of the Christian way of life. These have *not* become outmoded and anachronistic features of communal living. Indeed it is the deep caring work of many communities and groups, a caring which remains impatient even with a society that boasts a Welfare State, that gives point and legitimization to so much experimentation in community-making which might otherwise become narcissistic and parasitic.

Numerous intentional communities find that their own living together gives them a new insight into and empathy with those who come to them for help. Margaret Potts writes of St Julian's:

> Standing as we do in the midst of a wide network of personal relationships, we have discovered that the more we understand our own psychological make-up the more we can understand the hopes and fears and problems of those who come to us and the more we are able to give them the right kind of support.[68]

Others acknowledge how vital is the contribution to their own life and work of those for whom they care. Elizabeth Buckley of L'Arche, Inverness, repeatedly pays tribute to the joy and the fun, and indeed the insight that the more handicapped members give to the assistants and helpers. Thus both in giving and receiving, such groups as these are expressing something profound about our common humanity and the ability of every man to minister to his fellows.

Caring for the young

There are a number of Christian communities and groups which have sprung up in recent times to care for the young. Perhaps most significant has been work amongst homeless young people, especially those who have fallen victim to drugs.

Centrepoint is now well known to many people. It began at the end of 1969 in the basement of St Anne's House, Soho, to cater for young people at risk, especially those new to London. Its sponsorship is ecumenical and it has steadily developed first under the direction of Kenneth Leech and then of Bill Kirkpatrick, both priests of the Church of England. Currently, over 5,000 young people a year, mainly under seventeen years of age, are given shelter, and a dozen full-time staff are assisted by fifty volunteers. There is a short-stay hostel at Baron's Court which offers the possibility of more specialized help. The spirit of the work, also very relevant to the issues discussed in the first section of this chapter, is perhaps best summed up in Bill Kirkpatrick's report for 1974, in which he speaks of working for autonomy through caring:

> To love is to share unconditionally, to stretch out to the mystery that is the other person, and this in such a way that he can accept the mystery of his own existence. We all need to realize that effective caring only flows between persons who are not possessed by or

194

dominated by any authority, except that authentic authority of caring through sharing. Such authority encourages and assists us all to grow through the barrier of pain, be it physical, mental, or spiritual. The basic task of all caring personnel is to remain uniquely themselves for others, and insofar as we are released from fear, we shall together discover who we are. Every growth-enabling centre must evolve through the dignity of mutual concern.[69]

In many respects similar to the work of Centrepoint is that of St Basil's Centre (known better as The Boot) in central Birmingham, under the wardenship of another Anglican priest, Les Milner. The Boot is basically a night shelter for homeless young men, situated in a church hall in a dingy, highly industrialized part of the city. It began operations as such in 1972 and through many ups and downs has more recently been able to expand its work through the establishment of a boys' hostel and a girls' hostel, detached youth work notably amongst West Indians, and an advice kiosk in the Bull Ring shopping centre. The staff estimate that each year they work with some thousand young people in need.

One problem with The Boot night-shelter work has been that of gaining a balance between the community of young homeless and the community of the staff. At one point, allowing the young people to stay too long threatened to destroy the control of the more fluid staff group, working on a rota basis and with part-time volunteers. After a period of reappraisal, Les Milner was able to report:

The community that seems to be growing is the community of the staff, most of whom live in different houses in different parts of the city and yet have a common concern and common life around people who use the Night Shelter but whose life is not dominated by it.

If there is one kind of model which seems to describe the Night Shelter and its work and the relationships within it, it is the one of the family in which the staff are seen as elder brothers and sisters, aunts and uncles, mothers and fathers. As in any family that is working reasonably well there is an enormous amount of communication between 'parents', and this is known by the 'children' and known to be (however unpopular) in their interests, so that the Night Shelter seems to function.[70]

Working more specifically with the young drug addict, though Centrepoint and The Boot deal with many such, is Alpha House, discussed at the outset of this chapter, and, with a widely publicized

Christian aspect to its activities, the New Life Foundation founded by Vic Ramsey. Currently the latter has two community houses in England: the Red House at Kelham, near Newark, which is the main rehabilitation centre; and Vermont House in London which acts as a kind of halfway house for young adults from Kelham moving back into the city scene. The enterprise is founded on the assumption that full and effective treatment at some stage demands an explicit commitment from the young person to Christ, Vic Ramsey being quoted as saying that 'Christ is the only cure for drug addiction and alcoholism'.[71] Testimonies of residents who have become Christians whilst receiving treatment are regularly printed in publicity literature.

An organization of very similar style to the New Life Foundation is the Pye Barn Trust which at present has two houses, one in Clapham and one in Chiswick, accommodating some seventeen residents. John Harris, its house director, writes:

> We are motivated by our love for the Lord Jesus Christ to help young people with all kinds of problems, e.g. drug addiction, alcoholism, relationship problems, etc. We live as a community, sharing in all things and we aim to help those in our care to be able to once again take their place in society. The young people who come to live here are referred to us from Probation Services, Social Services, Voluntary Agencies, etc. Some of them stay with us for longer periods, depending on their particular needs.[72]

Other Christian communities also have their share of younger people in need passing through, some on drugs; in particular, Pilsdon and the Kingsway Community. From time to time Christian groups have also been active in catering for young people drifting out of the cities to find friendship and festivity, as with the summer Greenbus camp at Glastonbury from 1972 to 1975;[73] a project in 1974 in the Vicarage Centre at St Ives, Cornwall; and tent-based work in connection with several major pop festivals in recent years.[74]

One other notable service to young people has already been touched on, that of Corrymeela to children and adolescents mainly from Belfast. Alf McCreary describes how over the years the Ballycastle centre has been used again and again to respond to acute crises, including the occasional call for urgent evacuation of children from violent areas. He continues:

> The different strands of youth work come to a climax each summer

196

at Corrymeela and beyond. The many projects include holidays for handicapped and subnormal children, for small groups of special-care Protestant and Catholic children, and joint projects in the cities. A large number of volunteers are always needed to maintain and organize these activities, and Corrymeela depends greatly on young people from home and abroad.[75]

Commenting on the overall attitude to the work, he says:

There is no preaching or sermonizing or slickly presented philosophy. Corrymeela tries to speak for itself. Perhaps one of the reasons why it speaks and has spoken eloquently yet quietly to all sorts of people, is its basic foundation. And that foundation is its interpretation of Christianity. The theory and the practice of Corrymeela are totally interrelated.[76]

Caring for adults

The Church as a whole is engaged in an immense amount of caring for people in need, young and old, Christian and non-Christian, a fact which at this time, when it is being written off by many as anachronistic or redundant, should be taken extremely seriously. A great deal of this caring is focused on the obvious, yet still important, requirements of the young wife, the young mother and her child, and the elderly. Such needs are being met first and foremost in the local situation, but also through now well-established institutions such as homes for the aged. Though my main interest in this book is with the more intensive and extensive communal aspects of caring emerging in recent times, I want again to emphasize that this is not in any way to devalue much of the day-to-day social and pastoral work of the Church in the parish context.

There is a steadily growing number of communities and centres where those in need live and work alongside a core group of helpers, more intimately in some communities than in others but always in a mutually open and accepting manner. I have drawn attention to some of these in earlier chapters, but there are those communities whose especial *raison d'être* lies in this field.

Such a place is Pilsdon, though Percy Smith is clear as to 'what Pilsdon is not': 'It is not a rest home for aged and lonely people. Nor is it an annexe to a mental hospital. Every day we have to reply, with as much sympathy as we can, to many letters, saying that Pilsdon exists for an entirely different purpose.'[77] That purpose is the establishment of 'a religious community of a rather unusual kind', inspired by the example of Nicholas Ferrar's seventeenth-century family settlement at Little Gidding, 'where people are bound together in a relationship of work and voluntary prayer'.[78] Very much a part of this community of some thirty people in all are

> unmarried mothers with their children, husbands or wives whose marriages have broken up and men and women suffering from overstrain (who) may find in community a temporary retreat from the pressures of ordinary life. . . . [At Pilsdon] many who are defeated in the outside world are able to cope with the demands of life in what may be called 'a supportive, protective environment'.[79]

And at the heart of this ministry lies acceptance, as Percy Smith writes in one of his open letters:

> Thus we go on learning to 'accept' ourselves and one another, pooling our strengths and weaknesses, giving and receiving forgiveness, sometimes exasperated, sometimes slow to understand, but always helped by life in community, lived with a common purpose.[80]

Perhaps the words of a girl on heroin before she went to Pilsdon can give substance to these sentiments:

> Here I can start again. No one knows the things I've done in the past and the distrustful, lonely, rebellious young girl who came here a few weeks ago is changing. I still crave like hell, but I'm taking a chance. Like every addict, I still don't want to give up junk, but I will try because I want to live. When I leave here I can go forward or back, who knows. I hope it's forward, but if it's so it's mostly Pilsdon that's done this for me. Pilsdon is a home. A refuge when there's nowhere else. The people here don't judge. We work, we laugh, we all have our hang-ups, but we have them together. We are a community. We understand each other. We'll come through together. Yes, Pilsdon is a way of life – the best of life. It works and these are the words of a person who never would have thought it possible. I still can't believe it – I still don't know what the end will be, but if I fail it won't be through any fault of Pilsdon.[81]

Bystock Court is another such place, purchased in 1965 to provide a temporary home for women at a point of crisis in married life. Alastair Jamieson writes:

From the start ... mothers undergoing some form of marriage breakdown, or the unmarried mum or the prisoner's wife sought shelter with us. Conversion of the smaller rooms at the northern end of the house into units for mothers with children was the first task to be tackled. It seemed essential to give the broken family quarters of its own to enable the children to retain what was left of the family entity. Complete absorption into the larger community would, it was felt, be too disturbing for the children. Nine units were gradually formed comprising a combined kitchen/living room with one or more bedrooms as might be needed. During the week, community lunch is the only meal taken together but morning coffee, an afternoon cup of tea and coffee after Evening Prayers are the times when everyone meets together. The TV and quiet rooms bring the Community together as well as the swimming pool and outings to the beach and other places. We have up to six single men and women who use the house as a halfway home back to face life again after marital breakdowns, family rejections or convalescence. As a matter of policy it has been decided to restrict the number of guests to fifteen, plus children. It is recognized that should the numbers increase then the enlarged family concept would be lost and an institution formed. This small number would not be economic if salaries were paid to the staff. As it is, all work is done voluntarily and even the staff have paid for their accommodation up to the present. The guiding principle throughout is how would the normal Christian family behave.[82]

The intention of the staff group, some half-dozen people, all resident but some working full-time and some part-time at the Court, is to provide an ever-present support and ready ear for those in distress. Alastair Jamieson believes that the social worker's availability and often experience are inadequate to meet the needs of such women as Bystock cares for, needs which may be critical late at night or at weekends when professional help is almost impossible to obtain. He is convinced too that real therapy comes from being near enough to people over a long period to build trust and hope. Perhaps the ethos of Bystock Court is best summed up in the words one sees, when entering the house, in a frame on the far wall:

And the Lord said
'Behold I have set aside this house, and have blessed it,
That it may become a resting place
And a refuge for the weary.

Peace is to be found within its walls,
And friendship,
All who cross the threshold shall find welcome,
And a comforting hand to give fresh courage
In place of dark despair.
In this house shall My Name be glorified,
For that which is shattered
Shall be made whole.'[83]

The Kingsway Community began in the mid-1960s as an attempt to provide a friendly and tolerant group, based on essentially Christian principles, which was open to the disadvantaged, the dispossessed, and the drug addict. Their main work was centred on a somewhat dilapidated house in Chiswick and throughout, despite an attempt to structure the life of the community, there has been little planned policy or development except for certain limitations on who should join, for example on the proportion of drug addicts taken in. The community, now also with a centre at Keveral Farm in Cornwall, has struggled on through many difficulties, its main continuing thread being the presence of David Horn, his wife, and a handful of other people prepared to stick at the vision and the work. Despite all the setbacks, internal and external, there has been established at least some form of 'home' for many who would have totally rejected statutory or institutional provision. Its very fluidity, though causing great problems, has also offered a chance for some to penetrate a group within which they have tentatively been able to build some creative style of life.[84]

Another venture combining living together and caring is L'Arche, with its homes for the mentally retarded, referred to earlier in this chapter. I here want to stress the open and accepting nature of their communities, and the quality of loving concern that is expressed through them, a concern well summed up by Elizabeth Buckley:

In each L'Arche community are people who by their lives try to bridge the gulf, to surmount the barriers that keep men apart: the gulf of the intellectually gifted and non-gifted, of differing backgrounds, of differing religious beliefs or non-beliefs, the barriers erected by egoism, false values, fears – all that stands in the way of meeting one another in truth, justice, and peace. It is a day-by-day attempt through the common ordinary things of life – meals, work, play, prayer – to bring support and love a little more deeply into the world, so that no one may feel no one cares. It is supporting, caring and sustaining of each other through troubles and wounds.[85]

Similar to L'Arche, though this time dealing more with the homeless than the mentally retarded as such, are those groups and networks like the St Mungo Community, the Simon Community, and the Cyrenians, together with more locally based groups such as the Exeter Shilay Community. The Cyrenian communities are generally arranged on a three-tier system, with the first-tier accommodation offered in rough and ready overnight shelters, second-tier houses where it is hoped to provide a stable but unpressurized environment, and third-tier houses for those who seem likely to need an accepting house indefinitely. A self-sufficient fourth tier is under consideration, with no person being in the conventional worker role. The houses themselves usually contain some dozen residents together with a team of four workers, mainly young people over eighteen, who live in for a period of between six months and a year.

A worker's day will consist of many household chores; answering the telephone, driving the vehicle, helping an alcoholic to his clinic, visiting the hospital, settling tensions in the house and answering the door to those requesting food packs or a bed for the night. And, since he lives on the premises, the day is not necessarily over on going to bed – for even when he flops on his mattress at 1.00 a.m. he may have to listen to the man next to him; some individual who has remained reclusive for weeks, but who suddenly blurts out his life story.[86]

Tom Gifford, now designated Consultant to the Cyrenians, writes that 'the emphasis is on "community" rather than "hostel", on reducing barriers so that it is no longer "us" helping "them", on living together'.[87] Many men, socially very disoriented, have been given the first glimmer of hope through the Cyrenians and, in that context, it is worth noting Chris Blackwell's comment:

It is a principle of the Cyrenians that it derives from Christian inspiration. This is not merely a historical statement relating to the fact that the Cyrenian movement was founded largely by Christians. It also affirms that in the ongoing thinking-through of Cyrenian philosophy Christian theology has a vital contribution to make.[88]

There are other important projects where the core team and those cared-for work closely together but do not actually live on the same

201

premises: for example, at Community House, Glasgow, founded by the Iona Community as an expression of their concern for the inner city. Though a number of the staff, including the warden, live in, there is no permanent hostel accommodation for the homeless. The House, however, is a veritable hive of activity, some eighty organizations using the building at some time or other. Amongst other groups meeting regularly there in 1975 were Alcoholics Anonymous, Gamblers Anonymous, Agoraphobia, Glasgow Blind Association, One-Parent Friendship Group and Community Playschemes. There is a restaurant (where young people from community industry work), a lounge and a thrift-shop. The Glasgow homeless use the premises a great deal during the day, and the House believes it has a special duty to exercise a caring ministry to the many severely underprivileged people in and around the area.

At quite the other end of the scale in terms of location, size, and ethos is Llanerchwen, an eight-acre hill property just north of Brecon. In 1970 David Shapland and his family came to live there, together with a friend, an unmarried woman who occupied a cottage nearby. Another bungalow was built and was made available for the use of visitors seeking help or needing rest and quiet. An old cowshed became an oratory, a pigsty a study, part of the land was let to a local farmer, and the rest has been developed in keeping with the surrounding countryside.

> Over 200 people now visit Llanerchwen each year. Some just for the day but most to stay for a matter of days or longer. They come as individuals, or in family or other groups. They come from any religious tradition or none at all, and from all walks of life. A steady number of those who come are members of the helping professions – doctors and therapists, clergy and teachers. Their initial reasons for coming are equally diverse – for rest or retreat, for talk and discussion on both immediate and enduring issues, for help with spiritual, marital and other personal problems.[89]

One visitor typical of many writes:

> Here one can learn to *be* – something that just doesn't happen overnight; it can be a long and devastating struggle, but each hurdle can be faced by a wonderful compassionate loving. There is no being pushed into a corner by dogmatic statements, no feeling of drowning, just a gentle drawing into the reality of life. Llanerchwen is the grace

of God being shown forth in love, reaching out to all who come with their various needs.[90]

The 'open house' does not have to be a massive building in the heart of Glasgow or a small cottage in the hills of South Wales. It can also be in the midst of the unexceptional urban housing estate. As just one example, Jack Orr of the Iona Community writes of the work of street groups he initiated on a corporation housing scheme in Edinburgh. His aim was to enable the local church to be indigenous and not clergy-centred and, to this end, he writes:

I set about forming groups of interested people (church and non-church) in each street of the new scheme. Within a year some twelve street groups meeting monthly in houses were discussing, planning and taking action at various levels for the new community. For five years these street groups continued to meet, but still dependent to some extent on my organization and leadership.

Thereafter a smaller number of house groups came into being, but now completely autonomous and showing a new quality of initiative and leadership. Over the succeeding years these house groups (from three to six in number) have met fortnightly with no overall pattern or direction, some changing more than others in composition and form.

I would claim that the contribution and influence of these groups both in the community and in the church has been out of all proportion to the number of people involved at any time in them. Out of the street group meetings of the first five years came a concern for the welfare of the community expressed in working for the provision of local amenities, such as, for example, bus shelters and a local Post Office, and later a youth and community centre; and in providing for playgroups, clubs, etc., for young and old. Out of the later house church groups has come commitment and action at a deeper level for such things as War on Want, healing, Christian teaching, ecumenical progress, etc.; and conducting and leading the worship of the community in many different ways.[91]

Jack Orr's experience is being constantly repeated wherever Christians open their homes to enable groups to gather and engender that social energy vital to a lively community.[92] It is found that the house (sometimes an unoccupied one specially set aside for communal use) is often a far more conducive meeting place than the larger and more impersonal community centre.

In south Birmingham, Shenley House also worked along these lines.[93] Originally a manse owned by the Methodist Church, it became unoccupied as such and the circuit opened it up to a group of young people, at one point seven in number, who lived there and in one way and another sought to give time and energy to the needs of the surrounding estate. In 1973 a more formulated project was set up under the leadership of Joe Hasler, a full-time community worker, and his wife, Joy, who helped establish a number of useful and lively community groups in the surrounding neighbourhood. Despite differing views concerning the primary object of the exercise, those involved agree that the venture went a good way to encouraging a lively Christian presence in and social concern for the kind of area notoriously apathetic to normal church-based initiatives.

In addition to these caring activities of a more locally based and focused kind there is an increasing number of wider networks with which Christians have been closely associated: here I mention only the well-known telephone Samaritans. The Samaritans, founded in 1953 by a priest, Chad Varah, offer a telephone help service for the lonely, despairing, and suicidal, manned by unpaid volunteers, and available twenty-four hours a day all the year round. Keith Kimber spells out the parallels between the Samaritans, Christian in origin and pastoral in style yet firmly non-religious and non-partisan in approach, and the para-church. He writes:

Firstly there is the sense of mission, centred in the other person who calls. Then there is the fundamental principle of respect and acceptance, in which the other is encountered. There is the sense of unity in a local and universal community, an awareness of diversity of gifts and skills, and structures of leadership and responsibility (director, leader, member, helper). There is a sense of lay (as opposed to expert) participation in mission, the mutuality of the sharing, the commitment to growth in excellence, the diversity of the members' origins in outside society, and the practical (moral) rather than ideological basis of membership. (He who does the truth as opposed to talking about it.) What of the 'spiritual' and liturgical signs of the Church? Comparisons have been drawn between waiting upon God in contemplation and being on duty, or on call, waiting in readiness for someone to ring up. One shift follows another in succession, so that the vigil of waiting goes on. One volunteer can only experience a part of the whole enterprise at any time and yet the wholeness of the work goes on, just as with the activity of prayer and worship. Some Samaritans have said that they often experienced waiting and listening prayerfully – presumably because it is an act of outgoing loving concern, a beginning of experiencing God in the Other.

These signs may not be very adequate signs for some people; but are 'spiritual' and liturgical signs of the Church necessarily exclusive criteria of the authentic presence of the Church? The Samaritans are also truly ecumenical, in that they include Christians and non-Christians alike.[94]

Reconciliation

Many of the communities, groups, and networks I have described are not only involved in a ministry of caring, in acceptance and validation of individuals in deep personal need, but in the work of reconciliation. Wherever social barriers are crossed and anger and resentment and fear ended, there reconciliation occurs. So much of caring involves helping people to overcome their alienation from life, from society, and from themselves. Yet there remain one or two Christian communities and organizations especially dedicated to the work of reconciliation.

Before dealing with those engaged in rather more obvious fields of reconciliation, I include here a relatively small venture called the Six Circle Group.[95] It has been operating since 1970 and is interesting as a move towards breaking down barriers by 'twinning' groups of isolated people: in this case young offenders with the physically and mentally handicapped. Every year the Six Circle Group organizes camps (in 1975 on the island of Iona), which through a wide variety of activities enable the two groups, so far some ninety people in all, to mix freely with each other. The belief is, and has been borne out, that every individual has something to give to his fellow regardless of the severity of his problem. In 1975, as I mingled with the Six Circle Group on the Iona Community's weekly pilgrimage round the island, I could certainly bear witness to this, and not least to the fact that both groups were giving to visitors quite apart from each other.

One criterion of the choice of communities and groups covered in this book is that they have a positive orientation towards ecumenicity in its fullest sense. A place where this is no mere gesture of goodwill is of course Northern Ireland: for here to go ecumenical is really to risk much for the sake of the Gospel. Many groups, of many theological views,[96] are courageously involved in just such work and to describe one or two is not in any way to forget the efforts of those who perhaps dare not advertise their activities widely.

I have already referred numerous times to the work of the Corrymeela Community: I make no apology for doing so again, for, relatively small as it is, it remains a symbol of hope for many inside and outside Ireland. Their overall intention is clearly spelt out in a notice in the entrance hall of their Ballycastle House:

> Corrymeela is a Christian community believing itself to be 'called together as a community to be an instrument of God's peace, to serve our society, and to share in the life of the Church'. The community is committed to the work of reconciliation, in Ireland and beyond, to healing many breaches – social, religious, and political – which exist in Northern Ireland and throughout the world.

Corrymeela's work of reconciliation takes place on many fronts; as they would be the first to admit, sometimes with more success than others. There are the Corrymeela Encounter Projects and other conferences, the work camps and the children's holiday projects. Especially significant, however, are the family weeks, times of encounter for Catholic and Protestant families together, coming from very troubled areas or otherwise stressful backgrounds, and many of whom have lost husbands or sons in the recent violence. In September 1975, Mathilde Shär, the Corrymeela Secretary, cycled through dangerous parts of Belfast visiting twenty-four Catholic and Protestant homes to offer the hospitality of the Ballycastle House to those recently bereaved. The response to such invitations is limited, for many fear to leave their own homes, but the work of reconciliation still goes on.

Others in Northern Ireland are also offering this kind of ministry, within their own neighbourhoods and beyond, Roman Catholic and Protestant, and neither. Some work to encourage ecumenical meetings of a more religious kind, as with the Christian Renewal Centre at Rostrevor and with the small charismatic cells in numerous places. Others see reconciliation more as the consequence of corporate involvement in caring projects, such as the many summer holiday playschemes for children and the attempt of the Shankill Road Methodist Team Ministry to set up a community house as a base for neighbourhood service. In the Republic, the recently established Glencree Centre described in the previous chapter, not to mention the many groups in England, Wales, and Scotland who have given hospitality to Northern Irish children, all represent caring communities of significance.

So far I have made little reference to caring and reconciliation in the field of race relations. This is in fact because, outside of the work of the boards and committees of the main religious bodies (for example, the active Friends' Community Relations Committee), there is a very limited amount of genuinely interfaith activity. The black community has, on its side, its own style of religious practice and worship and is seeking, though with increasing difficulty, to retain its own cultural identity. The latter is generally much more family-oriented and close-knit than that of white Britain which has long since moved to a more mobile and individualistic way of life. There is, therefore, no great need or desire at this stage for black people to become involved in the sort of community-making ventures described in this book, though whether this will remain true as our society becomes increasingly cosmopolitan is anyone's guess. It may yet be the case, as a West Midlands ditty goes, that 'we will soon be able to tell a Brummy by the shamrock in his turban'!

That day is not yet here, however, and in the meantime a limited number of Christian people are involved in attempting to break down prejudice through experiencing and talking about the nature of cultures other than their own. One example of this is the Wolverhampton Interfaith Group, some twenty people from various races and faiths who for over two years have met monthly 'to encourage and promote understanding between the peoples of Wolverhampton whatever their religious tradition'.[97] The group works along the lines of both education and action. Tony Holden writes:

Since we are a religious group and not solely concerned with community relations, we try to develop interfaith dialogue. We meet in each other's centres and we have people speak about their faith. We had a 'bus-crawl' when we visited five centres: to stand with people of other faiths in a town-centre Anglican church and listen to the organ, to see the glitter of a Hindu temple, and the austerity of a Muslim mosque, to sit on the floor of a Sikh gurdwara, with men and women separated and with shoes off and heads covered, to share in silent worship at a Friends Meeting House, was to begin to be on the inside of religions. The speakers have added to this experience. We have heard a Christian talk about Easter, Sikhs explain their different groups' emphases, Sikhs and Hindus speak of their common festival of Basakhi, and a West Indian New Testament Church of God pastor lead us in a 'militant' act of Christian worship. We hope (in 1976) to help the Town Art Gallery put on an exhibition on the theme 'People and Faiths in our Town'.[98]

On the action side, members of the group have become involved in issues concerning homeless West Indians, the teaching of 'other' religions in RE in schools, and the need for local government plans to give proper attention to providing places of worship for minorities. The group is aware of the limited nature of its work, yet, within the realm of the possible, it is at least 'pointing the way and giving a sign'.[99]

Reconciliation on the international scene is really beyond the scope of this book. Yet I wish to emphasize that many communities and groups are very much aware of this dimension of concern, in their spirituality, in their ecological and economic interest, in their educational work, and in their caring. For example, a good number are active catalysts and stimulators with regard to promoting members' and visitors' consciences concerning the needs of the Third World.

With a more specific commitment for working towards international understanding and peace from a communal base, two kinds of group or network seem to exist. There are those involved in promoting the interchange of personnel, mutually to widen experience or offer service. Such a network is Servas, begun in 1949 as a movement called Peace Builders, to create 'a system of world-wide hospitality for travelling, open-minded, serious young people – a system of "bridges" between families and little groups that are kinds of oases of new life'.[100] The aim was to resist an expensive exchange service or to arrange this only as a tourist attraction. Instead, travellers were offered hospitality in the homes of the host community in exchange for the visitor communicating as much as possible about himself and his own country. Times have changed and the movement is reappraising how to match open homes with really deserving and interested travellers; but a great deal of good work has already been done to widen cultural horizons. Several other Christian organizations, with Christians Abroad playing a co-ordinating role, are providing job opportunities for young people willing to work overseas for periods of a year or two, in order to experience other countries at first hand. Notable among them is the Catholic Institute for International Relations. Major changes are afoot, however, with Third World countries amongst others taking only well-qualified personnel, especially those who can teach a skill rather than simply practise it. There is increasing concern that those who go overseas for short periods should first have community work experience at home; and the very concept of 'volunteer' is being questioned (their allowance often being greater than the pay of those with whom they work).

The other aspect of work to do with reconciliation concerns those groups and networks dedicated to the cause of international peace and the alleviation of persecution. The former include bodies such as the Fellowship of Reconciliation, the Iona Community, Pax Christi, and the London School of Non-Violence with which Christian Action has close associations. Concerned with unjust persecution is Amnesty International which began in Britain in 1961 as a one-year campaign. Its aim is to work for the release of men and women imprisoned because of their political, religious, or other conscientiously held beliefs, or because of their colour, language, or ethnic origin; provided they have neither used nor advocate violence. It opposes the death penalty and the torture or otherwise cruel, inhuman, or degrading punishment for all prisoners. It now has a membership of 3,000 in Britain (of more than 70,000 throughout the world) where there are over 130 so-called 'adoption groups' which work directly for the release of prisoners and for the relief of their families.

DIFFICULTIES

In a great deal of what has gone before I have attempted to draw attention to the very positive efforts of communities and groups to develop a form of caring which both met crises and enabled those helped to work towards the development of autonomy. I have stressed the depth of concern, the intensity of commitment, and the patient perseverance of many people in giving expression to their Christian convictions. It is 'good news' – and it rightly fills the bulk of this chapter. But there is also the 'bad news' – the great difficulties which those who dedicate themselves to the work of caring and reconciliation face, and which cannot be glossed over. I touch on some of these problems here in no sense of carping judgement on those giving of their time and energy so splendidly, but simply to point out difficulties, attention to which may help to make those committed more effective in their endeavours and those of us sitting comfortably on the sidelines more ready to get our hands dirty.

One major problem which caring communities in particular face is the considerable confusion of objectives and thus of roles. A number of groups set out both to live together, with a close-knit communal life-style, as well as to undertake a demanding programme of service to others, either as individuals (sometimes through full-time paid work) or as a whole group. They find it extremely tough going to sustain both. The Blackheath Commune found themselves increasingly impotent in the local neighbourhood and compelled to concentrate on keeping the community itself going, especially as needy visitors came for longer periods than expected. The venture lasted three years. The Bridge Community in East London[101] hardly got off the ground, amongst other reasons because the irregular working hours of the residents, some involved in social work, meant little choice to meet as a group during the week. Shenley House in Birmingham encountered similar problems, with some of its members able to give time to both the life of the House and the local community, others in their work and interests gradually being drawn away from both. The demands on Cyrenian workers (and others living with the homeless) are so great as to make the attempt to move from the hostel to community a very difficult one. It seems, in fact, that it is very hard to combine in one place a very demanding corporate caring (as opposed, for example, to teaching) ministry with a demanding form of communal living; the one or the other tends to lose out.

The most viable pattern seems to be, on the one hand, an intentional community which either gives itself over to a caring ministry 'in spurts', as some groups have given over a fortnight or a month to offer hospitality to children from Northern Ireland; or to 'sending out' its members to undertake their work of caring away from 'the mother house' as, for example, the Anglican Society of St Francis which has established a small group of brothers working just off the Shankill Road in Belfast. In a much more limited way the Iona Community also works along these lines. On the other hand, a group can combine intensively on a common task, as for example in the healing work at Burrswood or the social work at Community House, Glasgow, without themselves attempting to live communally in any very intimate manner. Where an intensive community life and an intensive caring ministry do go together, as with the Cyrenian houses, staff tend to stay for relatively short periods. Yet there are remarkable exceptions. A number of religious Orders succeed in combining this type of life and work and, amongst the basic communities I am concerned with in this book,

Pilsdon and L'Arche are outstanding. But I think these exceptions only go to prove the general rule.

One reason why problems arise when caring for others and residential community life are combined is that caring is a very exhausting business, however dedicated one may be. Those working at Corrymeela, and indeed over this side of the Irish Sea, speak of the great strain, even for short periods, of living with disoriented youngsters from the streets of Belfast, suddenly let loose in strange surroundings. A leading figure in the Religious Broadcasting for Schools Unit of the BBC, whom I met one summer on Iona, had beaten a hasty retreat from the Ballycastle House after only a couple of days, being unable to stand the din and the smell. Those working with the homeless and the alcoholic could offer similar experiences. At Bystock Court it is not only the mothers and families which consume energy, but the maintenance of the huge, rambling premises. At Centrepoint and The Boot, caring demands both day and night shifts. Furthermore, there are those with whom even the most stable communities know they cannot cope. Percy Smith of Pilsdon states quite honestly: 'There are some people whom we are not geared to help.'[102] Where such people are allowed in, as the Kingsway Community soon found out, life becomes intolerable for everyone.

Another difficulty is the quite straightforward one of lack of adequate resources, in staff or helpers, money and time (of course all interlinked). Many communities and groups depend on people free to help and with a vocation so to do; they are hard to come by. Whether it is staffing Centrepoint or the Cyrenian houses, finding informed people to take an active interest in Community Health Councils or volunteers for Good Neighbour Schemes, there is always a great shortage of reliable, committed helpers. And in particular the cry for the assistance of those with Christian convictions still goes out. In 1975 Alister Green wrote of Community House, Glasgow:

It is ironic that, as the ministry in the House develops, no member of the [Iona] Community serves on the House staff. It is sad indeed that so few members of the Community play any real part in the continuing life and ministry of the House. No more than one swallow makes a summer does one Daffodil Fair or one Thrift Shop contribution mean involvement or commitment.[103]

And it goes without saying that in times of severe inflation it is the sort of ventures I am concerned with that feel the pinch first.

The disadvantage of basic communities which rely so heavily on those committed by vocation, tested and untested, to their work is that adequate expertise and experience are often missing. The very attraction of the peer emphasis in re-evaluation counselling, for example, can have its own hazards if adequate professional supervision is not exercised at some point. The Cyrenians have to operate with workers often too young and too inexperienced to make up very stable core groups in each house: so much so that it is said by some that it is the homeless who minister to the workers! Of course many people naturally join communities not only to serve but to have their own needs more effectively met, a fact which can create difficulties when, for example, the desire for greater intimacy overwhelms the mature relationship required for creative caring.

The most crucial issue for my part, however, is how meeting crises and alleviating distress can be integrated with working for the autonomy of the individual, the twin aims of the caring ministry mentioned at the outset of this chapter. It is so often taken for granted that caring means immediately removing the cause of distress or giving unconditional help, and indeed this is sometimes the only thing one can do. But it is forgotten that autonomy can only be realized by an individual for himself, and thus it is vitally important *how* distress is eased and *how* we offer assistance. There are two extremes here, neither of which is an adequate way forward.

One is the way of caring within a context which overtly or subtly directs the person cared for to respond in a predetermined way, not least in a predetermined religious way. There was a hint of this in the earlier approach of the Clinical Theology Movement and it still remains in such groups as the New Life Foundation and the Pye Barn Trust. The other extreme is to believe that one can help people most by offering help within an unstructured or poorly organized context; groups operating towards this end of the scale would seem to be the Student Christian Movement as *movement* and the Kingsway Community. It is of course extremely difficult to get the right balance between direction and non-direction, structure and flexibility, but it remains essential if the person in need is not to be manipulated on the one hand, or allowed to flounder helplessly on the other. A basic requirement for any caring community or group to achieve this balance is to give adequate time to examining with honesty, and perhaps professional assistance, the nature and implications of its philosophy, objectives, and methods; too many are too busy for too long to appreciate this.

Achieving a balance between direction and non-direction is also a risky business, for it must be achieved for the sake of the cared-for and not the carer. It is to allow the former sufficient security to grow yet not so much support and guidance as to cramp or determine the nature and direction of that growth. Mary Charbonneau of the L'Arche house in Ottawa puts this point well:

> When a community grows to the point where the assistants in a sense overwhelm the handicapped person, then that person feels no particular need to accomplish a task; he may, in fact, be afraid to try because of the threat that comes from the greater ability of the assistant.

> Assistants and directors are called to provide the proper secure environment for our residents, so that they — and many of them have spent long years in hospitals — may feel safe enough to voice an opinion or a desire. It is also our responsibility to help them discover what these desires and choices could be, and to help encourage the self-reliance they will need to voice these.

> How prepared are we to take the risk that possibly some of our residents might turn against the values we have chosen and are trying to share, never to return? They may, on the other hand, return with an even deeper conviction, as this will have been their choice, not ours.[104]

Even then, however, the questions do not end, for all caring communities are part of a wider society and have to measure their endeavours against external norms. If they take these norms for granted or never enable those for whom they care to challenge them, then they are open to the criticism of being merely agents of social containment and social control.

On the one hand, they can be seen as conditioning those whom they serve to fit in with an unjust society, a society (wherein the Church remains a pillar of the Establishment) which in the end will keep them in a state of immature dependence. For example, the highly disciplined approach of Alpha House, like the public-school régime of the last century, could quite easily turn out good but over-conforming citizens. Many of the groups and centres working in the welfare field forget that healthy people ask searching questions about life. The negating of critical awareness is also a danger when lively initiatives become institutionalized. An appointment of a full-time Good Neighbour

Scheme liaison officer by a local authority or of full-time secretaries to Community Health Councils could be major steps in the right direction or withdrawal from the concept of community care in favour of institutionalized and easily controllable provision.

On the other hand, caring communities can be accused of removing from society the task of taking genuine responsibility for the disadvantaged and the distressed, as the Cyrenians believe is the danger in their work. The weakness in particular of Christian ventures in caring is that attention is so focused on the individual in need (as with the homeless, the drug user, the potential suicide case, or those in less dramatic need served by Good Neighbour Schemes) that little attention is given to pressing for social and political reforms to make such work less necessary. It is a feature of caring groups sponsored by or associated with the Church that they are rarely found taking a strong line in the name of social reform, at national but particularly at local level. Perhaps the problem is highlighted, though not solved, by the situation in Northern Ireland, where groups exercising a powerful caring ministry have been criticized for being politically soft and even impotent.

Part of the dilemma is not too hard to spot, for as soon as a strong political leaning emerges in caring groups, above all towards the political left, as in the case of the Student Christian Movement or of Community House, Glasgow (and indeed as in the earlier days of the Iona Community under George MacLeod), the institutional Church is quick to see a potential threat to the *status quo* and seeks to avert it either by open disapproval or by the quiet withdrawal of support and a policy of isolating the offending part. Nor need the 'offence' be political, as the ostracism of the divorced Christian or of the Christian homosexual, and disapproval of the mixed marriage, show.

Those working in the field of alternative welfare and caring provision thus walk the tight-rope between becoming so much a part of the Establishment, of State or Church, that they are gradually moulded by and absorbed into it, or becoming such a nuisance that they are effectively silenced. In the first case the great danger is that, however efficiently need is met, working for autonomy can go by the board. In the second case the problem is simply that of need being ignored altogether. Both occurrences are made all the more possible by the diverse and fragmented nature of the alternative caring scene, including the alternative Christian scene. There is, for example, a surprising number of separate homosexual groups in some way associated with the Church. There is vitality in a healthy pluralism but one wonders whether many basic communities in this field, as with the numerous counselling centres, could not considerably strengthen their hand without destroying the cause they further by a greater degree of co-operation, co-ordination, and the sharing of resources. At least they have in common a Christian philosophy of life on which to found an ecumenical quest for affirming the dignity of man in community.

So for some of the problems. But despite all these and against pretty considerable odds, the caring communities continue their impressive ministry.

7

NEIGHBOURHOODS AND NETWORKS

From neighbourhood to social network or from community of place to community of interest. This has been the inexorable trend since urbanization, industrialization, and bureaucratization[1] set in and since a highly mobile society became the order of the day. Add to this the process of secularization and it is only too evident why the local church so often feels itself to be stranded on an island past which a busy world sweeps, but on which only the immobile spend very much of their time.

My opening chapter suggested that because we have moved from a local to a cosmopolitan society, the local church as we know it is now in an anachronistic situation, where both message and medium are becoming increasingly parochial. My intention, therefore, was to look at the gradual growth of a different form of Christian presence termed basic communities, i.e. communities of interest not closely tied down to the neighbourhood, pioneering new styles of life and a fresh approach to questions of authority, the personal and the interpersonal.

In describing basic communities, I have by and large treated them as distinct entities and commented on those features most relevant to my theme. Yet such units rarely stand alone: in one way or another they are part of a wide network of related ventures in community-making with which they have much in common. The second part of this chapter is about these networks: the way they have built up round core groups; how such networks relate to each other; what their links are with the institutional Church. I shall also examine the relationship of these networks to the neighbourhood, arguing that each is a very important resource for the other.

First, however, I take a longer and harder look than hitherto in this book at the neighbourhood itself, community rooted in the locality, and discuss the extent to which some of those features so characteristic of the new networks are also beginning to manifest themselves within the parish. Has the local church remained impervious to major changes going on beyond it, or is evidence of the emergence of a new spirit and a new style of life found there too?

216

NEIGHBOURHOODS

In many places, far too many, the local church still remains stolidly conservative in ethos and outlook. Its style of leadership and organization, and the type of interpersonal experience it offers to members, have remained tied to a way of life far more meaningful to earlier centuries than to ours. The basic communities of interest and action discussed in this book are as remote to it as high-rise flats to the people of the Outer Hebrides.

Yet that is only one side of the coin. For slowly but surely, in all kinds of otherwise quite ordinary localities, there are signs of laity and clergy beginning to adopt a new stance to their own life as a congregation and to the area in which they live. The new shape of parish life emerging can be likened to a series of concentric circles, a phenomenon which I later show to be typical of the network as well as the neighbourhood. There is nothing particularly surprising about this concentric pattern, for the Church has often worked with a deeply committed core group round which others gather. What is noteworthy is the composition of these concentric circles and the way they relate to each other.

Ever since the Church set apart, trained, and ordained a full-time ministry, the latter has occupied the key position on the local scene. No inevitable problem here. But such a ministry has over time assumed a leadership role and status, which, even in the conformist tradition, have devalued the layman and in subtle ways reduced him to a position of immature spiritual dependence. Furthermore, the idea of a core group, as operated, for example, in the days of the early Church, has steadily been whittled down to one central person on whom the congregation has come to depend for all sacramental and pastoral ministrations. Thus the concentric pattern in many local churches today consists of an ordained minister at the centre, a small circle of hardworking lay people supporting him, mainly in an administrative capacity, with heterogeneous, loosely knit associations of less committed people beyond, many seeing their religious allegiance as an individual and occasional affair.

Team ministry

A major recent challenge to this mode of operating has come through the developing concept of team ministry, especially as pioneered in this country by the Methodist team of David Mason, Norwyn Denny, and Geoffrey Ainger which began work in the early 1960s in Notting Hill, London, following on the race riots there in 1958[2] and much inspired by the work of the Protestant parish in East Harlem, New York.[3] Methodism, historically accustomed to working something of a team (i.e. circuit) system of ordained men, made considerable strides in developing this concept of ministry throughout the 1960s[4] and still remains the only Church with a national team ministries committee.

Spurred on by the Paul Report,[5] the Anglican Church also began to take an active interest in team ministry, initially as a means of solving the manpower problem in rural areas such as Lincolnshire and East Anglia, but later to harness resources in New Towns, and older, decaying urban areas. The other Free Churches and the Roman Catholic Church have been less involved though they have played an increasingly active part in more loosely knit ecumenical teams. A report on team ministries[6] recorded 200 in existence in 1975, though this must be a minimum figure. They vary immensely in their composition, internal relationships, and ways of working, though certain common features emerge.

That which I am stressing here is the core *group* (as opposed to a key *individual*). The team rather than the individual operates at the centre of the life of the local church and in so doing opens doors to a new style of leadership and to ideas from fellow team members belonging to different denominations and with different personalities and outlook. Whilst a member of the Notting Hill team, Norwyn Denny wrote:

> Group Ministry has been a way for us in Notting Hill to find new roads to real community. It is the breakdown of the 'one man' situation, which fosters a peculiar mechanistic pattern of authority and responsibility, which has opened up the possibilities of other kinds of group relationship. Exploration has been made in new forms of ministerial work by working outwards from a group of ministers and wives, to new and developing relationships and style of life with many other people.[7]

The Notting Hill team were able to operate a most creative division of labour: David Mason involved in the Notting Hill Social Council, Norwyn Denny with multi-racial and pastoral concerns, and Geoffrey Ainger in the worship. Since then few teams have been able or willing to do this, Peter Croft reporting that of the 200 listed in the 1975 report 'only five share out work purely on the basis of function'.[8] The problem is that the team tends to work in a supplementary rather than a complementary way, that particular skills remain only partially utilized, and that too much time in the team meeting is spent on ecclesiastical concerns, with the organization of services dominating the agenda and even pastoral considerations getting short shrift.[9] None the less, the team concept gives the opportunity for a more corporate and balanced style of leadership to develop.

As with Notting Hill, nearly all teams are made up of ordained ministers, the attempt to involve laymen in team meetings (other than those working full-time for the local church, such as youth leaders) so far having been an almost total failure. The laity are often not available when the clergy want to meet and either cannot or do not wish to be involved in much of the week-to-week planning. There is thus the ever-present danger of the core group again becoming an élite and assuming a dependency rather than an enabling function. However, in many cases the clergy team is guided by a 'team council' in which laymen are fully involved and which has the task of formulating policy. This body, or other similar gathering (in Notting Hill it was a Leaders' Meeting made up of virtually all those holding leadership positions in the local congregation), forms a first circle of committed people in close contact with the core team. Of Notting Hill, Norwyn Denny writes:

> Most people assume that a core group of clerics will prevent other people having a say. This could be true but one is made so conscious of one's responsibility within the group that it would soon be obvious if one took too much autocratically upon oneself. The ease of relationships within the group and the freedom of spirit somehow better enables other people to make their own way and 'to do their own thing'. In fact the whole lay-clerical relationship loses its hard edges and is broken into a different life-style and a real community. Within the wider group which has come into being, and which is open-ended or at least undefined, it is no longer a question of doing things as parsons or laymen but as the persons best fitted to do the job.[10]

For many Anglicans in particular the establishment of team councils and the contribution that an active laity can play in the worship and life of the local church have been a revelation; in a few cases lay people are now being appointed as part-time or even full-time 'elders'. The Free Churches, more used to vigorous lay leadership at the local level, have been less surprised but have themselves been awakened both to the need to bridge the gap between minister and people which has developed over the years and to their neglect of the layman's contribution in extra-ecclesiastical spheres. One result has been the growth of a new sense of corporate responsibility for the life and witness of the local church and a deepening sense of the latter as a sharing community.

Small groups and extended households

Beyond the core team and the team council or its equivalent, there has developed in the more adventurous parishes a circle of active small groups. The latter, usually meeting in people's homes, first (re)appeared on the local scene in the mid-1950s through the work of a parish priest, Ernest Southcott, in Leeds.[11] Since then many churches have set up house groups (such as the LINK group described in Chapter 5), the development in this direction probably reaching its peak in the nationwide 'People Next Door' project mounted by the British Council of Churches in 1966.

In the Anglican and Roman Catholic traditions, the house group was sometimes the setting for the celebration of the Eucharist, helping to free people from the impersonality of large congregations or formal worship and enriching the Sacrament with a new intimacy and spontaneity. This practice has continued, even if it has not grown in popularity, but in no case has it gone further than with the 'para-church' set up at the end of 1973 by the Ashram Community in Sheffield. There a small group of some twenty people have become 'members' of the so-called 'Eucharist Congregation', linked to the Sheffield Inner City Ecumenical Mission and approved by a Sponsoring Committee representative of the main denominations. Members make a yearly commitment and are corporately sustained by a fortnightly Eucharist and meal, a fortnightly Congregation Meeting, and one or two weekends shared with the wider Ashram Community, as well as social outings amongst themselves. The aim has been to bring some of those unwilling to commit themselves to membership of a mainstream denomination into a strong yet open Christian fellowship. In a frank assessment of the problems facing such a para-church, John Vincent writes:

> The Congregation has plenty of defects. It is at the mercy of anyone who drops in, for we will be open to their influence, however nutty, prejudiced, or chip-on-shoulder. It is in danger of satisfying neither

those who want a rounded Church or Para-Church life, nor those who shy off at the remotest suggestion of 'churchiness'. It is a haven for talkers, extroverts, people with ideas but not always commitment. It is in peril of becoming too introvert, simply because people enjoy it and enjoy each other, and like doing things together. It could easily become as much a place of 'cheap grace' as the ordinary churches – in fact, it could be even cheaper, for nothing is asked of people in return, not even a membership commitment or a stewardship commitment. Its strong social conscience could easily avoid any strong corporate political activity. By affirming everyone as they are, it could become as much as the ordinary Church, a place where people could be shielded from the Gospel challenge to radical change, rather than a place where everyone is constantly exposed to it. By being 'footloose', not having a Church building, and avoiding real-estate, it could miss some of the elements of incarnation. By being all things to all people, it could avoid being anything in particular to anyone. But Eucharist Congregation has its strengths. About twenty people are seriously committed to it. It will go where those twenty people – and any more who join it – take it. That is its greatest strength.[12]

The novelty of the house-group type of meeting has now worn off and not a few groups, even where ecumenical, have played themselves out. Churches have only slowly grasped, if at all, that keeping small groups fresh and alive needs considerable skill, not least some knowledge of group dynamics, and that few satellite gatherings survive for long where the life and work of the core team are at a low ebb. Furthermore, and heeding the words of caution by John Vincent, the small group itself needs to be open and outward-looking, in thought or action, if it is to avoid becoming narcissistic. The Notting Hill team grasped this point fully for themselves as a group and were thus able to apply it to the numerous neighbourhood cells which they established. Norwyn Denny writes:

Our ministry is not just to the church, but to everyone with whom we come into contact. This has been a basic principle. No one has been able to shackle us to the church organization in opposition to other things. There has been plenty of real church commitment, especially in worship, pastoral matters, and administration, but there has always been the opportunity, which Group Ministry provides, for all of us to give a good deal of time to the people of the area. A commitment which is only to the church is an unbalanced view of evangelism which fails to hold together proclamation by word and by life.[13]

This approach has been hard for many churches to sustain and the house group has all too often become another traditional religious huddle. Overall the 1970s have seen a pause after the strenuous activity of, and at times disillusionment following, the 1960s. But in spite of fluctuating fortunes, the concept of a cluster of small neighbourhood groups surrounding a core team and a team council has survived. It is a pattern now being given fresh impetus by the charismatic movement which, looking especially to the parish of the Church of the Redeemer, Houston, as its prototype, is increasingly utilizing the concentric model as the shape of things to come.

Another dimension of neighbourhood church life is the community house or extended household, where members live and share their lives together in a far more intimate way than is possible in any house group. This development draws on one of the real strengths of the neighbourhood, its still being the place where the family as family has its base. It enables the family unit to be used as a whole and to offer its combined resources to others as a microcommunity of Christian people.

The first attempts at the establishment of such households did not meet with immediate success and a number of early ventures collapsed. Residents were often very young and inexperienced in communal living, they sought to combine the latter with occupations which demanded far too much of them, and they were often caught between their own and the local congregation's conflicting expectations of their role. But the vision and the enthusiasm remained and lessons were learnt; amongst others, that such community houses must be seen as an integral part of the life of the local church, neither being expected to do the latter's pastoral work for it and thus salving its conscience, nor keeping themselves to themselves, tucked away doing their own thing.

Recently there has been the emergence of a small number of satellite extended households relating closely to the core team and congregation. Churches inspired by charismatic renewal have been especially prominent here, stimulated by the example of the Community of Celebration, an offshoot of the Church of the Redeemer (though even their first attempt to establish community houses in Coventry was not very successful), and Post Green in Dorset. Notable neighbourhood experiments in establishing extended households in the English scene are taking place at St Cuthbert/St Michael-le-Belfrey in York,[14] St Hugh's, Lewsey, near Luton,[15] and an Anglican/Methodist venture (The Community of Hope)[16] on the Clifton Estate, Nottingham.

An interesting development in this connection has occurred at Brandhall Baptist Church in south Birmingham, where the minister John Bedford has over the last two years helped his members to establish six extended households (two semi-detached houses being given extra accommodation by the building of dormer rooms in the roof). Some forty members of the congregation now live in this way, sharing meals and a common purse. The households originally arose in response to personal needs of particular individuals, but are increasingly seen as ministering to all residents and through them to the total congregation. There is still a traditional approach to the leadership within each household, an emphasis on the somewhat autocratic authority of the male members, but there is no doubt about the vitality of the communal experience for all those involved and the renewal of congregational life as a whole.

Other houses, with no particular charismatic emphasis, have also been or are being set up in Shenley Hill, Birmingham (see Chapter 6), Beeston, Nottingham,[17] and Sparkbrook, Birmingham.[18] The Ashram Community houses fulfil something of this function even if the (para) congregation is of a type radically different from the norm. Such ventures indicate a growing momentum in the exploration of this dimension of Christian living which, though by no means suitable for all, can offer much to the life of both congregation and neighbourhood.

The outer circle of this concentric pattern of neighbourhood ministry consists of groups involved in exercising the usual kinds of groups, clubs, and youth organizations undertaking such work. But recently there has been a desire both to extend and enrich the quality of the service given (working for autonomy as well as responding to need) and the life of the Christian community from which activities spring. For example, the Notting Hill team eventually established round them some hundred laymen acting as 'community leaders' and visiting those in any way linked with the local church and doing 'invaluable work in creating real community in and around our gathering for worship',[19] as Geoffrey Ainger comments. Good Neighbour schemes and a few Community Development projects (see Chapter 6) have played their part in giving the outreach of the local church new point and purpose, such approaches being especially effective when linked to ventures like the

Shankhill Road Methodist Team Ministry's community house, where volunteers offer acceptance and help to those in distress in the area.

New forms of neighbourhood ministry: authority, the personal and the interpersonal

Authority and leadership

In Chapter 1 I made reference to Peter Rudge's five organizational models: the traditional, the charismatic, the classical (or bureaucratic), the human relations, and systematic.[20] The established style of parish organization is dominantly traditional; recently witnessing the attempt, though often a failure at the local level, to introduce more businesslike aspects of the classical model, and here and there revitalized by charismatic renewal. However, these three models assume a more or less autocratic form of leadership, a looking up to, and dependence upon, some person assumed to be above one, in most cases priest or minister, for spiritual assurance and direction.

The apparent advantages of this situation are numerous, not least that it is a relatively easy option all round. The clergy can play the 'father' role, enjoying the kudos whilst being protected from genuine encounter with people as people; the laity can escape from any real awareness of being the Church and the adventure of 'doing theology', into a privatized and easy-going form of Christianity. But this situation results in an inertia and passivity ('God's Frozen People', as Mark Gibbs and Ralph Morton once called it)[21] which in the end satisfies no one and leads to the death of community.

The significance of the new style of neighbourhood ministry steadily emerging is that it takes the human relations mode of operating very seriously and thus has the potential to call in question the kind of ecclesiastical leadership which has been far too clergy-centred and individualistic. Not that the human relations approach easily accomplishes change, for the concentric circle still relates to a centre, and escaping from the inbred belief that one key figure or an élite group is essential for survival and security is no easy task. There remains a very long way to go and the process of the delegation of authority and responsibility and enabling those assuming it to exercise it effectively and creatively is a slow and painful process: the building of the Notting Hill model (still unsurpassed as an example of how a total congregation can minister to an inner urban neighbourhood) took over a decade. Yet the new concept of leadership is gradually gaining ground, even in places of recent charismatic renewal where it is so easy for priests and ministers to be again thrust into the limelight.

The personal

The traditional form of neighbourhood ministry gives church members scope for the exercise of a very limited range of skills. The latter have to be church-centred: the administration of church affairs, the occasional conducting of services, or the exercise of a degree of pastoral oversight. The Free Churches believe in an actively involved laity, but by and large actively involved with church business. Yet times have changed and society now works on the principle of an intricate division of labour depending on a high level of education and specialization (a trend which in turn affects the increasing diversity of leisure pursuits). Traditional patterns of local church life in no way reflect the rich variety of opportunities offered the layman outside, and the few tasks he is called upon to perform can seem mundane and trivial, offering little opportunity for the genuine use of his talents and skills and giving little chance for self-expression or personal fulfilment.

The new pattern of neighbourhood church life at least goes some way to meeting this restrictive situation: first, and extremely important, for the clergy themselves who can no longer remain satisfied with traditional definitions of their role. This is not to deny the centrality of the ministry of Word and Sacrament and the importance of pastoral care; it is simply to state that such a definition of the function of the ordained ministry and the way this function has hitherto been expressed is now inadequate. The concept of team ministry at best opens up new and exciting possibilities. Where the team is willing and able to operate an enterprising division of labour, the clergy can opt for a ministry not just concerned with congregational worship and pastoral care but related to non-church sectors such as education, social welfare, and health wherein special skills can be developed and exercised.

However, there are problems. As a matter of fact, most teams have failed to develop a division of labour relevant to secular sectors. Once again Notting Hill was here way ahead of its time. Teams still apportion responsibilities largely by area and not by skills, a situation sometimes made inevitable by their having pastoral oversight of two or more congregations. Where responsibilities are shared out, they tend to be within the relatively narrow confines of the conduct of worship or, at best, related to attendance at various church committees.

A further difficulty, and this is much more fundamental, is the limitation imposed by the neighbourhood as neighbourhood. The latter is no longer a unit of self-contained community life, and residents travel out of it for work, recreation, and often schooling and medical attention. The core team is increasingly restricted in the scope and depth of specialization open to its members by this sociological fact of a mobile society. It is here that the more focused and specialized contribution of the developing networks of communities and small groups to the Church as a whole, and to the neighbourhood in particular, is of great significance. I return to this point later: here I simply wish to emphasize that a network of basic communities can give the Church the opportunity to break free from preoccupation with the parish system, at present consuming nearly all its institutional energies, into a society now shaped as much, if not more, by community of interest as community of place.

Just as the team concept gives some opportunity to the clergy for the exercise of a more diversified ministry, so the emergence of small cells, extended households, and the new modes of outreach already mentioned, give greater scope for the layman to offer his own specialisms and skills in the service of the local church. The breaking down of the worshipping congregation into small units with diversity of function means that the Church can begin to harness the considerable range of lay resources in its midst. Methodism now constitutionally requires each church to set up a Neighbourhood Committee on which sit, amongst others, 'one representative of each project for mission and service in the community in which the Local Church is involved'.[22] Yet once again, and even more so than in the case of the clergy, it has to be recognized that the layman lives a great deal of his life right outside the neighbourhood and his interests and thus his personal fulfilment can be only partially found within it.

The interpersonal

The traditional, and indeed classical, forms of ecclesiastical organization ensure that people meet in accordance with well-established norms; encounter is predictable and safe. At the same time, and despite the advantages of being able to build community slowly on the basis of a common heritage, there remains little openness to new experiences and relationships which might reveal possibilities within oneself and others as yet unrealized. It is assumed that the structured, formal organization of church life is the most suitable; a structure and

226

form which amongst other things keep priest and people distanced from one another.

The development of the team concept has helped to give clergy an experience of standing not in front of and above people but with them, initially with their fellow clergy, in a way that has opened up the challenge and the richness of a corporate approach to ministry. For challenge there is to those used for decades to being seen as 'set apart'. At the same time great gains accrue, as I have commented elsewhere:

> When a man joins a team ministry he is thrown together with others in a relationship which can bring great strength but which can also bring considerable strains and stresses. Tension can arise not only because of clashes of temperament, but because of difference of theological conviction, administrative ability and disagreements as to the time and effort that should be given to the various aspects of the work. Though each man has time and opportunity to pioneer new ventures in his own sector, there are occasions when the need for the general agreement of the team actually slows down decision-making and action and demands patience on the part of all concerned.

> But the advantages of team membership outweigh the difficulties. (If they do not, the team will quickly collapse.) There is a great sense of corporate endeavour and moral support in the good team. The discipline of listening to others and wrestling together for the best possible solution is both healthy and creative for the life of the individual and of the church as a whole.[23]

Within the new pattern of neighbourhood ministry, the sense of being a team, or, in theological language, the Body of Christ, also extends to the congregation, nourished by the more intimate fellowship of house groups and extended households. A kind of fusion takes place, seen currently in certain churches where charismatic renewal has occurred, though abundantly evident in the multi-racial Notting Hill congregation, which brings a new dynamic and vitality to worship and mission. As Norwyn Denny puts it: 'Celebration is the note of discovered community that we would want to strike above all others.'[24]

The test of this deep sense of corporateness, and of being open to others, lies not only in the quality of congregational life but in the local church's caring for the world beyond its doors. There is growing evidence that this pattern of the core team and concentric circles of groups and households gives far greater impetus to a lively concern for the total neighbourhood than traditional patterns of parish life.

The institutional Church and
new forms of neighbourhood ministry

The institutional Church, though making gestures of interest, has proved extremely slow to respond to the developing pattern of neighbourhood ministry. The former has stuck tenaciously to traditional and classical organizational models, apparently incapable of contemplating any real alternative. Economic anxieties and some uncertainty about the number and calibre of men offering for the ministry have sent the Church into retrenchment rather than persuaded it to explore imaginative ways forward.

The 1960s saw the Church delicately courting the team ministry idea. In Methodism a Connexional Team Ministries Committee produced some excellent documentation and argued convincingly for the Methodist Conference to press for the adaptation of the circuit system in this direction. And Methodism too had the impressive Notting Hill prototype to show what could be achieved. But no one grasped the nettle. The need to match men and teams, to support young teams through early teething troubles, and to defend a more specialized division of labour against those ministers who championed a monochromatic traditional role and laity possessive of their secular 'territory' proved too much, and the 1970s have so far seen team ministry still a Cinderella concept from Methodism's point of view.

After a slow start the Anglican Church has done somewhat better but, in spite of the legal framework offered by the Pastoral Measure, it too has failed in its understanding of the real implications of team ministry. Thus in many cases claims to being a team reveal little more than what can be found in an ordinary Methodist circuit; close-knit groups operating a genuine division of labour are hard to come by. On the ecumenical scene progress has also been limited, the high hopes associated with the formation of areas of ecumenical experiment[25] hardly having been realized, and ecumenical sponsoring bodies possessing insufficient authority to ensure vital continuity.[26] Ecumenical teams face exactly the same difficulties and opposition as denominational teams, only more so in that they are seeking to hold together organizations in which the authority and status of the ministry are so differently conceived. By and large, very few denominational or ecumenical teams have received the support and servicing necessary or help in the setting of objectives and in the working out of steps to reach these.

A possibility of new moves may be at hand. In June 1976 over 150 members of team ministries met at Swanwick under the auspices of ONE for Christian Renewal (an organization which I comment on later). It is interesting to note that one of the main recommendations was to ask 'that the Methodist Team Ministries Committee . . . should take a lead in ensuring that an interdenominational body should be set up to co-ordinate and service team ministries'.[27]

The Church's response to the growth of house groups (it is too early yet to assess reaction to extended households as such) has been much more positive, if only because it seems to threaten traditional patterns less. Groups have been seen as a means of helping to educate the laity through Bible study and discussion, the full potential of the interpersonal dimension having so far been given very little attention, though it should be added that the Roman Catholics have gone a good way here in connection with their network of family groups, as for example those sponsored by the Grail. The Church has raised its eyebrows with the emergence of house communions, but the presence of clergy on most occasions has so far been enough to assuage fears.

Attitudes to the wider circle of community involvement, through such approaches as community development, have caused more debate (again because resources of men and money are often involved), especially where there is little immediate return in terms of recruitment to the ranks of the institution. As mentioned in the previous chapter, Shenley House in Birmingham encountered opposition, despite undertaking some excellent community work in the area, simply because it failed to 'produce the goods' (i.e. more church members) expected by some members of the local congregation to which it was closely linked.

The response of the Church at all levels to new patterns of neighbourhood ministry has so far been guarded, certainly lacking in really positive and practical support, and occasionally downright hostile. The trough in ecumenical enthusiasm has not helped to keep things as fluid and flexible as many hoped and the majority of teams and house groups remain drawn from or dominated by a single denomination. Despite this, the winds of change are blowing, perhaps more strongly now than for some years, and the fact that the new neighbourhood ventures of which I have written are developing slowly but surely is a sign that something of enduring significance is afoot. As Norwyn Denny states: 'There is no "blueprint"; the individual situation has to be dealt with faithfully and as a unique phenomenon.'[28] Yet new patterns of ministry are emerging on the local scene and, despite the inherent limitations of neighbourhood work, may well be revealing something very exciting about the shape of the Church to come.

NETWORKS

The basic communities I have been concerned with in this book are not neighbourhood-centred. They have emerged because of the growth of communities of interest rather than communities of place. Yet as they have developed in number and influence, the same kind of concentric organizational network, evident in new forms of neighbourhood ministry, has manifest itself; in this case not contained within local geographical boundaries but extending over large parts of the country.

The concentric network

There are a number of communities existing on their own, often caught up in the pursuit of self-sufficiency and in the creation of a self-contained life-style, having little, as a body, which they want to advertise to the outside world. Examples would be such non-religious communities as Birchwood Hall near Malvern and Postlip Hall in Gloucestershire and, with a more religious orientation, Taena in Gloucestershire and at present Lothlorien in Kirkcudbrightshire. Their purpose is above all to exist; to experience the joy and pain of community living to the full and through this to discover sufficient corporate solidarity and individual significance to fulfil the needs of members.

None the less, most communities, by accident or design, soon attract other groups and individuals to them. It is at this point that the 'concentric network' begins to develop. By 'concentric network' I mean a core community or group surrounded by circles of associates, friends, or supporters, themselves linked both to the centre and to each other.

Core community/network of communities

One type of network is that of a central community to which are linked a number of 'sister' houses. Post Green is a good example, with a group containing the most influential leaders residing in the main house whilst the rest of the community live in some half-dozen houses situated largely on the estate. In 1975 the Community of Celebration at Yeldall

Manor had another community house nearby and was contemplating leaving the Manor to move into smaller units (this has in fact now taken place). Another major part of the community is established on the Isle of Cumbrae, with a mainland house in Largs.

Noel Stanton, the leader of the Jesus Fellowship in Bugbrooke, lives with a few members in a small house next door to the chapel, whilst a number of other houses, termed 'Jesus Central Homes' for 'those who have important ministries in the Body of Christ'[29] and 'Jesus Family Homes' (extended households), some small and some as large as the farm with twenty-five residents and the Hall with forty-five residents, are situated in the village itself. Closely associated with these, but farther afield in Northampton, Daventry, and Banbury are 'Jesus Welcome Homes', described as 'frontline homes of evangelism and compassion, with a "screening" ministry where the needy people are made welcome on a short-stay basis . . . and then passed to Jesus Family Homes'.[30] Extending over an even wider area than the Bugbrooke network are the sister houses of the Student Christian Movement, with its headquarters and central resident community now at Wick Court, near Bristol. Currently satellite houses exist in Oxford, Birmingham,[31] Bristol, and Dublin (with attempts being made to establish one in Belfast), though the fluctuating fortunes of the SCM have made the future of some of these ventures uncertain.

Federation of communities

A few networks operate on a more federal than concentric principle, usually being linked together by the work of a small central administrative staff and by occasional get-togethers. The Cyrenian houses are set up on this basis, as are the homes associated with L'Arche in this and other countries. The Ashram Community houses connect in a similar way.

Core community/network of groups

Operating on the concentric principle again are two or three established communities which are supported not by sister houses but by a network of small groups which meet regularly in their own localities. The Iona Community works on this basis with a small core community on the island (as well as administrative staff in Edinburgh and Community House in Glasgow), with which as many as possible of the 140 full members link up for one week each year. The latter are themselves divided into family groupings which seek to meet regularly in their own

231

areas. The Grail operates on similar lines through the very large number of family circles which it has helped to set up and which it services in various ways by means of publications and gatherings at Waxwell, although circle members are not formally linked to the central community. Corrymeela is hoping to adopt this pattern and extend its small network of groups in order to ground the work done at Ballycastle more firmly in the local situation, above all in Belfast. (The London Corrymeela Group has had fluctuating fortunes.)

Core community/network of individuals

Many basic communities, including a number of those already mentioned, are supported by individuals scattered all over the country who gain inspiration and encouragement from association with a core unit. There are concentric circles of such people ranging from those who wish to be very strongly committed to the community's vision and ideals, to those who simply wish to be kept informed of its doings.

The most committed 'second circle' existing at present is perhaps that of the Grail 'Companions',[32] some thirty women working away from Pinner in secular jobs, who nevertheless undertake to follow an explicit and quite demanding rule of life closely linked to that of the core community. Any would-be Companion has a period of over three years to prepare for her dedication which includes amongst other things celibacy, and commitment to her fellow Companions and the Grail Community as well as to material simplicity of life-style. This dedication is made for one year at a time and usually reaffirmed at an annual gathering at Waxwell.

The Farncombe Community has about a hundred 'Companions', but these are much less involved with the small core group than in the case of the Grail. The Companions 'commit themselves to the aim and ideals of the Community as a whole, to co-operating with members of other Churches as they are able, and undertake to keep a simple rule of life and prayer according to their circumstances'.[33] Beyond the Companions is a 'Fellowship of Prayer' which consists of people supporting the community by their prayers and gifts but who cannot be more specifically committed. The Iona Community's innermost circle of supporters are some 600 'Associates' who link themselves as fully as possible with the aims, life, and work of the community. They are dedicated to sustaining a disciplined life of daily prayer and Bible study and some also participate in the community's economic rule. The

'Friends' of Iona are connected with the work mainly through financial contributions. Lee Abbey's closest sympathizers are some 8,000 'Friends' throughout the world who support the centre in Lynton through prayer and financial contributions: beyond these are 'Associates' who follow the fortunes of the community with interest but without commitment.

So one could go on. Most communities or groups with a distinctive ethos have one or more categories of supporters: Scargill with its 'Partners', Burrswood's 'International Fellowship', and the 'Friends of Hengrave'. In these cases, and many others where an even more informal link with sympathizers exists, some form of magazine or newsletter is distributed with news about the core unit and sometimes articles of more general interest. The Grail produces *In Touch*, the Farncombe Community its Newsletter, Iona *The Coracle*, and Lee Abbey *Christian Witness*. Such publications vary in circulation from hundreds, in the case of Farncombe, to several thousand, as with the *Burrswood Herald*.

Centres of learning or caring/network of students or clients

There are other centres which I have discussed in this book which, though not having a core group of a communally very distinctive kind, nevertheless draw in a wide variety of interested people and steadily develop their own particular ethos and reputation. These fall mainly into two categories: communities and centres of learning as discussed in Chapter 5, and the caring communities and groups described in Chapter 6. In the former category come places such as Ringsfield Hall, Dartmouth House, St George's House in Windsor, and Glencree. In the latter category come places like Pilsdon, Bystock Court, Burrswood, and Alpha House. These centres do not operate so closely to the concentric pattern but over the years have built up a large number of contacts who look to them as places of inspiration and stimulation, or support and caring.

Networks of groups

Finally there exists a number of networks of small non-residential groups occasionally linked through a central group, or more often by a co-ordinating central staff. The Servants of Christ the King operate on the former principle. Each 'company', a local group of about a dozen members, 'is autonomous. A central company acts as a clearing house for information and ideas and links companies for mutual support, but there is no kind of central direction.'[34] SCK also has an annual conference at which members of all the companies meet. Some networks of groups are co-ordinated by a central team, often small, such as those associated with the Re-evaluation Counselling Movement, the Clinical Theology Association, the Compassionate Friends, the Julian Meetings, Katimavik, the Pilgrims of St Francis, and Amnesty International.

Despite the variations found in the organization of those networks which I have described, I want here to emphasize the overall dominance of the concentric pattern; the core community, group, or administrative team pursuing a distinctive style of life, ministry, or cause, and in the process drawing round it and enlisting the interest and support of followers, some more, some less openly committed to the concerns of the central unit. Such followers rarely reside within narrow geographical limits; their allegiance crosses local and sometimes national boundaries with ease. Community of place has given way to community of interest.

The symbolic gathering

One feature of the way networks are sustained is what I want to call 'the symbolic gathering', fulfilling something of the same function as 'symbolic place' discussed in Chapter 4. This is a large gathering held once a year or even less often, which brings together those in any way associated with the network as a whole. It is a very different kind of meeting from the annual get-together of full members of the community on Iona or the conference of staff and Companions at the Grail, and even from the summer holiday which members of the Ashram Community sometimes take together. It is an event rather than a conference; a happening rather than an assembly. Its function is not just to keep members of the network in touch with the centre and each other, though the dissemination of information of all kinds through formal and informal contacts on such occasions is important enough. It is more to reaffirm those attending in their commitment to a particular ministry or cause through a visible demonstration of the commitment of many others, and to rekindle enthusiasm through the medium of the mass meeting, with its openness to 'charismatic' leadership and potential for engendering powerful feelings of solidarity. Such symbolic gatherings are occasions for the setting aside of doubts and the reviving of hope springing from new visions of kingdom and world. The atmosphere is certainly intense but typified by spontaneity and sometimes exuberance rather than formality and solemnity.

Though I am not concerned in this book with events outside Britain, one obvious prototype for this kind of symbolic gathering is Taizé's Council of Youth and the assemblies leading up to its inauguration. As Andrew Lockley writes, the gatherings, especially at the opening of the Council in August 1974, had all the features of both pop festival and pilgrimage.[35] The Roman Catholic Focolare operates in a similar way, and writes about its annual Mariapolis (City of Mary) gathering in August 1975 as follows:

> About 600 people, lay, religious, men, women, children from all denominations and widely differing backgrounds, converged on Middleton, Manchester, for the summer meeting of the Movement. For five days the de la Salle training college presented the unusual spectacle of dogs and children playing among the tents and caravans which housed some of the overflow; while their parents, clergy and sisters conferred in small groups and young people sang to guitars or prepared sketches or mimes for an evening entertainment. This was a family gathering in every sense of the word. As with the early church, there had to be community of goods and this meant we had a large contingent of families from Glasgow. Living the life of the Gospel together people experienced how barriers of age, class, and creed broke down ' . . . That they all may be one' no longer seemed a prayer for the future but something to be worked for now.[36]

Katimavik is an Eskimo word meaning 'meeting place', describing a movement which is characterized by a series of gatherings of a similar kind up and down the country. The group writes:

> (Katimavik) is a gathering of the young and the young in heart who want to share a few days together searching for Jesus . . . yearning to be closer to him, meeting him through the Gospels and in each other . . . meeting him in silence and in prayerful sharing together. Katimavik is open to all, but it is basically rooted in the Catholic Church. It is the growth of a community over a few days, spilling over into the continued growth of smaller communities of prayer and commitment.[37]

A somewhat more structured annual event, though still possessing something of the spirit of the symbolic gathering, is the International

Ecumenical Fellowship's conference. In 1975 the seventh such event was held in York:

> The 350 members taking part came from most European countries, the United States, and the Far East, and spent a week together in the traditional IEF pattern of worship, study, workshops, and interest groups. . . . One day was spent outside York on pilgrimage to various places – Ampleforth, Fountains Abbey, Rievaulx Abbey, Ripon Cathedral, and the Ecumenical Centre at Woodhall. . . . The Eucharist was celebrated each day according to a different rite – Methodist, Lutheran, United Reformed, and Roman Catholic. The Orthodox liturgy, celebrated in the choir of York Minster, was attended by His Grace Archbishop Basil of Brussels, John Bishop of Finland and members of the Nikaean Club. . . . The 'fun evening' brought to light much hidden talent as did the Sunday afternoon concert; the conference closed with the now traditional 'service of light'.[38]

At the more radical end of the theological spectrum the Student Christian Movement set up two symbolic gatherings in true festival style. In the winter of 1972 a freely organized event entitled 'Seeds of Liberation', and concerned with the spiritual dimension to political struggle, attracted 400 people to Huddersfield, whilst in January 1974, 250 people met in Birmingham for 'A Celebration of Free Communities'.[39]

The evangelical wing of the Church of England through its numerous youth rallies and musicals and, in particular, the charismatic movement, has thrived on symbolic gatherings of a wide variety, the latter movement notably through its large international assemblies held over the years at Guildford, Nottingham, and Westminster, as well as what was described as 'the most representative body of Christians from every part of Ireland that has ever met in this land', when 3,700 people gathered in Dublin in September 1975.[40] Two extended gatherings organized by the London Ecumenical Centre, 'That's the Spirit' and 'Exploring the Ways of the Spirit', the latter congress attended by over 7,000 people, have been referred to in previous chapters.

One feature of these British gatherings is that, unlike Taizé, they are not usually associated with networks which have a strong core community. As such they at times run the risk of symbolizing an unearthed vision, not least an unearthed ecumenical vision. The vision is crucial, without it 'the people perish', but the grounding of that vision in ongoing communities in which Christians are fully engaged, is just as crucial.

If the symbolic gathering has a good deal of the festival about it, the pilgrimage element is not unimportant. As Andrew Lockley points out, what draws many to Taizé is the desire to discover and share an authentic Christian life-style. Many of the network gatherings just mentioned have an air of simple joy and simple living about them. Other groups have on a smaller scale found this through the pilgrimage, notably the Pilgrims of St Francis whose communal experience is based fully on this kind of gathering. Of their international pilgrimage from Norwich to Walsingham in 1976, attended by some 300 people, they wrote:

> The pilgrimage can give to each what he needs, but only if each is prepared to give himself in service to God and to others in the group and those whom they meet on the way. It is an exercise in community living in the spirit of St Francis. Those who come on pilgrimage must be prepared to be completely immersed in the life of the group. They must be prepared to accept other people as different from themselves, but complementary to themselves. They must be ready to accept the demands of communal sharing of responsibilities even if this means personal material discomfort! The pilgrimage is a microcosm of our whole life's pilgrimage with its difficulties and joys and opportunities for service. It is an enjoyable holiday, but it is much more than that. It is an ACT OF WORSHIP.[41]

The Iona and Othona Communities, and the Institute of Christian Studies, all have days or longer periods on pilgrimage, as does Katimavik. In August 1975 Christians at Glastonbury invited those interested to travel there and camp in order to celebrate the Feast of the Transfiguration and to 'let there be Life from the ruins'. Such pilgrimages symbolize a people with a common heritage on the move, in faith and hope, to find new inspiration and new strength in the quest for authentic community.

Authority, the personal and the interpersonal: the organizational dimension

The basic communities which are our subject usually extend their influence and gain support through developing a form of concentric

237

network, sometimes focused in symbolic gatherings. It is a pattern which in our day and age seems to work and as such is worth noting by those concerned with the renewal of ecclesiastical (or indeed other) structures. But to draw attention to this overall pattern says little about the way leadership is exercised, the place given to the individual, or the nature of interpersonal relations within each community or group or throughout the network as a whole. And it is these features which are of paramount importance.

The ways in which authority, the personal and the interpersonal, are related to each other lead to the emergence of certain basic organizational models or types such as those described by Peter Rudge. A majority of communities, groups, and networks which I have dealt with have most in common with Rudge's human relations model and it is translating the latter into practice which I believe gives the community movement its importance at this point in history. Of course all our communities, groups, and networks also possess features of the traditional, classical, and charismatic models, for no actual organization is 'pure' in the literal sense. But it is those features characteristic of the human relations model which are the most prominent and of the most significance.

If, however, there is another organizational model of particular consequence for the community movement, it is the charismatic. What appears to be going on at the present time is the slow growth of networks of an essentially human relations kind, a number of which, as with the Community of Celebration, have been given initial impetus by some form of charismatic renewal. To assess the significance of this situation I first examine the main contribution of the human relations type of network to the Church and inquire what the charismatic dimension adds to this. I then look at the relation of the human relations model to the traditional and classical types of organization.

The concentric network in relation to the human relations and charismatic models

By way of illustration it may be of value to place a few of the networks of basic communities described in this chapter more specifically into the human relations or charismatic categories, before going on to look in more detail at the particular features of each model. I do so, emphasizing two things: one, that the organization of quite a number of individual basic communities, as opposed to networks, can also be thus categorized (and I will refer to a few of these below); the other, that such categorization is inevitably simplistic in that it ignores the reality of the mixed model.

Networks of intentional communities falling under the human relations head would include the Student Christian Movement, the Cyrenians, L'Arche, and the Ashram Community houses. Networks of non-residential groups would include Re-evaluation Counselling communities, the Compassionate Friends, the Julian Meetings, the Servants of Christ the King, the Pilgrims of St Francis and Amnesty International.

Illustrations of networks of the charismatic type are as yet more difficult to discover. Nearest here would be the Children of God and Bugbrooke though both, with their reference back to the ecclesiology of the early Church, possess many traditional features. The Community of Celebration, though springing from charismatic renewal in Houston, has more recently seen interesting developments. The early and more dramatic charismatic features of its life and worship have now been so assimilated that they are much less obvious to the visitor, though the spirit of renewal remains very much alive. At the same time the organization of the community had by 1976 drawn nearer to the corporate and flexible human relations model, though the paternal influence of Graham Pulkingham remains, the community feeling freer to initiate change when he is present and can in effect sanction what is being proposed, than when he is absent. Other networks with a charismatic style of *leadership*, though here more in the organizational than strictly religious sense of the term, would be L'Arche, the Ashram Community, and even the Alternative Society. Networks more reflective of the charismatic model at the *interpersonal* level would be those associated with Focolare, Katimavik, and Post Green, though the last also possesses many human relations features.

Authority and leadership

Within the human relations network there are evident two aspects of leadership: one relating to the community or group as a whole, the other to the member cast in the role of 'the leader' within it. Such aspects may appear contradictory; in fact they are complementary. The outstanding feature of the first aspect is that leadership is a corporate phenomenon. Each member is recognized as having leadership potential, given the appropriate situation, and the aim is to come to decisions through a common mind, if at all possible. Typical here would be the companies of the Servants of Christ the King and, a more recent development, the community houses associated with the Student Christian Movement and the Ashram Community. L'Arche communities have no hesitation in seeing this move towards corporate leadership as a step towards maturity; as Alain Saint-Marcary of Trosly writes: 'A community which becomes mature passes imperceptibly from the monarchical to the democratic model.'[42] And their members should know, for they are seeking to explore this mode of operating under very demanding conditions. One outstanding feature of the corporate aspect of leadership within the human relations model is that it is predominantly lay leadership. The role of the professional, especially one whose status is ascribed rather than achieved (as is frequently the case with priest and minister) is not a thing which in itself carries much weight. This does not mean that expertise is devalued but emphasizes that each member of the group has expertise of one kind or another to offer. Such would be the case with the Re-evaluation Counselling Movement and the Compassionate Friends with their insistence on peer support.

The other aspect of leadership, that relating to the individual who notwithstanding the corporate emphasis comes to be designated as overall 'leader', underlines the role of co-ordinator as a key function. The fundamental importance of the skilled co-ordinator within the human relations model, and thus for the future shape of Church and society, cannot be overemphasized. It is difficult to list names here, for by definition such people often work as low-profile enablers, but communities operating this kind of leadership would currently include Iona, the Cyrenians, and Corrymeela. Characteristic also of this style of leadership is its non-directive yet enabling nature, in no sense implying a *laissez-faire* attitude but being an attempt to help groups and individuals to take as much responsibility as possible for their own personal and corporate development.

If the charismatic model has anything to add to these human relations aspects of leadership, it would be an inspirational and at times prophetic dimension. Leadership within the human relations network can sometimes lack that dynamic and vision which can rouse men to great endeavour and give them the enthusiasm and courage to press on in the face of considerable odds. One example of such a figure would be Jean Vanier, whose dedication and inspiration have enabled Christians in many countries to commit themselves wholeheartedly to sharing their lives with the mentally handicapped. Graham Pulkingham of the Community of Celebration has in his way also inspired those on both sides of the Atlantic to see the vision of the Church as 'a community of brothers . . . an incarnate, warm, human, touching, caring, affectionate involvement of person with person . . . a careful commitment of humanity to humanity, a tender giving of self to others'.[43]

There are of course problems with charismatic leadership; it can be highly directive and brook no questioning. The leader-follower relationship can be highly unstable, with an overdependence on both sides that can result from deep fear of rejection or of losing a cause. But here I am concerned mainly with the human relations model at the heart of the community movement and the positive contributions of more charismatic figures.

The personal

The human relations network stresses the personal, so much so that it has been criticized as being 'pan-human'.[44] But in an age of bureaucratization and high mobility, it is the human, the personal dimension of living that has suffered most. The human relations model stresses the uniqueness of the individual and the unrealized potential of man. It is intent, therefore, on providing the opportunity for radical means of self-fulfilment. It is a model based on belief in the inherent 'glory of man'[45] and the 'optimism of grace'.[46] An individual so believed in by others, or one who comes to believe in himself, is found to be capable of intense commitment to this cause or that interest. Thus one important feature of the communities and groups I have dealt with is the deep involvement with, and extreme dedication of members to, a common concern and each other. This holds true whether one is speaking of those engaged in communal living, exploring new experiences of spirituality, venturing into self-sufficiency, committed to personal growth within the human potential movement, giving time and energy caring for the disadvantaged, or pleading for the socially wronged.

The human relations network is thus characterized by the word 'self', not in the pejorative sense but indicating its potentiality. It is an organizational model committed to self-awareness and self-affirmation in relation to body, mind, and spirit. Of these three I want at this point to stress 'mind', which in the preceding pages may have seemed to take a subordinate place to feeling. A feature of the human relations model is that it depends on people who are prepared to think for themselves, those who are capable and articulate enough to work out their own ways of doing things. Typical here would be the community of women at St Julian's, Coolham, in their sophisticated approach to personal development, the articulate members of the various Open Centres, and the cultured, extended family building its log home and developing the land at Lothlorien.

Creativity too is an aspect of the human relations network, a creativity which shows itself through people discovering, cultivating, and utilizing talents and skills not realized before or little validated in our prefabricated society. This is most clearly seen in the emergence of a wide variety of crafts and artistic or musical skills: spinning and weaving at the Grail, woodcarving at Taena, pottery at Post Green, jigsaw-making at Keveral Farm, music, dance, and drama at the Community of Celebration. And allied to this affirmation of the individual are activities associated with self-sufficiency, self-help (especially in relation to communities of caring), and self-determination, all equally relevant to the nature of authority and the interpersonal.

In connection with the personal, the charismatic organization possesses numerous features akin to those of the human relations. It stresses the personal dimension of life in an intensive and at times dramatic manner and attempts to meet deep individual needs, in this case of the less as well as the more able. But it tends to do this on its own terms and to select only those whose concerns match its potentially narrow outlook. It stresses self-awareness, but often places the emphasis on the emotional and the intuitive at the expense of the cognitive. But, with its stress on spontaneity, the active response of man as he feels, with inhibitions relaxed, to the experience of being alive and open to the Spirit, it has a major contribution to make to the human relations approach. This is seen above all in charismatic worship where, at its best, there is the release of enthusiasm, a sense of exhilaration, and a consequent feeling of deep and intensely moving involvement. Of course this can become narcissistic and stylized. On the other hand it can, at its best, enrich people's offering to God, break down the formal barriers which prevent true human encounter in worship, and facilitate a quite new and inspirational feeling of being the Church. Such is the experience of many at the symbolic gatherings described earlier in this chapter. Spontaneity of human greeting and exchange is also typical of most charismatic communities and groups outside of worship, making their fellowship one in which both member and stranger can feel personally valued and equally welcome, as I have experienced on numerous occasions even at places with a theology as exclusive as Bugbrooke's.

The interpersonal

An outstanding aspect of the human relations model in the context of the interpersonal is that it is oriented towards 'the kind of pluralistic posture which is essential to the development of any form of democracy'.[47] This emerges through the commitment of those involved to particular areas of concern, the mobility of people in modern society and the means of rapid communication enabling participants to create networks around the kinds of interests and needs discussed in previous chapters. Because such involvement is voluntary and vigorous, basic communities of the human relations type generate a vitality and drive so often lacking in other models apart from the charismatic. This impetus is not just in relation to religious matters, it engages with a whole range of secular interests and issues too.

At the same time basic communities forming round strong common interests generate a high degree of mutual acceptance, in part because there is considerable 'match' between their own concerns and attitudes and in part because the latter reflect a valuing of the individual as individual. This is the case with open networks like the Compassionate Friends, the Association of Interchurch Families, and, on an international scale, Servas. Such acceptance often carries over to those not belonging to the basic community itself, especially where the purpose of living life together is to express some form of caring or therapeutic ministry. This can be seen operating in situations like Bystock Court, Corrymeela, the Samaritans, and Amnesty International.

Within the accepting primary group typical of the human relations organization there is considerable intimacy between participants. This occurs naturally in communities such as those associated with the Student Christian Movement, with some 200 visitors a month passing through Wick Court, or L'Arche, and is more deliberately fostered in those educational networks employing growth techniques derived from the human potential movement which were described in Chapter 5.

The charismatic style of organization likewise encourages a high degree of involvement and a drive to pursue powerful common interests. However, such interests, within a major part of the charismatic movement at present, are specifically religious and directed towards proclaiming the Gospel in one way or another. Although participation is voluntary, there is considerable pressure in charismatically inclined communities and groups to conform to normative patterns of regular

243

Bible reading, prayer, and, indeed, 'loving one's neighbour'. There is also an inevitable onus on wives or husbands whose partners have been 'baptized in the Spirit' to discover the same experience fairly rapidly. Caroline Urquhart, wife of Colin Urquhart whose notable charismatic ministry of St Hugh's, Luton, is described in his book *When the Spirit Comes*,[48] writes:

> In Luton life began changing almost immediately. Colin was obviously moving into a deeper relationship with God, leaving me far behind spiritually. I was not unduly worried – after all it was his job! But as he changed I found I couldn't handle this new person. . . . Fortunately my love for Colin did not lessen, and he seemed to love me with greater intensity than before. But somehow I was unable to respond in the way I wanted. Finally, I realized that something had to happen to change me. Obviously I could not expect Colin to revert back to what he was before, especially as his ministry was so much more fruitful now. Therefore I would have to join him in this Holy Spirit business. 'If you can't beat 'em, join 'em!'[49]

My point here is not to query the validity of any charismatic experience, but simply to comment that in this intense situation a 'blessing' for one partner can leave the other in a position of painful spiritual isolation, with the attendant temptation to surrender integrity for the sake of peace and security.

One impressive feature of charismatic communities and groups is their readiness to adopt a simplicity of life-style, sitting lightly to material possessions through a sense of detachment from the worship of worldly wealth. This is especially impressive with the Jesus Fellowship at Bugbrooke where members have surrendered their claims on all personal belongings and are seeking to exist on half the normal cost of living in order to give the surplus to the work of the community. Yet it should be added that some of those involved in the human relations networks, though not practising a simplicity of life-style and a sharing of goods as extreme as that at Bugbrooke, also live with few luxuries and to some extent share incomes or belongings. This is the case, for example, with the Student Christian Movement community at Wick Court, the Kingsway Community, and the Ashram Community houses.

In this comparison of the human relations model with the charismatic I have noted a number of important and at times impressive features characterizing the latter. None the less, I would argue that the human relations approach is the one which is likely to make the more fundamental contribution to the shape of Church and society at this point in time. This is because its features are vital to the development of mature individuals and humanized institutions. Its concept of authority at the level of the total group stresses the corporate and lay, whilst in the case of individual leadership overall it gives priority to the role of co-ordinator and non-directive enabler. It is a model which affirms the unique value of the individual and the centrality of the personal. In relation to the interpersonal it encourages a dynamically participatory and pluralistic community life whilst at the same time fostering within each group and network an accepting and intimate yet open pattern of relationships.

Limitations of the human relations approach in relation to the traditional and classical models

Though the human relations model can greatly benefit from seeking to assimilate certain features of the charismatic, there are also aspects of the traditional (which I here want to associate mainly with the parish system) and classical (bureaucratic) models which it needs to see as complementary. Some would even go as far as to judge the human relations type of community, group, or network as parasitic, a view more often found amongst those fearful of change than those eager for renewal. Another more positive attitude is to see what organizations of a (local) traditional or classical kind have to offer, and to begin to explore ways of combining the most important characteristics of each with the human relations network without destroying the nature of the latter.

The human relations network and the traditional organization

When compared with the traditional organization, the human relations network has three major limitations: it is based on interests of a sometimes very narrow kind and attracts a socially restricted membership; it lacks an easily identifiable geographical base; and it can miss out on a sense of history and a common heritage. An antidote to some of these deficiencies can be, though by no means always is, found in the parish situation.

Communities and groups of a human relations kind thrive on the enthusiasm and drive resulting from the sharing of a particular and powerful common concern. This excites, extends, and fulfils those for whom the local scene seems claustrophobic and literally parochial. But it can lead to the creation of networks of people dominantly from one section of the class spectrum and generally at the younger end of the age range. Sustaining such networks necessitates communicating and travelling over large distances and demands time, energy, and money. This greatly restricts the field of possible participants and can mean that the latter withdraw from the relatively more heterogeneous life of the neighbourhood, cutting their links with the wider cross-section of people of all ages and occupations still found worshipping in the local church. This can also mean a neglect of 'the people next door'. Where communities have sought to retain or recapture something of the ethos of the more locally oriented extended family, as with places like Taena, Scoraig in Wester Ross, Keveral Farm, and Lothlorien, they have often moved into secluded rural parts, thereby also limiting contacts.

The human relations network lacks an easily identifiable geographical base. Of course communities have a physical home, but they have often been established in relation to the current availability of property and personnel. As such they are not easy for the 'man in the street' to locate, can be known to only a few people even living in the immediate vicinity, and lack an identity which gives them the credibility and acceptability sometimes needed for survival. Networks of groups can suffer the fate of anonymity and can find themselves strung out across the country with all the associated problems of communication, recruitment, and harnessing resources. It is probable that many readers will have heard of only a few of even the more well-established basic communities mentioned in this book. On the other hand, it is fully predictable that each neighbourhood will have its local church, the identity and function of which both Christians and non-Christians alike recognize. However much it may be struggling to hold its own in this day and age, it is not only a symbolic reminder of a spiritual dimension to life, but an organization to which both religious and non-religious look in order to gain support and recruit help for a wide range of community activities from local concerts to holiday play schemes.

The third limitation is the lack of a sense of history and common heritage amongst certain basic communities of the human relations kind. This is perhaps less of a weakness than might initially be supposed in that a number of networks with human relations features have sprung out of an attempt to rediscover and redefine for our generation something of the spiritual riches of the past. Such is the case with Iona, looking back to a long monastic heritage starting with St Columba, and with those communities seeking to emulate the example of Nicholas Ferrar, like Pilsdon and Little Gidding. (A number of groups gain an identity through their association with symbolic places, as discussed in Chapter 4.) Other networks of a more fully human relations type, for example the Servants of Christ the King, the Cyrenians, the Julian Meetings, and the Pilgrims of St Francis, similarly take their bearings from past as well as present.

None the less, because many of these groups are still very young, because their interests and concerns are relatively narrow, and because participants are often strenuously engaged in them, they can easily neglect or fail to appreciate the extent to which they draw on a Christian heritage embodied in the multitude of worshipping congregations in neighbourhoods throughout the land, a heritage sustained by the continuing ministry of Word and Sacrament, pastoral caring, and the spiritual support of men and women throughout the whole of life. The young community or group can further fail to appreciate its indebtedness to those who have told the Christian story down the ages and who over the centuries have hammered out a meaningful theology which the local church, however inadequately, seeks week by week to interpret and transmit.

For their part the human relations basic communities and networks have a vital contribution to make to the traditional parish system (and thus to other traditionally oriented parts of the Church). They have to offer that approach to authority and leadership already discussed. They can utilize the energy of many who have more particular interests, concerns, and skills. They can lead the Christian into active involvement with areas of exploration, discovery, and action at the frontiers of communal living, spirituality, ecology, education, caring, and politics in a way the local church cannot match. They have an interpersonal freedom and openness which local congregations often lack. And they are not encumbered by the upkeep of ecclesiastical buildings and of a full-time paid ministry.

What is now needed is the much deeper appreciation of each of these organizational approaches by the other and an attempt to link networks of basic communities and neighbourhoods in a way which can sustain and support the former whilst freeing and mobilizing the resources of the latter. Moves have been made in both directions. Basic communities have made deliberate efforts to keep in regular touch with their local churches and to worship there as frequently as possible, even though they may have chapels of their own set aside for daily devotions.

This goes not only for the more traditionally oriented communities, such as Farncombe, and for certain of those with a charismatic emphasis, such as the Community of Celebration and Post Green, but also for more fully human relations units such as the Blackheath Commune in its day and Bystock Court. Many networks such as those associated with the Grail, Iona, the Julian Meetings, Katimavik, and Amnesty International, are very aware of the importance of earthing their interests and concerns in the neighbourhood, even if as yet their membership is inevitably spread thinly. The International Ecumenical Fellowship is a good example of the continuing move in this direction. In 1976 their chairman wrote:

> By and large those who had not been present at International Conferences have missed out on talks and discussions which have been an important influence in the thinking and development of the Fellowship. . . . Now we find ourselves in a situation when not even all those who apply for places at International Conferences can attend—even when there is more than one such conference during the year. This is why I welcome the idea that the whole Fellowship should be meeting together in small groups whenever possible. . . . Local groups are in fact coming into being.[50]

The Community of Celebration in 1976 took a major step towards planting the seeds of a new Christian life-style in the neighbourhood when it transferred two of its households 'of renewal and healing' from Yeldall Manor to Beaconsfield Baptist Church and St Mary's parish, Wargrave.[51]

Likewise, local congregations sometimes take an interest in nearby communities: 15,000 people from the area and beyond attended the healing services at Burrswood in 1975, members of all churches gather weekly for worship at the Christian Renewal Centre at Rostrevor in Northern Ireland, and Lothlorien had a well-attended open day in the summer of 1975 when people from far and wide came to share in seeing and talking about the enterprise. Most communities and centres of learning play host to parish groups and the Grubb Institute in particular has given a central place in its philosophy to the importance of the local church and its minister. The Movement for a Better World, following the steadily growing Roman Catholic awareness of the importance of basic communities, is now turning its attention to using its retreats to give the initial vision of 'a new style of parish' and encourage the adoption of 'a pastoral strategy which envisages and promotes the emergence of these basic groups. This calls for the priests and others engaged in the pastoral work of the parish to re-think their priorities and pastoral methods.'[52]

Yet despite this encouraging two-way traffic, there are still many doubts and prejudices to be removed. It often takes communities some time to overcome the stigma of being labelled as a bunch of dissolute weirdies, a suspicion originally encountered by groups as different as Keveral Farm, the Wick Court residents, and Lothlorien. But on a deeper level members of some basic communities, especially of the human relations type, do in fact find that they are pursuing a style of life which is in genuine contrast to, if not in conflict with, that of the locals, including local churchgoers, and that communication all too often breaks down. Father McDyer discovered this with his co-operative enterprise in Glencolumbkille, those at Glastonbury caring for the young wanderers found it in relation to certain townsfolk and local churchgoers, the Iona Community finds it with regard to a few of the indigenous islanders, and Lee Abbey encounters difficulties in enabling those associated with it to fit easily into their local congregations back home. In this sense many of the groups mentioned in this book remain what Rosemary Haughton terms a 'sign of contradiction'.[53]

The human relations approach and the classical organization

The classical organization has in recent years received a bad press, so much so that the term 'bureaucratic' is now condemnatory rather than descriptive. Yet this model, as Weber realized, is the rational outcome of man seeking to survive in a highly complex, technological society. And because the Church is an institution along with other institutions it too has found itself taking on more and more features of the classical type of organization.

There are many obvious weaknesses inherent in this mechanistic approach to human affairs. It is by definition hierarchical, with authority concentrated in the upper echelons and (almost) absolute power at the peak of the pyramid, bringing problems ranging from autocracy at the top to a sense of helplessness and hopelessness at the bottom. One's status accords with one's role, defined in terms of the good 'organization man'. The professional and the expert are always preferred to the non-professional and the laymen. Relationships are structured according to the system and breaking protocol is a major offence. Encounter is contained and restricted by the 'primary task' (i.e. what the organization must do to survive in its environment) of the enterprise.[54] Above all bureaucracy, with its rigid controls and tight sanctions, gets a bad name because it is built on 'the pessimism of nature',[55] on the belief that man is essentially selfish, unreliable, and lazy and must thus be strictly supervised.

The human relations approach attempts to challenge outright or to alleviate many of these assumptions about the nature and potential of so-called organization man. But the classical model also has its virtues and there are aspects of a more positive kind which the human relations approach neglects to its cost. I would highlight in particular the ability of a bureaucracy to co-ordinate and combine a multitude of highly specialized and complicated functions in the pursuit of a definite objective. To this end the hierarchical mode of organization, at best, produces clearly defined levels of command (people know where they stand), facilitates quick communication between all parts of the organization, enables those with abilities and expertise in different fields to utilize their skills to the full, and integrates people into an often large and complex enterprise.

Most of the major denominations at this point in history, though still retaining many traditional features, demonstrate characteristics of a classical type. Certain basic communities recognize that there are advantages in being associated with their denominational machinery, not only in terms of resources available and institutional credibility, but of communicating their message and co-ordinating their networks. They thus implicitly if not explicitly acknowledge the value of the classical model; but at a price. The price is the retention of much closer denominational monitoring and the exercise of more denominational constraints than in the case of other more independent human relations networks. There comes too a tacit condoning of the negative as well as the positive aspects of bureaucratic organizations.

This is especially true of Roman Catholic ventures such as the Grail, Focolare, the Movement for a Better World, the Christian Life Movement, L'Arche, and Katimavik. All affirm their strong connection with the Roman Catholic Church and, in some cases, as with the Focolare and the Movement for a Better World, they make a good deal of the hierarchy's official blessing. This enhances their acceptability at parish level, on which for example the Movement for a Better World depends to carry through its special retreats, and the Grail to establish family circles. Such groups also utilize international as well as national Catholic channels of communication and are thus able to extend their influence in a way impossible for many non-Catholic networks. But the situation is inherently contradictory and the tension great, for the endeavour is being made to work with two kinds of organizational model; internally a human relations approach is being developed, externally the support of a dominantly classical organization is being relied on. The result is so often compromise or confusion.

Those networks working more independently on a human relations basis, and as a consequence treating association with bureaucratic denominationalism with caution, in their turn suffer from the withdrawal or lack of institutional support and credibility. They struggle not only with having to convince the regular churchgoer of their relevance and with obtaining the wherewithal to survive, but with the need to work out a system of communication and collaboration which can end their sense of isolation without encompassing all the negative aspects of the bureaucratic régime. Human relations networks engaged in this exercise are seeking, however tentatively, to operate a pluralistic organizational model so far little explored and ill-defined. No wonder that some recent endeavours are as yet fragile constructions, even if they hold a good deal of promise.

A network of networks

Contact and co-ordination

The attempt to build a viable network of networks of an essentially human relations kind (below I shall also touch on one or two co-ordinating ventures working with networks of a more traditional or charismatic kind) is at present like trying to take men beyond the moon; we have neither achieved it nor yet know whether it can be successfully accomplished. But this book is about people beginning to move forward in a variety of ways, spurred on by the conviction that what they are about is a profoundly Christian, above all a genuinely human, undertaking.

Links are being established between basic communities and their networks in a multitude of ways. First, there are those informal, unplanned encounters between members of communities and of groups living in close proximity. Then there are persons operating in related fields who find advantages in an increasingly close liaison. This is now the case with Iona and Corrymeela, members of each linking up with one another on various occasions. Corrymeela is also closely associated with Coventry Cathedral and with communities on the Continent such as Agape and Taizé. L'Arche houses are the focus of prayer and giving by those associated with Katimavik, whilst L'Arche and the Cyrenians are increasingly exchanging ideas. In 1976 a few members from the Community of Celebration in Cumbrae and the Post Green Community in Dorset exchanged communities, and the Community of Celebration moved some of its office work and its British Fisherfolk team to Post Green. The Community of Celebration and the Open Centres also have links with members on the staff of Coventry Cathedral.

Those involved in community-building assemble at occasional large gatherings such as the ones mentioned earlier in this chapter. Those sponsored by the Student Christian Movement, the London Ecumenical Centre and, most recently, Glencree were particularly heterogeneous in character. Shaun Curran writes of the Glencree happening:

> (It was) an international gathering of people, real people, searching for something better than society now offers. A representative gathering. Many would be called 'drop-outs' by our more sophisticated society; yet sprinkled with the unexpected, a millionaire businessman, the abbot of a monastery, university professors and such like. . . . They worked on urban communes, rural communes, alternative technology, alternative medicine, Yoga, Transcendental Meditation, organic gardening, health foods, etc. . . . Many professed atheism yet never was Christ so present in Glencree. Here was a caring community, even though there were many more than two or three gathered together. . . .[56]

Here I draw attention not so much to the symbolic nature of this gathering as to the simple fact of some 500 participants meeting together to exchange ideas and concerns.

Those engaged in community-making also meet at events arranged by certain of the centres of learning described in Chapter 5. They naturally gather round themes of especial interest to them though such meetings do sometimes bring people from different networks together, for example those involved in caring and those concerned with community living, or those interested in spirituality and those active in politics.

These comings and goings are important but most are one-off events which cannot establish any continuous linking of networks or begin to set co-operation and co-ordination on a firm footing. Are there attempts being made to do just this? Denominational machinery as such cannot easily operate here because most of the human relations (and indeed charismatic) networks concerned are strongly ecumenical in intent. Even if a denomination were persuaded to offer resources in order to facilitate the linking of networks, it would be seen by many as denominational imperialism and regarded with great suspicion. This situation already poses problems for the Roman Catholic groups mentioned. The British Council of Churches fares somewhat better and has been able to promote a limited degree of exchange, but its work lies mainly within the established structures, and conferences of a more open kind, for example in the youth field, are often successful but still *ad hoc* events.

A beginning along more realistic lines has been made by the one or two co-ordinating bodies which have been set up to link basic communities working within the same spheres of interest. Some of these have been mentioned already, like the Association for Pastoral Care and Counselling and the Churches' Council for Health and Healing. Linking groups operating in the spirituality field, most with a more traditional approach, is the Association for Promoting Retreats, with over fifty years' work behind it, with 'aims to foster the growth of spiritual life by the practice of retreats and to introduce retreats to those who do not know of them'.[57] This it does mainly through a now annual publication, *The Vision*, an ecumenical journal which contains a full list of retreat houses and conferences. In addition it holds an annual festival-cum conference and arranges occasional courses for training retreat leaders.

The charismatic movement has seen the growth of an increasingly influential and active co-ordinating body in the Fountain Trust. It began in the autumn of 1964 in a flat in New Cavendish Street, London, really gathered momentum in the early 1970s, with a major conference at Guildford in 1971 being something of a turning point, and since the Nottingham conference in 1973 has found itself ministering to an exploding international movement. Under the directorship of Michael Harper and now Tom Smail, it has not only organized three mammoth assemblies in the United Kingdom but has sponsored regional conferences of all kinds and training courses in charismatic leadership, servicing these with tapes, records, and a multitude of publications of which its bi-monthly *Renewal*, with a circulation of some 10,000, is now the main channel of communication. In 1975 it issued a first small *Charismatic Directory* covering churches and centres where renewal had occurred. The Fountain Trust sees its work as 'Christ-centred . . .

253

charismatic . . . corporate . . . and compassionate'.[58] Of the corporate emphasis *Renewal* states that the Fountain Trust 'sees renewal chiefly in corporate rather than merely personal terms. Its main concern is to see churches of all denominations rather than individuals renewed by the Spirit, while recognizing that God brings renewal through individuals.'[59] There is no doubt that the Trust has so far undertaken with great efficiency an invaluable task of co-ordination at the heart of the charismatic movement.

Amongst those networks of a more distinctively human relations kind, the British Group of Leaders of Laity Centres, with some forty members from many of the centres mentioned in Chapter 5, fulfils a useful function. It is as yet a rather loosely knit group with little corporate identity or overall policy but it has value as a forum for the exchange of ideas and as a means of linking the British centres with those on the Continent. In 1975 an occasional mailing called *Laity Exchange* was started to facilitate the communication of information about the centres and of other relevant material for those specializing in various kinds of adult Christian education. *Laity Exchange* is issued by the Audenshaw Foundation as part of the Audenshaw Project in Laity Education. This Foundation, an independent charity, has since 1966 produced a series of *Audenshaw Papers*, edited by Mark Gibbs, containing informed comment on current issues relating to laity education; and a series of *Audenshaw Documents* on similar themes but with a more definite focus and a more restricted circulation. The Project spans the Atlantic and links readers in Britain, the United States, and Canada. The 'fundamental objective is to encourage the education and support of the laity—all God's people in all the churches and outside them, whether they are contented or restless or bitterly critical, as they struggle to understand and apply the Christian faith as they see it in the everyday world of today and tomorrow'.[60] The emphasis should be put on 'all God's people' for here, and likewise true of all ventures described in this book, the establishment of 'a laity cult' would be as damaging to the emergence of a new quality of community life as 'the clergy cult' has been in the past.

The Student Christian Movement produces an occasional *Directory of Christian Alternatives*, currently into a third edition, which lists a large number of the ventures mentioned in this book, but as an attempt to co-ordinate networks goes no further than this.

There remain three other organizations of note attempting to service and link communities and networks of an essentially human relations kind: ONE for Christian Renewal, the William Temple Foundation, and the Alternative Society. ONE for Christian Renewal emerged in January 1970 out of an amalgamation of most of the denominational renewal groups of the 1960s: the Congregational Church Order Group, the Methodist Renewal Group, the Friends of Reunion, Parish and People, the Baptist Renewal Group, and the Catholic Renewal Movement (though the latter retained its ongoing identity). It has a radical declaration:

> As members of a world in revolution, a divided church, a generation for which forgiveness and love alone have authority, we commit ourselves
>> to accept one another in Christ
>>
>> to study together the nature of our responsibility for God's world
>>
>> to combat poverty, racialism and oppression through social and political action
>>
>> to help in re-creating the one church—new in witness, worship and life
>>
>> to support actively those doing the work of Christ inside or outside the institutional church
>>
>> to ground the action for renewal in our own situation
>>
>> to underwrite this commitment financially.[61]

ONE soon ran into difficulties, for the collapse of the Anglican-Methodist unity negotiations prevented the major breakthrough hoped for on the ecclesiastical scene in England and failed to produce any dynamic alternative in reaction to this ecumenical setback. Instead, disillusionment with the ability of the Church to achieve doctrinal agreement or structural renewal led to a time of perplexity and apathy, the emergence of the charismatic movement being the only genuine spark of hope for many. ONE survived this period and resisted the temptation to throw in its lot with any single group or network, however worthy its cause, slowly establishing as its primary function the linking of Christians involved in diverse human relations type ventures across the country. Its co-ordinating work is undertaken through a few regional groups but mainly through its valuable mailing which contains news and views about a wide range of radical Christian concerns. ONE is steadily gaining momentum and, whilst continuing to support individuals linked with it (there are some 1,000 members), is giving very serious consideration to how best to service networks such as those described in this book. At the same time it continues to work for the renewal of denominational structures through a number of denominational sub-groups (such as the Anglican Parish and People) which remain an integral part of ONE.

ONE also sponsors the *Community* magazine from which much of the material in this book has been drawn. *Community*, which I edit, initially with the able assistance of Emmanuel Sullivan, a Roman Catholic Franciscan and until recently chaplain of the Hengrave Hall Centre, and Norman James, a Congregational minister and warden of Benefold, the Ecumenical House of Prayer, until it closed, began in the autumn of 1971. It was an attempt to bring together stories of Christians involved in establishing basic communities of all kinds, especially in the human relations style. The magazine now contains 'a switchboard' of current news from a wide variety of communities. It is published three times a year and reaches about 1,000 individuals and groups. In April 1975 a gathering representative of over thirty basic communities was held in Birmingham, the major value of which was time to exchange experiences and ideas in an unhurried manner.[62] In conjunction with ONE, the linking-up of networks of very varied kinds through *Community* is steadily gaining ground, with future plans to involve the religious Orders much more fully. Early in 1977 a resource centre containing literature and information about new ventures in community was established in Selly Oak, Birmingham, the aim being to give those involved or interested a continuing point of contact.

The work of the two other co-ordinating groups of note, the William Temple Foundation and the Alternative Society, the latter basically a secular enterprise though having many Christians involved within it, I have discussed in earlier chapters. Both are concerned to promote the development of groups of people with areas of specialized knowledge who can work out realistic alternatives to the present highly centralized, impersonal, bureaucratic system. However, David Jenkins, director of the William Temple Foundation, writes:

> It seems clear that the Foundation should reject the notion, for the present at any rate, that it should set out to establish and service a wide network of people or that it should attempt to be the centre of something that might become a movement. The present task is to develop projects which can be the source of information and insights in the central area of the Foundation's concern, which is that of

exploring the relationship of the Christian faith and the Christian church to the ways in which institutions make it possible or impossible to further truly human values.[63]

The Alternative Society is now seeking to establish a 'Foundation for Alternatives', the trustees of which will administer funds to help sponsor practical alternative projects.[64]

The shape of things to come

It is too early to predict how successful these co-ordinating groups will be in knitting together diverse networks into some form of mutually supportive movement which can effectively influence for the better certain of the more negative aspects of the current ecclesiastical machine. The Fountain Trust, in the name of the charismatic movement, has so far come nearest to challenging the institution, at times meeting a good deal of hostility from the evangelical wing of the Church of England and from those suspicious of its connections with Rome, even though it has criticized the latter for adhering to certain fundamental beliefs which are major stumbling blocks to Protestants. ONE for Christian Renewal has not yet gained sufficient following to challenge the institutional Church as it stands, though its slow growth may in the end prove to be its strength rather than its weakness. The William Temple Foundation and the Alternative Society are concerned first and foremost with societal renewal and have as yet been clearing the decks for action, though that in itself is no mean achievement.

Of course there are those within basic communities, not least of a human relations orientation, who still treat with great suspicion the emergence of any kind of co-ordinating body, though they are prepared to subscribe to information-giving publications such as *Community*. Some are resistant to anything more than this developing because they simply wish to 'do their own thing' in relative isolation and are unconcerned about any kind of wider reform or renewal, ecclesiastical or societal. There are a number of people so involved with their own particular interests and hobbies, for example in the field of alternative technology, that talk about social or political aspects of change seems irrelevant. There are others who feel that the way forward is to continue quietly to be an example and who work on the principle of the leaven or the mustard seed. Rosemary Haughton writes from Lothlorien in this vein:

257

The community movement, in fact, doesn't have to *find* a role, it *has* one, and it is unavoidable. It is a 'sign of contradiction', as effective symbols are bound to be, but for those who are feeling, however tentatively or semi-consciously, for a way ahead, they are a bridge to a more human future, a fallible but courageous attempt to be what people must be to each other – brethren, one family, expressed in the solidarity of small groups who work and live together for the sake of all. But whether that role is played well or ill depends on the degree of understanding and acceptance which individuals, and individual communities, bring to the playing of it. The numbers so far are tiny, the resources ludicrously small, but the symbolic value is potentially enormous. Which of the many experienced forms of community will endure remains to be seen. What matters is that the very existence of such communities means, 'people can make lives for themselves, we don't have to wait for the dictators – little or big – we are human, therefore, *together*, we can make a future fit for humans'.[65]

Ian Fraser also expresses the views of not a few when he writes at the end of his book on examples of radical Christian renewal across the world: 'We have had enough of co-ordinating organizations which soon put on institutional weight and secure their own place and future – that death-in-life. What may be needed is sources for the nourishment of vision.'[66]

Yet the truth as far as the British community scene is concerned is that there is only a tiny handful of co-ordinating publications (note the demise of such switchboard-type journals as *New Christian, Christian Renewal, Frontier,* and *Roadrunner*), let alone groups, in existence and what few there are struggle on with very limited resources to undertake the task, often with little support from the Church or the networks. It is my conviction that if Rosemary Haughton's final *'together'* is to have any real force, then sooner or later alternative networks, not least those in which Christian men and women are active, will have to become more fully involved with a world in which the bureaucratic machine, with its ability to manipulate wealth, power, and influence, calls the tune, or remain innocuously tagged on to the fringe of Church and society. Kenneth Leech, in his comprehensive analysis of the youth scene, argues that 'the counter-culture has emphasized liberation, expansion of consciousness and aesthetics, but neglected the creation of new institutions'.[67] Geoffrey Corry, at the end of his account of the once vigorous Jesus Movement in this country, writes that the participants 'have failed to understand the power of individual man to change political reality and have opted out of tackling the structures of evil'.[68] 'Light-hearted we must be if we want to elude the manipulators and survive; but let us never forget the ruthlessness of those principalities and powers against which we fight',[69] comments John Taylor. To have any hope of survival in such an engagement, basic communities and their networks will need to communicate efficiently, share resources, and combine efforts in every way possible. Some really effective means of co-ordination will be essential and not an optional extra.

The task of co-ordination needs to operate in three ways. One is to relate the experiences and insights of those involved in building new models of community in such a way as to contribute towards the articulation of a coherent alternative to the present organization of ecclesiastical institutions. In this connection there are signs of a new and exciting concept of ecumenicity emerging, now based not on the closer association of Christians as denominational animals but as human beings engaged in different aspects of renewal across a whole spectrum of concerns. It makes the first priority the Christian's engagement with life rather than religious institutions, with the Kingdom rather than the Church. It takes seriously the range of abilities and skills given to an individual, seeks their fullest possible development and expression, but insists that these must not become the exclusive possession of this or that community, group, network, profession, or institution. Those concerned with the integration of human relations networks are in a position to pursue a genuine ecumenicity; not one which restricts it to some kind of ecclesiastical joinery or jamboree, but that which respects and honours men first as human beings, with all their unique potentialities, and then sets about the painstaking task of enabling them to face, come to terms with and where possible overcome genuine divisions and conflicts, no longer dressed up in outmoded doctrinal formulations and obscured by a dead theology. It is an immense undertaking, literally a 'man-sized' one which no longer debases the meaning of the word ecumenical. It means that mission is no longer the false endeavour to move men from being human to being Christian, but to demonstrate to them that our being Christian is a sign and seal of our being committed to the journey which enables us all to become, individually and corporately, fully human.

The second aspect of co-ordination is the communication of this understanding of ecumenicity to, and fostering it within, the neighbourhood and the local church. The more free-floating networks need to be complemented by the sometimes more solidly earthed expression of Christian commitment at parish level, still the base camp for family life. This means a meeting and mutual appreciation of the part to be played in the total drama by network and neighbourhood. But a neighbourhood now itself moving, as described at the outset of this chapter, towards integrating the assets of the traditional with the attributes of the human relations approach. For just as ecumenicity must now shake clear of its denominational strait-jacket, so too it must break out of its parochial prison and outmoded definitions of the segregated roles of clergy and laity to embrace the Christian's engagement in life beyond the traditional and the local. This does not deny the importance of the latter; it is to argue that without some association with wider networks of concern and involvement, the Christian can fail to take seriously great sectors of life, and his understanding of ecumenicity and mission can become increasingly trivial.

The third aspect of co-ordination involves the building of bridges between the new models expressive of Christian commitment in both network and neighbourhood and the institutional Church as such, especially as manifest in the ecclesiastical corridors of power. This is a task as yet hardly begun, for the community movement is still a relatively young phenomenon and the Establishment as a whole has little intention of encouraging it to grow very fast or very strong, just because it contains the seeds of revolutionary change. But there are those bearing the burden of ecclesiastical leadership who are fully aware of the dehumanizing effect of the machine they have been given to administer and open to the movement of the Spirit. It is for these to listen; whilst those small bridge-building groups and publications seeking to link and interpret the pluralistic and kaleidoscopic community movement, even when accused on the one hand of building empires and on the other of castles in the air, must have the courage to speak. For they are involved in telling stories not about what might be but what is, and to those stories any with ears to hear will listen.

Despite all the protests to the contrary, it would seem that what we lack at this point is not so much visions and dreams, though these are necessary, and not now even people who have the commitment to earth these in the life of community or group in neighbourhood or network, but the courage to risk all the dangers entailed in piecing together a new model of Church and society which can enable the riches of the human relations philosophy to be combined with the wisdom of the traditional and the dynamic of the charismatic into truly human organizations free from the suffocating stranglehold of bureaucracy. It is not the destruction of institutions that is required, but the creation of infinitely better ones.

The religious Orders

This book has been about new ventures in community-making which have a predominantly lay and ecumenical emphasis. It has so far made no explicit reference to a similar network of communities of a much more historic nature, the religious Orders. Yet they have for centuries been regarded as the epitome of Christian community and it would be a major omission to make no comment about them. In what follows I make a few points regarding the similarities and differences between the religious Orders and the human relations type of network and about possible future links between them.

The religious Orders developed from small groups and communities into very much the same sort of concentric networks (only with a great deal more wealth and power) as those I have been discussing. A mother house was established (Cluny, the Grande Chartreuse, Citeaux) which then provided the inspiration and support for the founding of sister houses. But this says little about the all-important issues of the nature of authority, the personal and the interpersonal which characterized those networks.

With regard to authority it is interesting to note that, akin to the modern human relations organization, the monastic movement was originally something of a lay protest against being excluded from the highest prizes of the Christian calling. The lay emphasis remained encouraged by the sixth-century Rule of St Benedict until well into the Middle Ages, when the ordained monk came to be the norm. None the less, as Michael Hill states, 'full lay participation has remained as an ideal throughout the history of religious Orders and has been restated in some very recent reforms'.[70]

The actual nature of leadership within the religious Orders is not as easy to pin down as might at first be thought. There was an undoubtedly charismatic element, which drew people to figures such as Bernard of Clairvaux and Francis of Assisi (for I include the friars in this discussion). But it was a charisma very different from that which characterized the leaders of the millenarian movements of the late Middle Ages, as so dramatically described by Norman Cohn.[71] The

261

Orders accepted what Hill talks of as being leadership by 'the religious virtuoso', and he writes: 'Virtuoso religion typically refers back to a strongly valued source of tradition which it restates in its pristine purity and seeks to emulate by means of ethical rigorism.'[72] In this respect leadership, in the first instance, also contained powerful traditional elements. However, as Orders grew in size and complexity they developed a rigid hierarchical structure of their own, within and between houses, and, as with the Roman Church itself, the classical pattern came very much to dominate the scene. It is only very recently that this organizational model has been questioned and that the first hint of the human relations approach, with its corporate form of leadership and decision-making, appeared, minorities no longer being silenced in the name of holy obedience.

With regard to the personal, the religious Orders, like the human relations network, gave participants a rich opportunity for self-expression and self-fulfilment. It is noteworthy that the Orders were able to provide people with the opportunity to specialize in most of the fields mentioned in this book: communal living, spirituality, self-sufficiency, arts and crafts, learning and caring. The Orders, too, like most human relations networks, were the place to which the intelligent and the articulate members of society found their way to create and enjoy a culturally advanced life-style. They were an élite and, because the only means of expressing themselves adequately was through the ecclesiastical institution, a religious élite, as witnessed particularly with Orders like the Cistercians and, later, the Franciscans and Dominicans.

Despite this emphasis on intellectual acumen and dexterity of hand and eye, the Orders also stressed the importance of the emotions, even if through structure and form rather than spontaneous exuberance. The liturgy and private prayer, their music, art, and literary pursuits, touched the heights of man's search for aesthetic sustenance. Yet there was a difference here from most human relations communities and groups of today for the Orders, above all else, directed the emotional energies of men into the quest for holiness; fulfilment was defined in terms of personal sanctity over against a morally lax or religiously apathetic society. In the modern community movement there are no such powerful ethical undertones to personal fulfilment: the religious pilgrimage has given way to the human pilgrimage. It is being human rather than being holy which motivates those adopting the human relations approach to community.

At the level of the interpersonal, the Orders are often regarded as

262

demonstrating the zenith of Christian community and in certain respects their attainments were prodigious. Poverty, until overtaken by corporate wealth earned by assiduous endeavour or heaped on them for a variety of motives by rich patrons, was a key to their appeal. The way of simplicity and sharing set a glowing example to a Church preoccupied with status and material possessions. The Orders also set an example of hospitality and caring for the needy which has been unequalled in history. Like many modern communities of caring they dealt generously with the poorest and compassionately with the weakest members of society.

Yet the interpersonal dimension of life within the Orders remained shaped by a pattern of life which deliberately restricted vital areas of experience. One was sexual: strictly delimited by the words 'chastity' and 'celibacy'. Not that, as the writings of St John of the Cross or Julian of Norwich show, monks and nuns were sexually frigid.[73] Far from it! But so destructive of community was the overt physical expression of sexual attraction felt to be that its manifestation on the interpersonal level was deliberately screened out at every point. One consequence of this was a spirituality that sought passionate personal communion between the soul and God but ruled out all open expressions of intimacy between an individual and his fellows. The religious Orders became places within which deep interpersonal relationships were seen more as a stumbling block to sanctity than as a means of grace. Because the sort of open, intimate relationships found between many members of the human relations networks today were terrifying to monks and nuns, the structure came to preserve and protect an often immature community in the realm of the interpersonal.

The religious Orders carry with them, despite the vicissitudes of the centuries, a rich experience of communal life to which those in the human relations networks today do well to pay heed. Their members have been in many ways the spiritual athletes of the Church. But that very designation has been a problem, for two reasons. One is that their very existence has been a way for a threatened Church to divert zeal into safe channels. The Orders have then provided a pool of cheap labour, salved through the vicarious nature of their good works the conscience of the guilty, and unwittingly deflated any challenge to the traditional and classical manifestations of the institution. The other problem, as Max Delespesse writes, is that the Orders 'have sometimes siphoned off for themselves, without realizing it, the community ideal which belongs to the whole Church'.[74] The light is slowly dawning and the Orders are coming to appreciate that if they still have a role to play, it is that of helping to strengthen fellowship throughout the entire Church.

A few tentative steps have been taken in this direction. As mentioned in Chapter 2, religious and lay have been seeking to pioneer a shared community life at Hengrave Hall. At Ammerdown, a Methodist lay warden and his wife and Roman Catholic sisters combine to run the centre. The Society of the Sacred Mission now not only have Companions, similar to the Tertiaries of other Orders, but have established a group of lay Associates who are more fully committed than Companions yet still have considerable personal freedom. At the same time other Orders, notably the Franciscans, are playing an increasingly active role alongside lay Christians, be that at the Centrepoint shelter for young people in Soho or on the Shankill Road in Belfast. These are small beginnings but they are beginnings.

At the same time the Orders have a good deal to learn from the current community movement, young as it is. They have to face fairly and squarely the challenge to old patterns of authority within community and the rediscovery of what the personal and interpersonal dimensions of life are all about for our age. A first step is the drawing closer together of members of religious Orders (male and female) and basic communities in a continuing dialogue as Alan Harrison, Secretary of the Advisory Council for (Anglican) Religious Communities, suggests:

> The modern experiments in community living are exciting and obviously full of possibilities. The traditional Orders and Religious Communities whether Monastic or Apostolic need to be able to share the insights being gained in the communes, extended families and whatever. Similarly the new forms of community life at their peril neglect to learn from the experience of centuries enshrined in the traditional communities and now being modified in the light of renewal. It is time those who bear witness to the common life of faith talked to each other.[75]

Moves are in fact now under way to enable this to happen.

8

YES

Yes and the personal

i thank You God for most this amazing
day: for the leaping greenly spirits of trees
and a blue true dream of sky; and for everything
which is natural which is infinite which is yes

(i who have died am alive again today,
and this is the sun's birthday; this is the birth
day of life and of love and wings: and of the gay
great happening illimitably earth)

how should tasting touching hearing seeing
breathing any – lifted from the no
of all nothing – human merely being
doubt unimaginable You?

(now the ears of my ears awake and
now the eyes of my eyes are opened)[1]

This book is about people saying yes – to themselves, to their fellows, to life, to God. And not just saying it but living out to the full what it means in everyday events and relationships. Many in our impersonal technological society have given up or 'died', but those of whom I have written are 'alive again today' and celebrate 'the sun's birthday'.

Those who say yes have names – personal names. They are not men and women in general or even 'that kind of a man' or 'that sort of a woman'. They have discovered and affirmed their own individuality and significance and value in a way that cannot be denied them. For all this, their yes is a response to the yes of others often spoken before consciousness fully dawned. For the Christian it is above all a response to the yes of God. As Alan Ecclestone writes:

When we strive to know ourselves, we are seeking to know not a

265

speck of dust nor the species man but the Word that was spoken and took our flesh, the Yes that permitted us to be. We are seeking to know it because we are sought-out, because we are named as persons are named, because to be persons at all is to find in our hearts the Yes that strives to reply. We are that Yes, not of ourselves alone, but in Him and by Him and through Him in eternity.[2]

This yes is born of an awareness of living, of the realization of vitality within. It is a vitality that has given many of those creating community an energy and endurance which they never imagined possible: to sustain the emotional demands in every intentional community of living cheek-by-jowl with those whose habits and attitudes differ greatly from their own; to endure cold, rain, and mud at Keveral Farm and Lothlorien; to cope with hard manual work at Pilsdon and Scoraig; to take the wear and tear of being on hand to deal with the needs of broken families at Bystock Court, of the homeless in the Cyrenian shelters, and of those disoriented by violence at Corrymeela. These and many other such experiences have been lived through strenuously and creatively because those involved have so possessed that inner awareness of their own and others' value that they have been able to commit themselves wholeheartedly to life and to living wherever that may take them.

Their yes to life is, however, more than vigorous activity: it is fun! Analysis and discussion must never be allowed to detract from the sheer enjoyment within the community movement today. There is fun in plenty. Not in the trivial sense, but in that which Transactional Analysis seeks to describe when it talks about the full-blooded *joie de vivre* of the 'Free Child'. Thomas Harris goes so far as to suggest that, though theoretical dialogue is essentially an 'Adult' (i.e. purely rational) activity, 'it may be that religious experience is totally Child'.[3] And if we dismiss such a possibility with disdain, let us not forget that it was once said that 'whoever does not receive the kingdom of God like a child shall not enter it'.[4] It is not surprising, therefore, to find many of those exploring new paths into community possessed of an *élan* and enthusiasm which are an authentic mark of a genuine yes to life: not childish but childlike. This is no self-generated *bonhomie* but springs from 'the optimism of grace'.

Such enjoyment and laughter is catching. Many have been taken by surprise, in excitement or embarrassment, by its appearance. We have been made so cynical by the cruelty and destructiveness of man that it has become almost a blasphemy to declare, with the writer of Genesis, that the universe is 'very good'. But, as Harvey Cox reminds us, 'both for Christianity and for cosmic sensibility nothing in life should be taken too seriously. The world is important but not ultimately so.'[5] It is that liberating sentiment which releases mirth and the ability to celebrate life without ignoring the still crying needs of an imperfect world. 'Where it is real, laughter is the voice of faith.'[6]

Many basic communities know full well the meaning of joy and how to express it. They do so spontaneously in their daily conversation, especially over meals which they prepare and share together. They do so in their social gatherings, be these regular weekly events or more special occasions such as the parties or outings planned by caring groups. They do so in their worship; in music, song, and dance, believing that 'if God returns we may have to meet him first in the dance before we can define him in the doctrine'.[7]

If the yes to life is spoken vigorously and joyously, it is also felt and expressed in quieter ways. One theme running throughout the expression of new life-styles is that of a deeper appreciation of beauty in all its forms. If this sometimes becomes cultic, as perhaps at Findhorn and in some of the more pantheistically inclined groups, it is simply because urbanized man has for so long denied all but synthetic and mass-produced substitutes for truly aesthetic experience.

This yes to life through beauty is found in the desire of many communities to rediscover and reaffirm their oneness with the natural world. When at Scoraig in Wester Ross one watches the sunset over Little Loch Broom, it does not take much imagination to understand what keeps people there for many years, despite the strains and stresses of such a physically tough and socially isolated existence. The yes is also expressed, though as yet less often, through an awareness of the beauty of the human body in form and movement, in the old as well as the young.[8] There is little attempt to adorn or embellish the body artificially; where this does occur it seems natural enough. 'I saw a girl walking along, naked from the waist up and with her breasts decorated as flowers. She looked unusual but quite attractive',[9] writes Derek Stirman of the Isle of Wight Festival of Music, adding that he laughed outright 'when reading that a press photographer was the only man on the beach wearing trousers!'[10] The yes to beauty through art and craftsmanship I have already spoken of many times, the eager care of those at work at the Dove Centre near Glastonbury or the workshop at Findhorn remaining in my mind as impressive witness to this.

Vigour, laughter, beauty: these are things which give the community movement immense appeal to the individual. They are dynamic and exciting attributes for which it is worth sacrificing a very great deal. Yet sacrifice there is and it would be naive to imagine that any quest for a deeper sense of significance and for personal fulfilment could avoid the rigour of 'the agonizing journey of self-awareness',[11] as Monica Furlong describes especially its spiritual aspect. This journey is one which does not allow us to dodge the Jungian 'shadow' without encountering which 'we are at the mercy of our own projections'.[12] No wonder then that pioneering new styles of life and new dimensions of community has brought many to near despair; about their fellow human beings but especially about themselves. It has exposed the weakness of all individual intentions, however sincere, and the frailty of all corporate endeavours, however noble. It reveals our inability to face the demands of community, bringing the realization that, in Tillich's phrase, man finds it desperately difficult to be true to himself yet true as a part. It shows how little courage we really have when faced with what at times is crucifixion, being spreadeagled between the apparent annihilation of our individuality on the one side and of our world on the other. It is an experience which the Psalmists in their wisdom knew only too well and which today we forget is still part of the spiritual journey.

Yet one of the redeeming features of the lives of those involved in the ventures described is that they have said yes not only to the good and beautiful within themselves but to the shadow also. They are learning to own their projections. They are whole people just because they have refused to run away from the darker side of human nature. They have said yes, not to condone or excuse but because that is where self-acceptance and self-affirmation begin and because, without these, acceptance and affirmation of others, in their weakness as well as their strength, is impossible and community a sham.

Yes and the interpersonal

The yes to life through the personal is richly interwoven with the yes to life through the interpersonal. Eric Fromm puts it thus:

> Love is possible only if two persons communicate with each other from the centre of their existence, hence if each one of them experiences himself from the centre of his existence. Only in this

'central experience' is human reality, only here is aliveness, only here is the basis for love.[13]

'Love' is another way of describing the yes given to the interpersonal experiences of living and it is the fuller expression of this that the most noteworthy ventures in creating community are all about. There can be no vitality, fun, or appreciation of beauty which does not in some way relate back to a loving relationship. 'Laughter in solitude turns bitter as it grows insecure; for lasting mirth we need the company of others',[14] writes John Taylor. 'One has only to consider how cold and desolate the fairest face of nature can seem to a man left utterly alone, willing to exchange the whole sum of natural beauty for a single human face,'[15] states Alan Watts. Our conviction as Christians is that the ultimate source of the yes lies in God's yes to man, seen above all in that affirmatory Word made flesh. The yes is God's offer of community with and for man, now and eternally.

The yes to life, to others, and to God through the interpersonal can only be born out of a relationship of passion, so perceptively described by Rosemary Haughton in her book *On Trying to Be Human*.[16] 'Passion' in her sense is that powerful emotion, even or turbulent, which drives the individual to identify with and in some sense to possess a person beyond himself. Because it is an essentially lawless phenomenon, it enables those experiencing it to break out of their accustomed way of seeing things and people into new worlds of activity and relationship. Passion breaks a man open to the priceless nature of the personal and to the profound depth and liberating breadth of the interpersonal. It is the stuff of which visions are born: it separates the 'Why?' from the 'Why not?' of experience.

The wealth of activity and relationships which passion generates depends on its source. If this has been the readiness of two people to say an unconditional yes to each other in loving trust, be that mother and child, friend and friend, loved and beloved, or man and God, then the scene is set for the revelation of a quality of community quite incomprehensible to the apathetic, the rejected, or the fearful. It is this discovery that those involved in the community movement are making simply because they have committed themselves in courageous openness to life and love in and through their fellow men.

Passion is not synonymous with sexual desire. Today a whole range of sexual experiences is being publicly marketed and privately engaged in without the presence of that passion of which I am speaking. But such passion, as the substance of visions and great endeavours not least in community-making, is powerfully infused by the sexual quality of the interpersonal in its fullest sense. It is because we have so misunderstood, suppressed, or abused this aspect of being human and this gift of God that we have on our hands today a hopeless Church and a joyless society. From a psychoanalytic standpoint Wilfred Bion has described this aspect of saying yes to the interpersonal as 'pairing',[17] an experience which can occur between those of the same as well as the opposite sex. It is an encounter possessing a dynamic sexual content which gives birth to affection, vitality, and hope.

One key feature of the community movement of our day is this passionate drive towards 'pairing' in a society starved of affection and slowly breaking away from a state of passive dependence on impersonal institutions. This liberation, for so it is, expressed through such apparently diverse, yet in reality closely linked phenomena as the human potential movement on the one hand and the charismatic movement on the other, is lifting man's eyes to new horizons and especially to a new understanding of community. It is producing both the excitement and the power not only to dream but also to be and to do.

This sort of upswing in the aspirations of men is not unique. Alan Ecclestone reminds us how the twelfth-century devotion to the Blessed Virgin produced an outpouring of energy that led to the building of some eighty cathedrals and hundreds of vast churches, kindled a great enterprise of human reason, and inspired a new wave of lyrical delight.[18] In our day the pairing phenomenon has so far kept clearer of the veneration of individuals, though the guru is still a compelling figure for some. Nor do I think that for our age it is essentially a one-way drive, from man to woman, though the anima, in Jung's sense, is certainly very active. (As Jessie Bernard points out, it is all too easy for the passionate male to draw the female into a life-style which, still in part tied to traditionally defined roles, can physically and emotionally overwhelm her.)[19] We, however, are not witnessing a drive towards the building of cathedrals but one of community; not so much a reaching up to heaven and eternity as a search to discover the meaning of being human in the here and the now. And, hopefully, not just as men or women but as those who treasure individuality in all.

Many basic communities have realized the significance of this. Despite the inevitable constraints and inhibitions they inherit as members of a Church and society which have distorted and suppressed the potential of passion, sexuality, and love, they have said a forthright yes to the interpersonal aspect of community. The members of the Grail, for example, write: 'To commit ourselves to Christ through the channel of the Grail makes certain demands on us. . . . It asks us to recognize the importance of sexuality in all relationships, learning to release and redirect our power of loving in warm, deep and trusting friendships.'[20]

Yet there is still a world of possibilities to explore and the ever-increasing involvement of Christians in intentional communities and extended households demonstrates that they are intent on being at the frontiers of experience. They are aware of the need for real meeting and would uphold Tillich's conviction that 'only in the continuous encounter with other persons does the person become and remain a person'.[21] They are about rediscovering the art of loving, of giving creative expression to passion and sexuality, intensively and extensively; an art which Alan Watts thinks the West has relegated 'far below cookery'![22] If, as Alan Ecclestone argues, 'our Yes in sexuality has been long delayed, and even now is pronounced in hesitant fashion',[23] then at least through one means or another those involved in the creation of community are learning to speak with a clearer voice. They are saying that the human, the sexual, and the religious have far more in common than many wish or dare to believe and that the realization of this fact, with all its disturbing as well as exciting implications, is one avenue into the renewal of Church and society.

Visions and dreams, passion and sexuality sound all very well but where do they stand in the cold light of day: against the grief of the bereaved parent in Birmingham or the slaughter of the innocent in Belfast, against the helplessness of the mentally handicapped in Inverness or the plight of the homeless in London? As Wilfred Bion knew, pairing can as easily divert men's energies from the task in hand as give them the inspiration to work at it. Are not these interpersonal experiences just another trip into fantasy, distracting us from the hard realities of life, and do they not cause more chaos than community? Alan Ecclestone pertinently comments:

Passion without engagement is a display of fireworks, a waste of energy, a self-abuse, 'full of sound and fury, signifying nothing'. It burns itself out to leave only ashes. Its intensity can scorch and scar but not transfigure. It knows and offers no guide to the worth of what it touches. Its most unlovely forms appear in sexual jealousy and religious bigotry, its most arid in sentimentality and wishful thinking.

271

It can distort and wreck the best engagements of men's lives by vehement importunity and blind desire.[24]

The evidence of these pages, however, is that members of basic communities *are* so engaged, in a way which at times shames those of us sitting cosily in our armchairs watching the tragedies of the world flash entertainingly by, in colour if we can afford it, on our television screens. They are engaged in communal living, sticking with relationships when most of us regularly escape into less demanding encounters. They are sharing their possessions readily whilst we hoard and covet. They are expending great efforts to conserve the resources and beauty of a world we are busy wasting and polluting. It is they who are challenging us to educate ourselves in a deeper appreciation of the personal and interpersonal dimensions of life when we would rest content with our ignorance and prejudice. They are tending the sick, caring for the lost, supporting the bereaved, and striving to enable men to be free, when we are taken up with ourselves and our trivial ailments and anxieties. They are daring enough to laugh and dance in the presence of the Almighty when we prefer the safe prison of the church pew screwed firmly to the floor. Can we then have the effrontery to say that these people are all vision and passion and no engagement? It is we who have surrendered humanity and community for we have neither vision, passion, nor engagement!

The interpersonal aspect of the community movement is about love; passion and engagement. The yes to others in word and deed is enabling a new appreciation of the human and communal to grow. Alan Watts writes that 'love brings the real, and not just the ideal, vision of what others are'.[25]

Those involved in the community movement are not for ever harking back to a golden age, because they know there never was such. They are rather in the present declaring, as the Gospel has always done, the possibility of the apparently impossible. As yet they are doing so with reference to no theory or theology but by offering as their credentials the evidence of that quality of community life which they are creating. For them, community is its own symbol.

Yes and authority

The pioneers of a new vision of the personal and interpersonal, of a new sense of significance and solidarity for man, of a new quality of community, have taken it upon themselves to say yes. They have neither depended on others to say yes for them, and thus escaped responsibility for their decisions, nor been prepared to accept a yes thrust upon them. Their yes is an autonomous yes. It is a yes which comes, as Anna describes it to Fynn, from knowing 'Mister God in my middle in your middle'.[26] Their authority is not 'out there' or 'up there' but 'in here'.

To take authority to oneself is a dangerous matter; Church and society would say pretentious if not downright subversive. It is dangerous because to move beyond social and religious norms is to leave behind all the familiar landmarks; in the end, as Tillich writes, it is to find oneself in a place 'without a name, a church, a cult, a theology'.[27] Whatever is there discovered is one's own discovery, and whatever thereon built is one's own construction. Nevertheless, for those really wrestling to find new expressions of community, this is what the business is all about, for themselves and for others. It is not, however, a state of anomie, total confusion leading to loss of all norms, but one of choosing for oneself, with one's fellow travellers, what the new norms shall be, and holding them flexible and responsive to developing experience.

Those basic communities which rate autonomy highly find themselves standing over against Church and society not because they are by nature radical or revolutionary but because they have espoused values which traditional and bureaucratic institutions find extremely difficult to assimilate. One set of values surrounds their understanding of significance and the personal. Where they are working for the right and responsibility of the individual to choose for himself, they find that they are up against institutions which have a totally different view of the person, judging his worth according to his position in the traditional order or on the hierarchical ladder. It is not that they envy the power and status enjoyed by those officially in control, but that they abhor the treatment of people as if they were babes in arms or cogs in wheels, an attitude which seems to carry over into every aspect of life. They do not object to the exercise of authority but to its being exercised in a paternalistic or autocratic way that refuses people space to grow, on the grounds that they will always refuse or abuse freedom of choice.

At present the community movement in its championing of the personal finds itself in a position akin to Wilfred Bion's 'fight/flight'[28] position over against normative social structures. It can 'flight' in frustration or disgust from an increasingly dehumanizing Church and society, or it can gather its resources to 'fight' the powers that be. In fact, I see few members of basic communities flighting from the task of affirming the value of the individual. Rather I find people deeply concerned, be it in urban or rural settings, through one kind of communal life-style and activity or another, striving to overcome impersonality and the threat of insignificance. The differences at present come in how that fight should be conducted both within their own ranks and in relation to the world beyond.

That authority which takes upon itself the responsibility of saying yes to the value of the person also takes upon itself the right to affirm the depth and the comprehensiveness of the interpersonal. Here again the community movement stands over against a Church and society which, through fear and vested interest, refuse to allow men to explore new patterns of human relationship. The power of pairing and passion is, as we have seen, 'essentially lawless'.[29] It is a threat to the established order because on the one hand it challenges the exploitation of groups easily exposed to manipulation, such as the isolated nuclear family, and on the other seeks to break down those barriers that would deliberately keep man divided from man on the basis of pride and prejudice.

The exploration of new dimensions of communal living in relation to the family is still a wisp of smoke on the horizon, but without doubt far-reaching changes are under way.[30] I have touched on some of the social issues relevant to family life in Chapter 2, and on a number of related economic concerns in Chapter 4. Though the scene is changing slowly, especially as far as the Christian is concerned, and few would go as far as Wilhelm Reich who saw the family as the instrument by which the State subdued its citizens,[31] we are already witnessing a backlash from the guardians of established mores. The irony is that while many communities and groups are developing their own relationships with care and maturity, it is society itself wherein the real dehumanization of family life, not least of the wife and mother as a person, is occurring.

The power of pairing and passion also threatens the legitimacy of those authorities who would raise irrational barriers between men. It could be argued that members of basic communities are of a relatively homogeneous social type and thus in reality do not practise what they preach. But to believe wholeheartedly in the community of man does not mean that one forces oneself to deny one's origins and cultural identity. What it does mean is the breaking down of constraints and prejudices that make it impossible to choose to live, work, worship, or play with and care for any man, woman, or child as a person. This

274

commitment of the community movement to hold to the ideal of an open Church and society is one which many public figures outwardly applaud while in practice treating it with great suspicion in case established ways and vested interests are threatened.

Basic communities and the Church

These points are especially relevant to the Church as an institution. We in the West are inheritors of a theology which, in Transactional Analysis terms, has cancelled out the 'Adult' in favour of the 'Critical Parent'. Thomas Harris writes:

> Central to most religious practices is a Child acceptance of authoritarian dogma as an act of faith, with limited, if not absent, involvement of the Adult. Thus, when morality is encased in the structure of religion, it is essentially Parent. It is dated, frequently unexamined, and often contradictory.[32]

The result is a laity who, on the one hand, are bemused or frustrated by the supposed mystique of religious dogma and, on the other, in such a position of infantile dependence that they are unwilling or unable to do anything constructive about their situation. No more pertinent yet tragic example is the state of the Church in Northern Ireland.

We are members of an ecclesiastical institution which denies the very truth for which it stands. We are supposed to be a pilgrim people unencumbered and on the move yet we are chained to plant and property; we proclaim the hollowness of riches yet still have great wealth. The Church preaches about servanthood and humility yet is classically hierarchical; it offers wholeness to man yet ministers to only a fraction of his personality and needs; it speaks about love and reconciliation yet is as divided and divisive as any other institution. Charles Davis puts it thus: 'The present social structure of the Church is no longer adequately a living institution, in as much as it no longer adequately embodies Christian experience. It is an antiquated structure out of harmony with the thinking, needs, and desires of active Christians today.'[33] There is plenty of frantic activity going on, with straws by the dozen being clutched at, be these visions of massive charismatic revival or appeals to the nation. But the Church, as Western man has known it, cannot continue as it is without being a denial of the Gospel for our age. It has to change, and to change in a fundamental way, if it is to avoid being itself an heretical social system.

This is not mere rhetoric. It is obvious to any feeling and thinking Christian with an appreciation of what humanity and community are all about.

The direction of authentic change will be towards that quality of life which those described in this book are seeking to express. As yet the path is indistinct and the landmarks few, but the basic communities of which I have written are undoubtedly blazing a trail. None of them knows all the answers; indeed none of them knows all the questions. But within their life, organization, and activity is to be seen a foretaste of things to come.

The Church has hitherto been unable to respond because it is caught looking the wrong way. It is looking the wrong way in its clinging on to the separate and segregated role of the clergy with which an increasing number of basic communities will have nothing to do. As the traditional role of the Church in society declines, so inevitably does that of the ordained ministry; and there is no going back. The future must see, as in so many examples quoted in this book, clergy and laity working together in an equally diversified and mutually supportive ministry. It must see clergy and laity freeing themselves from their collusion in an immature relationship, in order to be the Church in the world.

The Church is looking the wrong way in its worship and its spirituality. Neither liturgical renewal nor charismatic revival can bring back vitality and meaning unless body, mind, and spirit are fully engaged in thanksgiving to God. This means the Church taking very seriously the growth of greater self-awareness and self-affirmation amongst members of the community movement, and the demonstration of how worship and encounter can again infuse each other. There is no way to the rediscovery of the meaning of spirituality until holy communion is born out of holy community. It is the sterile formality or flippant superficiality of what today passes for worship that has set going the exciting explorations on which I have touched. Not least, let it be said, seized with a genuine festivity which 'is in its very essence participatory and anti-authoritarian'.[34]

The Church is looking the wrong way in its appreciation of the wholeness of life. Dogged by the Western world's propensity to split everything from the atom outwards, it has fallen victim to the paralysis of analysis which separates man from his environment, and mind from body and spirit. It has, for example, by worshipping within four solid walls screened out the beauty of a living world. (Go to the chapel at St Julian's and rejoice in a great window, from floor to roof behind the altar, by means of which their beautiful garden becomes part of the sanctuary.) Some of our basic communities, prompted by the message of the Eastern religions, are attempting to show that Christian man has lost touch with the very substance of which he is made and without an awareness of which his full humanity is lost. They are not devaluing the intellect as some would assume but affirming that true wholeness of being without which salvation has little meaning.

The Church has turned its back on the liberation offered through learning and education. It has contracted out of telling its story, and of communicating it in a way that its Founder demonstrated again and again. It has sought to instruct and train, sometimes to indoctrinate, but rarely to educate. It has been obsessed with 'religious knowledge', as if that were anything but part of what life and man's response to it were all about. Not all the communities of learning described in this book have shaken clear of traditional approaches but most are endeavouring to do so, some with impressive success. They are grappling with the mysteries and complexities of the world in which man lives and the ultimate questions about it. They are enabling us to tell each other stories and to listen attentively: they are realizing that there are no answers or endings other than those which the listener discovers for himself. There is the speaking of the yes, the truth as they know it, but not the speaking of the truth as it must be received by others.

The Church is looking the wrong way in its concern for those in need. It persists in the belief that the institutional and professional are more necessary than community care. It remains jammed, though perhaps a little less firmly here than in other fields, in the mould of earlier centuries. It cannot comprehend that people are actually able to minister to people: it constantly intrudes with its outmoded, patronizing, pastoral models of intervention. By no means all the caring communities and groups escape such paternalism, for ready response to crisis can make men deaf to the often weak cry for autonomy. But here and there the ability of the layman to minister to the layman and even of the disadvantaged is being recognized and acted upon.

The Church has turned its back on politics because it does not wish to acknowledge that its activities are just as political as those of any other institution. In doing so it has mythologized its worship and its teaching whilst surrendering its credibility to call in question the type of society and economy of which it is an integral part. It has washed its hands of the world of industry and commerce. It has contracted out of seriously wrestling with the social and economic issues of the day and resorted to platitudes and simplistic exhortation. If it does now and then go public in an articulate manner it is largely through the few clergy it has set aside to salve its conscience, whilst its laity (its real political spokesmen) are kept busy giving out the hymnbooks or raising funds for the restoration of the spire. Basic communities have by no means yet remedied this situation but many of them are applying their energies to major economic issues in a world fast using up its natural resources, to the meaning of participation in work as well as worship, to the association of spirituality with politics and to the cause of justice for the prisoner, the persecuted, and the poor. They are not experts; they are people concerned about people and seeing these activities as an authentic, indeed compelling, expression of their faith.

In some ways dominating all the other issues, the Church is facing the wrong way in its understanding of ecumenicity. It is still tied to the concept of unity based on the merger of declining and now outmoded denominations. Such unity can do no more than replace several anachronisms by a single crippling one. For those things which divide men no longer need the language of bygone days to cloak them; they are of the warp and woof of conflicts which have now emerged infinitely more explicitly and starkly in secular form. The community movement still looks to its religious heritage and respects it out of loyalty. But most are aware that the deep things that divide men only originate there in the imagination of the theologians. They are conscious that it is more fundamental matters than creeds and dogmas which really separate mankind, that ecumenicity is not about the discovery of compromise religious formulas or ecclesiastical joinery, and that the real business of reconciliation concerns treating people as human not treating them as Christians. Ask Corrymeela about that.

Winds of change

The Church is a conservative institution. In some respects it is properly so because it is the guardian and vehicle of the story of how man, through the joy and agony of human experience, has sought to give meaning and purpose to his existence. It is conservative because for many it provides a clearly recognizable and eternally secure sanctuary amidst 'the changes and chances of this fleeting world'. As we have seen in Chapter 5, even those experienced in the field of group dynamics can argue that the Church's primary task is to be a dependable institution, above all through its clergy as symbolic figures and through its worship.

It is thus understandable why the contract between minister and laity should be a 'no change' one, why the initial response to suggestions of minor change are cautious and to major change downright aggressive. For change in this situation threatens not just an institution but a total way of interpreting and living life built up over generations if not centuries.

I do not quarrel with man's need for that on which he can depend, not least the Christian's God. But what has happened is that the Church and priesthood as institutions have usurped this role and reduced man to a state of immature and at times infantile dependence. The Church has ceased to be a people on the move, with no abiding city within which to shelter, constantly declaring the provisional nature of all social systems including its own. It has literally become 'established', so indistinguishable from other institutions in its form and mode of operating that, instead of being free to lead man to a deeper and more comprehensive awareness of community, it is the last to feel the winds of change.

Yet the winds of change have been blowing for some time, given impetus by the rising tempo of mobility – spatial, social, and cognitive – and through a few prophetic voices, many not Christian, the meaning of humanity and community is being radically questioned and searchingly reappraised. And who can argue that a Church which has always claimed to offer the key to the truly human and to represent the fullness of community should not be especially ready to welcome such a challenge? The basic communities of which I have written are but a very small part of a much larger 'movement of fire' running across many continents.[35]

For the Church in this country, however, they are, in conjunction with their counterparts in the secular sectors, the part that counts. Their first endeavour has been to find the space and resources to establish themselves with some hope of survival; their second object to begin to build alternative models of community which others can see and understand; their third to work, by means of their own example and endeavour, for the re-creation of a Church and society which gives new meaning to the personal and interpersonal dimensions of life. These communal alternatives are still in the process of growth and development. Many have not taken root; others have fallen by the wayside. But an increasing number, across the whole spectrum of society's interests and concerns, are not only taking hold but beginning to blossom. As yet we have a kaleidoscope of colours and a changing

279

pattern to the overall picture, but necessarily so if this movement is in the end going to provide the means to the lasting attainment of a new dimension of community.

One major question as yet unanswered concerns not the nature of change, with which this book has been mainly involved, but its means. Is change to come through co-operation and consensus or through confrontation and conflict? Can the Church be reformed or must it be bypassed?[36] Charles Davis writes: 'The real question . . . is whether the Christian revolution now gathering force will succeed in breaking up and reshaping the present structures or, resisted to the end, sweep past them to leave them as quaint, meaningless relics.'[37]

Indeed, what power have these seemingly puny ventures in community got to promote any change at all? The Marxist would write them off as at best Utopian socialism and argue that should 'Utopian experiments disturb the existing Capitalist system to any significant degree then the Capitalist state would destroy the Utopian Communities by violence'.[38] Others, however, see it differently, for their aim is not to match the violence of Church and society with their own brand of aggression, but to live out their vision as best they can, believing wholeheartedly in the power of example, the redemptive nature of suffering, and the grace of God. In Keith Kimber's words, they are 'communities of protest' whose 'spirit cannot be destroyed by oppression, but rather is that which will give life to all new movements which emerge in the hope of transforming our future'.[39] For the Christian at least the means of change has somewhere within it a cross, and that a symbol not of sentimentality but of saying a genuine yes out of the midst of 'the darkness that covers the world with fearful hatred and horror'.[40]

I include just one example of what this can mean in practice. Bob Livingstone writes 'from the heart of the Shankill':[41]

Since the present conflict in Northern Ireland is waged between working people, the Shankill area is in the front line of the battle. Across the so-called 'peace line' lies the Falls District, as traditionally Catholic as the Shankill is Protestant. So the scene is set for confrontation. Added to the chaos produced by violence is the devastation caused by re-development. Over half the houses in the Shankill area are scheduled for demolition and replacement. The demolition has gone ahead, but violence has delayed the replacement, with the result that the more progressive elements of the community have moved out, leaving behind the elderly, the backward and the anti-social. Set down in the midst of this human deprivation, distress and depravity are the five members of the two-year-old Shankill Methodist Team Ministry. They are convinced that one of the crying needs of the moment is for a community house where voluntary workers could come and live together for longer or shorter periods, offering acceptance and service to those around them. A house in the adjoining non-development area is now [autumn 1975] available, but the Shankill Team Ministry has neither the money to purchase and repair it, nor the workers to use it. The leader of the Team Ministry, the Rev. Robert Livingstone, cries from the heart of the Shankill to the readers of *Community* to help with gifts of money and voluntary workers.[42]

Within a short time the relatively small, and not particularly affluent, readership of the *Community* magazine had donated £500 and a number of young people have since volunteered to live in the house and work in the area. The project continues.

The community movement faces many pitfalls, within and without. Internally it walks the knife-edge between activism and passivity. As with those groups involved in caring and political concerns, for example, the response to crises and fighting blatant injustices can obscure the deeper search for a society wherein the person is valued as a person and the interpersonal expressed as an all-encompassing engagement. 'Even the commitment to politics', writes Paul Oestreicher, 'can be and often is an escape into mere activism if love of persons, immersion in the mystery of God in a little child, in every child, is not at the heart of the desired revolution.'[43] On the other hand, there is the temptation, as in the case of some new forms of spirituality, to escape into passivity, to cease responding to the events of a world beyond one's self and immediate circle. Or to pretend, as certain interfaith groups have at times tried to do, that differences of attitude and custom have little consequence with regard to creating community. But therein no genuine renewal is to be found. Keith Kimber writes:

The communities of protest which remove themselves from inter-action with society by creating alternative life-styles of ideologies which deliver them from the sphere of society's influence, like the Pilgrim Fathers or underground secret sects, suffer the ossification of their way of life. Once they cease to threaten they can be absorbed or accommodated into society at little cost. The dialogue of protest *has*

281

to be manifest and *has* to continue if the life of communities of protest is to be sustained.[44]

From without, the community movement faces many threats. The Church in particular has the ability to seem to condone whilst in fact condemning. One example of this is the process which Sumner termed 'conventionalization'.[45] New ventures in community are called 'experiments' (a word I have tried to avoid in this book); in reality indicating that the sincerity and efforts of those involved gain token acknowledgement, thereby deflecting any major critique of the system. This has been a feature of the ecumenical scene, not least in connection with the concept of team ministry and 'areas of ecumenical experiment'. It is currently occurring with regard to the charismatic movement which will soon be 'blessed to death'. Even more pertinent to my theme, Pope Paul himself at the end of 1975 commended *communidades de base* as destined to be 'special beneficiaries of evangelization and at the same time evangelizers themselves',[46] apparently unaware of the fundamental challenge that basic communites pose to a Church established on dominantly classical lines.

Another threat comes from any Church which, having mis-understood what the prophets are saying, attempts to use its authority to compel people to set about re-creating community. The Second Vatican Council was for many Roman Catholics a milestone in renewal but there are indications, for example within the religious Orders, that communities have sought to reform simply because they have been instructed to reform. Such a mode of operating produces the very antithesis of autonomy. Structure and organization are very necessary but, in our terms, they can do no more than give men the space to discover themselves and the quality of life community can offer. When the Church seeks to force growth or impose community, it merely reinforces that sense of dependence which is the very thing being human and thus Christian is *not* about. 'The revolution which is not created by people themselves is but another form of oppression.'[47]

Where now?

The community movement in which many Christians are involved has a narrow path to tread if it is to realize the visions which it has not only espoused but begun with courage to work out in practice. It needs the encouragement of the many as yet not directly involved, but who are aware of the winds of change beginning to blow through the Church and world at gale force. It does not want to be paternalistically protected nor prematurely idealized; it is robust enough to stand up for itself and it openly acknowledges that it has already run into all the problems associated with that type of human endeavour which risks going out into the unknown.

None the less, it is important that an open dialogue should continue between those involved in this movement and those at present living within the mainstream of Church and society. It is a dialogue which in the end will have to fashion a new philosophy and a new theology to enable the current experience of community to be interpreted and communicated to the many at present who are quite unaware of what is happening. The community movement must be true to itself and, without loss of conviction and identity, enter into partnership with all those ready like itself to see, hear, and learn.

Such a partnership includes not only the Christian but the non-Christian. For though this book has been focused on the Christian active in pioneering new life-styles, Paul Oestreicher is absolutely right when he states: '"Religious community" is precisely what the Christian faith is NOT about. It is about the transformation of secular communities into the Kingdom of God.'[48] In that task the Church is only one institution amongst many and the Christian only one sort of person amongst others. Where there are people in whatever sector of society and with whatever faith, or none, so committed, then they too are fellow travellers.

The movement for the discovery of a new dimension to the meaning of being human and of community here described, with the Church as backcloth, is also occurring in relation to other institutions in our society: the family, the school, the factory, the hospital, and government itself. The search is of a similar kind, the issues and the questions are basically the same. The search for a fully personal and a richly interpersonal quality of life is identical, for I have been talking first about the business of being human and only then of being Christian. The Christian is involved not because he has a monopoly of truth or wisdom but because he too has freely chosen to be in on 'the dawn-chorus of a new creation'.[49]

NOTES

CHAPTER 1
NEW PERSPECTIVES ON COMMUNITY

1 Merton, R. K., *Social Theory and Social Structure*, New York, The Free Press, revised edn (1957), pp. 387–420.

2 Ibid., p. 393.

3 Cf. Clark, D. B., 'Local and Cosmopolitan Aspects of Religious Activity in a Northern Suburb', in Martin, D., and Hill, M. (eds.), *A Sociological Yearbook of Religion in Britain*, vol. 3, SCM Press (1970), pp. 45–64.

4 See Clark, D. B., 'The Concept of Community: a Re-Examination', in *The Sociological Review*, vol. 21, no. 3, University of Keele (August 1973), pp. 397–416.

5 Plant, R., *Community and Ideology*, Routledge and Kegan Paul (1974).

6 Clark, 'The Concept of Community', op. cit., pp. 399–400.

7 Ibid., pp. 400–2.

8 Ibid., pp. 402–5.

9 Ibid., p. 409.

10 Niebuhr, Reinhold, *Moral Man and Immoral Society*, SCM Press (1963).

11 Jenkins, D., *What is Man?*, SCM Press (1970), p. 81.

12 Ibid., p. 89.

13 Berger, P., *A Rumour of Angels*, Pelican (1971), pp. 66–96.

14 See Williams, C. W., *John Wesley's Theology Today*, Epworth Press (1960).

15 Furlong, M., *The End of Our Exploring*, Hodder and Stoughton (1973).

16 Jenkins, op. cit., p. 109.

17 Tillich, P., *The Courage to Be*, Fontana, Collins (1962), p. 30.

18 Ecclestone, A., *Yes to God*, Darton, Longman and Todd (1975), p. 106.

19 Ibid., p. 111.

20 Tillich, op. cit., pp. 114–51.

21 Watts, A. W., *Nature, Man and Woman*, Wildwood House (1973), p. 43.

22 Ibid., pp. 25ff.

23 Ibid., pp. 142–3.

24 Ibid., p. 43.

25 The Holy Bible (RSV), Thomas Nelson (1952), John 3.8.

26 Buber, M., *I and Thou*, T. and T. Clark (1958).

27 Cox, H., *The Secular City*, SCM Press (1965), pp. 48–9, 263ff.

28 Tillich, op. cit., pp. 89–113.

29 Dahrendorf, R., *The New Liberty*, Routledge and Kegan Paul (1975), p. 44.

30 Harris, T. A., *I'm OK – You're OK*, Pan Books (1973), p. 217.

31 Ibid., p. 229.

32 Berne, E., *Sex in Human Loving*, Penguin (1973), p. 127.

33 Ibid., pp. 129–30.

34 See, for example, Bonhoeffer, D., *Letters and Papers from Prison*, Fontana, Collins (1959), p. 108.

35 Wright, D., *The Psychology of Moral Behaviour*, Penguin (1971), pp. 222–8.

36 Smith, P., *Letters from Pilsdon*, Pilsdon, Dorset (December 1967).

37 Harris, op. cit., p. 211.

38 Rudge, P. F., *Ministry and Management*, Tavistock (1968), particularly the chart on pp. 32–3.

39 Mannheim, K., *Ideology and Utopia*, Routledge and Kegan Paul (1936), pp. 226–7.

40 Ineson, G., *Community Journey*, Sheed and Ward (1956), p. 33.

41 Haughton, R., *On Trying to Be Human*, Geoffrey Chapman (1966), p. 136.

42 Jenkins, op. cit., p. 114.

CHAPTER 2
INTENTIONAL COMMUNITIES

1 *A Society of Lay People*, The Grail (1974), pp. 9–11.

2 Rigby, A., *Communes in Britain*, Routledge and Kegan Paul (1974), p. 26.

3 Author of *Pop Goes Jesus*, Mowbrays (1972). In personal correspondence.

4 Corry, G., *Jesus Bubble or Jesus Revolution?*, British Council of Churches (1973), p. 19.

5 *Community*, no. 11 (Spring 1975), p. 3.

6 *In Touch*, no. 27 (December 1974), p. 18.

7 *In Touch*, no. 28 (March 1975), p. 11.

8 *The Rule of Life of the Hengrave Community* (1974), section 1.

9 *Community*, no. 7 (Winter 1973), pp. 9–10.

10 *Community*, no. 10 (Winter 1974), p. 15.

11 *Community*, no. 11 (Spring 1975), p. 3.

12 Ineson, G., *Suggestions for an 'Ashram' at Taena*, Taena (July 1975), p. 3.

13 Knowles, D., *Christian Monasticism*, Weidenfeld and Nicolson (1969), p. 230.

14 Leech, K., *Youthquake*, Sheldon Press (1973), p. 156.

15 *In Touch*, no. 27 (December 1974), p. 1.

16 Leach, M. M., *My Name Shall Be There*, Scargill Publications (1971), 2nd edn, p. 45.

17 Rigby, op. cit., p. 80.

18 Ibid., pp. 40–67.

19 Pamphlet on *Pilsdon*, Bridport, Dorset (n.d.).

20 *Community*, no. 2 (Winter 1972), pp. 5–6.

21 *A Society of Lay People*, op. cit.

22 Ibid., pp. 23–4.

23 Corry, op. cit., pp. 25–6.

24 *Towards Renewal*, no. 1 (n.d.), p. 7.

25 *Community*, no. 15 (Summer 1976), pp. 10–11.

26 Rigby, op. cit., p. 141.

27 *Crusade* (May 1974), p. 22.

28 *Community*, no. 11 (Spring 1975), p. 7.

29 Blackwell, C., *Cyrenian Principles*, The Cyrenians, Canterbury (1973), p. 10.

30 Corry, op. cit., p. 40.

31 *Community*, no. 6 (Summer 1973), p. 10.

32 Schutz, W., *Elements of Encounter*, Joy Press (1973), pp. 53–6.

33 Bradford, L. P., Gibb, J. R., and Benne, K. D., *T-Group Theory and Laboratory Method*, New York, John Wiley (1964), pp. 248–78.

34 Clark, D. B., 'Local and Cosmopolitan Aspects of Religious Activity in a Northern Suburb', in *A Sociological Yearbook of Religion in Britain*, no. 3, SCM Press (1970), pp. 45–64.

35 Lockley, A., *Christian Communes*, SCM Press (1976), p. 88.

36 Cooper, D., *The Death of the Family*, Penguin (1972), p. 41.

37 Potts, M. I., *St Julian's*, SCM Press (1968), p. 52.

38 *A Society of Lay People*, op. cit., p. 14.

39 Withey, V., *Towards Renewal*, no. 4, Post Green (Autumn 1975), p. 13.

40 O'Neill, N. and G., *Open Marriage*, Abacus (1975).

41 See Gordon, M. (ed.) *The Nuclear Family in Crisis: the Search for an Alternative*, New York, Harper and Row (1972), pp. 204–22.

42 Bernard, J., *The Future of Marriage*, Pelican (1976), pp. 281, 292.

43 Ibid., p. 208.

44 Broido, M. (ed.), *Communal Housing*, a report by a Chimera working group, Sussex University (1971), pp. 10–11.

45 *Community*, no. 4 (Autumn 1972), p. 2.

46 *Community*, no. 6 (Summer 1973), p. 13.

47 *Crusade* (May 1974), p. 24.

48 Taylor, J. V., *Enough is Enough*, SCM Press (1975), p. 14.

49 *Community*, no. 15 (Summer 1976), p. 17.

50 Broido, op. cit., pp. 11–12.

51 Bernard, op. cit., p. 254.

52 *New Covenant* (November 1974), pp. 6–7.

53 Potts, op. cit., p. 37.

54 Ibid., p. 38.

55 Ibid., p. 40.

56 Ibid., pp. 40–1.

57 Ineson, op. cit., p. 3.

58 Ineson, G., *Community Journey*, Sheed and Ward (1956), p. 64.

59 Rigby, op. cit., p. 104.

60 Haughton, R., *On Trying to Be Human*, Geoffrey Chapman (1966), p. 135.

61 *The Little Gidding Way*, Little Gidding (Spring 1976).

62 Rigby, op. cit., p. 73.

63 *A Society of Lay People*, op. cit., p. 22.

64 *Community*, no. 7 (Winter 1973), p. 10.

65 *Community*, no. 6 (Summer 1973), pp. 13–14.

66 *A Society of Lay People*, op. cit., p. 35.

67 *Community*, no. 5 (Spring 1973), p. 9.

68 Abrams, P. and McCulloch, A., *Communes, Sociology and Society*, Cambridge University Press (1976).

69 Bernard, op. cit., pp. 207–9.

70 Abrams and McCulloch, op. cit., p. 211.

CHAPTER 3

SPIRITUALITY

1 Webb, P., *Salvation Today*, SCM Press (1974), p. 100.

2 New English Bible, Eph. 1.18.

3 Douglas, M., *Natural Symbols*, The Cresset Press (1970), p. 50. Published by Galliards Printers, Queen Anne's Road, Great Yarmouth, Norfolk.

4 Walsh, M. L., 'Celebrations in the Age of Aquarius', in *Movement*, no. 12, SCM Press (1973), p. 19.

5 Leaflet on the Community of the Transfiguration, Roslin, near Edinburgh.

6 *Community*, no. 2 (Winter 1972), p. 5.

7 *Community*, no. 5 (Spring 1973), p. 15.

8 *What? Why? How? You!*, Iona Community leaflet.

9 *A Common Discipline*, Coventry Cathedral Staff, II: 'The Practice of the Discipline', sections 1, 3, and 6.

10 Potts, M. I., *St Julian's*, SCM Press (1968), Appendix I.

11 *ACT*, journal of the Ashram Community Trust, Sheffield, no. 7 (May 1974), p. 7.

12 *Community*, no. 3 (Summer 1972), p. 5.

13 *Community*, no. 1 (Autumn 1971), pp. 13–14.

14 *Community*, no. 1 (Autumn 1971), p. 14.

15 Corry, G., *Jesus Bubble or Jesus Revolution?*, British Council of Churches (1973), pp. 25–6.

16 *Towards Renewal*, no. 1 (n.d.), p. 2.

17 Ibid., p. 14.

18 *Focolare*, pamphlet, p. 6.

19 Elixir, *God Spoke to Me*, Part I (n.d.), Findhorn Publications, p. 24.

20 Ibid., p. 31.

21 Klein, J., *Samples from English Cultures*, vol. I, Routledge and Kegan Paul (1965), p. 95.

22 Ecclestone, A., *Yes to God*, Darton, Longman and Todd, p. 43.

23 Nicholson, J., 'Belief Today', from a talk given at the Evangelische Akademie Arnoldshain (Whitsun 1975).

24 Ineson, G., *Suggestions for an 'Ashram' at Taena*, Taena (July 1975), p. 2.

25 *Community*, no. 12 (Summer 1975), p. 4.

26 *Towards Renewal*, op. cit., pp. 2 and 9.

27 *Katimavik*, booklet (1975), p. 1.

28 Lanier, J., *Gestalt Paraphrases* (n.d.), Malaga, Spain, p. 1.

29 Hebblethwaite, P., 'New Forms of Worship', in *Movement*, no. 12, SCM Press (1973), p. 21.

30 *A Society of Lay People*, The Grail (1974), p. 29.

31 Cooke, J. A., 'An Analysis of Modern Worship Experiments', in *Facets*, no. 3 (Winter 1973), p. 25.

32 Hengrave Hall Newsletter, no. 3 (June 1975).

33 *Lively Worship*, ONE for Christian Renewal (March 1975), Case-study 2.

34 *Renewal*, Magazine of the Fountain Trust, London, no. 59, p. 8.

35 *Community*, no. 8 (Spring 1974), p. 6.

36 *Movement*, op. cit., p. 23.

37 *A Society of Lay People*, op. cit., pp. 35–6.

38 Ibid., p. 36.

39 *What is Transcendental Meditation?*, Spiritual Regeneration Movement of Great Britain (n.d.), p. 3.

40 Ibid., p. 5.

41 Leech, K., *Youthquake*, Sheldon Press (1973), pp. 70, 73.

42 Ibid., p. 85.

43 *The Guardian* (5 August 1975).

44 Ibid.

45 Leech, op. cit., p. 98.

46 Wrekin Trust Programme of conferences (1975).

47 Happold, F. C., *The Journey Inwards*, Darton, Longman and Todd (1968), p. 13.

48 *The Vision*, journal of the Association for Promoting Retreats (July 1975), p. 6.

49 *Katimavik*, op. cit., p. 4.

50 *Community*, no. 6 (Summer 1973), p. 13.

51 Ibid.

52 *Community*, no. 5 (Spring 1973), p. 14.

53 *The Vision*, Association for Promoting Retreats (January 1976), p. 5.

54 Ibid., pp. 5–6.

55 *Community*, no. 10 (Winter 1974), p. 15.

56 Servants of Christ the King Newsletter, no. 8 (August 1974), p. 1.

57 Ibid., p. 2.

58 *What is I.E.F.?*, pamphlet on the International Ecumenical Fellowship, Crutched Friars, London (n.d.).

59 Cox, H., *The Feast of Fools*, Harvard University Press (1969), p. 47.

60 Leach, M., *My Name Shall Be There*, Scargill Publications (1971), 2nd edn, p. 38.

61 *Towards Renewal*, op. cit., p. 8.

62 Corry, op. cit., p. 29.

63 *The Way*, Magazine of the Pilgrims of St Francis, no. 19 (April 1975), p. 5.

64 *Community*, no. 9 (Summer 1974), p. 14.

65 *Community*, no. 3 (Summer 1972), p. 11.

66 *Facets*, op. cit., p. 27.

67 *Observer Supplement* (8 September 1974), p. 48.

68 *Movement*, op. cit., p. 22.

69 *Renewal*, magazine of the Fountain Trust.

70 Sullivan, E., *Can the Pentecostal Movement Renew the Churches?*, British Council of Churches (1972); *Study Encounter*, vol. VIII/no. 4 (1972).

71 *Renewal*, no. 58 (August/September 1975), p. 4.

72 *A Society of Lay People*, op. cit., p. 8.

73 *Renewal*, no. 51 (June/July 1974), pp. 2–4.

74 Sullivan, op. cit., p. 9.

75 Ibid., p. 6.

76 Cox, op. cit., p. 28.

77 *Lively Worship*, op. cit., Case-study 4.

78 Douglas, op. cit., p. 155.

CHAPTER 4
ENVIRONMENTAL AND ECONOMIC ASPECTS OF COMMUNITY

1 (June 1975), Dartmouth House, Dartmouth Row, London SE10 8AW.

2 See Rivers, P., *The Survivalists*, Eyre Methuen (1975), pp. 53–4.

3 Schumacher, E. F., *Small is Beautiful*, Blond and Briggs (1973), pp. 275–9.

4 Taylor, J. V., *Enough is Enough*, SCM Press (1975).

5 Dahrendorf, R., *The New Liberty*, Routledge and Kegan Paul (1975), p. 10.

6 Dickson, D., *Alternative Technology and the Politics of Technical Change*, Fontana, Collins (1974).

7 Taylor, op. cit., p. 12.

8 Ibid., p. 14.

9 Dahrendorf, op. cit, p. 22.

10 Dickson, op. cit., p. 64.

11 Ibid., p. 43.

12 Dahrendorf, op. cit., p. 27.

13 Ibid., p. 32.

14 Ibid., p. 28.

15 Dickson, op. cit., p. 89.

16 Ibid., pp. 186–7.

17 Ibid., p. 55.

18 Ibid., p. 11.

19 Schumacher, op. cit., p. 244.

20 Tillich, P., *The Courage to Be*, Fontana, Collins (1962), p. 30.

21 Dickson, op. cit., p. 38.

22 *Towards Life Together – Letters from Community*, Pilsdon (1958–67).

23 *Movement*, no. 20, SCM Press (April/May 1975), p. viii.

24 *The Earth, and why it needs you for a friend*, Friends of the Earth, 9 Poland Street, London W1V 3DG (n.d.).

25 Elliott, D., 'Working on All Fronts', in *Undercurrents*, no. 16 (June/July 1976), p. 14.

26 Ibid.

27 Leaflet, *The Conservation Society for Survival*, London (n.d.).

28 Taylor, op. cit., pp. 22–39.

29 Ibid., p. 104.

30 Dammers, H., *Life Style – a Word to the Wise*, Bristol (1974).

31 Ibid.

32 *ACT*, journal of the Ashram Community Trust, Sheffield, no. 11 (1975).

33 Ineson, G., *Suggestions for an 'Ashram' at Taena*, Taena (July 1975), p. 2.

34 Crowther, G., 'Self-Sufficient. Rural Commune – Special Offer', in *BIT Better*, BIT, 146 Great Western Road, London W11 (1975), p. 14.

35 Elliott, op. cit., p. 13.

36 Schumacher, op. cit.

37 *Community*, no. 5 (Spring 1973), p. 8.

38 Seymour, J., *The Fat of the Land*, Faber and Faber (1961), p. 9.

39 Warren, D. S. and L. J., The New Villages Association, 3 Salubrious, Broadway, Worcs. (n.d.).

40 Crowther, op. cit., p. 14.

41 Ibid., p. 15.

42 Elliott, D., 'How the Land Turned Sour', in *Undercurrents*, no. 11 (May/June 1975), p. 15.

43 Ibid., p. 15.

44 McDyer, J., Glencolumbkille Report, *Donegal Democrat*, Donegal (n.d.).

45 Ibid., pp. 21–2.

46 Ibid., p. 20.

47 Wilson, D., 'Christians in North have not read Signs of the Times', *Irish News*, Belfast (10 February 1975).

48 Ibid.

49 Warren, D. S., *The Community Land Trust*, 3 Salubrious, Broadway, Worcs. (n.d.).

50 Sawtell, R., *How to Change to Common Ownership*, Industrial Common Ownership Movement, 8 Sussex Street, London SW1 (1975), and *This is ICOM*, London (1974).

51 Schumacher, op. cit., p. 264.

52 Ibid., p. 264.

53 Crowther, op. cit., p. 13.

54 Dahrendorf, op. cit., p. 40.

55 *Community*, no. 13 (Autumn 1975), p. 13.

56 Wright, B. and Worsley, C. (eds.), *Alternative Scotland*, Wildwood House (1975), p. 148.

57 *Country Women*, no. 4 (June 1975), p. 12.

58 Wright and Worsley, op. cit., p. 143.

59 *Country Women*, op. cit., p. 4.

60 Ibid., p. 3.

61 *Communes Journal*, no. 39 (August 1972), p. 13.

62 *Community*, no. 2 (Winter 1972), p. 9.

63 *Community*, no. 9 (Summer 1974), p. 2.

64 *Community*, no. 5 (Spring 1973), p. 15. Cf. Abrams, P. and McCulloch, A., *Communes, Sociology and Society*, Cambridge University Press (1976), pp. 30ff, where they draw attention to the great importance of 'place-making' as a communal activity.

65 Ibid.

66 'Towards Life Together', op. cit. (March 1960).

67 Ibid. (October 1960).

68 Dickson, op. cit. (p. 69).

69 Moore, W. E., *Man, Time and Society*, New York, John Wiley (1963), pp. 44–52.

70 Jenkins, D., *What is Man?*, SCM Press (1970), p. 43.

71 Wright and Worsley, op. cit., p. 142.

72 Potts, M. I., *St Julian's*, SCM Press (1968), pp. 16–17.

73 *Community*, no. 5 (Spring 1973), p. 15.

74 Roszak, T., *The Making of a Counter Culture*, Faber and Faber (1970), p. 228.

75 *Dove One*, Butleigh, Glastonbury (1973), p. 12.

76 Hawken, P., 'The Magic of Findhorn Gardens', reprinted from *East West Journal*, Boston (n.d.), p. 7.

77 *Community*, no. 10 (Winter 1974), p. 15.

78 Dickson, op. cit., p. 12.

79 *Community*, no. 12 (Summer 1975), p. 3.

80 Broido, M. (ed.), *Communal Housing*, a report by a Chimera working group, Sussex University (1971), p. 23.

81 Ibid., p. 12.

82 See *Legal Frameworks Handbook*, Laurieston Hall, Kirkcudbrightshire (1975), pp. 27–30.

83 Ibid., p. 29.

84 Fromm, E., *The Art of Loving*, Allen and Unwin (1962), pp. 62–77, 92–5.

85 Taylor, op. cit., p. 69.

86 Herbert, G., 'The Neighbourhood Unit Principle and Organic Theory', in the *Sociological Review*, vol. 11, no. 2 (July 1963), p. 206.

87 Clark, D. B., 'The Church as Symbolic Place', in the *Epworth Review*, vol. 1, no. 2 (May 1974), p. 7.

88 Herbert, op. cit., p. 202, quoting Smithson, A. and Smithson, P., 'Fix', in the *Architectural Review* (July 1961), p. 439.

89 Clark, K., *Civilisation*, BBC and John Murray (1969), p. 7.

90 See the chapter on the Glastonbury Greenbus in Lockley, A., *Christian Communes*, SCM Press (1976), pp. 28–39.

91 Elen, R., 'Mysterious Energies', in *Undercurrents*, no. 11 (May/June 1975), pp. 18–20.

92 McDyer, op. cit., p. 2.

93 Wright, K., *International Ministry – A Brief Report, Coventry Cathedral* (1976).

94 Ineson, op. cit., p. 3.

95 Hand-out about Lothlorien, Kirkcudbrightshire (1975).

96 Crowther, op. cit., pp. 15–16.

CHAPTER 5
COMMUNITIES OF LEARNING

1 *Symposium – Christian Community and the Arts*, Post Green (1974), p. 2.

2 *Community*, no. 11 (Spring 1975), p. 2.

3 Ibid.

4 *Community*, no. 6 (Summer 1973), p. 13.

5 In personal correspondence (February 1976).

6 Rigby, A., *Communes in Britain*, Routledge and Kegan Paul (1974), p. 138.

7 *Open Letter*, no. 1 (December 1974), Findhorn, p. 5.

8 Leaflets from Findhorn (1976).

9 *Open Letter*, op. cit., p. 5.

10 *Community*, no. 10 (Winter 1974), p. 15.

11 *Community*, no. 13 (Autumn 1975), p. 16.

12 Martyn, M., *Lee Abbey – A Venture of Faith*, Lee Abbey (1974), p. 13.

13 *Community*, no. 8 (Spring 1974), p. 4.

14 *A Society of Lay People*, The Grail (1974), p. 33.

15 *Community*, no. 6 (Summer 1973), p. 12.

16 Morton, T. R., *The Future of the Iona Community*, Audenshaw Paper no. 32, (1974), p. 3.

17 Ibid., p. 6.

18 Ibid.

19 McCreary, A., *Corrymeela – The Search for Peace*, Christian Journals, Belfast (1975), pp. 71, 73.

20 *Causeway*, Corrymeela (1975), p. 2.

21 Corrymeela conference leaflet (October–December 1974).

22 *Community*, no. 14 (Spring 1976), p. 15.

23 Lindley Lodge leaflet (n.d.).

24 Ibid.

25 Lindley Lodge publicity brochure (n.d.).

26 *Community*, no. 4 (Autumn 1972), p. 15.

27 Ibid., p. 16.

28 *Community*, no. 14 (Spring 1976), p. 17.

29 Prospectus, Institute of Christian Studies, London (1975/1976), p. 4.

30 Ibid., pp. 7, 8.

31 Ibid., p. 19.

32 Ibid., p. 26.

33 Ibid., pp. 4–5.

34 Leaflet about the London Ecumenical Centre, 1976.

35 *Community*, no. 11 (Spring 1975), p. 13.

36 'Centre Self-Portraits', in *Laity Exchange*, no. 2, The Audenshaw Foundation (November 1975).

37 In private correspondence from a Methodist minister attending a course at St George's House, Windsor, in 1976.

38 Ibid.

39 Paper on the Urban Ministry Project, Morden (1976).

40 Brochure on the Urban Ministry Project (n.d.).

41 *City Forum*, no. 2, Oxford Institute of Church and Society (May 1976), pp. 6–7.

42 *Community*, no. 13 (Autumn 1975), p. 11.

43 Ibid.

44 *Community*, no. 6 (Summer 1973), p. 7.

45 Ibid., p. 6.

46 *The Action/Research Programme*, Glencree, Co. Wicklow (1976).

47 Newell, R. D., Notes on the Social Studies Centre, East End Mission, London (May 1976).

48 Leaflet from the East End Mission, London (n.d.).

49 Leaflet of the Wrekin Trust, Hereford (1976).

50 *Community*, no. 14 (Spring 1976), p. 9.

51 *Dialogue*, Movement for a Better World, Southport (February 1976).

52 *Aims and Projects*, William Temple Foundation, Manchester, 1975.

53 Miller-Bakewell, J., 'Consultants Put a Professional Polish on Charities', in *The Times* (10 November 1975).

54 *Community*, no. 6 (Summer 1973), p. 12.

55 *Community*, no. 12 (Summer 1975), pp. 1–3.

56 Leaflet on The Teilhard Centre for the Future of Man, London (n.d.).

57 *Community*, no. 1 (Autumn 1971), p. 13.

58 Ibid., p. 14.

59 *Towards Renewal*, no. 4 (Autumn 1975), p. 11.

60 *Community*, no. 8 (Spring 1974), p. 5.

61 Ibid., pp. 5–6.

62 Ibid., p. 6.

63 Bion, W. R., *Experiences in Groups*, Tavistock (1961).

64 Lieberman, M. A., Yalom, I. D., Miles, M. B., *Encounter Groups: First Facts*, New York, Basic Books (1973), p. 5.

65 Schutz, W. C., *Elements of Encounter*, Joy Press (1973), p. 3.

66 Rogers, C. R., *Encounter Groups*, Pelican (1973).

67 Schutz, op. cit., p. 5.

68 His most well-known book is *Games People Play*, Penguin (1968).

69 Perls, F., Hefferline, R. F., Goodman, P., *Gestalt Therapy*, Pelican (1973), p. 361n.

70 Ibid., p. 327.

71 Cooper, C. L., 'How Psychologically Dangerous are T-Groups and Encounter Groups?', in *Human Relations*, vol. 28, no. 3 (April 1975), p. 258.

72 *Community*, no. 6 (Summer 1973), p. 4.

73 Ibid.

74 Ibid.

75 Ibid.

76 Ibid., p. 3.

77 Bion, op. cit.

78 Reed, B., *Going to Church*, Grubb Institute, London (1970).

79 Cox, H., *The Feast of Fools*, Harvard University Press (1969), p. 162.

80 For example, see Higgin, G., 'The Scandinavians Rehearse the Liberation', *The Journal of Applied Behavioural Science*, vol. 8, no. 6 (1972), pp. 643–63.

CHAPTER 6
CARING COMMUNITIES

1 Klein, J., *Training for the New Helping Professions – Community and Youth Work*, University of London Goldsmith's College (1973), p. 9.
2 Ibid.
3 Rudge, P. F., *Ministry and Management*, Tavistock (1968).
4 Creed, A. and Matthews, G., *Community or Hostel . . . ?*, Cyrenian paper, Canterbury (n.d.).
5 Jackins, H., *Fundamentals of Co-counselling Manual*, Seattle, Rational Island Publishers (1970) (revised edn).
6 *Community*, no. 10 (Winter 1974), p. 14.
7 Ibid., p. 13.
8 *Community*, no. 15 (Summer 1976), pp. 5–6.
9 See Re-evaluation Counselling magazines: Rational Island Publishers, PO Box 2081, Main Office Station, Seattle, Washington 98111, USA.
10 See article in *Community*, no. 10 (Winter 1974), pp. 11–12.
11 *Community*, no. 11 (Spring 1975), pp. 3–5.
12 Ibid., p. 4.
13 Alpha House, Detailed Information for Counsellors, Hampshire County Council Department of Social Services (n.d.).
14 *Community*, no. 11 (Spring 1975), p. 5.
15 Ibid.
16 *Letters from L'Arche*, no. 7 (Summer 1974), pp. 4–5.
17 Ibid., p. 8.
18 Ibid., p. 5.
19 *Community*, no. 11 (Spring 1975), p. 5.
20 See, for example, Vanier, J., *Tears of Silence*, Darton, Longman and Todd (1973).
21 Blackwell, C., *Cyrenian Principles*, The Cyrenians, Canterbury (1973), p. 8.
22 *Guidelines for Cyrenian Houses*, Cyrenian paper, Canterbury (1976).
23 *People's Church*, Directory of Christian Alternatives, SCM Press (1974), p. 13.
24 Ibid., p. 24.
25 *Community*, no. 11 (Spring 1975), p. 1.
26 *Two-Church Families*, Association of Interchurch Families, London (n.d.), p. 36.
27 Ibid., p. 37.
28 *Responsibility in the Welfare State?*, Birmingham Council of Christian Churches (1961).

29 Ibid., p. 7.

30 *The Caring Community*, National Council of Social Service (1966). See also *Time to Care*, National Council of Social Service (1972).

31 See, for example, Batten, T. R., *Communities and Their Development*, Oxford University Press (1957), and Batten, T. R., *The Non-Directive Approach in Group and Community Work*, Oxford University Press (1967).

32 See the numerous reports on *Project 70–75*, Grail Publications (1970 onwards). See also Lovell, G., *The Church and Community Development*, Grail/Chester House Publications (1972), p. 35.

33 *Community Work and the Churches*, Working Group Report, British Council of Churches (1976). *The William Temple Foundation*, Bulletin 2 (April 1976), p. 31.

34 Wilson, M., *Health is for People*, Darton, Longman and Todd (1975), p. 105.

35 Elliott, C., *Inflation and the Compromised Church*, Christian Journals, Belfast (1975), p. 145.

36 Ibid., p. 146.

37 Leech, K., paper on The Jubilee Group, London (1975).

38 *Community*, no. 1 (Autumn 1971), p. 4.

39 Ibid., pp. 4–5.

40 See, for example, *Community*, no. 8 (Spring 1974), pp. 16–17.

41 Wilson, op. cit., p. 117.

42 Ibid., pp. 113, 108.

43 Furlong, M., *The End of Our Exploring*, Hodder and Stoughton (1973), p. 33.

44 *Community*, no. 5 (Spring 1973), p. 14.

45 Ibid.

46 Ibid.

47 Ibid.

48 Ibid.

49 *St Christopher's Hospice*, leaflet, London (1973).

50 Ibid.

51 *Guild of Health Handbook*, London (1974), p. 2.

52 Ibid., p. 5.

53 Lyall, D., *Resources in Pastoral Care and Counselling*, ONE for Christian Renewal (1975).

54 *Towards Renewal*, no. 1 (n.d.), p. 7.

55 *The Coracle*, Iona Community (October 1974), p. 18.

56 Trimmer, D., circular letter concerning 'The Christian Adventure and Arts Project' (May 1974).

57 *New Society* (1 January 1970), p. 5.

58 See, for example, Harris, T. A., *I'm OK – You're OK*, Pan Books (1973), pp. 207–37. James, M., *Born to Love*, Transactional Analysis in the Church,

Massachusetts, Addison-Wesley (1973). *Community*, no. 13 (Autumn 1975), pp. 13–15.

59 Letter from Archie Mills, Church of Scotland Counselling, Development and Training Centre (13 December 1976).

60 *Community*, no. 11 (Spring 1975), p. 10.

61 *The Dympna Centre*, leaflet (1975).

62 Halmos, P., *The Faith of the Counsellors*, Constable (1965).

63 Lanier, J., *Gestalt Paraphrases* (n.d.), Malaga, Spain, pp. 2, 4.

64 *Community*, no. 10 (Winter 1974), pp. 13–14.

65 *Community*, no. 15 (Summer 1976), p. 13.

66 Lake, F., *Clinical Theology: a theological and psychiatric basis to clinical pastoral care*, Darton, Longman and Todd (1966).

67 *Clinical Theology News*, no. 2, Nottingham (August 1975), p. 3.

68 Potts, M. I., *St Julian's*, SCM Press (1968), p. 53.

69 Centrepoint, Annual Report, Soho, London (1974), p. 15.

70 *Community*, no. 9 (Summer 1974), p. 15.

71 *The Outstretched Hand*, New Life Foundation Trust, London (1973).

72 In correspondence from John Harris, Pye Barn Trust (15 June 1976).

73 Lockley, A., *Christian Communes*, SCM Press (1976), pp. 28–39.

74 Papers on the pop scene and various pop festivals (Isle of Wight Festival, Reading Festival, Glastonbury Fair), Department of Mission and Unity, British Council of Churches, London (1971).

75 McCreary, A., *Corrymeela – The Search for Peace*, Christian Journals, Belfast (1975), pp. 66–7.

76 Ibid., p. 57.

77 *Community*, no. 5 (Spring 1973), p. 16.

78 Ibid.

79 Ibid., p. 15.

80 Smith, P., *Letters from Pilsdon* (February 1959).

81 Fairfield, R., *Communes in Europe*, San Francisco, Alternatives Foundation (1972), p. 94.

82 *Community*, no. 7 (Winter 1973), p. 7.

83 Ibid., p. 8.

84 Rigby, A., *Communes in Britain*, Routledge and Kegan Paul (1974), pp. 68–88.

85 *Community*, no. 11 (Spring 1975), p. 5.

86 *Community*, no. 8 (Spring 1974), p. 9.

87 Ibid.

88 Blackwell, op. cit., p. 14.

89 *Community*, no. 15 (Summer 1976), p. 8.

90 Ibid.

91 *Community*, no. 4 (Autumn 1972), p. 10.

92 See also John Newby's experience at Cantril Farm, Liverpool, in *Community*, no. 12 (Summer 1975), pp. 13–15.

93 *Community*, no. 14 (Spring 1976), pp. 5–6.

94 *Community*, no. 13 (Autumn 1975), p. 5.

95 *Community*, no. 14 (Spring 1976), pp. 12–13.

96 See the article on Northern Ireland in *Community*, no. 13 (Autumn 1975), pp. 1–3.

97 *Community*, no. 13 (Autumn 1975), p. 8.

98 Ibid.

99 Ibid.

100 *Community*, no. 3 (Summer 1972), p. 13.

101 On the Bridge Community, see *Community*, no. 11 (Spring 1975), pp. 6–7.

102 Smith, op. cit. (June 1959).

103 *Community House*, A Report of the Work in 1974–5, Glasgow (July 1975).

104 *Letters from L'Arche*, op. cit., p. 20.

CHAPTER 7
NEIGHBOURHOODS AND NETWORKS

1 See the argument in Stein, M. R., *The Eclipse of Community*, Princeton (1960), pp. 5ff.

2 Mason, D., Ainger, G., and Denny, N., *News from Notting Hill*, Epworth Press (1967).

3 Kenrick, B., *Come Out the Wilderness*, Collins (1965).

4 *Team Ministry*, Methodist Church Home Mission Department (April 1972).

5 Paul, L., *The Deployment and Payment of the Clergy*, Church Information Office (1964).

6 Croft, P., *The State of the Teams, 1975*, ONE for Christian Renewal (1975).

7 *Community*, no. 3 (Summer 1972), p. 9.

8 Croft, op. cit., p. 2.

9 Ibid., p. 3.

10 *Community*, no. 3 (Summer 1972), pp. 9–10.

11 Southcott, E., *The Parish Comes Alive*, Mowbrays (1957).

12 Vincent, J. J., *A Para-Church in Sheffield*, Studies in Mission, Methodist Church Home Mission Division (September 1975). Cf. Vincent, J. J., *Alternative Church*, Christian Journals, Belfast (1976), pp. 60–76.

13 *Community*, no. 3 (Summer 1972), p. 10.

14 *Towards Renewal*, Post Green, no. 3 (Summer 1975), pp. 13–19.

15 *Towards Renewal*, Post Green, no. 5 (Winter 1976), pp. 19–20.

16 *The Community of Hope*, leaflet from St Francis' Vicarage, Southchurch Drive, Clifton, Nottingham NG11 8AQ (1976).

17 Chilwell Road Methodist Church newsletter, Beeston, Nottingham (Autumn 1976).

18 *Community*, no. 11 (Spring 1975), p. 11.

19 See *Community*, no. 13 (Autumn 1975), p. 4.

20 Rudge, P. F., *Ministry and Management*, Tavistock (1968).

21 Gibbs, M., and Morton, T. R., *God's Frozen People*, Fontana, Collins (1964).

22 *The Constitutional Practice and Discipline of the Methodist Church*, Methodist Publishing House, 6th edn (1974), p. 297.

23 *Team Ministry*, op. cit., pp. 20–1.

24 *Community*, no. 3 (Summer 1972), p. 11.

25 Jeffrey, R. M. C., *Areas of Ecumenical Experiment*, British Council of Churches (1968).

26 *Community*, no. 6 (Summer 1973), p. 14.

27 'Team Ministries Look to Methodism for a Lead', *Methodist Recorder* (8 July 1976).

28 *Community*, no. 3 (Summer 1972), p. 11.

29 *Jesus Reality*, no. 3, Bugbrooke (1975), p. 8.

30 Ibid.

31 See the description of this venture in Lockley, A., *Christian Communes*, SCM Press (1976), pp. 54–64.

32 *A Society of Lay People*, The Grail (1974), pp. 40–51.

33 *Community*, no. 2 (Winter 1972), p. 5.

34 *Community*, no. 3 (Summer 1972), p. 5.

35 *Community*, no. 10 (Winter 1974), p. 10.

36 *Community*, no. 14 (Spring 1976), p. 16.

37 *Community*, no. 11 (Spring 1975), p. 19.

38 *Community*, no. 13 (Autumn 1975), p. 18.

39 *Community*, no. 8 (Spring 1974), pp. 19–20.

40 *Renewal*, no. 60 (December 1975/January 1976), Fountain Trust, p. 4.

41 The Pilgrims of St Francis, leaflet on their international pilgrimage (1976).

42 *Letters from L'Arche*, no. 7 (Summer 1974), p. 21.

43 *Towards Renewal*, Post Green, no. 6 (Spring 1976), p. 11.

44 Martin, D., 'The Church in Modern Society: the Familiar Unknown Quantity', *Crucible*, SPCK (January–March 1975), p. 8.

45 Jenkins, D., *The Glory of Man*, SCM Press (1967).

46 Williams, C. M., *John Wesley's Theology Today*, Epworth Press (1960), pp. 125, 190.

47 Robertson, R., *The Sociological Interpretation of Religion*, Basil Blackwell (1970), p. 179.

48 Urquhart, C., *When the Spirit Comes*, Hodder and Stoughton (1974).

49 *Towards Renewal*, Post Green, no. 6 (Spring 1976), pp. 6–7.

50 *Community*, no. 15 (Summer 1976), p. 18.

51 Ibid., p. 16.

52 *Dialogue*, newsletter of the Movement for a Better World, Southport (May 1976), p. 6.

53 *Community*, no. 14 (Spring 1976), p. 3.

54 Rice, A. K., *The Enterprise and its Environment*, Tavistock (1963), p. 13.

55 Williams, op. cit., p. 190.

56 *Community*, no. 15 (Summer 1976), p. 17.

57 *The Vision*, Association for Promoting Retreats, London (regular inset).

58 *Renewal*, op. cit. (regular inset).

59 Ibid.

60 Gibbs, M., and Morton, R. M., 'The Audenshaw Foundation', in *Audenshaw Papers*, no. 30 (1972), Muker (N. Yorkshire).

61 *ONE for Christian Renewal Declaration* (leaflet).

62 *Community*, no. 12 (Summer 1975), pp. 6–8.

63 The William Temple Foundation Bulletin 2, Manchester (April 1976), p. 6.

64 Annual Report 1975, Alternative Society, Kidlington (Oxford), pp. 20–3.

65 *Community*, no. 14 (Spring 1976), p. 3.

66 Fraser, I. M., *The Fire Runs*, SCM Press (1975), p. 152.

67 Leech, K., *Youthquake*, Sheldon Press (1973), p. 139.

68 Corry, G., *Jesus Bubble or Jesus Revolution?*, British Council of Churches (1973), p. 40.

69 Taylor, J. V., *Enough is Enough*, SCM Press (1975), p. 69.

70 Hill, M., *The Religious Order*, Heinemann (1973), p. 67.

71 Cohn, N., *The Pursuit of the Millennium*, Paladin Books (1970).

72 Hill, op. cit., p. 3.

73 Furlong, M., *The End of Our Exploring*, Hodder and Stoughton (1973), pp. 80–2.

74 Delespesse, M., *The Church Community – Leaven and Life Style*, Ottawa, The Catholic Centre of St Paul University (1969), p. 73.

75 *Community*, no. 15 (Summer 1976), p. 2.

CHAPTER 8
YES

1 Cummings, E. E., *Selected Poems 1923–1958*, Faber and Faber (1969), p. 76.

2 Ecclestone, A., *Yes to God*, Darton, Longman and Todd (1975).

3 Harris, T. A., *I'm OK – You're OK*, Pan Books (1973), p. 229.

4 The Holy Bible (RSV), Thomas Nelson (1952): Mark 10.15.

5 Cox, H., *The Feast of Fools*, Harvard University Press (1969), p. 152.

6 Ibid., p. 154.

7 Ibid., p. 28.

8 On the beauty of the body in old as well as young, see Franck, F., *The Zen of Seeing*, Wildwood House (1973), pp. 65–79.

9 Stirman, D., *The Third Isle of Wight Festival of Music*, British Council of Churches Department of Mission and Unity, papers published 1971, p. 2.

10 Ibid., p. 3.

11 Furlong, M., *The End of Our Exploring*, Hodder and Stoughton (1973), p. 92.

12 Ibid., p. 43.

13 Fromm, E., *The Art of Loving*, Allen and Unwin (1962), p. 75.

14 Taylor, J. V., *Enough is Enough*, SCM Press (1975), p. 100.

15 Watts, A. W., *Nature, Man and Woman*, Wildwood House (1973), p. 29.

16 Haughton, R., *On Trying to Be Human*, Geoffrey Chapman (1966).

17 Bion, W. R., *Experiences in Groups*, Tavistock (1961).

18 Ecclestone, op. cit., p. 95.

19 See Bernard, J., *The Future of Marriage*, Penguin (1976), pp. 208, 251–3.

20 *A Society of Lay People*, The Grail (1974), pp. 13–14.

21 Tillich, P., *The Courage to Be*, Fontana, Collins (1962), p. 93.

22 Watts, op. cit., p. 12.

23 Ecclestone, op. cit., p. 99.

24 Ibid., pp. 10–11.

25 Watts, op. cit., p. 184.

26 Fynn, *Mister God, This is Anna*, Collins, London (1974), p. 85.

27 Tillich, op. cit., p. 182.

28 Bion, op. cit.

29 Haughton, op. cit., p. 93.

30 See, for example, Bernard, op. cit., and O'Neill, N. and G., *Open Marriage*, Abacus (1975).

31 See, for example, Cattier, M., *The Life and Work of Wilhelm Reich*, New York, Avon Books (1973).

32 Harris, op. cit., p. 220.

33 Davis, C., *A Question of Conscience*, Hodder and Stoughton (1967), p. 76.

34 Cox, op. cit., p. 118.

35 Fraser, I. M., *The Fire Runs*, SCM Press (1975).

36 For processes of change on the local church scene, see Clark, D. B., 'Local and Cosmopolitan Aspects of Religious Activity in a Northern Suburb: Processes of Change', in Martin, D., and Hill, M. (eds.), *A Sociological Yearbook of Religion in Britain*, vol. 4, SCM Press (1971), pp. 141–59.

37 Davis, op. cit., p. 190.

38 *Community*, no. 9 (Summer 1974), p. 3.

39 *Community*, no. 10 (Winter 1974), p. 2.

40 Ecclestone, op. cit., p. 132.

41 *Community*, no. 13 (Autumn 1975), p. 4.

42 Ibid.

43 *Community*, no. 5 (Spring 1973), p. 4.

44 *Community*, no. 10 (Winter 1974), p. 2.

45 See Sumner, W. G., *Folkways*, New York, Dover Publications (New Dover edn, 1959).

46 Pope Paul VI, *On Evangelization in the Modern World* (8 December 1975), para. 58.

47 *Community*, no. 10 (Winter 1974). p. 1.

48 *Community*, no. 5 (Spring 1973), p. 2.

49 Ecclestone, op. cit., p. 125.

ANNOTATED LIST
OF BASIC COMMUNITIES AND
NETWORKS

The following is a list of all the basic communities and networks mentioned in this book. The notes are limited to giving only a very brief profile; further information can be obtained from the addresses indicated (on sending a stamped, addressed envelope). Many of the ventures have been more fully described in the *Community* magazine (see entry under that heading). The information is as up to date as known on 1 January 1977.

Advisory Council for Religious Communities   264

Set up in 1935 to advise the bishops and others concerned about the formation of new communities and on the life of existing communities, especially where questions about Regulations arise. Anglican. Secretary: Revd Alan Harrison. Address: St Anselm's House, Ham Common, Richmond, Surrey TW10 7JG. Tel. 01-948 0775

Alpha House   171–2, 190, 213, 233

Began in 1968. A residential community, on a self-help basis, for the social rehabilitation of ex-drug misusers. No particular religious affiliation. Residence divided into Phase I (inside) and Phase II (living in but working out). House Director: Jean Stubbs. Address: Alpha House, Wickham Road, Droxford, Southampton, Hampshire. Tel. 048-97 478.

Alternative Society   53, 105, 147–8, 162, 164, 166, 239, 255, 256, 257

Set up in 1972 to provide a communication network for all those who, in different fields, are working to create the cells of a new society. No particular religious affiliation. Weekend conferences, community craft camps, international summer school. Projects: housing, probation work, neighbourhood health, land trusts. Seeking to establish a Foundation for Alternatives. Co-ordinator: Stan Windass. Address: The Rookery, Adderbury, Nr. Banbury, Oxfordshire. Tel. 0295 810706.

In 1975 the Society opened a Centre for Alternatives in Urban Development at Lower Shaw Farm, Shaw, Swindon, Wilts. SN5 9PJ. Tel. 0793 771080.

Ammerdown   25, 28, 99, 135, 264

Opened in 1973. Conference centre situated on the estate of Lord Hylton. To help people to study personal and community problems, and aspects of their work, in a

Christian setting which is not doctrinaire. Interdenominational. Warden: Andrew Aldrich. Address: Ammerdown, Radstock, Bath BA3 5SW. Tel. 076-13 3709.

Amnesty International   138, 142, 182, 209, 234, 239, 243, 248

Started in Britain in 1961. Now international. Campaigns for basic human rights for all non-violent prisoners of conscience. Some 130 'adoption' groups in Britain. Periodical: *British Amnesty*. Chairman of the British Section: Revd Paul Oestreicher. Address: Amnesty International, 55 Theobald's Road, London WC1X 8SP. Tel. 01-242 1871.

The Anchorhold   74

Began in 1969. A centre to develop prayer, meditation, and physical movement as part of a search for a richer Anglican spirituality. House belongs to the Society of St John the Evangelist. Lay community apart from its leader, Father Herbert Slade, SSJE. Address: The Anchorhold, Paddockhall Road, Haywards Heath, Sussex RH16 1HN. Tel. 0444 52468.

Ann Arbor   84

Originated from a university-based Pentecostal group in 1967. A community of Christian love expressed especially through extended households. Charismatic and basically Roman Catholic. About 750 strong, with some 50 residential households. Periodical: *New Covenant*. Address: PO Box 87, Ann Arbor, Michigan 48107, USA.

Argyll Hotel   137

Runs two five-day residential conferences per year to bring together those seeking a new understanding of the relationship between spirituality and the world in which we live. Proprietor and organizer of conferences: John Walters. Address: Argyll Hotel, Isle of Iona, Argyll PA76 6SJ. Tel. 068-17 334.

Ashram Community Trust   23, 26, 36, 55, 61, 71, 99, 220, 223, 231, 234, 239, 240, 244

Set up in 1967. Aims to discover new implications of the way of Jesus for today's world, especially through a contemporary Christian life-style. Originally mainly Methodist, but now other denominations are represented. Ashram Community households in four places (see below). Residential conferences. Periodical: *ACT*. Organizing Secretary: Grace Vincent. Address: Ashram Community Trust, 239 Abbeyfield Road, Sheffield S4 7AW. Tel. 0742 386688.
Ashram Community houses:
  17 King Street South, Rochdale OL11 3TR. Tel. 0706 48922.
  84 Andover Street, Sheffield S3 9EH. Tel. 0742 26170.
  56 Woodlands Road, Middlesbrough TS1 3B.
  36 Key House, Bowling Green Street, London SE11. Tel. 01-582 0238.

The Association for Pastoral Care and Counselling   193, 253

Informal meetings began in 1970. To link clergy and laity with a particular concern for the development of training in pastoral skills. Interdenominational. Secretary: Revd Leslie Virgo. Address: The Rectory, Skibb's Lane, Chelsfield, Kent BRG 7RH. Tel. 0689 25749.

The Association for Promoting Retreats   253

Its periodical *The Vision* (a major aspect of its work containing lists of centres in Britain) first appeared in 1920. Works with communities and groups running retreat houses or offering accommodation for retreats and conferences. Ecumenical, but especially strong Anglican and Roman Catholic connections. Occasional training course for retreat leaders. An autumn festival. Secretary: Penelope Eckersley. Address: Church House, Newton Road, London W2 5LS. Tel. 01-727 7924.

Association of Interchurch Families   176–7, 243

Formed 1968. To offer mutual support in the problems brought by a mixed marriage and to bring pressure to bear for creative change. Membership mainly of couples one of whom is usually Roman Catholic. About 200 members in England and Wales who meet in area groups and at an annual conference. Contact persons: Revd Martin and Ruth Reardon. Address: 23 Drury Lane, Lincoln LN1 3BN. Tel. 0522 23227.

Audenshaw Foundation   254

Established 1964. To encourage the education and support of the laity. Ecumenical. Information service. Consultancy. Periodicals: *Audenshaw Papers* and *Audenshaw Documents*. Contact person: Mark Gibbs. Address: Muker, Richmond, North Yorkshire DL11 6QQ. Tel. 0748-86 315.

The Barnabas Fellowship   44–5, 54, 78, 86, 127–8, 132, 163, 166

Established 1971. Conference centre opened 1972. To work within the whole Church to encourage Christians and help renew their faith through the power of the Holy Spirit. Mainly Anglican. House staffed by a community of some 10 adults. Warden: Revd Reg East. Address: Whatcombe House, Winterbourne Whitechurch, Nr Blandford Forum, Dorset DT11 OPB. Tel. 025-888 280.

The Beeston Christian Community House   223

Established in 1975. A group committed to community living in the household; to the support in the group of at least one person in personal need; to regular worship together. Ecumenical. One couple and four single people – early 20s. Contact person: John Pursey. Address: 4 Grange Avenue, Beeston, Nottingham. Tel. 0602 223886.

Birchwood Hall   25, 40, 43, 44, 45, 49–50, 51, 53, 117, 119, 230

Community set up in 1971. A group of friends wanting to live together in a rural setting. No religious connections. About 25 people in all (including children). Address: Birchwood Hall, Storridge, Nr Malvern, Worcs. Tel. 088-64 203.

The Blackheath Commune   22, 25, 31, 36, 55, 66, 180–1, 210, 248

Existed 1969–71. Aimed to establish a Christian yet open community to be a base for radical political activity in the surrounding neighbourhood. 8 regular members. Address: Blackheath Rise, London SE13.

The Boot Night Shelter   195–6, 211

In existence as a night shelter since 1971. To provide for homeless young men in the context of a caring community. Anglican premises. Part of a larger organization concerned with accommodation and help for young people. Warden and Team Leader:

Revd Les Milner. Address: St Basil's Centre, Heathmill Lane, Deritend, Birmingham B9 4AX. Tel. 021-772 2483/8540.

Brandhall Baptist Church   223

Extended households established from 1974 to provide communities of fellowship and caring within the life of a local church. Baptist. 6 households. Minister: Revd John Bedford. Address: 53 Kings Way, Oldbury, Warley, West Midlands. Tel. 021-422 6254.

Bridge   36–7, 210

A community house which lasted from 1974 to 1975. Aimed to provide a point of contact between the traditional Church and those 'outside' who shared its concerns. Anglican premises and mainly Anglican group of some 10 young adults. Address: The Vicarage, Follett Street, London E14.

The British Group of Leaders of Laity Centres   254

Originated in 1965. To facilitate the exchange of ideas and information between directors and wardens of laity centres in Britain. Ecumenical. Some 40 members. Annual gathering. Periodical: *Laity Exchange*. Secretary: Mark Gibbs. Address: Muker, Richmond, North Yorkshire DL11 6QQ. Tel 074886 315.

The Bruderhof   19

Established by Eberhard Arnold at Sannery in Hesse, Germany, in 1920. First English community set up in Ashton Keynes in 1936. Pacifist, communistic, communitarian. Present address in England: Darvell Community, Robertsbridge, Sussex. Tel. 0580 626/7.

Bugbrooke – The Jesus Fellowship   23, 28, 34–5, 36, 44, 52, 63, 102–3, 231, 239, 242, 244

Community living began in 1973. Aim to be one family in the Lord Jesus through complete surrender to the will of God. Interdenominational. Extended households, farm, shops – in Northampton and other towns. Some 300 members. Periodical: *Jesus Reality*. Leader: Noel Stanton. Address: 35 High Street, Bugbrooke, Northampton. Tel. 0604 830223.

Burrswood   78, 184–5, 186, 210, 233, 248

Founded by Dorothy Kerin in 1947. A home of healing, working for wholeness of body, mind, and soul in accordance with God's will and man's response to the Divine love. Interdenominational. About 1,000 admissions a year. Some 15,000 received the laying-on-of-hands in their Church of Christ the Healer in 1975. Periodical: *Burrswood Herald*. Warden: Dr Kenneth G. Cuming. Address: Groombridge, Nr Tunbridge Wells, Kent TN3 9PY. Tel. 089-276 353.

Bystock Court   28, 38, 43–4, 47, 50, 51, 190, 198–200, 211, 233, 243, 248, 266

House opened 1965 to give continuing support through a core Christian community to women and their children in acute need through marital or other relationship problems. Interdenominational. Core community, about 6 adults. Some 9 units of accommodation for mothers. Accommodation for youth groups. Chairman: Alastair Jamieson. Address: Bystock Court, Withycombe, Exmouth, Devon. Tel. 039-52 6605.

Catholic Institute for International Relations   113, 208

Work in Britain and the Third World for justice and peace through a programme of development education and an overseas volunteer organization in Latin America and the Yemen Arab Republic. Roman Catholic (but the volunteers are from all Churches). Periodical: *Comment*. General Secretary: Mildred Neville. Address: 1 Cambridge Terrace, Regent's Park, London NW1 4Jl. Tel. 01-487 4431 (educational); 01-487 4397 (volunteers).

Catholic People's Weeks   151

Began in 1945. To add the dimension of learning and liturgy to holiday weeks. Roman Catholic. Holidays arranged in various centres throughout the country. Secretary: Bernard Hypher. Address: 7 Dashwood Close, West Byfleet, Weybridge, Surrey KT14 6QH. Tel. 09323 45254.

Centrepoint   194–5, 211, 264

Established 1969. To provide temporary accommodation and assistance to young people who are new to and/or are at risk in the West End. A basically Christian organization but open to all. Short-stay hostel in St Anne's House dealt with 5,000 young people in 1975. Some 50 volunteer helpers. Co-ordinator: Nic Fenton. Address: St Anne's House, 57 Dean Street, London W1V 5HH. Tel. 01-734 1075. Night Shelter Address: 65a Shaftesbury Avenue, London W1. Tel. 01-734 1075.

Children of God   23, 30, 34, 39–40, 46–7, 52, 63, 103, 108, 239

Began in 1968 as part of the Jesus Revolution in the USA. Fervent evangelical concern based on a strict community life. Interdenominational. Moved their international headquarters to London in 1971. Some 10 colonies and 200 members in Britain. Periodicals: *New Nation News* and *Letters of Mo*. Leader: David Berg ('Moses'). Address: PO Box 31, London WC2E 7LX. Tel. 01-458 1766.

Christian Action   181, 209

Originated from a large meeting in Oxford in 1946 led by Canon John Collins. To promote peace and understanding between rival groups and nations. Ecumenical. Projects include Homeless (women) in Britain; the London School of Non-violence; Radical Alternatives to Prison (see below). Executive Officer: Graham Bann. Address: Christian Action, Eastbourne House, Bullard's Place, London E2. Tel. 01-981 0041.

Christian Concern for Southern Africa   182

Began 1972. To examine the implications of British involvement in the commercial and industrial life of South Africa and Namibia from a Christian standpoint. Advisory service, especially on investment issues. Ecumenical though strong Methodist backing. Secretary: Tim Sheehy. Address: 1 Cambridge Terrace, Regent's Park, London NW1 4JL. Tel. 01-935 5260.

Christian Fellowship House (Love of God Community)   22–3

Established in 1974. To build a model of the Church based on the communal style of life characteristic of the early Christians. Interdenominational. 6 extended households. Address: 6 Willow Avenue, Edgbaston, Birmingham B17 8HD. Tel. 021-429 3703.

Christian Organizations Research and Advisory Trust (CORAT) 150

Began in 1967; first team in 1970. An advisory service on organization and administration to enable dedicated manpower to be used more effectively. Mainly Anglican. Seminars, summer schools, research. Director: John Miller-Bakewell. Address: Berkeley Road, Boars Hill, Oxford OX1 5ET. Tel. 0865 735579.

Christian Outdoor Pursuits and Arts Scheme (COPAS) 187–8

Ran first course in Derbyshire in 1973. To provide courses for deprived children and introduce them to some new experience of outdoor and arts activities in the context of a Christian community. Interdenominational. A fortnight's summer camp each year. Chairman: David Trimmer. Address: 19 Crimmond Rise, Belle Vue, Halesowen, Birmingham. Tel. 021-550 8847.

Churches' Council for Health and Healing 186, 193, 253

Founded by Archbishop William Temple in 1944. To link the Church and the medical profession in the care of the sick and for the advancement of healing techniques and practices. Ecumenical. Acting Secretary: Janet Lacey. Address: St Peter's Vestry, Hobart Place, London SW1W OHH. Tel. 01-235 3305.

Church of the Redeemer, Houston 27, 84, 222, 239

Revd Graham Pulkingham became rector in 1963 and about a year later the church and parish entered a period of renewal, with many charismatic features. From this church originated the Community of Celebration (see below). Rector: Revd Jeff Schiffmayer. Address: The Episcopal Church of the Redeemer, 5511 Dallas Avenue, Houston, Texas, USA.

The Clinical Theology Association 192, 212, 234

Formed in 1962 from interdisciplinary seminars begun in 1958. To provide opportunities for training in pastoral care and counselling and to set up or support counselling facilities. Strong Anglican connections. Courses and conferences. Director: Dr Frank Lake. Address: Lingdale, Weston Avenue, Mount Hooton Road, Nottingham NG7 4BA. Tel. 0602 75475.

Commune Movement 100, 107

Small beginnings in 1965; rapid growth 1970–3. Aimed to create a federal society of communities. No religious connections. Now inactive as such; replaced early in 1975 by a loose-knit Commune Network. Periodical: *Communes* now replaced by a newsletter, *Commune Network*. Contact person: Tony Kelly, Selene Community, Can-y-Lloer, Ffarmers, Llanwrda, Dyfed, Wales or Laurieston Hall (see below).

Community 256, 257, 281

A periodical which was started in 1971. Aims to act as a switchboard of information and comment about basic communities and networks especially where Christians are involved. Sponsored by ONE for Christian Renewal (see below). Has published articles on many of the ventures described in this book. Editor: David Clark. Editor's address:

Westhill College, Weoley Park Road, Birmingham B29 6LL. Tel. 021-472 7245. Address for subscriptions: 169 Forest Road, Loughborough, Leics. LE11 3HS. Tel. 0509 63321. A *resource centre* of magazines and articles about community in Britain has just been established. Contact person: Joy Hasler. Address: 126 Oak Tree Lane, Selly Oak, Birmingham B29 6HY. Tel. 021-472 0878.

Community Development   177, 178–9, 223

A means of social intervention which seeks to foster democratic participation and self-development especially at the neighbourhood level. Got under way in this country in the mid 1960s. Amongst church groups with a particular interest in this approach are the British Council of Churches, Project '70–'75 (see below) and the William Temple Foundation (see below). BCC Community Work Secretary: Revd Tony Addy. Address: 10 Eaton Gate, London SW1W 9BT. Tel. 01-730 9611.

Community Education Centre   144–5, 146, 163, 164, 165

Opened in 1972 and closed in 1976. Aimed to foster greater awareness of the issues that arise in the inner urban community through a residential and experiential training programme. A project sponsored by the Student Christian Movement (see below). Courses mainly for students from colleges of education. Leaders for the first three years: Revd Bob and Maggi Whyte. Address: 13 Northbrook Road, London SE13 5QT.

Community Health Councils   177, 179, 211

First established as a result of the reorganization of the National Health Service in 1974. To represent the entry of the 'democratic voice' into the running of the Health Service. One for each Health District. Members appointed by local authorities, voluntary organizations, and the Regional Health Authority. Periodical: *Community Health Council News*. Address: obtainable from the local telephone directory.

The Community Land Trust   105, 119

In the process of being established. Aims to set up a quasi-public body, chartered to hold land in stewardship for all mankind, present and future, while protecting the legitimate use-rights of its residents. No religious connections. Address: contact through the Food and Energy Research Centre, Evesham Road, Cleeve Prior, Evesham, Worcs.

The Community of Celebration   24, 25, 26, 27, 30–1, 35, 36, 41–2, 44, 46, 49, 50, 51, 54, 56, 61, 63–4, 68, 78, 81–2, 99, 127, 162, 165, 187, 222, 230–1, 238, 239, 240–1, 242, 248, 252

Grew out of the Church of the Redeemer, Houston, Texas (see above). First community in England set up in Coventry in 1972 but soon moved to Yeldall Manor in Berkshire. This in turn has now been vacated and the group is located at the addresses given below. A caring community evolving a life-style relevant to our age and working for the renewal of the Church through visiting teams conducting a multi-faceted training programme for Church leaders. Very strong Episcopalian element from Houston, but there are members of other denominations and nationalities. Fisherfolk (English and International) music and singing group. Leader: Revd W. Graham Pulkingham, Provost of the Cathedral of the Isles. Address: Cathedral of the Isles, Millport, Isle of

Cumbrae, Scotland KA28 OHE. Tel. 047-553 353. Second largest group has linked up with Post Green (see below), Lytchett Minster, Poole, Dorset BH16 6AP. Tel. 020-122 2317. Separate households now linked to Beaconsfield Baptist Church and St Mary's Parish Church, Wargrave.

Community of Hope 223

In the process of being set up. A dozen members intending to serve the local church and neighbourhood and eventually to live communally in an extended household. Ecumenical. Contact person: Revd Frank Crowther. Address: St Francis' Vicarage, Southchurch Drive, Clifton, Nottingham NG11 8AQ. Tel. 0602 212446.

The Community of the Word of God 36, 44

Established 1973. Aims to integrate the concept of the religious life and the covenant community in the service of Church and society. Anglican. Some 10 adults living in 3 houses. Contact person: Vera Brandon. Address: 74 Elderfield Road, Clapton, London E5 OLF. Tel. 01-986 6709.

The Compassionate Friends 170–1, 234, 239, 240, 243

Founded 1969. Now an international organization of bereaved parents offering friendship and understanding to other bereaved parents. Strong Christian base but open to all. Some 35 branches in Britain. Periodical: *The Compassionate Friends Newsletter*. Secretary: Joan Wills. Address: 50 Woodwaye, Watford, Herts. WD1 4NW. Tel. 0923 24279.

The Conservation Society 98

Established 1966. To inform people of the dangers associated with high technology, resources depletion and world-wide population increase, and to persuade them to work for alternative life-styles which will ensure a stable and harmonious relationship between man and the environment. No religious connections. Working parties and published papers. Periodical: *Conservation News*. Director: Dr John Davoll. Address: 12 London Street, Chertsey, Surrey KT16 8AA. Tel. 093-28 60975.

Co-operatives – Northern Ireland 104–5

Contact person: Father Des Wilson. Address: 123 Springhill Avenue, Belfast BT12 7QF. Tel. 0232 26722.

Corrymeela Community 19, 112, 122, 132, 133–5, 162, 163, 166, 196–7, 206, 211, 232, 240, 243, 251, 266, 278

Grew out of a group of Presbyterian students meeting at Queen's University, Belfast in 1964. Ballycastle house bought in 1965; conferences began there in 1966. A community of Christian men and women committed to healing the many divisions – social, religious, and political – which exist in Northern Ireland. Strong Presbyterian element, but increasingly ecumenical. Some 80 community- members. Groups in Belfast. At Ballycastle: conferences, meetings, family weeks, work camps. Periodical: *Causeway*. Director: Revd Ray Davey. Addresses: Corrymeela House, 8 Upper Crescent, Belfast BT7 1NT. Tel. 0232 25008. The Corrymeela Centre, Ballycastle BT54 6QU. Tel. 026-57 62626. Support group in England: Corrymeela Link, PO Box 118, Reading, Berks.

Counselling, Development and Training – Church of Scotland 189

The unit aims to enable people to anticipate and cope with stress, and to release men and women to grow into the fullness of the life of Christ within the unique experience of creative Christian community. Church of Scotland. Courses in counselling and group work. Especial use of Transactional Analysis (see below). Director: Revd Dr Archie Mills. Address: Simpson House, 52 Queen Street, Edinburgh EH2 3NS. Tel. 031-225 1054.

Coventry Cathedral 60–1, 80–1, 87, 122–3, 145–6, 163, 164, 165, 251, 252

The new cathedral was consecrated in 1962. The cathedral staff has established a centre of Christian education and discipline expressing the desire of those involved in the rebuilding to discover a way to international reconciliation and the renewal of urban life. Work co-ordinated by its Centre of Studies and including the International Development Centre and John F. Kennedy House, especially concerned with residential courses for young people. Base for the Community of the Cross of Nails, open to all those (now some 50) groups committed to reconciliation and a simple Christian life-style. Address: Cathedral Office, Coventry CV1 5ES. Tel. 0203 27597.

The Cyrenians 24, 26, 28, 36, 37, 173, 174–5, 201, 210, 211, 212, 214, 231, 239, 240, 247, 252, 266

Offshoot from the Simon Community (see below) in 1970. Aims to help single homeless people unable to cope without support. Christian base, but very open. Some 40 local projects – residential houses and night shelters. Volunteers work for 6 to 12 months as project staff. Periodical: *The Cyrenian*. Secretary: Brigid Gifford. Consultant: Tom Gifford. Address: 13 Wincheap, Canterbury, Kent CT1 3TB. Tel. 0227 51641.

Dartmouth House 66, 71–2, 91, 99, 111, 140–1, 162, 166, 233

A residential conference centre belonging to the Diocese of Southwark. Anglican. Aims to be a setting for meeting and discussion, relaxation or retreat for those within and outside the churches. Warden until autumn 1976 was John Nicholson. Deputy Warden: Diana Eeles. Address: Dartmouth House, Dartmouth Row, London SE10 8AW. Tel. 01-692 3620.

Divine Light Mission 75–6

Aims to initiate aspirants into the 'Knowledge', a pursuit of ancient Eastern origin. This mission was established by Sri Hans Ji Maharaj, the father of the present Master. The Mission came to the West in 1969. The Master: Guru Maharaj Ji. British centre: 131 Clapham High Street, London SE4. Tel. 01-622 9261/3.

The Dove Centre 116, 117, 267

Established 1972. A centre to practise and teach crafts within the context of community living. No religious connections. Community emphasis declined and craftwork and teaching predominated after the first year or two. Address: The Dove Centre, Butleigh, Glastonbury, Somerset. Tel. 045-85 682.

The Dympna Centre 189

Opened 1971. For the spiritual care of those suffering from emotional disturbance and spiritual conflict. Roman Catholic foundation. Counselling and training in counselling. Director: Revd Louis Marteau. Address: 24 Blandford Street, London W1H 3HA. Tel. 01-486 1592.

East Bergholt 50

Community in a large country house began in 1974. To live communally on the basis of a socially supportive and ecologically sound style of life. No particular religious connections. Some 35 adults and their children. Contact person: John Gamlin. Address: Old Hall, East Bergholt, Colchester CO7 6TQ. Tel. 020–629 294.

End Loans to South Africa (ELTSA) 182

Set up in 1974. To seek to prevent banks from lending to the South African government. Strong Methodist element, but open to all concerned. Secretary: Revd David Haslam. Address: 134 Wrottesley Road, London NW10 5XR. Tel. 01-965 7454.

Ettrick Shaws – Open Centre 74, 129–30

Open centre incorporated into the hotel programme in 1974. For those seeking inner truth; for discussion and meditation within a framework of a disciplined way of life. In the summer the centre is run as a hotel; in the winter and spring, as an open centre (see also the Salisbury Centre, below). Will cease functioning as an open centre in 1977 owing to financial difficulties. Contact person: Ludi How. Address: Pine Lodge, Ettrick Bridge, Selkirk TD7 5HW. Tel. 075-05 229.

The Farncombe Community 25, 26, 33, 46, 52, 60, 73, 232, 233, 248

House was dedicated in 1964. A fellowship of prayer for the furtherance of Christian unity. Ecumenical. Core community of 5 sisters. Wider circle of Companions and a Fellowship of Prayer. Periodical: *Newsletter*. Contact person: Dorothy Bee. Address: 5 Wolseley Road, Farncombe, Godalming, Surrey GU7 3DX. Tel. 048-68 7253.

Fellowship of Reconciliation 209

Established 1914. To work for peace, in every way possible, not least by non-violent witness and example. Strong Christian basis, but open to all. Some 5,000 members and 60 local groups in Britain. Periodicals: *Reconciliation Quarterly* and *Newspeace*. Secretary: Richard Sandbrook. Address: 9 Coombe Road, New Malden, Surrey KT3 4QA. Tel. 01-942 6521.

Findhorn Foundation 25, 26, 27, 46, 50, 56, 65, 76, 81, 96, 97, 99, 100, 117, 125, 128–9, 148, 161, 165, 267

Small beginnings in 1962. Main growth from 1969 onwards. In 1975 purchased the Cluny Hill Hotel as an extension for its work. Pioneering community living to demonstrate and proclaim the spirit of the New Age. Open to all sharing their New Age philosophy. Community now some 200 strong. Theatre, craft studios, garden. publishing. A University of Light. Periodical: *Open Letter*. Leader: Peter Caddy. Address: The Findhorn Foundation, The Park, Findhorn Bay, Forres, Moray, Inverness IV36 0TZ. Tel. Findhorn 311.

Focolare   52, 64, 70, 87, 152, 235, 239, 250

Began in the town of Trent, northern Italy, in 1943. For those committed to mutual love in Christ and to unity across all barriers. Predominantly Roman Catholic. The Focolarini are committed to poverty, chastity, obedience: live in Focolares (3 women's and 2 men's Focolares in Britain). Wider circle of linked families and young people. A large summer gathering (Mariapolis) of up to 500 in England each year. Contact person: Dimitri Bregant. Address: 57 Twyford Avenue, London W3 9PZ. Tel. 01-992 7666.

Fountain Trust   72, 84, 85, 236, 253–4, 257

Established 1964. For Christ-centred, charismatic, corporate, compassionate renewal. Ecumenical. Conferences, public gatherings, tapes. Periodical: *Renewal*. Director: Revd Thomas A. Smail. Address: 3a High Street, Esher, Surrey KT10 9RP. Tel. 0372 67331. Core community lives at 23 Spencer Road, East Molesey, Surrey, KT8 0SP. Tel. 01-979 1798.

Friends of the Earth   97–8

Began in the USA in 1969; in Britain in 1970. Committed to the conservation, restoration, and rational use of our natural environment and resources. No religious connections. Operating in some 10 countries. 150 local groups in Britain in 1975. Address: 9 Poland Street, London W1V 3DG. Tel. 01-434 1684.

Froddle Crook – Community of Christian Love   137–8, 162

Formed in 1956; centre purchased in 1965. Searching for a more balanced religious life and working for a more democratic international order. Ecumenical. Small group administer the centre. Conferences, retreats. Founder/Secretary: Alice Stephens. Address: The Father Bernard Delany Ecumenical Centre, Froddle Crook, Armathwaite, Cumbria.

General Synod Board of Education – Church of England   152, 160, 165

Set up the first conference on the Church and group life in 1957. Aims to bring to bear the insights and skills of modern group work on education within the life of the Church, especially in relationship to personal development and leadership. Anglican. Workshops. Group work (three-stage course), couples, family life, worship. Gradually decentralizing its activities. Contact person: Canon Stephen Burnett. Address: Church House, Dean's Yard, London SW1P 3NZ. Tel. 01-222 9011.

Glencolumbkille   97, 103–4, 107, 122, 249

Co-operative parish venture developed after 1945. Aiming to revive, on community development principles, a rural parish and realize its potential as a co-operative undertaking. Farming, small industries, home crafts, fishing, tourism. Leader: Father James McDyer. Address: Cashel, Glencolumbkille, Co Donegal, Republic of Ireland.

Glencree Centre for Reconciliation   146, 162, 163, 206, 233, 252

Established 1974. A community who have been moved by Christ's concern for reconciliation, justice, and peace to attempt the role of peace making. Core group largely Roman Catholic, but exercising an ecumenical ministry. Training, study

313

projects, hospitality, youth work, community action. Leader: Shaun Curran, SJ. Address: (Dublin Office), 129 St Stephen's Green, Dublin 2. Tel. Dublin 753775. Glencree Centre, Glencree, Bray, Co Wicklow, Republic of Ireland. Tel. Dublin 860963.

Good Neighbour Scheme, Sheffield   178, 211, 213–14, 223

Started in 1962. A voluntary neighbourhood-based service for those in personal or domestic need. Interdenominational. Liaison officers and teams of helpers throughout the city. Contact person: Eileen Simpson. Address: Sheffield Churches' Council for Community Care, 19 Division Street, Sheffield S1 4GE. Tel. 0742 79452.

The Grail   21, 25, 27, 30, 33–4, 37, 41, 52, 54, 70, 73, 77, 85, 87, 131–2, 151, 162, 164, 166, 179, 229, 232, 233, 234, 242, 248, 250, 271

Pioneered by James van Ginneken, a Dutch Jesuit, in Holland in 1921. To England in 1932. To work to build a society based on loving relationships between God and man and between man and man, and to demonstrate this ministry through the authenticity of their own communal life. A Roman Catholic community of women. Run Waxwell House as a 'home' and conference centre. Catechetical work. Centre of a nationwide network of Family Circles (Roman Catholic). In 1975 started a scheme for volunteers to share in the work of the Grail for up to a year. Periodical: *In Touch*. Contact person: Jackie Rolo. Address: Waxwell Farm House, 125 Waxwell Lane, Pinner, Middlesex HA5 3ER. Tel. 01-866 2195/0505.

Greenbus, Glastonbury   68, 121–2, 196, 237, 249

A series of summer camps which began in 1972. To offer tent accommodation to young people coming to Glastonbury during the summer season; the camp staffed by a core Christian community of about a dozen people. Ecumenical. Administrative difficulties led to only a two-week camp being set up in 1975. Contact person: Jim Nagel. Address: PO Box 10, Glastonbury, Somerset BA6 9YG.

The Grubb Institute   157–60, 162–3, 165, 248

Established in 1957 as the Christian Teamwork Trust. In 1963 began collaboration with the Tavistock Institute of Human Relations. In 1969 assumed its present title. Aims to promote a deeper understanding of the nature of authority and dependence by those in leadership roles through conferences, consultancy, and research. Strong Anglican connections but services offered to all. Executive Chairman: Revd Bruce Reed. Address: EWR Centre, Cloudesley Street, London N1 0HU. Tel. 01-278 4224.

Guild of Health   186

Established in 1904. To help restore the healing ministry of Christ through the Church; to bring together all branches of the medical and caring professions to work for the health of individual and community. Strong Anglican connections but an ecumenical ministry. Local groups. Periodical: *Way of Life*. Secretary: Miss G. M. Herington. Address: Edward Wilson House, 26 Queen Anne Street, London W1M 9LB. Tel. 01-580 2492.

Hengrave Hall Centre   25–6, 30, 52, 53, 54, 71, 131, 132, 162, 166, 233, 256, 264

Community established in the centre in 1974. A conference and retreat centre aiming to renew the Church by community witness and to promote programmes of ecumenical education and spiritual and social renewal. Strong Roman Catholic connections, but ecumenical community and ministry. Sisters of the Assumption, several families and a Franciscan priest; some 15 in all. Co-ordinator: Revd Donald Rogers. Address: Hengrave Hall Centre, Bury St Edmunds, Suffolk IP28 6LZ. Tel. 028-484 721/2.

Highgate Counselling Centre   189

Set up in 1960. To help those with personal problems. Strong Christian base, but open to all. Counsels and trains counsellors. Chairman/Director: Revd Denis Duncan. Address: Highgate Counselling Centre, Child Guidance Centre, Tetherdown, London N10. Tel. 01-263 2690.

Hildenborough Hall   130

Opened for present work in 1963. To work from the base of a Christian community for the communication of the Gospel, especially amongst young people. Interdenominational. House community of some 25. 'Open House' weekends. Musical teams into schools. General Director: Justyn H. Rees. Address: Hildenborough Hall, Otford Hills, Sevenoaks, Kent. Tel. 0732 61030.

Houses of Prayer Ecumenical (HOPE)   78–9

Began in England in 1975. To enable people from different walks of life to live together for a short time to learn about prayer and community in Christ. Ecumenical. Many participants originally from the religious Orders, but steadily broadening its base. Time together anything up to six weeks. Contact person: Helen Allan. Address: 89 High Street, Kidlington, Oxford OX5 2DR. Tel. 086-75 6231.

Human Potential Movement   69, 86, 154–61, 162–3, 164–5, 190–2

Originated in the States especially after 1945. Embracing a wide range of therapeutic and groupwork techniques (including Encounter and Bio-energetics) emphasizing man's potential to choose and to change himself. Main points of contact in England: Clinical Theology Association (see above); General Synod Board of Education (see above); Association of Humanistic Psychology, 57 Minster Road, London NW2 3RE. Tel. 01-435 9200; Group Relations Training Association. Secretary: Keith Turner. Address: Brackenber Hall, Appleby-in-Westmorland, Cumbria CA16 6LP. Tel. 0930 51124; Quaesitor (wide variety of courses), 187 Walm Lane, London NW2. Tel. 01-452 8489.

Industrial Common Ownership Movement   106, 108

Set up in 1958 as the Society for Democratic Integration in Industry. In 1971 assumed present title. Aims to help start new enterprises in and to transform existing companies to common ownership. No religious connections. 13 independent member companies in September 1975. Co-ordinator: Anita Renicks. Address: 31 Hare Street, Woolwich, London SE8 6JN. Tel. 01-855 4099.

Institute of Christian Studies   *138–9, 163, 164, 165, 237*

Began about 1970. Aims to provide a community where men and women can be free to share in the adventure of study, prayer, and fellowship. Anglican base, but open to all. Courses, lectures, workshops, seminars. Restaurant and bar. Periodical: *Christian.* Principal: Revd John Slater. Address: 84 Margaret Street, London W1. Tel. 01-637 3526.

International Ecumenical Fellowship   *80, 235–6, 248*

Started in 1967 in Switzerland. To enable Christians to meet on the basis of friendship and equality; to foster common worship and private prayer; to encourage informal discussion in the pursuit of unity. Ecumenical. Annual international conference. Secretary: Susan Richardson. Address: 42 Crutched Friars, London EC3N 2AL. Tel. 01-481 8277.

The Iona Community   *19, 38, 60, 72, 73, 87, 112, 121, 132–3, 137, 152, 161, 163, 164, 187, 202, 203, 209, 210, 211, 214, 231, 232–3, 237, 240, 246, 248, 249, 251*

Founded in 1938 by George MacLeod. To work for the renewal of the life of the Church in the service of the world; symbolized by the rebuilding of the living quarters of the Abbey on Iona (work completed 1966). Church of Scotland, but an ecumenical ministry. Some 140 full community members; core group lives in the Abbey. In 1976 the first Roman Catholic member joined the community. On Iona, study weeks, youth camps. Beyond Iona, local groups, centres in Edinburgh and Glasgow. Periodical: *The Coracle.* Leader: Revd Graeme Brown. Address: Community House, 214 Clyde Street, Glasgow G1 4JZ. Tel. 041-221 4921. Edinburgh Offices: Candlemakers' Hall, 36 Candlemaker Row, Edinburgh EH1 2QF. Tel. 031-225 1135. Iona: The Abbey, Iona, Argyll PA76 6SN. Tel. 068-17 314.

Islington – community house   *45*

Set up in 1970. The group aims to live communally as Christians in order more effectively to carry out their everyday work. Roman Catholic. 6 adults and 2 children. Contact person: James Pitt. Address: 157 Copenhagen Street, London N1. Tel. 01-278 5643.

The Jesus Family (Lonesome Stone)   *23, 27, 54, 82*

Originated in the USA in 1971. One team came to Europe and settled in London in 1972. Aims to communicate the Gospel message to young people outside the Church. Interdenominational. About 25 members. Launched a multi-media musical, *Lonesome Stone*, in 1973. Periodical: *Everyman.* Leader: Jim Polosaari. Address: 56 Beulah Hill, Upper Norwood, London SE19. Tel. 01-771 9642.

Jubilee Group   *180*

Originated from discussions in 1974. Aims to renew the Catholic Movement within the Church of England. Especial concern for the integration of contemplation and radical political activity. Anglican. Predominantly clergy members. Operates mainly through the circulation of papers. Co-ordinator: Revd Kenneth Leech. Address: St Matthew's Rectory, Bethnal Green, London E2 6EX. Tel. 01-739 4730.

The Julian Meetings   74, 77, 78, 87, 152, 234, 239, 247, 248

Began in 1973. Aims to establish groups for the practice of contemplative prayer and a deeper spirituality. Ecumenical. A network of small groups throughout the country. Contact person: Hilary Wakeman. Address: Kents, Great Chesterford, Saffron Walden, Essex CB10 1PL. Tel. 079-983 461.

Katimavik   68–9, 70, 77, 87, 152, 234, 235, 237, 239, 248, 250, 252

First gathering at Abbeville in northern France in 1971. In England first gathering in Haywards Heath in 1973. Aims to heighten awareness of the living power of Jesus. Roman Catholic, but gatherings open to all Christians. Gatherings and meetings for worship and fellowship. Contact person: Shelagh Lindsay. Address: The House of Light, 114 Thornlaw Road, West Norwood, London SE27 0SB. Tel. 01-670 1445.

The Kibbutz   45

Originated in Palestine in 1909. A voluntary society based on communal property, production, and labour as well as communal eating and living arrangements. Predominantly Jewish. There are currently some 235 kibbutzim in Israel, with a total population of over 90,000. For further information contact Kibbutz Representatives, 1 King Street, St James, London SW1 6BB. Tel. 01-930 6181.

The Kingsway Community (and Keveral Farm)   26, 28, 31, 36, 37, 50, 51, 53–4, 55, 66, 108, 110, 115, 116, 190, 196, 200, 211, 212, 242, 244, 246, 249, 266

Informal group discussions began in 1965. Chiswick house leased in 1969. To offer the support of community living to the weak and the exploited. Original Christian basis now much less evident. Three houses – Keveral Farm in Cornwall, housing 6 adults with children. The Community is now administered by Patchwork, but all households retain their autonomy. Leader: David Horn. Addresses: 23 Sutton Court Road, Chiswick, London W4; 101 Rushmore Road, London E5; Keveral Farm, St Martin-by-Looe, Cornwall Tel. 050-35 215.

L'Arche   70, 72, 173–4, 190, 194, 200–1, 211, 213, 231, 239, 240, 243, 250, 251–2

Originated through the work of Jean Vanier in France in 1964. First British house opened in Kent in 1974. A Christian interfaith community which creates home-life and work situations for mentally handicapped adults. Predominantly Roman Catholic, but open to all. Some 30 houses in 10 different countries. (Two British houses but plans to open others in Lambeth and Liverpool.) Periodical: Letters of L'Arche. Addresses: Secretariat at 14 London Road, Beccles, Suffolk Tel. 0502-71 5329. Residential houses – Little Ewell Old Rectory, Barfrestone, Nr Dover, Kent CT15 7JJ. Tel. 0304 830930. Braerannoch, 13 Drummond Crescent, Inverness IV2 4QR. Tel. 0463 38921. The Anchorage, 25 Fairfield Crescent, Newsham Park, Liverpool 6. Tel. 051-228 3526.

Laurieston Hall   43, 50, 54–5, 56, 97, 98, 110, 119

Community took over the hall in 1972. To live communally and simply in a rural setting; to promote a radical critique of society. No religious connections. 15 adults and 10 children in 1975. Strong Women's Liberation element. Runs an 'alternative university' in the summer. Address: Laurieston Hall, Castle Douglas, Kirkcudbrightshire. Tel. Laurieston 275.

The Laxton Distributist Community   101

Developed from a group of families which settled in Laxton (offshoot from a pre-existing community at Colchester) in 1935. Aim to further the wide distribution of productive property in small units and demonstrate in their own way of life its economic and spiritual viability. Predominantly Roman Catholic. Leader: Harold McCrone. Address: The Laxton Distributist Community, Laxton, Nr Corby, Northants.

Lee Abbey   24, 31, 34, 38, 44, 53, 54, 74, 86, 130–1, 162, 163, 166, 233, 249

House opened in 1946. A centre for evangelism and lay training in a holiday setting enriched by a shared community life. Basically Anglican, but ecumenical ministry. Residential community of some 80 people, mostly single. Summer camps. Hostel for 200 students from overseas in London was opened in 1964. Warden at Lynton: Revd John Perry. Address: Lee Abbey, Lynton, North Devon EX35 6JJ. Tel. 059-85 2303. Lee Abbey International Students Club, 26–27 Courtfield Gardens, London SW5. Tel. 01-373 7286.

Life Style   98–9

Set up in 1972. To encourage a simplicity of life which is generous to others and content with enough rather than with excess. Ecumenical. Asks for an individual and informal commitment to a simple rule of life. Co-ordinator: Revd Horace Dammers, Dean of Bristol. Address: Bristol Cathedral, College Green, Bristol BS1 5TJ. Tel. 0272 24879.

Lindley Lodge   135–7, 162

Organization set up in 1967. Nuneaton house was opened in 1970. To provide an opportunity for young people in their early years of employment to examine and develop their attitudes towards work and society, and to give them a greater understanding of other people and their problems. Interdenominational, open to all. (Courses for young people from industry.) Now 2 houses. Core community at Nuneaton of some 20. Nuneaton house Director: John Moore. Address: Lindley Lodge, Watling Street, Nuneaton CV10 0TZ. Tel. 0682 68128/9. Masham house: Lindley Lodge, Masham, Nr Ripon, Yorkshire HG4 4JJ. Tel. 0765-82 254.

Link Group   62, 152–3, 164

Began in the mid 1950s. To discuss current issues in the light of the Christian faith. Ecumenical. Monthly meetings of 15–20 people. Contact person: Revd Brian Woodcock. Address: St Mark's Manse, Ashburnham Place, London SE10. Tel. 01-858 6214.

The Link – street warden scheme, Bristol   178

Set up in 1964. To meet requests for personal or domestic help from those with needs outside the immediate concern of the helping professions. No particular religious connections. Uses some 1,000 volunteers. Liaison officer: Bernard Brooks. Address: Department of Social Services, Metropolitan House, Prince Street, Bristol BS1 4BA. Tel. 0272 29481.

Little Gidding   *38, 44, 51, 96, 107, 110, 122, 198, 247*

The seventeenth-century home of Nicholas Ferrar and his community of family and friends from which the present community takes its inspiration. First meetings in 1969. Moved into farmhouse in 1972. Aims to hold in balance the need to be with God in prayer and man's struggle to survive without exploitation of the earth or his fellows. Predominantly Anglican, but open to all. Core community runs the farm, in 1976 promoting a simple rule for other members. Quiet days, family days, members' fortnight, work camps. Periodical: *Newsletter.* Leader: Revd Tony Hodgson. Address: Manor Farm, Little Gidding, Huntingdon. Tel. 08323 383.

Llanerchwen   *202–3*

Established in 1970. To offer a caring and beautiful environment wherein there is space to discover security, meaning, and purpose and to grow in maturity and union with God. Basically Anglican, but open to all. An eight-acre hill property with core group of 3 adults and 2 children. 200 visitors a year. Contact person: Revd David Shapland. Address: Llanerchwen, Llandefaelog, Brecon. Tel. 0874 2902.

London Ecumenical Centre   *141–2, 163, 164, 236, 252*

Developed out of the Notting Hill Ecumenical Centre which began in the mid 1960s. Moved to Jermyn Street and adopted present title in 1974. A place of meeting for people willing to listen to and learn from each other, and for Christians who seek unity for Christ's work in the world. Ecumenical, with Methodist origins. Projects: worship and prayer resource centre, training in multi-cultural awareness, group exploration of the changing roles of men and women. Link with Amnesty International (see above). Programme Director: Brian Frost. Address: 35 Jermyn Street, London SW1. Tel. 01-437 0235.

Lothlorien   *97, 110, 111, 113, 123–4, 230, 242, 246, 248, 249, 257, 266*

Community formed in 1974. Aims to provide a centre for informal education, especially amongst young people from urban environments, in the setting of a rural community of as self-sufficient a kind as possible. Roman Catholic nucleus, but open to all. One large family with relatives and friends make up the resident community of about 20. Currently building their home, a big log-house. Volunteers work there for shorter periods. Contact persons: Rosemary and Algy Haughton. Address: Lothlorien, Corsock, Castle Douglas, Kirkcudbrightshire.

Luton Industrial College   *143*

Established 1955. For the furtherance of industrial mission through consultation, study, and research, and through the mutual co-operation of those working in industry towards this end. Methodist centre and staff but open to all. Supports the work of some 170 Methodist industrial chaplains throughout the country. New extension opened 1976. Principal: Revd William Gowland. Address: Luton Industrial College, Chapel Street, Luton LU1 2SE. Tel. 0582 29374.

Maharishi International College (Transcendental Meditation)   *74–5*

Formerly the Spiritual Regeneration Movement of Great Britain. Derived from the teachings of Marharishi Mahesh Yogi about the mid 1960s. Aims to provide a simple natural technique for the progressive refinement of the nervous system through the regular alternation of meditation and activity. Now working for a World Government for the Age of Enlightenment. Some 60 World Plan Centres in Britain. A conference centre at Royden Hall, East Peckham, Nr Tonbridge, Kent. Tel. 0622 812121/812438. Administrative headquarters: 32 Cranbourn Street, London WC2H 7EY. Tel. 01-240 3103.

Marygate House 122

House into full use in 1971. A Christian conference and retreat centre. Anglican and Methodist, but ecumenical ministry. Warden: Douglas Graham. Address: Marygate House, Holy Island, Berwick-upon-Tweed, Northumberland. Tel. 0289 246.

Methodist Connexional Team Ministries Committee 228–9

Set up by the Methodist Conference in the mid 1960s. Aims to support and link the work of Methodist team ministries and encourage the establishment of new teams. Secretary: Revd Denis Gardiner. Address: 169 Forest Road, Loughborough, Leics. LE11 3HS. Tel. 0509 63321.

Metropolitan Community Church 176, 214–15

Established in the USA by Revd Troy Perry in 1968. Aims to be an open Christian community especially serving those rejected by their fellow Christians because of their sexual situation. Strong homosexual membership; smaller number of lesbian members. Several centres in Britain including Birmingham, Bath, and Bristol. Contact person: Ken Taylor. Address: 94 Goldhurst Terrace, London NW6 3HS. Tel. 01-624 2185. For general information on the gay Christian scene, contact the Gay Christian Movement. Secretary: Jim Cotter. Address: c/o 15 Bermuda Road, Cambridge, CB3 3JX.

Movement for a Better World 148–9, 163, 248, 250

Established in 1952 by an Italian Jesuit, Father Riccardo Lombardi. Aims to renew the Church for mission. Roman Catholic, with ecumenical orientation. International. Especial use of a 'basic' retreat – an intensive shared experience of reflection, prayer, and discussion. Director in Britain: Father James Sweeney, CP. Address: 23 Weld Road, Southport, Merseyside PR8 2JP. Tel. 0704 65928.

The Netherbow 142

Opened in 1974. Aims to link the Church and the world of the arts. Church of Scotland. Studio theatre, exhibition gallery, books, coffee bar. Director: Revd Dr Gordon Strachan. Address: 43 High Street, Edinburgh 1. Tel. 031-556 9579.

Newhaven 22, 31

Community house, formed in 1971. Now disbanded. Radical student Christian group, fairly rapid turnover of residents. Location: Edinburgh.

New Life Foundation 196, 212

Began in mid 1960s. A Christian ministry to reach and help drug addicts. Interdenominational. Deals especially with young adults between 17 and 25. Two houses. Founder and leader: Revd Vic Ramsey. Administrative headquarters: PO Box 166, London SE19 3TG. Tel. 01-653 2485. Residential community: The Red House, Kelham, Newark NG23 5QP. Tel. 0636 2807.

New Villages Association   102, 105

Set up in 1975. To establish land-based villages where people can live and produce as much as possible of their own food, clothing, and other necessities locally, and recycle their wastes. No religious connections. Secretary: Don Warren. Address: New Villages Association, Food and Energy Research Centre, Evesham Road, Cleeve Prior, Evesham, Worcs.

Notting Hill Group Ministry   82–3, 84, 141, 218–19, 221–2, 223, 224, 225, 227, 228

Began in 1960. To express the fullness of Christian community within a large multi-racial congregation. Methodist ministers and congregation, but very open. Contact person: Revd Donald Eadie. Address: c/o 9 Denbigh Road, London W11 2SJ. Tel. 01-229 7728.

ONE for Christian Renewal   71, 151, 255–6, 257

Set up in 1970. A radical network of individuals and groups to facilitate study and action for the renewal of Church and society. Ecumenical; originally a merger of several denominational 'renewal groups' of the 1960s. Membership of about 1,000. Major triennial conference. Sponsors *Community* magazine (see above). Periodical: A folder of articles and news items. Chairman: Revd Denis Gardiner. Address: 169 Forest Road, Loughborough, Leics. LE11 3HS. Tel. 0509 63321.

Open Centres   27, 28, 50, 66, 74, 77, 79, 129, 163, 242, 252

See references to Ettrick Shaws and the Salisbury Centre. For further information contact Cara Voelcker (Secretary to the Open Centres), Avils Farm, Lower Stanton, Chippenham, Wilts. Tel. 024-972 202.

Orkney Community (Rainbow Lighthouse)   109–10

Set up in 1969 and dispersed in 1974. Nucleus of 3 couples with children living communally, simply, and 'near to nature'. Location: one of the northern islands of the Orkneys, Scotland.

Orr, Jack – house groups   203

A network of house groups established on a corporation housing estate near Edinburgh, now having been operating for a number of years. Church of Scotland. Minister of the parish (St John's, Oxgangs): Revd Jack Orr. Address: 2 Caiystane Terrace, Edinburgh E10 6SR. Tel. 031-445 1688.

The Othona Community   137, 237

Set up in 1946. To strengthen international relations; to foster Christian unity; to encourage a deeper experience of Christian community; to study the relation of faith and life with a view to action. Anglican nucleus, but now very open. Periodical: *Newsletter*. Leader: Canon Norman Motley. Address: St Michael's Vestry, Cornhill, London EC3V 9DU. Tel. 01-626 8841. Two centres: Othona Community House, Burton Bradstock, Bridport, Dorset. Tel. 030-889 338; East Hall Farm, Bradwell-on-Sea, Southminster, Essex. Wardens: Colin and Kate Hodgetts.

Pax Christi   138, 209

Founded in France at the end of the Second World War. Initially aimed for German/French reconciliation, now works for a greater sense of Christian responsibility on issues of war, peace, and international relations. Roman Catholic. British section has some 600 members. Strong emphasis on its educational programme. Periodical: *Justpeace*. Address: Pax Christi Centre, Blackfriars Hall, Southampton Road, London NW5. Tel. 01-485 7977.

Phoenix House   171

Offshoot of Synanon, established in 1958. Aims to offer a new way of life to disorientated young adults, particularly those addicted to drugs. No religious connections. Alpha House (see above) modelled on this community. Contact person: Dr Mitch Rosenthal. Address: Phoenix House, 164 West 74th Street, New York 10023, USA. Tel. 212-595 5810. (Synanon address: 6055 Marshall-Petaluma Road, PO Box 786, Marshall, California 94940, USA. Tel. 415-663 8111.)

The Pilgrims of St Francis   72, 82, 84, 121, 234, 237, 239, 247

Set up in 1927 by French and German laymen working for reconciliation after the First World War. Aims now to work for peace and social justice; spirit of fellowship fostered by regular 'pilgrimages' in various countries. Originally Roman Catholic, now ecumenical. An international pilgrimage held in Britain in 1976. Periodical: *The Way*. Information Secretary: Kathleen Holford, 140 The Avenue, Aylesford, Maidstone, Kent ME20 7RL. Tel. 0622 70765.

Pilsdon   15, 28, 33, 38, 43–4, 50, 52, 53, 54, 60, 87, 96, 110, 113–14, 115, 116, 190, 196, 197–8, 211, 233, 247, 266

Country house purchased in 1958. Aims to offer unconditional friendship to all who come, however defeated, that by sharing in the life of the community, healing may take place and artificial barriers be broken down. Takes its inspiration from the seventeenth-century community established by Nicholas Ferrar at Little Gidding (see above). Anglican, but open to all. Emphasizes the importance of a regular rhythm of work and worship. Periodical: *Letters from Pilsdon*. Leader: Canon Percy Smith. Address: Pilsdon, by Bridport, Dorset. Tel. 030-86 308.

Post Green   24, 25, 26, 28, 30, 35, 36, 42, 43, 44, 49, 51, 54, 56, 63, 68, 78, 81, 99, 126–7, 162, 163, 165, 222, 230, 239, 242, 248, 252

Grew out of a healing and teaching ministry based on the estate of Sir Thomas and Lady Faith Lees which began in 1968. Development of extended family households from 1973. Aims to exercise a teaching and caring ministry for the renewal of parish life from a community of the Spirit. Strong Anglican nucleus, but ecumenical in orientation. Meetings, camps, workshops. Part of the Community of Celebration (see above) joined them in 1976. Periodical: *Towards Renewal*. Contact person: Sir Thomas Lees. Address: Post Green, Lytchett Minster, Poole, Dorset BH16 6AP. Tel. 020-122 2317.

Postlip Hall   51, 119, 230

Community formed in 1970. A convenient and interesting living arrangement in a large country house. No religious connections. Some 4 families with one or two others living in separate accommodation units in the hall but who come together for various activities when they wish. Address: Postlip Hall, Winchcombe, Glos. GL54 5AQ. Tel 0242-602 720.

Project '70 – '75   170–5, 179

Ran from 1970 until 1976. A five-year action research programme designed to explore the practical, technical, and theoretical implications of the churches becoming involved in community development work. Carried out in a west London borough. Led to the establishment of a Service Agency for Church and Community Work in late 1976. Contact persons: Revd Dr George Lovell or Miss C. Widdicombe. Address: 125 Waxwell Lane, Pinner, Middlesex HA5 3ER. Tel. 01-866 2195/0505.

Pye Barn Trust   196, 212

Established about 1970. To help young people with personal problems through the means of a caring Christian community. Interdenominational. Two houses. Director: John Harris. Address: 16 The Chase, Clapham Common, London SW4. Tel. 01-622 4870.

Quaker Group, Glasgow   22, 26

Group formed in 1974. Aim to live together on a communal basis. Society of friends. Six members in a large flat. Location: central Glasgow.

Radical Alternatives to Prison   181–2

Established in 1971. Aims to research and advocate rational and humane community-based alternatives to prison with a view to the eventual abolition of imprisonment. Christian basis, but open to all. Talks, papers, teaching kits. Associated with Christian Action (see above). Periodical: Newsletter. Contact person: Gail Coles. Address: Eastbourne House, Bullards Place, London E2. Tel. 01-981 0041.

Reach   175–6, 214–15

Established in 1971. Aims to encourage the Church to re-examine sexuality in general and the homosexuality issue in particular. Ecumenical. Day seminars and working parties. Director: Revd Dennis Nadin. Address: 27 Blackfriars Road, Salford M3 7AQ. (No telephone number published.)

Re-evaluation Counselling   169–70, 191–2, 234, 239, 240

Started in the USA by Harvey Jackins in the mid 1950s. Arrived in this country early 1970s. A method of personal growth which aims at enabling people to recover what are believed to be innate qualities of creative intelligence, the capacity for warmth, loving relationships, and zest for living. No particular religious connections, but many see in it affinities with the pastoral work of the Church. Operates on a peer counselling basis. Participants often belonged to non-residential communities which meet regularly. Contact person: Audrey Shilling. Address: Oxford House, Derbyshire Street, Bethnal Green, London E26 HG. Tel. 01-739 9093/4.

The Richmond Fellowship   188

Established in 1959. Works for the welfare and rehabilitation, especially through residential communities, of those suffering from mental breakdown. No particular religious connections. Over 20 houses. College set up in 1966 for courses in human relations. Founder and Director: Elly Jansen. Address: 8 Addison Road, London W14 8DL. Tel. 01-603 6373/5.

Ringsfield Hall   45, 110, 135, 166, 233

Established in the early 1970s. A core community run a centre, and smallholding, to which groups from schools and churches come for study and recreation. Anglican emphasis, but open to all. Core group of 5 adults and 5 children. Leader: Revd Peter Langford. Address: Ringsfield Hall, Beccles, Suffolk NR34 8JR. Tel. 0502 713020.

The Roadrunners   55, 181, 258

Operating in 1973. A small group of young adults living in a community house. Amongst other activities produced the *Catonsville Roadrunner* (radical Christian magazine) for a period. Address: 28 Brundetts Road, Manchester 21. Tel. 061-881 0477. Last group known to be producing the magazine was Some Friends (see below).

The Roslin Community   25, 30, 50, 52, 60, 73

Set up in 1965. Aims to live a life of intercession and prayer in the midst of the secular. Ecumenical. A group of brothers; some 6 members. Sisters and lay companions also linked. Poverty, chastity, obedience. Rule of regular worship and work. Address: 23 Manse Road, Roslin, Midlothian.

Rostrevor (Centre for Christian Renewal)   52, 63, 85–6, 187, 206, 248

Established in 1974; grew out of a charismatic group meeting in Belfast. Aims to be a centre of prayer, renewal, and reconciliation. Core community of some 10 adults with children. Conferences, retreat days, prayer meetings, counselling, healing. Leader: Revd Cecil Kerr. Address: Centre for Christian Renewal, Shore Road, Rostrevor, Co. Down, Northern Ireland. Tel. 069373 492.

St Christopher's Hospice   184, 185–6

Opened in 1967. A Christian and medical foundation caring for those suffering because of advanced cancer or other long-term illnesses. Open to all. Staff operate as a caring community; some 80 volunteers visit patients each week. Medical Director: Dr Cicely Saunders. Address: 51–53 Lawrie Park Road, Sydenham, London SE26 6DZ. Tel. 01-778 9252.

St George's House, Windsor   125, 142–3, 162, 165, 166, 233

Conference centre opened in 1966. To be a centre where people in positions of leadership in industrial, professional, artistic, and church life can come together to discuss major issues in modern society. Anglican. Warden: Vice-Admiral D. H. Mason. Address: Windsor Castle, Berkshire SL4 1NJ. Tel. 075-35 61341.

St Hugh's Lewsey   223, 244

Parish charismatically renewed in the early 1970s. Established a number of extended households. Vicar: Revd Philip Rumsey. Address: St Hugh's Vicarage, Leagrave High Street, Lewsey, Luton, Beds. Tel. 0582 64433.

St Julian's   25, 38, 40–1, 48, 54, 61, 115, 194, 242, 276–7

Community established in 1941 under the leadership of Florence Allshorn. Present house and farm from 1950. Aims to provide a place of retreat and recreation for those returning from work overseas and, increasingly, for those wanting a break from work in this country. Anglican, but open to all. A core community of some dozen women. House in Kenya also. Periodical: *Community Review*. Leader: Barbara Rutherford. Address: Coolham, Horsham, Sussex RH13 8QL. Tel. 040-387 220.

St Michael-le-Belfrey with St Cuthbert's, York 81, 223

Parish charismatically renewed in the early 1970s. A number of extended households set up. Vicar: Revd David Watson. Address: 86 East Parade, York. Tel. 0904 24190.

St Mungo Community Trust 174, 201

Soup run began in Battersea in 1969. In addition aims to provide residential caring communities for homeless men in London. No particular religious connections. Night shelters, longer-term care, action research. Director: Jim Horne. Address: The Old Charing Cross Hospital, PO Box 94, William IV Street, London WC2N 4LP. Tel. 01-240 5431/2.

The Salisbury Centre 50, 74, 79, 117, 129

Opened 1973. Aims to give people the opportunity to live and search together to discover in themselves real love and openness and the true nature of work, so that each person can become a more integrated individual and a more effective instrument of service in the world. An open centre, like Ettrick Shaws (see above). Small core residential community. Meditation, prayer, crafts, painting, encounter, study of Christian and Sufi mystics. Address: 2 Salisbury Road, Edinburgh EH16 5AB. Tel. 031-667 5438.

The Samaritans 190, 204–5, 243

Started by Revd Chad Varah in 1953. Aims to provide a telephone help service for the lonely, despairing, and suicidal. Christian origins, but open to all. Service manned by some 20,000 volunteers. Address: 17 Uxbridge Road, Slough SL1 1SN. Tel. 0753 32713/4.

Scargill House 24, 31, 54, 61, 74, 81, 86, 131, 163, 165, 166, 233

Opened in 1959. A conference centre for those seeking relaxation and the exploration of current concerns within the context of a Christian community. Anglican, but open to all. Resident community staffs the centre, mainly single young adults. Warden: Patrick Marsh. Address: Scargill House, Kettlewell, Skipton, Yorks BD23 5HU. Tel. 075-676 234.

Scoraig 45, 51, 55, 96, 97, 102, 107, 110–11, 115, 122, 246, 266, 267

Crofting community set up from the mid 1960s. To promote a simple life-style based on the conservationist philosophy of life. Some Christian families. Small 'village' of some 2 dozen adults with children. Contact person: Tom Forsyth. Address: Ruigh' Riabmach, Dundonnell, Garve, Wester Ross, Scotland.

Scott Bader Commonwealth 106, 107

Commonwealth set up in 1951. Aims to set an example of and promote the movement towards common ownership in industry. No particular religious connections. Workforce about 400; produces chemicals and plastics. Company limited by guarantee, with no share capital. Address: Wollaston, Northants NN9 7RL. Tel. 0933 71100.

Scottish Churches House   143, 163

Opened in 1961. An ecumenical centre for the Scottish Churches organizing conferences on various aspects of social and political concern. The house Council represents all major denominations except the Roman Catholics. Warden: Revd J. Wilson McLeod. Address: Kirk Street, Dunblane, Perthshire FK15 0AJ. Tel. 0786 3588.

The Servants of Christ the King   61–2, 77–8, 79–80, 152, 233–4, 239, 240, 247

Originated from an Oxford conference in 1943. Aims to offer to God small communities bound together in a common fellowship. Originally Anglican, but went ecumenical by open decision in 1964. A network of 'companies' – some 60 in Britain and 25 overseas – with about a dozen members in each. 'Waiting on God', discussion, action. Secretary: Jim Brierley. Address: 16 Coppice Walk, London N20 8BZ. Tel. 01-445 2824.

Servas (Peace Builders)   208, 243

Began in 1949 as Peace Builders; took current title in 1952. To enable active workers for peace to travel between different countries, study them, and share experiences. No particular religious connections. A system of world-wide hospitality with branches in some 30 countries. Had 130 hosts in Britain in 1976. Periodical: *Servas International News*. British Secretary: Barbara Acquah. Address: 194 Moor Lane, Great Crosby, Liverpool L23 2UH. Tel. 051-924 9082.

Seymour, John – farm   101–2

Originally began farming in Suffolk in the mid 1950s. Now runs a school in self-sufficiency on his farm at Fachongle Isaf, Newport, Pembrokeshire, Dyfed, Wales.

Shankill Team Ministry – community house   224, 280–1

Opened in 1976. To provide a place where voluntary workers could come and live together, offering acceptance and help to those around them. Methodist nucleus, but open to all. Leader: Revd Robert Livingstone. Address: 168 Agnes Street, Belfast BT13 1GN. Tel. 0232 28981.

Sheffield Inner City Ecumenical Mission   220–1

Established in 1971. To develop a new style of ministry to an inner city area. Methodist origins but now ecumenical. Links 4 churches, the Ashram Community house (see above) and the Urban Theology Unit (see below). Leader: Revd Dr John Vincent. Address: 239 Abbeyfield Road, Sheffield S4 7AW. Tel. 0742 386688.

Shenley House   23, 204, 210, 223, 229

Community established there in 1969; disbanded in 1976. To develop a sense of community within a suburban council estate through a core Christian group resident in the area. House owned by Methodism; community ecumenical. Between 4 and 7 young adult members over the years; one a professional community worker. Contact persons: Joe and Joy Hasler. Address: 126 Oak Tree Lane, Selly Oak, Birmingham, B29 6HY. Tel. 021-472 0878.

Shilay Community   201

Established in the mid 1960s. To provide shelter for single homeless men. No particular religious connections. Three-tier rehabilitation process. Warden: Martin Daly. Address: St Nicholas School, Holloway Street, Exeter. Tel. 0392 73896.

Shrubb Family   31, 50, 53, 98, 115, 119

House obtained and community formed in 1970. To enjoy living together in a simple style away from 'straight' society. No religious connections. Fairly rapid turnover of members. Address: Shrubb Farm Cottages, Larling, Nr Thetford, Norfolk.

Simon Community   28, 174, 201

Established in 1963. To meet the needs of the homeless and socially disadvantaged. Strong Roman Catholic connections. Volunteer workers staff the residential houses. Founder and Leader: Anton Wallich-Clifford. Periodical: *Simon Star*. Address: Challenge House, 118 Grove Green Road, London E11. Tel. 01-539 0541/2/3.

Six Circle Group   205

Established in 1969. To promote camps shared by Borstal boys and those young people in need of special care due to physical or mental handicap. No particular religious connections. Chairman: Charles W. Hills. Address: HM Borstal, Brightons, Nr Falkirk, Stirlingshire, Scotland. Tel. 0324 711558.

Social Studies Centre – East End Mission   147

Phase I, opened in 1967. Aims to provide the opportunity for different groups to engage in social studies in an inner city area. Three-phase operation. Phase I (referred to in this book) provides social and remedial education for secondary-school children in the area. Phase II provides A-level courses for resident students. Phase III offers facilities for visiting groups to the East End. Tutor Warden of Phase I: Revd Roy D. Newell. Address: East End Mission, 583 Commercial Road, London E1. Tel. 01-790 3366.

Society of St Francis   210, 264

Anglican religious Order with a small community house at 51 Morpeth Street, Belfast BT13 2HZ. Tel. 0232 27680. Headquarters at 42 Balaam Street, Plaistow, London E13 8AQ. Tel. 01-476 5189.

Society of the Sacred Mission   264

Anglican religious Order with a house at the SSM Priory, Willen, Milton Keynes, Bucks MK15 9AA. Tel. 0908 611749.

Some Friends   22, 26

Operating since 1974. Community of some 12 young adults. Society of Friends; radical orientation. Last group to produce the *Catonsville Roadrunner*. Address: 128 Bethnal Green Road, London E2 6DG. Tel. 01-739 2301.

Sparkbrook – community house   22, 223

Operating from 1974 to 1976. To link an experiment in communal living with the life of the neighbourhood and local churches. Methodist venture. Six members. Hoping to operate again as a community linked to the Ashram Community Trust (see above) in 1977. Address: 1 Anderton Road, Sparkbrook, Birmingham 11.

Student Christian Movement   *22, 26, 54, 66, 97, 135, 144, 160–1, 181, 212, 214, 231, 236, 239, 240, 243, 244, 249, 252, 254*

Founded in 1889. Currently aims to interpret and communicate through study and action the revolutionary significance of Christ for our age in social, political, religious, and cultural terms. Ecumenical. Radical Christian core community established in the new headquarters in Wick in 1974. Offers hospitality, consultations, conferences in the Tatlow Centre (Wick address). Half a dozen community houses. Work in schools and higher education through itinerant staff. Periodical: *Movement*. Headquarters address: Wick Court, Wick, Nr Bristol. Tel. 027-582 3377.

Taena   *24, 26, 29, 38, 40, 45, 46, 48, 53, 62, 67, 83, 97, 99, 110, 116, 123, 230, 242, 246*

Began in Cornwall in 1941. To Forest of Dean in 1943 and present location in 1952. Originated as a left-wing pacifist farming community with common ownership. Became predominantly Roman Catholic in 1950. Reverted economically to individual units in 1961. Some half-dozen families. Some have an especial interest in craft and meditation. Contact person: George Ineson. Address: Whitley Court, Upton St Leonards, Glos. GL4 8EB. Tel. 0452 68346.

Taizé   *23, 235, 236, 237, 251*

Began during the Second World War. First profession by the Brothers in 1949. Lutheran/Calvinist/Anglican. Sponsored the World Council of Youth which started in 1970; the first stage culminated in 1974 when some 40,000 young adults gathered in Taizé. Key theme: struggle and contemplation. Periodical: *Letter from Taizé*. Prior: Roger Schutz. Address: F-71460 Taizé Community, France.

The Teilhard Centre for the Future of Man   *152*

Began in 1965. Aims to make Teilhard de Chardin's thought more widely accessible and more readily understood. Ecumenical. Study groups, library, publications. Periodical: *The Teilhard Review*. Address: 81 Cromwell Road, London SW7 5BW. Tel. 01-370 6660.

Transactional Analysis   *11–12, 156, 160, 188–9, 266, 275*

Originated through the work of Eric Berne in the USA from the late 1950s. Aims to provide a systematic framework for understanding personality and relationships. A method of personal development through group experience and an analytic, therapeutic technique. No religious connections. Addresses: Institute of Transactional Analysis, 52 Cranley Gardens, Palmers Green, London N13 4LS. Tel. 01-889 4311; Hallam Centre for Transactional Analysis and Related Studies, Weston House, West Barr Green, Sheffield S1 2DL. Tel. 0742 20869.

Urban Ministry Project (UMP)   *144, 145, 163, 164*

Began in 1968. Aims to provide field-work experience and analysis, with theological reflection, related to working with people in an urban situation. Anglican. In London and Ripon College, Cuddesdon. Courses involve 'the Plunge' and situation analysis. In 1976 began to move away from simply training clergy and ordinands. Now linked with the Oxford Institute for Church and Society. Periodical: *City Forum*. Director: Revd

Donald Reeves. Address: St Peter's Vicarage, Bishopsford Road, St Helier, Morden, Surrey. Tel. 01-648 6050.

Urban Theology Unit (UTU)   139–40, 162, 163, 164, 166

Formed in 1969. Moved its headquarters to the Pitsmoor Study House in 1974. Aims to bring the study of theology and society together to serve the Church and the city. Methodist origins; ecumenical ministry. Part of the Sheffield Inner City Ecumenical Mission (see above). Study weeks, consultations, reading weeks, post-graduate year. Director: Revd Dr John Vincent. Address. Pitsmoor Study House, 210 Abbeyfield Road, Sheffield S4 7AZ. Tel. 0742 388035.

West London Chaplaincy   73, 153–4, 164

Began in the early 1960s. To enable a Christian presence to grow within the ordinary structures of college life. Anglican but ecumenical outreach. Based on Imperial and Queen Elizabeth Colleges, Kensington. Network of groups and 2 community houses. Chaplain: Revd David Ashforth. Address: 25 Campden Hill Square, London W8. Tel. 01-727 3804.

Westminster Pastoral Foundation   189–90

Opened in 1970. To provide a counselling service and training programme on the basis of a continuing link between the religious outlook and the behavioural sciences. Methodist basis, but ecumenical ministry. Counselling service and training programme. Some 16 affiliated centres throughout the country. Director: Revd Dr William Kyle. Address: Central Hall, Matthew Parker Street, Westminster, London SW1H 9NH. Tel. 01-930 6676/7.

William Temple Foundation   149–50, 163, 179, 255, 256–7.

College founded 1947. College closed and Foundation moved operations to Manchester in 1971. Aims to develop a network of reflective and hopeful change agents; to help build an adequate theology for lay involvement in society; to help renew the institutions of the Church. Anglican, but ecumenical ministry. Projects related to industry, health, the young disadvantaged, community development. Periodical: Bulletin. Director: Canon David Jenkins. Address: Manchester Business School, Manchester M15 6PB. Tel. 061-273 8228.

Wolverhampton Interfaith Group   207–8

Started in 1973. To encourage and promote understanding between all people of Wolverhampton whatever their religious tradition. Group drawn from different races and faiths. Some 20 people meet monthly. Contact person: Revd Neville Platten. Address: 3 Stratton Street, Wolverhampton WV10 9AJ. Tel. 0902 55931.

Wrekin Trust   76, 148, 165

Established in 1971. To understand and disseminate the ageless wisdom of the centuries to which the great Spirit of the Universe is reawakening mankind. Open to all interested in the New Age philosophy. Courses, lectures in various centres. Director: Sir George Trevelyan. Address: Bowers House, Bowers Lane, Bridstow, Ross-on-Wye, Herefordshire H59 6JX. Tel. 0989 4853.